Networking the Macintosh

Networking the Macintosh

**A Step-by-Step Guide
to Using AppleTalk
in Business Environments**

Bill Woodcock

McGraw-Hill, Inc.

New York   San Francisco   Washington, D.C.   Auckland   Bogotá
Caracas   Lisbon   London   Madrid   Mexico City   Milan
Montreal   New Delhi   San Juan   Singapore
Sydney   Tokyo   Toronto

Library of Congress Cataloging-in-Publication Data

Woodcock, Bill.
    Networking the Macintosh : a step-by-step guide to using AppleTalk
in business environments / by Bill Woodcock.
        p.   cm.
    Includes index.
    ISBN 0-07-071683-8 — ISBN 0-07-071684-6 (pbk.)
    1. AppleTalk. 2. Local area networks (Computer networks)-
-Management. 3. Macintosh (Computer) I. Title.
TK5105.8.A77W66   1993
004.6'165—dc20   93-24613
                                                CIP

1 2 3 4 5 6 7 8 9 0 DOH/DOH 9 9 8 7 6 5 4 3

ISBN 0-07-071683-8 (hc)
ISBN 0-07-071684-6 (pbk.)

*The sponsoring editor for this book was Daniel A. Gonneau, the editing
supervisor was Christine H. Furry, and the production supervisor was
Donald Schmidt. This book was set in Century Schoolbook by North
Market Street Graphics.*

Printed and bound by R. R. Donnelley & Sons Company.

Contents

Preface

What *Networking the Macintosh* Covers

This book follows the development of a model network from its inception with just two devices, a Macintosh and a laser printer, up to about two hundred devices, both Macintoshes and Unix machines, spanning several varieties of network system and several cities.

The progress is paralleled by notes on the important issues to keep in mind, options available at each juncture, and helpful examples referring directly to the model network.

Specifically, topics covered include:

- Creation of small networks of a dozen or fewer devices
- Specifying and installing building wiring for much larger networks
- Understanding the data that flows across the network
- Supporting client-server file sharing and electronic mail
- Upgrading your network to high-performance Ethernet media
- Making Unix services available to Macintosh users
- Network management and user technical support concerns
- Network security and legal issues

A test-bed network was constructed during the course of the writing of this book, employing the techniques described, to assure their validity and mutual compatibility. It was constructed along the lines of the model network described in the book, and it's from this test-bed network that the examples used in the book were taken.

Who Can Profit by Reading This Book

Since the development of the LAN, or "Local Area Network," composed of a number of desktop computers, network administration is no longer the realm of highly trained specialists with degrees in computer science and information systems management. Instead, it's now thrust, often unwanted, upon a computer user within the company who seems to be more comfortable with technical issues than other users. If you're such a user, accustomed to being accosted in hallways by coworkers with technical questions, you probably already know it. You may not, however, know what direction to proceed in networking your company's computers.

This book is intended to serve as an introduction to the Macintosh's networking capabilities, and as a guide to help you decide when and how to expand your network from each level of functionality and service to the next.

For network administrators who have already begun this process, the linear organization is designed to facilitate entry at whatever point you find yourself.

Bill Woodcock

Acknowledgments

In writing this book, I've had the invaluable assistance of many people. My thanks are extended to Kee Nethery of Kagi Engineering, for contributing many suggestions throughout the book's creation; and to Mark Vinsel of Farallon Computing, for sharing some of his cabling expertise. My thanks as well to Chris Carothers and Kevin Karplus for helping me find the time to write the book. Also to Kurt Vandersluis of The Network Group and Bernard Aboba of MailCom, for providing inspirational authorial role models (most of the time, anyway); and to David Burk, Yara Sellin, and my family for moral support and encouragement at various times during my writing.

I also owe many thanks to the vendors and vendor representatives who loaned products for the building of the test-bed network which paralleled the writing of the book. These include Mike Zivkovic and Robin Anderson of Apple USA; Scott Petry and Martha Steffen of Apple Computer; Wilson Farrar of Cayman Systems; Brita Meng and Dave Harrison of Shiva; Trudy Edelson of Farallon Computing; Will Herlan of Microsoft; Rusty Rahm, Scott Steward, and Jim Persky of StarNine Technologies; Walt Hays of Dantz Development; Dominique Ducasse of Advanced Software Concepts; Barbara Maxwell of Synergy Software; Kim Agricola of On Technology; Throop Wilder and Jeff Osborn of Wilder Systems; and Elyssa Edwards of Neon Software.

For the timely provision of information during the course of my writing, I'd like to thank Erik Fair, Paul Hudspeth, Kevin Mellander, and Alex Rosenberg, all of Apple Computer.

For loaning me the use of their names (or, rather, insisting that they appear) in my book, I'd like to thank Mark Unruh, Liza Denis, and Cathy Serventi.

Last, I'd like to thank Jeff Logullo of Apple Computer, Stephen Howard of MacWEEK, Ron Gibbs of Dow Chemical, Morris Balamut of Hughes Aircraft, and others already mentioned who read the book while still in draft and provided technical criticism, the value of which was beyond measure. Obviously I am entirely to blame for any mistakes or inaccuracies which may still remain.

Network: Anything reticulated or decussated, at equal distances, with interstices between the intersections. SAMUEL JOHNSON
Dictionary of the English Language, 1755

Don't be too proud of this mechanical terror you've created! DARTH VADER
Star Wars, 1977

Networking the Macintosh

1

Introduction

1.1 Background

At its most basic level, any network is basically a system of plumbing—pipes laid between devices to facilitate the flow of data. But that's as simplistic as saying that speech is a way of causing pressure waves to move through the air. The formation of a network, like speech, is driven not by desire for a process, but to fill a functional need. Speech is used to share all sorts of information and knowledge, both concrete and abstract. Networks are also used to share information and knowledge, and they're used to share access to physical devices as well.

In both information and device-sharing capacities, networks have evolved greatly over the past twenty years. The first computers were huge devices, unconnected to anything else and accessible by only one person at a time. These "mainframe" computers gradually added text-terminals, with screens and keyboards, each connected by a cable which led directly back to the computer. Later, the terminals escaped from the "computer room" out into the rest of the office, but they still consisted of nothing more than a screen and keyboard. All the computing was done centrally, and only text from the keyboard to the computer, and from the computer to the screen, flowed over the cables. Eventually, the unit cost of making small processors fell, as production technology was spun off from the development of state-of-the-art, high-performance processors, which remained relatively expensive. Availability of low-cost processors, in combination with people's growing frustration with having to wait for the central computer whenever they wanted to do anything, led to the development of smaller and smaller mainframe-style computers and, perhaps more importantly, standalone microcomputers like the original Apple II and IBM PC.

The machines which evolved in response to demand for smaller mainframe-style computers continued to use the same kinds of operating systems and software, and continued to require terminals for input and output. The first generation of these were called minicomputers, and lowered the price of mainframe-style computing by one order of magnitude. As they became affordable enough that single companies could possess more than one at any location, networking technologies developed to interconnect them. True to form, these networks were high-performance, difficult to configure, and very fragile. As the scientific and large-business market continued to demand smaller, but still powerful machines, the "workstation" was developed, another order of magnitude cheaper. A kind of hybrid of minicomputer and terminal technology, workstations possess their own screens and keyboards, but still use the same complicated software and high-performance networks and, moreover, continue to support terminals while simultaneously rendering them unnecessary.

The machines which grew out of the first microcomputers, on the other hand, were small, cheap (three orders of magnitude cheaper than mainframes), and eminently easy to use. They catered to the populist tastes of home and small-business users, and spread rapidly. As the cost of making processors which are small and slow, relative to the state-of-the art, continued to drop, microcomputers were the main beneficiaries, growing more and more powerful each year. As microcomputers, or "desktop computers" as they came to be called, proliferated in business environments, Apple Computer perceived a need for network capabilities like larger computers had, and developed Apple Talk, an inexpensive networking technology, which could be included in every computer they built.

Although the whole scale of computing has changed exponentially over this period, the tasks for which computers are used have changed slowly. Many of the number-crunching tasks which once occupied teams of programmers with mainframe computers for days can now be accomplished in minutes on desktop computers, using inexpensive commercially developed software. On the other hand, people are now realizing that computers' greatest advantages are often realized in facilitating the most mundane office tasks, like the typing and delivery of memos and correspondence, the totting-up of figures, and coordinating of calendars. The need for large centralized processors has dwindled, while the demand for desktop processing power has grown greatly.

Today, the demand for greater processor power in microcomputers and lower cost in workstations has caused microcomputer and workstation vendors to converge upon exactly the same processors: the Motorola 68000 series, Intel's 80X86 series, and RISC, or "Reduced Instruction Set Computing" processors made by both those and other vendors. The prices, as well, have converged: the majority of the microcomputer and workstations sold to business are in exactly the same price range. As the processors and price become more and more similar, so to do other features, like physical configuration, operating systems, and networking. Today's high-end microcomputers are virtually indistinguishable in appearance from low-end workstations, featuring similar cases and similar video displays. The operating systems of microcomputers and workstations, the basic operating software which computers require to run, have been converging in appearance and function, as well. Workstations now uniformly sport mice and graphically oriented "windowing" interfaces, while most microcomputers, the Macintosh included, can run Unix, the standard operating system used by workstations and most of today's mainframe analogs. The Macintosh's built-in networking capabilities have been emulated by other microcomputer and workstation vendors alike, and Apple is forging ahead by including built-in support for Ethernet, the standard high-speed workstation and mainframe network system, in new models of Macintosh and LaserWriter.

Although the shift from mainframes to microcomputers is often seen as a natural part of the "downsizing" movement in business, in actuality, it's a massive *increase* in the amount of processor power companies possess, disguised by the transition from centralized to distributed computing systems. Instead of a hundred $500 terminals connected to a single multi-million dollar mainframe via direct cables, a company is now likely to have a hundred $5,000 workstations and microcomputers communicating with each other as peers, over a parallel network, and this network of microcomputers is likely to possess many times the processor power of the original mainframe.

1.2   So What Is AppleTalk?

AppleTalk, the network system Apple Computer developed in 1983 and 1984 for inclusion in their new Macintosh computer line, was originally developed ·as a response to the network technologies which had evolved in the workstation market, which were fast, but terribly expensive, fragile, and difficult to understand and use. Moreover, implementations of the workstation networking technologies differed significantly between vendors, and compatibility between devices from different vendors was far from assured. Any configuration task required expert knowledge, and there were few experts in the young field.

AppleTalk was designed to be congenial to the user in all ways, rather than provide the highest raw data transmission rate without regard to expense. By using a lower-frequency electrical signal, fewer data-carrying modulations were possible in any given timeframe, but the network was extremely "robust," or foolproof, and resistant to damage and interference. In combination with Apple's inclusion of the network hardware inside the case of the computer, and thoughtful design of the cable components, this robustness meant that anyone, regardless of prior experience, could physically connect devices into a fully functional network, over long distances and through bad conditions which would render the use of workstation networking technologies unthinkable.

On the software side, all the configuration tasks which made mainframes and workstations so difficult to interconnect were simplified, automated, and hidden from the user. Thus initial configuration of a newly connected machine was made as easy as turning it on. The selection of services to connect to across the network was also made easy, this time through extension of the Macintosh's easy-to-use graphical interface. Instead of editing many interconnected files full of obscure commands in cryptic terminology, a user could simply open a window and click on an icon or the name of a device.

Since its inception, AppleTalk has developed in both its hardware and software aspects. AppleTalk can now run not only over its original media, now called "LocalTalk," but over Ethernet, conferring all its benefits to that system, and Token Ring, IBM's proprietary network system. Its software aspect has gone through one major overhaul, necessary to support extremely large networks of thousands (and potentially millions) of Macintoshes, and now includes support for TCP/IP, the Unix workstation networking software; SNA, which is used by IBMs; DECnet and LAT, which are used by many Digital Equipment mainframes and workstations; and a host of other network systems too many in number to list here.

It's the stated goal of Apple's Enterprise Systems Division to make the Macintosh "the perfect client" to network services provided by other types of networked computers, interoperating seamlessly, regardless of vendor or model. At the same time, Apple's Networking and Communications group has worked to make the Macintosh a strong network service provider among workstations and microcomputers. Together, this makes the Macintosh an excellent choice of network computing platform, regardless of whether you're in a company with an existing network of other types of machines, or are just beginning to build a new network which may contain only Macintoshes for some time. The Macintosh is adaptable to its situation; if it finds itself in the presence of more powerful computers which are providing services, it can take full advantage of those services. If, on the other hand, it finds itself to be the most powerful computer on its network, it can provide those same services to other computers. The Macintosh is unique in possessing this level of flexibility.

The flexibility and power that AppleTalk now provide come at the cost of increasing complexity and an increased base of knowledge needed to expand AppleTalk networks beyond their basic capabilities. This book is intended to present the complex elements of AppleTalk networking in as simple a form as possible, serve as a planning resource, and provide network administrators with a reference source for AppleTalk technical information, know-how, and tips.

2

The Minimal Network

2.1 The Problem

Let's join Mark Unruh, the unfortunate soul who's just been dubbed network administrator of the business that'll be used in our examples, the American Grommet Company, as he deliberates over the first of the problems which make this book necessary: Mark has been assigned to explore the possibility of tying together the few computers his company already owns, and those it expects to purchase in the future, to form a network. He's had a Macintosh for more than a year, and has come to rely upon it for many of his business tasks, writing memos, calculating spreadsheets, and doing materials analysis on the brass bushings which were his particular specialty before his network administration fate overtook him. He's never tried connecting it to anything other than a simple dot-matrix printer, so he decides that his first step will be to explore the Macintosh's networking capabilities at their very most basic level.

2.2 The Macintosh

The Macintosh is, in many ways, the most "connectable" computer on the market. This support for connectivity is built into every Macintosh sold, in the form of AppleTalk drivers and a LocalTalk port. The AppleTalk driver, the software which moderates any transactions in which your machine may participate on the network, is resident in the Macintosh's Read Only Memory. Different models have different versions of AppleTalk, depending upon when they were first released, but Apple's System 7 contains an AppleTalk "patch" which overrides ROM resident software and loads itself into RAM if it finds that it is more recent than the version contained in the ROMs. Although all versions of AppleTalk are compatible, and devices on your network can communicate with each other regardless of which version is built into them, newer versions increase efficiency, add new features and protocols, and make large networks more stable. In addition to the AppleTalk driver, your Macintosh's ROMs contain drivers for the LocalTalk port. The LocalTalk port is often called the "printer port" because it can be used to drive a serial printer if it's not being used for an AppleTalk connection, and is marked with a small printer icon on the back of your Macintosh. The port is an RS-422 compliant serial port, and uses a Mini-DIN 8 connector.

The LocalTalk driver takes formatted AppleTalk packets from the AppleTalk driver, and is charged with using a speed- and media-dependent Link Access Protocol to send them across a specific media, in this case LocalTalk. A binary digital waveform is created, split into positive and negative electrical signals, and sent out two pins of the Mini-DIN 8 jack on the back of the machine. The driver also interprets signals on two other pins of the jack as the positive and negative components of incoming messages, but it is unable to send and receive simultaneously.

All Macintoshes come from the factory with AppleTalk turned off in the Chooser, so this is always something to check when preparing a machine for connection to a network. To turn AppleTalk on, start the machine, go to the Apple menu, and open the Chooser.

In the Chooser, there is a radio button which toggles between "AppleTalk Active" and "AppleTalk Inactive." AppleTalk can be turned off to allow the connection of a serial printer like an ImageWriter to the printer port, but must be turned on if the machine is to be able to access any network services or devices. If AppleTalk is inactive, and you turn it on, the Mac displays an alert which warns you to "Please make sure the Macintosh is connected to an AppleTalk network." Clicking "Continue" to dismiss the alert completes the switch-over.

2.3   The Cable

There are several options in choosing a LocalTalk cable medium. Apple uses the generic term, "LocalTalk connectors," to identify their own connectors, while Farallon Computing sells "PhoneNet connectors." These two are the most widely used, but there are clones of each sold by other vendors, and there are other products which use different media, like fiber optic cable, or run at slightly different speeds.

For the purposes of this book, we'll be using PhoneNet connectors, which are the most common type of LocalTalk connector in use, and a de facto standard. Unlike Apple's connectors, which use a proprietary Mini-DIN 4 cable, and work in only one wiring topology, or physical layout, PhoneNet LocalTalk connectors use common telephone cabling and connectors, and can be arranged in a wide array of topologies.

The connector itself has a pigtail on one side, with a Mini-DIN 8 plug at the end to attach to your Macintosh's LocalTalk or "Printer" port, and has two telephone-style RJ-14 jacks on the other side. Depending upon how you buy it, it usually comes with a length of modular telephone cable and something called a terminating resistor as well.

LocalTalk connectors (used henceforth in the generic sense to refer to PhoneNet-type connectors, rather than to Apple's connectors of that particular name) have two main functions: they combine the positive and negative components of the transmitted signals into a single balanced signal and split those

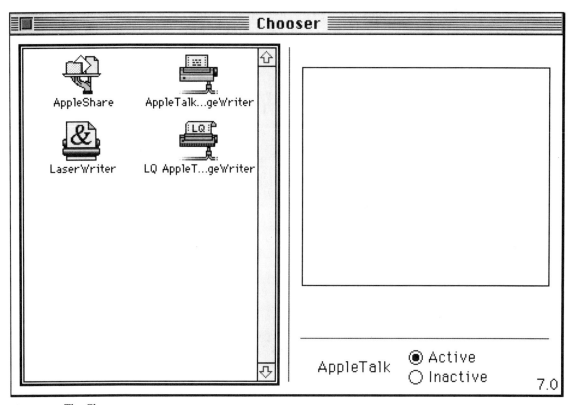

Figure 2.1   The Chooser.

components out of received signals, and they provide surge suppression. As mentioned above, the Macintosh sends LocalTalk messages out its serial port on two pins, and receives messages on two other pins. LocalTalk networks, however, only require a total of two conductors. The LocalTalk connector combines outgoing signals and splits incoming signals to effect the change. As for surge suppression, you may have heard that if you just want to connect two machines, you can use an ImageWriter-type serial cable instead of a pair of LocalTalk connectors and a phone cable. While it's true that this will work, cables connecting computers act as antennas and pick up current from magnetic fields around them, and the longer the cable is the more current it will pick up, especially if it's near power wiring. Thus the surge suppression inside LocalTalk connectors acts as an insurance policy: it's a lot cheaper to replace a LocalTalk connector that has been damaged by an electrical spike than it is to replace a computer that's similarly damaged.

2.4   The Printer

Like Macintoshes, many printers have LocalTalk ports. In this book we'll be using Apple LaserWriters, which are networkable and use the PostScript page description language, but many other printer manufacturers make networkable laser printers, and some make ink-jet printers which can be put on LocalTalk networks as well. Apple even makes an inexpensive AppleTalk expansion card for its ImageWriter II dot matrix and ImageWriter LQ wide-carriage printers.

Some Apple LaserWriters use SCSI or serial connections, and are not PostScript capable, but all can be upgraded by exchanging the motherboard, which is a single slide-out card, with jacks on the back.

Unlike Macintoshes, LaserWriters have no need for serial communication on their DIN-8 jacks, so they have dedicated LocalTalk ports, and there is no need to make AppleTalk active when connecting them. Many PostScript printers support protocols other than AppleTalk on a separate RS-232 port however, and have some kind of selector (usually a set of DIP switches or jumpers, or a dial) which tells the printer which port to watch for incoming print jobs. If your printer has any jacks on it which you can't identify, or suspect may be for other protocols, you should consult the printer's manual to find out how to confirm that the LocalTalk port is selected and active.

2.5   The Physical Connection

Once you've got LocalTalk connectors plugged into the LocalTalk ports of both the Macintosh and the LaserWriter, you can use a piece of modular telephone cable to interconnect the two LocalTalk connectors. Each connector has two RJ-14 jacks. The two jacks are identical and are connected to each other inside the box, so it doesn't matter which you use. If the cable that came with the connectors isn't long enough, any standard telephone cable will work, as long as it's got an RJ-14 plug on each end and has four conductors inside. LocalTalk connectors use what's called the *outside pair* of conductors in modular cables, so that they won't interfere with any telephones you may be using on the same cable, which use the *inside pair*. Some modular cables don't have an outside pair of conductors, but these are relatively uncommon and easily identified by their thinner cords and often blue-tinted plugs. Telephone handset cords will not work, because their plugs are narrower than standard RJ-14 plugs.

Once the two LocalTalk connectors are interconnected, depending upon the brand of the connectors you're using, you may need to use terminating plugs to terminate the network. Termination just means placing resistors across the two conductors of the network to keep signals from reflecting back across the wires once they've reached the end of the cable. To install the terminating plugs, simply put them into the two RJ-14 jacks which are still unused, one on each LocalTalk connector. The reasons for termination and methods of determining where termination is needed on larger networks are discussed further in Chaps. 3 and 4. This completes the physical connection.

2.6   Names and Addresses

Devices on an AppleTalk network, like your Macintosh and LaserWriter, have both names and addresses. AppleTalk uses dynamic addressing, which means

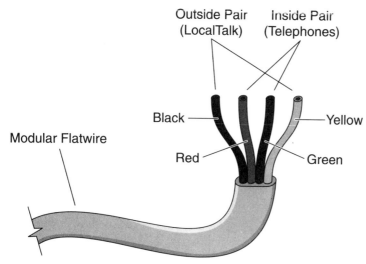

Outside Pair
(LocalTalk)

Inside Pair
(Telephones)

Black

Yellow

Red

Green

Modular Flatwire

Figure 2.2   Inside and outside pairs.

that each time a device is turned on it picks a unique numerical address, which is used by other machines that want to send it messages. The advantage of dynamic addressing is that it's completely "transparent." That is, it requires no configuration or action on the part of the user. The drawback is that since the choice of address is performed randomly at startup, there is a chance that a device may not be able to get the same address the next time it is turned on, if another device has claimed the address while the first was turned off; so another means of identification is needed, and that's the device name. Most devices are able to register some kind of alphanumeric name, along with their address. The name of our printer, as it came from Apple, is "LaserWriter II NTX." LaserWriters print their names across the top of the startup page which is printed out each time the printer is powered up. The odometer, or number of pages that have been printed since the LaserWriter left the factory, appears at the bottom of the startup page.

Make sure that both the Macintosh and LaserWriter are turned off, and that their LocalTalk connectors are interconnected, and then turn them both on. When a machine is turned on, it checks for a "hint" in its Parameter RAM, to see what address (or "node number") it had last, and inquires after a device with that address on the network. If no machine is already using that address, the new machine will receive no reply, and go ahead and use that address itself. If, on the other hand, it does get a reply, it will select a new number and repeat the process until it finds a unique address.

It's important that machines never be attached to an existing network after they've been turned on, since they will have already selected numeric addresses, which may already be in use on the existing network. If this happens, the newly added machine and the one which already had its address number will both try to respond to messages with that address number, and conflicts will result.

This is not as remote a prospect as it may sound. With only 254 possible addresses on any single local network (many of which can be interconnected to form a company-wide network, as we'll see in later chapters), the chance of this happening is one in [254 divided by the number of existing devices], and there are constraints on the address numbers that certain kinds of nodes may take, which makes this even more likely under some circumstances.

Once both machines have started, open the Chooser again, and highlight the LaserWriter icon. After the LaserWriter has printed out its test page and its lights have stopped blinking, if you've successfully connected the two machines, and AppleTalk is turned on, or *active,* you should see the name of the LaserWriter appear in the field at the top right side of the Chooser window. If you had more than one printer on your network, all their names would appear in this list. In large networks, the choice of descriptive printer names can be crucial. If we were to add a second printer of the same model to our network at this point, the two would be indistinguishable, since they have the same name. That being the case, we can use LaserWriter Utility, a utility which comes with Apple LaserWriters, to change the name of this printer to "MIS LaserWriter x1209". As I said before, the choice of a descriptive name is crucial; in this case, I've selected one composed of the department in which the printer is located, MIS; the type of device it is, LaserWriter; and a telephone extension number which will reach the person who is responsible for it. Criteria for the choice of device names are discussed further in the next chapter.

To change the name of a LaserWriter, open LaserWriter Utility and select "Rename Printer . . ." from the "Utilities" menu. It will present a dialog like the one illustrated in Fig. 2.3. Type the new name you wish to assign the printer in the field in the middle, and press the "Rename" button. The LaserWriter Utility can also be used to turn off the startup page (which is normally printed every time the printer is started) to save time and paper, it can collect configuration information, and it can list the fonts installed in the printer.

If we open the Chooser again, or restart the printer, and look at the startup page, we'll see the new name in effect.

2.7   The Logical Connection

As discussed in the first chapter, communication between machines is achieved by sending discrete packets of data across the network, and I've just described two actions in which devices use packets to communicate over the network: the choosing of a unique address, and using the Chooser to find a list of printers available. The way in which these packets operate, moving information between machines on a network, is something not all network administrators bother to examine. Nonetheless, a packet-level understanding of the way your network functions is crucial to the maintenance and troubleshooting you'll be called upon to perform as your network grows beyond the present nascent state of our example.

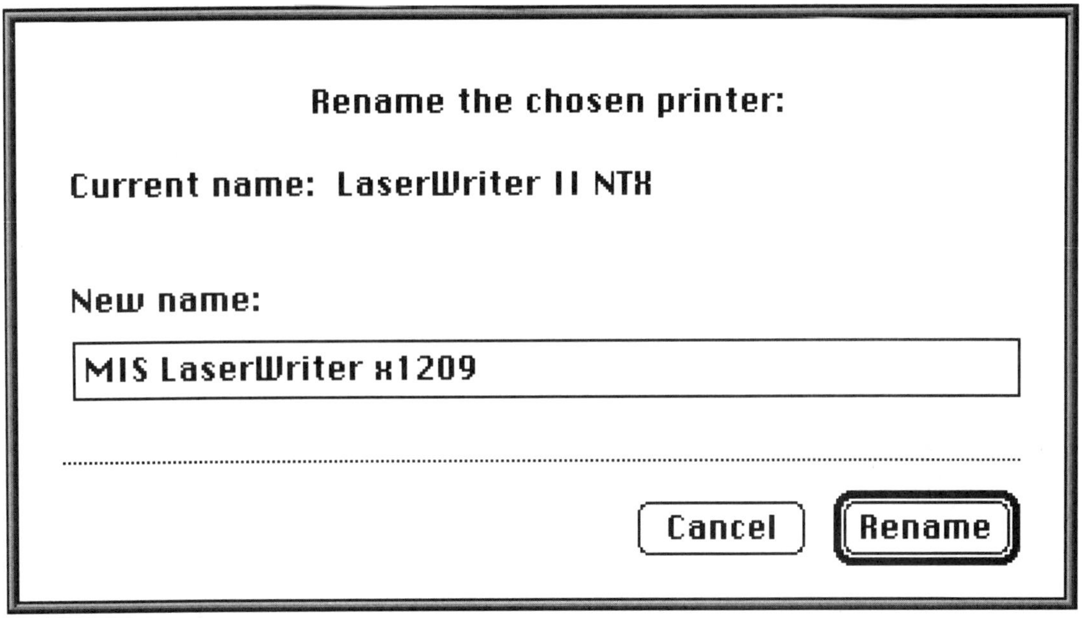

```
┌─────────────────────────────────────────────────────────────┐
│ ┌───────────────────────────────────────────────────────────┐ │
│ │                                                           │ │
│ │           Rename the chosen printer:                      │ │
│ │                                                           │ │
│ │  Current name: LaserWriter II NTH                         │ │
│ │                                                           │ │
│ │                                                           │ │
│ │  New name:                                                │ │
│ │                                                           │ │
│ │  ┌──────────────────────────────────────────────────────┐ │ │
│ │  │ MIS LaserWriter #1209                                │ │ │
│ │  └──────────────────────────────────────────────────────┘ │ │
│ │                                                           │ │
│ │  ....................................................     │ │
│ │                                                           │ │
│ │                        ( Cancel )  (( Rename ))           │ │
│ │                                                           │ │
│ └───────────────────────────────────────────────────────────┘ │
└─────────────────────────────────────────────────────────────┘
```

Figure 2.3   LaserWriter Utility.

Packet-capturing utilities—in this case, the AG Group's LocalPeek—generally require the presence of an additional computer on the network, which can be used to observe the operation of all the others. The method of addition of the third and subsequent devices to your network will be discussed in the following chapter.

By running a packet-capturing utility on our first machine, we can watch packets going by on the network as we turn the second machine on, and record them for analysis. After doing so, we get six hundred and forty-eight packets, in four groups of similar packets. The packets themselves are binary digital waveforms, which have to be interpreted by fitting each bit into place in a template. The packet is arranged like an onionskin, in that the sending device takes the raw data it wants to send and first wraps a "high-level" header around it, then another header around the whole thing, then a third, and so on, where the number and kinds of headers used are dependent upon what kind of data is being sent. Since we're using the LocalTalk protocols which are built into the Macintosh, we know that the outermost header, which was the last to be put on the packet and the first to be removed, is in LocalTalk Link Access Protocol format. At the end of this header, there are bits which tell us what kind of header the next one we'll encounter is, and how large it is. With this information, we could proceed to interpret it. Similarly, at the end of the second header, there will be the necessary information to determine what template to use in decoding the third header, and so on, until we strip all the headers off, exposing the data.

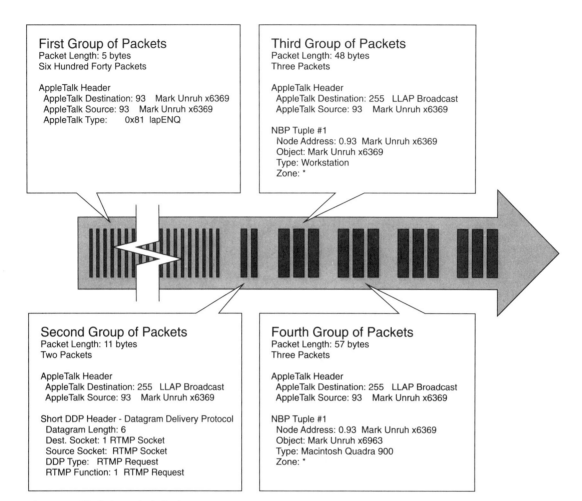

Figure 2.4   Packets sent at startup.

Fortunately, the capturing utility does this for us, but if we didn't have access to such software, the interpretation could be done by hand, using Apple's *Inside AppleTalk* for reference.

In the first group, there are six hundred and forty very small packets, each only five bytes long, which are addressed to node 93, the same as the sender address. These are called LAP Enq, or Link Access Protocol enquiry control packets. Their purpose is to alert other devices on the network that the Macintosh is about to go online using a particular node address—in this case, node 93. Since the packets are addressed to node 93, however, only another node that had already chosen that node number would receive them. If this were to happen, the machine which had seniority would respond with a LAP Ack, or acknowledge control packet, saying, in effect, "sorry, that number's already taken," whereupon the newly started Macintosh would increment the node number to 94, and try again. If, after any string of LAP Enq packets, it hears no response, it can be fairly sure that the number it's chosen is free for use.

The second group contains only two packets of eleven bytes each, addressed to node 255, which is the LocalTalk "broadcast address." Any packet sent to node 255 will be received by all nodes. Node 255 is therefore "reserved," and cannot be chosen as the specific address of any particular machine. The packets are coming from node 93, which we can surmise to be the address that the machine we've just turned on has tentatively chosen for itself. The next line tells us that the information that follows will be interpreted as a Datagram Delivery Protocol header. The DDP header tells us three things: that it's addressed to the RTMP socket on the receiving device, that the return address is the RTMP socket on the sending device, and that the packet type is an RTMP Request, a type of packet which doesn't have any data other than the information found in the header. There is, therefore, no need for further interpretation, and there is no further data to interpret. RTMP stands for Routing Table Maintenance Protocol. RTMP packets are sent to and by routers, which are a type of network device which will be discussed in Chap. 8. In these first two packets, the Macintosh is broadcasting a query packet, looking for any routers which may be present on the network, and querying them for an RTMP Response packet. Since we don't have any routers on our network, there is no response.

In the third group, there are three slightly longer packets, which are also sent to node 255, the broadcast address. I've removed two layers of headers, the DDP header and one called an NBP header, to simplify the diagram, leaving an NBP Tuple, which is the data contained in the packets. NBP stands for Name Binding Protocol, and is a type of packet used any time a device wants to find the alphanumeric name associated with a particular network node number. Several NBP queries or responses can be contained in a single packet; thus, we're looking at tuple one of one. If there were more tuples, or records, they would follow in exactly the same format. Since this is a query, the first field of the record, the Node Address field, has the address of the device to which responses should be sent, node 93. The Object field contains the name of the device for which we're looking. In this field we find "Mark Unruh x6369". In the Type field we find "Workstation" and in the Zone field we find an asterisk, which means "the same as this" in the obscure language of Name Binding. The Macintosh is looking for any other nodes that have registered names that are the same as those it wishes to use for itself, in much the same way that the LAP Enqs were used. This is what a node must do to perform NBP registration, which means "publishing" the NBP names to which it intends to respond.

The fourth group of packets are similar to those in the second, except that they're publishing an NBP record of type "Macintosh Quadra 900," rather than "Workstation." As many iterations of this three-packet pattern will be broadcast as are necessary to NBP register all the different network-oriented software processes running on the machine.

While the last packet capture demonstrated the use of NBP packets by a negative example, if we open the Chooser on our second machine, and select the LaserWriter driver icon, we can expect a more positive response.

In this transaction, we have NBP LookUp, or query, packets which are broadcast by the Macintosh while the Chooser is in use, and we have NBP Response packets returning from the devices being queried for. In this case, we are looking for LaserWriters, and there is only one on our network. Thus we have a packet being broadcast every one and a half seconds by node 93, immediately followed by a response from node 129 directly to node 93. These pairs will continue in exactly the same fashion as long as the Chooser is open. As we now have packets traveling in two directions, I've colored the packets being sent by the Macintosh dark gray, while the ones sent by the LaserWriter are white. As before, the arrow denotes the passage of time.

As we can see from the packet capture, the lookup is 33 bytes and the response is 54 bytes, for a total of 87 bytes every second and a half, or 58 bytes per second, or 464 bits per second. As the total bandwidth of the LocalTalk medium is 230,400 bits per second, keeping the Chooser open on this one machine is consuming 0.20%, or one five-hundredth of our network bandwidth. This figure increases with the number of devices responding. The phrase "MIS LaserWriter x4527" is 21 characters, or 21 bytes, and the Type code, "LaserWriter", is 11. Say we had eight different file servers responding to a lookup, and their names averaged 20 characters in length. The type code for file servers is "AFPServer", so we can calculate that the response packets would be about 51 bytes, while the lookup would be 31 bytes. In this scenario, each open Chooser would use 1.02% of the available bandwidth.

In the AppleTalk header of the lookup packet we see the broadcast address, the return address, and the instruction to interpret the next header in the Datagram Delivery Protocol format. In the DDP header we see that we should interpret the next header in accordance with the Name Binding Protocol format. In the NBP header, we see that this is an NBP Function 2, or NBP LookUp packet, with only one tuple. We know to expect the tuple next, and to interpret the first record as a return address, rather than part of a query, since this is a lookup rather than a reply. The next field specifies an object named "=" which seems a rather unlikely name for a printer. It is in fact another reserved item. Just as the asterisk meant "the same as this," the equals sign means "any." The Type field contains the string "LaserWriter", and the Zone field contains an asterisk. Thus we're looking for LaserWriters in this zone, with any name.

The packet we get back in response from the LaserWriter is fairly straightforward. In the AppleTalk header we can see that the packet is addressed to node 93, the node that was specified as the return address at the beginning of the lookup tuple in the querying packet. The packet is coming from node 129, the address of the LaserWriter, and again the next header is in DDP format. The DDP header tells us to interpret the next header in NBP format, and the NBP header tells us that the packet is an NBP Function 3, or LookUp-Reply packet. The response tuple contains the address of the responding LaserWriter, its name, its type, and the asterisk for the zone name.

After the System software on our second Macintosh has interpreted and stripped off all the headers, it delivers the tuple to the Chooser software, which

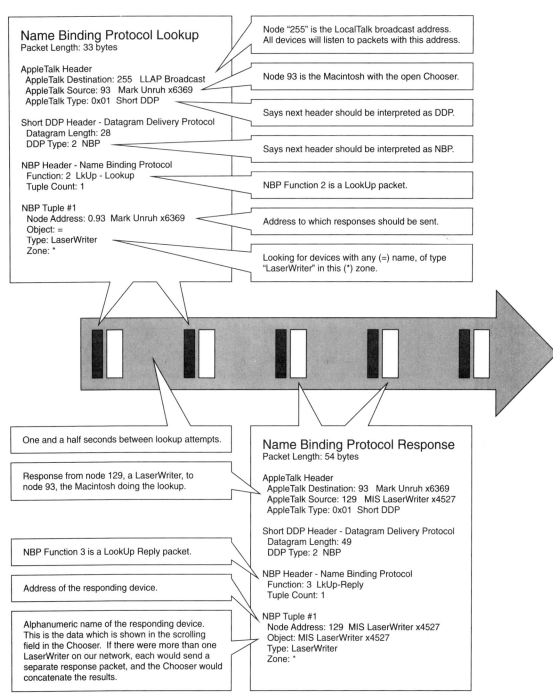

Name Binding Protocol Lookup
Packet Length: 33 bytes

AppleTalk Header
  AppleTalk Destination: 255   LLAP Broadcast
  AppleTalk Source: 93   Mark Unruh x6369
  AppleTalk Type: 0x01   Short DDP

Short DDP Header - Datagram Delivery Protocol
  Datagram Length: 28
  DDP Type: 2 NBP

NBP Header - Name Binding Protocol
  Function: 2 LkUp - Lookup
  Tuple Count: 1

NBP Tuple #1
  Node Address: 0.93 Mark Unruh x6369
  Object: =
  Type: LaserWriter
  Zone: *

Node "255" is the LocalTalk broadcast address. All devices will listen to packets with this address.

Node 93 is the Macintosh with the open Chooser.

Says next header should be interpreted as DDP.

Says next header should be interpreted as NBP.

NBP Function 2 is a LookUp packet.

Address to which responses should be sent.

Looking for devices with any (=) name, of type "LaserWriter" in this (*) zone.

One and a half seconds between lookup attempts.

Response from node 129, a LaserWriter, to node 93, the Macintosh doing the lookup.

NBP Function 3 is a LookUp Reply packet.

Address of the responding device.

Alphanumeric name of the responding device. This is the data which is shown in the scrolling field in the Chooser. If there were more than one LaserWriter on our network, each would send a separate response packet, and the Chooser would concatenate the results.

Name Binding Protocol Response
Packet Length: 54 bytes

AppleTalk Header
  AppleTalk Destination: 93   Mark Unruh x6369
  AppleTalk Source: 129   MIS LaserWriter x4527
  AppleTalk Type: 0x01 Short DDP

Short DDP Header - Datagram Delivery Protocol
  Datagram Length: 49
  DDP Type: 2 NBP

NBP Header - Name Binding Protocol
  Function: 3 LkUp-Reply
  Tuple Count: 1

NBP Tuple #1
  Node Address: 129 MIS LaserWriter x4527
  Object: MIS LaserWriter x4527
  Type: LaserWriter
  Zone: *

Figure 2.5   Packets used by the Chooser.

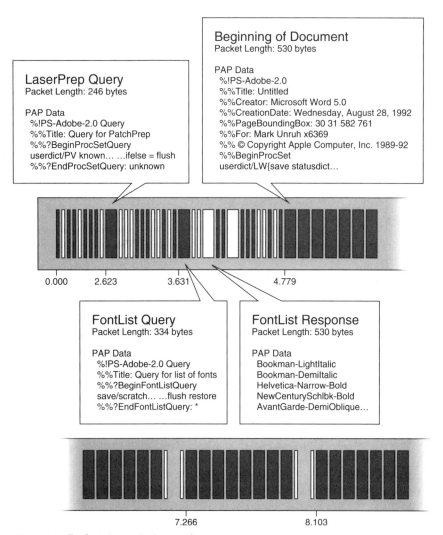

Figure 2.6 Packets in a printing session.

displays the name of the responding device in the scrolling field at the right of the Chooser window, and remembers what node number was associated with the name it put into the list. If several devices had responded to our lookup, they would all appear in the field, and the Chooser would keep track of all their node numbers, so that when we choose one from the list and close the Chooser, it could report back to the System software the address of the device to send print jobs to.

Now I'm going to create a simple Microsoft Word document on our second Macintosh, print it, and watch the flow of information between that Macintosh and our LaserWriter. The document will simply consist of the sentence "This is a sample."

This packet dump is much larger than either of the previous two. This transaction consisted of 124 packets, totaling over 42 kilobytes. Unlike the AppleTalk activity at startup and created by the Chooser, the bulk of this transaction consists of data, rather than AppleTalk header information.

When a user prints a document on a Macintosh, the operating system converts it to PostScript, the "page description language" used by nearly all high-end printers. PostScript is a programming language, just like C, Pascal, or Fortran, but it isn't designed to be run on Macintoshes. In response to a "Print" command, the user's Macintosh creates a PostScript program which is down-

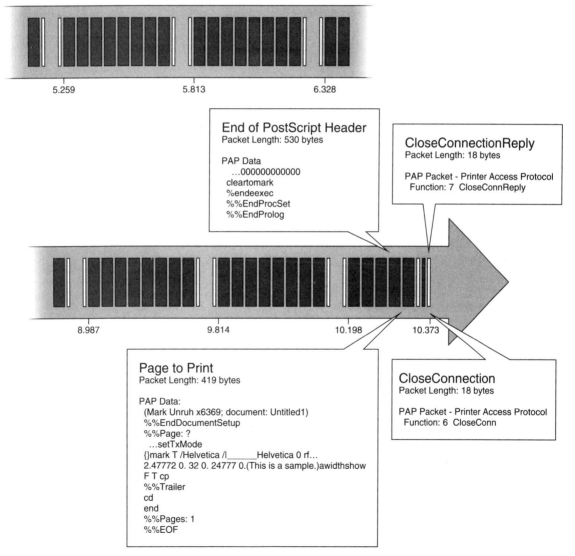

Figure 2.6 *(Continued)*

loaded through the network to the LaserWriter. The program is executed on the processor in the printer, and the output, or result, of the program is in the form of a printed page.

The data in the packets of this printing session is a PostScript program being sent to the LaserWriter. The data is enclosed in four layers of headers: first, the LLAP or LocalTalk Link Access Protocol header, necessary because we're on a LocalTalk network; second, the Short DDP or Datagram Delivery Protocol header, which mostly specifies what kind of data is being sent; third, either an ATP or AppleTalk Transaction Protocol, or an NBP or Name Binding Protocol header. The first two packets of the transaction are NBP LookUp and Reply packets and, after that, all are ATP packets. The AppleTalk Transaction Protocol allows specific query-and-response transactions to occur "reliably." That is, the protocol includes provision for lost packets, and can retransmit either a query or response if it detects an error, leaving applications free from the burden of monitoring the status of individual transactions. The fourth header is a PAP or Printer Access Protocol header, a type used only in printing. The PostScript program that's being sent has its own form of headers, but as they aren't network-related, we won't delve into them very far. Within the PAP header is the PAP Data, which is the PostScript itself. As before, in all but the last two packets, I've deleted the headers, leaving only the PAP Data in the illustration.

In the illustration, I've broken out eight packets of particular interest. The first, which is the tenth packet in the session, is also the first large packet, of 246 bytes in length. It contains a very short PostScript program which, when executed by the printer, will result in a response over the network, addressed to the sending Macintosh. As you can see in the second line of the PAP Data, the "title" of the PostScript program is "Query for PatchPrep". The Macintosh is finding out whether the printer has been "initialized" since it was last powered up, and if so, whether that initialization was done by a Macintosh using a compatible version of PostScript. The initialization serves the printer in somewhat the same way that operating system software serves a Macintosh. That is, printers contain PostScript interpreters and basic instructions in their ROMs, but they need specific instructions "patching" over their old ones to make them compatible with the latest version of PostScript being used by the Macintoshes they serve. The instructions which tell the Macintosh how to initialize a LaserWriter are contained in the LaserWriter rdev, or driver, found in the Extensions folder. In Systems previous to 7.0, it was in a separate file called "Laser Prep". In either case, all the Macintoshes using any particular printer should have the same version of this file, or "initialization wars," in which a printer is reinitialized each time it's used, can result. Since the initialization process can add tens of seconds and hundreds of kilobytes of traffic to each print job, this is a highly undesirable state.

The second highlighted packet is also a query by the Macintosh, this time for a list of the fonts which the printer has PostScript descriptions of, and thus already knows how to print. These may be temporarily stored in RAM, or permanently contained in its ROMs or stored on a directly connected SCSI hard disk. Again, the answer is important, because a lot of time and traffic are dependent upon it. If the document which is being printed contains typefaces which the LaserWriter doesn't know about, the "LaserWriter Fonts" corresponding to each of those typefaces must be downloaded from the Macintosh's Extensions folder to the LaserWriter, consuming both time and network bandwidth. If the font isn't found in the LaserWriter, and isn't contained in the Extensions folder of the printing Macintosh, the Macintosh has to generate a bitmap for each character and download each one to the printer, which is terribly inefficient and results in unattractive output.

The third packet, entitled "FontList Response," is the first of two large packets addressed to the printing Macintosh which contain a list of the fonts available in the printer's ROMs. The size of the first packet, 530 bytes, is significant in that this is the maximum size of a PAP packet. On each end, at the Macintosh and at the LaserWriter, memory is being reserved for incoming packets. Since, as we've seen, the transaction is generating quite a bit of traffic, and memory is usually a valuable commodity, a system of memory buffers is associated with the ATP protocol. The buffers are allocated in 512-byte quanta, and a maximum of eight buffers can be allocated to any one ATP transaction. If you subtract the LLAP, DDP, ATP, and PAP headers, you find 512 data bytes in a 530-byte PAP packet. The allocation mechanism serves as a kind of "flow control," ensuring that buffer space is not allocated until the receiving machine is ready to deal with more data, and that the sending machine knows when it can continue to send.

Thus, beginning at the 4.779 second mark, we see the fourth marked packet, which is the beginning of the PostScript page description itself, and also marks the beginning of a series of these maximum-size ATP transactions. Each transaction is characterized by a short ATP Request packet from the LaserWriter to the Macintosh, notifying that Macintosh that another eight 512-byte buffers have been allocated. This is followed immediately by eight 530-byte ATP Transaction Response packets, which contain 512 bytes of PAP data, from the Macintosh back to the LaserWriter, followed by an ATP Transaction Release, which serves as a receipt for the data, sent back from the LaserWriter to the Macintosh. A short delay follows, about a half second in our case, while the LaserWriter processes the received data, and then the cycle repeats with another ATP Request from the printer. In this packet, we can see the beginning of the PostScript header in the PAP data, in which the version of the PostScript language (Adobe-2.0) is specified, the document is named ("Untitled" because we didn't save it on the Macintosh before printing it), the name of the application sending the document (Microsoft Word 4.0) is identified, the creation date is specified, and the Owner Name of the person who created the document is specified.

The PostScript code which follows is usually in the form of an extremely large header, designed to take care of any odd things being done with the typesetting or illustrations in the document itself. The fifth marked packet, nearly five and a half seconds and 39 kilobytes later, is the end of this header.

The sixth packet contains the entire page description. After the "EndDocumentSetup" line, we see a setTxMode, which tells the LaserWriter to shift from line-drawing mode to typesetting mode. The next line selects Helvetica font, the line after that positions the origin on the page and specifies the text to be typeset, and the document ends soon after. There follows an ATP Transaction Release, ending that particular ATP Transaction.

In the seventh packet, the PAP header specifies a PAP Function 6, which is CloseConnection, and there is no PAP data. In the eighth packet, the LaserWriter responds with a PAP Function 7 packet, which is a CloseConnectionReply, and the print session is ended. The LaserWriter will now wait for two seconds, listening for new print jobs, ensuring that it sees packets from all the waiting machines, and can successfully select the one that's been waiting longest for the next print job.

2.8   The Solution

Having successfully gotten his Macintosh connected to a newly acquired LaserWriter and printed a few documents on it, Mark was quite impressed by the quality of the output and became fascinated by the wide range of typefaces available. He spent several days drafting and printing memos, each with a multitude of fonts, before the aghast looks these inspired in his coworkers convinced him that he really wasn't cut out to be a desktop publisher. Having gotten this out of his system he realized that, no matter how much he'd like to keep the LaserWriter for himself, his best option would be to make it available to other computer users in the company. After doing so, he could institute an interdepartmental chargeback scheme when they became similarly hooked, recoup his investment in the laser printer, and make his fledgling MIS (Management Information Systems, an inflated and somewhat egoistic term for network and computer management) department a profit center from the start.

To further his primary goal of understanding how Macintoshes are networked, Mark inquired among more expert friends, who directed him to purchase a "packet analyzer." So armed, he spent some time snooping among the packets exchanged by his Macintosh and the LaserWriter, until he became fairly certain he had some glimmering of what went on behind the scenes when he pressed the "Print" button or opened the Chooser.

3

Adding the Next Machine

3.1 The Problem

Mark decided that the first unwitting conscript to be attached to his fledgling network would be his assistant Luis. To that end, he began to investigate the physical problems to be overcome in adding another device to his network, and the benefits that this would provide to him and to the reluctant victim.

3.2 The Daisy-Chain Network

The simple two-node network created in Chap. 2 was a *daisy-chain* network. Daisy-chains are the easiest to implement of the LocalTalk topologies, and are frequently used where there are just a few machines grouped in a small area. There are two ways to add a new device to a daisy chain: to one end, or into some point in the middle.

For now, let's add the second user to the end of our network, next to the first user. To do so, we must first set up the new machine, and plug in a LocalTalk connector. Plug a new modular cable into one of the RJ-11 jacks on the new LocalTalk connector, and put a terminating resistor into the other jack. Move to the first user's workstation, remove the terminating resistor from the LocalTalk connector on that machine, and plug in the other end of the second modular cable. When you're sure you've got both ends connected, go back and turn on the second workstation.

The simplest way to determine whether you've succeeded in adding a new user to a simple network is to open the Chooser on the new workstation and see whether you're able to "see" the same services on the network that can be "seen" from existing machines on the same network. In the case of the example we've been developing, you would look in the new machine's Chooser for the LaserWriter which we configured in the last chapter. If it doesn't appear, first make sure that it really is turned on, and can be seen from the rest of the network, then check your new connections.

Since the daisy-chain network is providing us with service in serial, rather than parallel form, we can add to one end without much trouble, but if we add to the middle, we will have to cut our existing user off from the printer for a short period of time. In general, if this is done while users are working—during the middle of the day, for instance—you run the risk of disrupting currently running print jobs and any other network services which may be in use.

3.3 Peer-to-Peer File Sharing

When you install the operating System 7.0 or later onto a Macintosh, the installer program will put the files necessary for peer-to-peer file sharing onto that Macintosh by default. Three Control Panel Devices provide the interface to this functionality.

The first, Sharing Setup, allows you to assign a name to the Macintosh by which it will be recognized on the network. The second, Users & Groups, allows you to assign different access privileges or levels to different individual users who may try to access the Macintosh, and to whole groups of users. The third, File Sharing Monitor, allows you to see what volumes or directories you are currently advertising as available on the network, and who is currently using them, as well as allowing you to break the connection with any of those people.

The Sharing Setup cdev, or Control Panel Device, acts as a set of master switches for the file-sharing functions of your Macintosh. In the first field, you can assign yourself a name. This is the name which the Macintosh will default to in identifying you, the user. As we saw in Chap. 2, when a PostScript program is generated, as in printing a document, the name of the person who is sending the print job is inserted into the code. In the example in Chap. 2, we saw the phrase "%%For: Mark Unruh x6369". That information was obtained from the "Owner Name" which is kept in the Macintosh's parameter RAM. On machines running versions of the operating system prior to System 7, the owner name was called the "Chooser Name," because it was defined in the Chooser desk accessory, in an otherwise unchanged process.

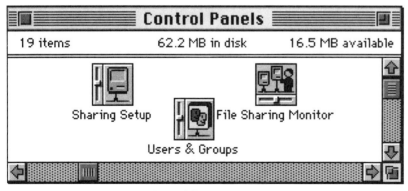

Figure 3.1 File Sharing Control Panel devices.

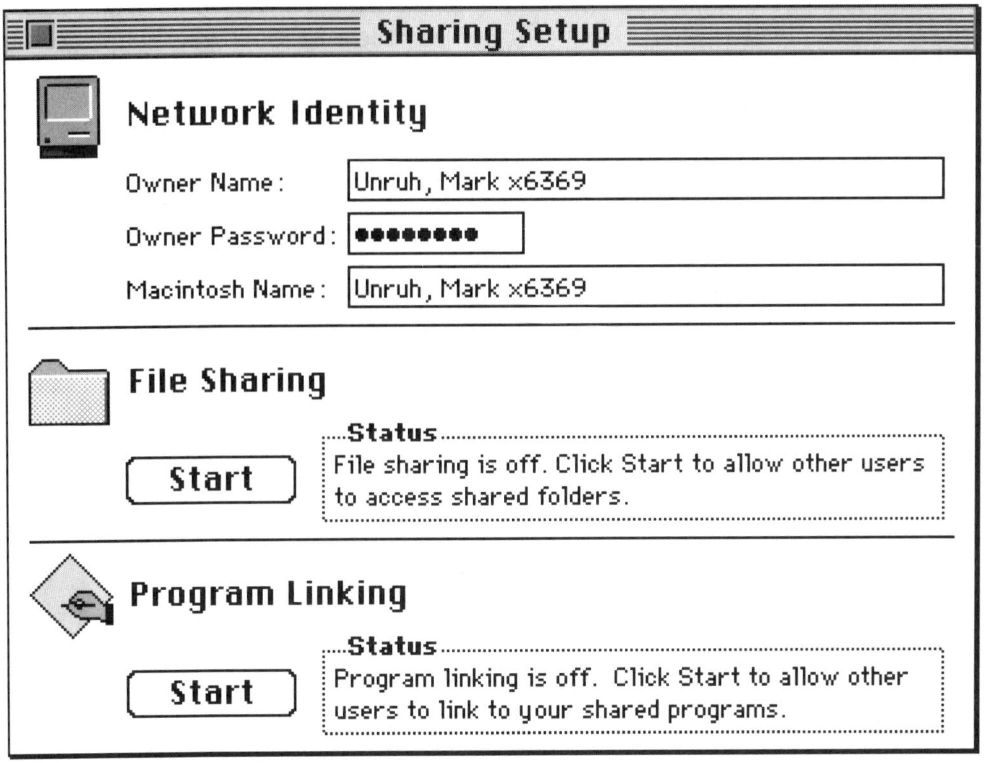

Figure 3.2   Sharing Setup Control Panel device.

In the second field, you can enter a master File Sharing password. With the Owner Name and the Owner Password, we can log into this Macintosh from anywhere on the network, and access all the volumes attached to it, shared or not, if File Sharing is turned on. Unfortunately, this password is limited to eight characters in length. Each character of the password is replaced by a dot when you leave the password field, so that it cannot be read by other people.

The next item, File Sharing, turns the sharing of folders and volumes on and off. It takes a few moments to take effect, either after being tuned on in the Control Panel, or after restarting the machine subsequently. When File Sharing is turned off (the button reads "Start"), the Macintosh is not visible in the Choosers of other users' computers.

The last item, Program Linking, turns interapplication communication on and off with respect to other users. Interapplication communication is what it sounds like: messages passed back and forth between two different programs, rather than between a program and the user. If Program Linking is active, programs on other users' machines could theoretically send these "AppleEvent" messages to any applications for which you've enabled Linking. These messages would typically take the form of commands (menu items, for instance) to be executed by the receiving program, data to be entered in it, or queries to which it should respond. At the time of this writing, AppleEvents are not supported in software applications, so it's of only theoretical interest and won't be discussed in any further detail.

The Users & Groups Control Panel is a window in which you define user accounts. There are four types of accounts which can be defined. From left to right in this example, we have Guest, Owner, User, and Group. Double-clicking on any of these icons brings up the appropriate definitions window.

The Guest user is simply an account which doesn't require a password, and has only the lowest level of access to files on shared volumes. In this window, you can turn guest privileges on and off. The name "<Guest>" cannot be changed.

The Owner definition icon is distinguished from the others by its heavy black border. Opening it brings up this window. Like the <Guest> definition, the Owner name and password cannot be changed from within this Control Panel, but are dependent upon the Owner Name and Owner Password strings, which

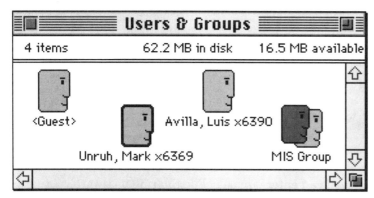

Figure 3.3 The Users & Groups control panel.

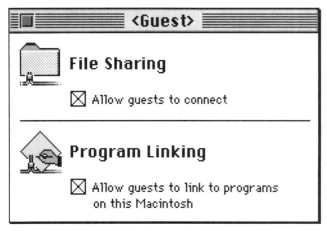

Figure 3.4 Guest definition.

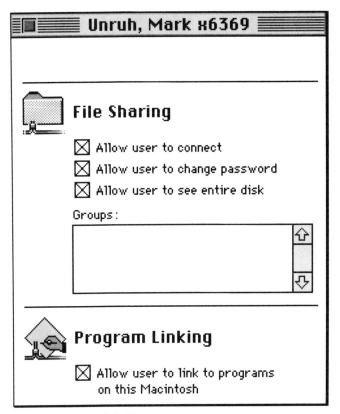

Figure 3.5 Owner definition.

are defined in the Sharing Setup Control Panel. Also, this is the only type of definition which has a "see entire disk" option.

Selecting "New User" from the File menu creates a new User icon, with the name highlighted. Type the name of the user whom you want to be able to access your shared directories, and then double-click on the icon. In this window (Fig. 3.6), you can create a password for the user, or you can leave the password field empty and the "allow user to change password" box checked so the user can create his or her own password. As in the Sharing Setup Control Panel, the password is displayed as dots after it's been entered either by you, or remotely by the user.

New Groups are created with the "New Group" item in the File menu. They're named like new Users, but double-clicking on them brings up an empty window. Users are added to groups by dragging their icons from the Users & Groups window into the specific Group window. Users can be deleted from Groups by dragging them from the Group window to the trash can, and both Users and Groups can be deleted by dragging their icons from the Users & Groups window to the trash.

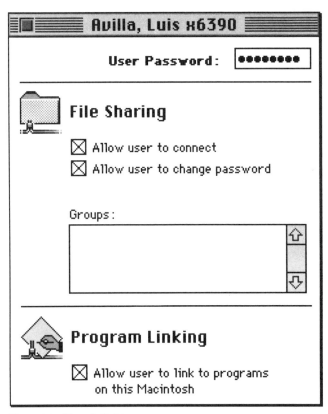

Figure 3.6 User definition.

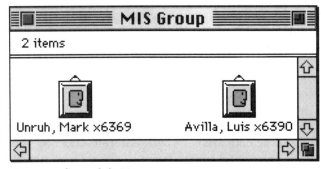

Figure 3.7 Group definition.

The third Control Panel is used for monitoring the status of file sharing going on on your Macintosh. The left field lists all directories currently being shared, while the right field lists all the other users who are currently sharing files from your machine. The "Disconnect" button allows you to cut off service to any of the currently logged-in users, while the "File Sharing Activity" ther-

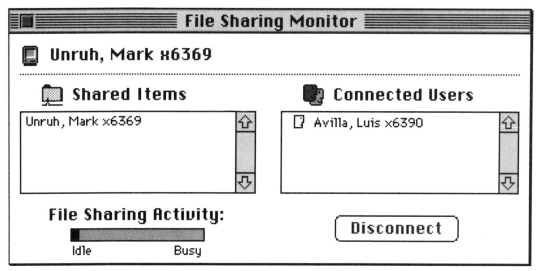

Figure 3.8   The File Sharing Monitor Control Panel.

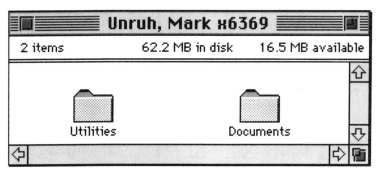

Figure 3.9   Creating a shared folder.

mometer gives a rough indication of how heavily your Macintosh is being used by remote users.

Back in the Finder, we can create a new folder and, for the purposes of this example, give it the same name as my Macintosh Name. Then put a few items to share with other people into it, and drag it onto the desktop. Highlighting its icon and selecting "Sharing . . ." from the File menu brings up a window which allows us to share that particular folder, and to set user privileges for it.

In this window we've shared the folder by checking the first check box. Different privileges have then been specified by unchecking different boxes in the privileges matrix, and selected a Group to which they should apply. By unchecking "Make Changes," we've write-protected the folder so that no one other than Mark can change any items in it, or add new items. By unchecking "See Files," we've made individual files invisible to people who aren't in the

"MIS" Group. We can also reassign ownership so that someone else has complete control over the folder. These options will be discussed in greater detail in Chap. 6. After closing this window, the folder will be available to other users on the network.

As soon as the File Sharing process has successfully made it available on the network, the folder's icon will change to a folder with network cables depending from it to indicate that the folder is currently being shared. When another user mounts the folder to their own desktop, the folder's icon will change again, adding the User "faces." If all users unmount the shared folder, it will return to its second state.

To mount a folder that's being shared from another user's machine, open your Chooser, select the AppleShare icon, and double-click on the name of the user's Macintosh from the list in the file server window.

The first dialog to come up in the login procedure will default to "Registered User" mode. That is, it assumes that you have a User definition on the machine

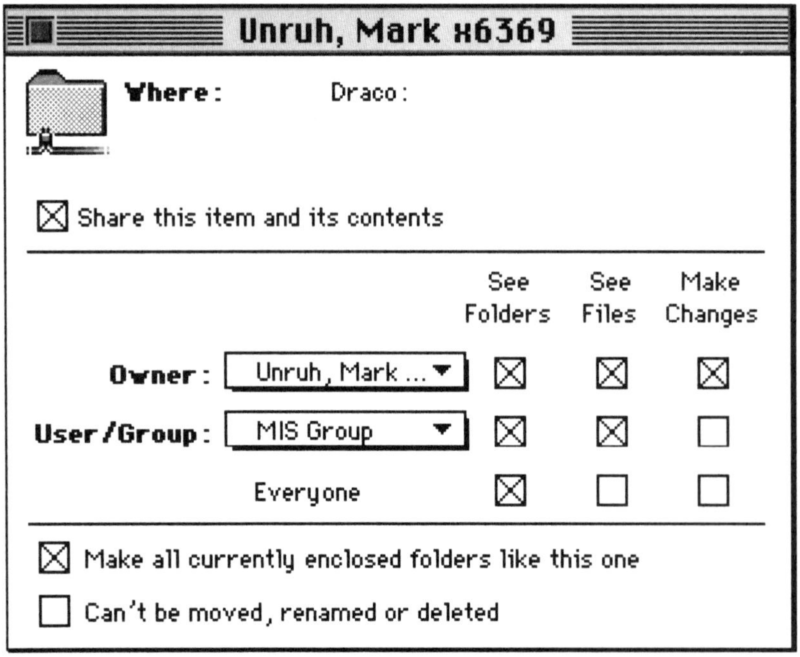

```
╔══════════════ Unruh, Mark x6369 ══════════════╗

     ┌──┐
     │  │   Where:        Draco:
     └──┘

   ☒ Share this item and its contents
   ─────────────────────────────────────────────
                              See      See     Make
                            Folders   Files  Changes

     Owner:  [ Unruh, Mark ... ▼]     ☒       ☒       ☒

 User/Group:  [ MIS Group      ▼]     ☒       ☒       ☐

             Everyone                 ☒       ☐       ☐
   ─────────────────────────────────────────────
   ☒ Make all currently enclosed folders like this one
   ☐ Can't be moved, renamed or deleted
```

Figure 3.10   Sharing a folder.

Unshared Folder   Shared Folder   Currently in Use

Figure 3.11   Shared folder icons.

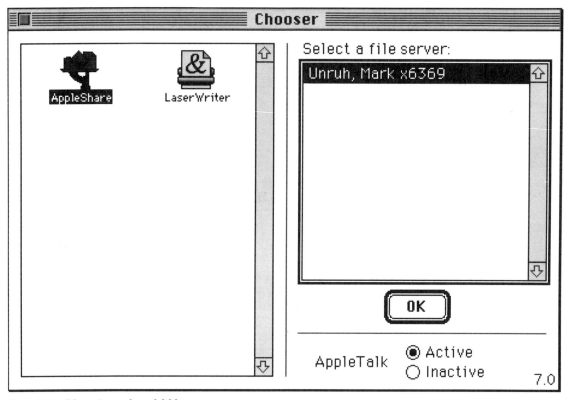

Figure 3.12   Mounting a shared folder.

that you're trying to log into. If that is not the case, select "Guest". The Name field will contain either the Owner Name from the machine you're currently on, or the name of the last person to use it to log into another machine. The cursor will be in the Password field.

If this is the first time you've logged into this particular server, you may want to assign yourself a new password. To do so, press the "Set Password" button, and enter both the old and new passwords. You will be asked to confirm your choice of new password.

Once you've logged in, you'll be presented with a list of currently served volumes or folders. Since the machine we're logging into has only one available, it's selected. In lists of several available volumes, the first one will be selected. By checking the box after the name, we can indicate that we want this volume to be automatically mounted to our desktop every time we start our Macintosh, provided it's available on the network at that time. We then have two options: Save Name Only, and Save Name and Password. If we select Name Only, we will be prompted for the user password next time we start our machine, while Save Name and Password makes the login process completely transparent.

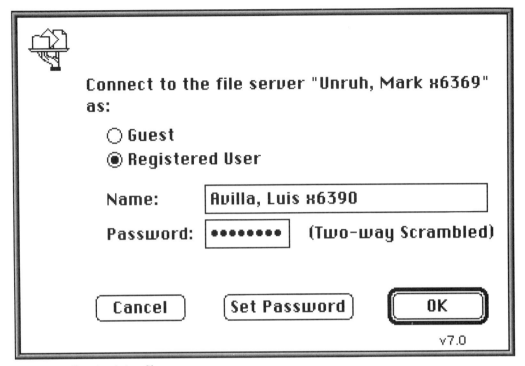

Figure 3.13 Logging into a file server.

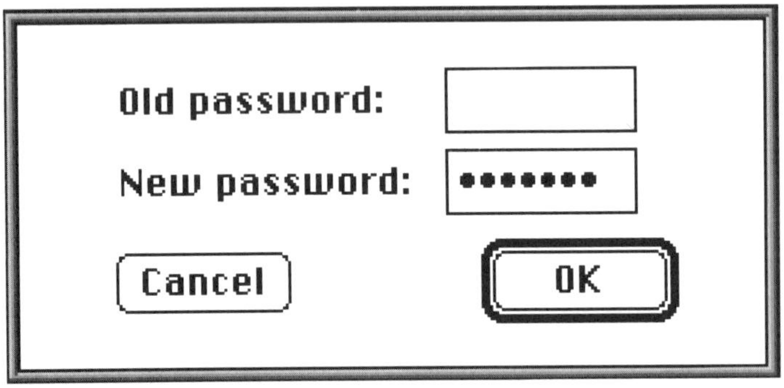

Figure 3.14 Changing a user password remotely.

3.4 Client Names as Identifiers

As you will soon see, the careful selection and organization of folders to be shared greatly simplifies the process of networked file sharing in large environments.

After we've clicked "OK" to dismiss the server volume dialog box, and returned to the finder, a new icon has been mounted on our desktop. An icon

Figure 3.15 Selecting a server volume.

Unruh, Mark x6369   Unruh, Mark x6369

Figure 3.16 Client and host views of served folders.

of a platter with a folder, an application, and a file on it represents a server volume.

Since the Finder allows multiple volumes with the same name on the desktop, and many people name folders in similar ways, the potential for disorder is greatly increased by peer-to-peer file sharing. If, for instance, three different people on the network were sharing folders called "Documents" and we mounted all of them, we would have no immediately visible means of telling them apart once they were all mounted on our desktop.

If, however, we place all the folders we're interested in sharing in one folder, give that folder the same name as we're using for our Owner Name and Macintosh Name, and share that folder only, other people will only have to mount a single volume from our machine, thus saving screen real-estate on their own desktops and avoiding clutter. Most importantly, that volume is guaranteed a unique and inherently informative name.

Unique and informative naming schemes are an invaluable aid in network administration. For the examples in this book, I've picked a rather simple scheme, but one which is typical of those used in many companies which enforce naming conventions. A full name, followed by a telephone extension number, is a good choice, and one which can be used in one of two ways, depending upon whether you wish to provide yourself, or your users, with more information. The telephone extension number can either be the one belonging to whomever is responsible for the device, or it can be one uniquely associated with the wires by which the device is connected to the network. In the first instance, the telephone extension of a responsible party allows users some immediately identifiable recourse and source of information, if they run into trouble with some device. If, for instance, a user were to double-click on an alias to a file residing on a remote hard drive, and encounter the error message "The shared disk 'Mark Unruh x6369' could not be found on the network," they would know exactly who to contact about their problem. In the second instance, the number would coincide not with an extension of telephone service, but with a cable inside your walls, leading to the corresponding device. This form of "cable management" will be discussed at length in Chap. 5. Some advanced PBXes, or "Private Branch Exchanges" as business telephone switches are called, provide aliasing features. If this is the case with your PBX, you may be able to provide yourself and your users with the advantages of both schemes, in that cable identification numbers could be aliased to the extensions of the responsible parties in a table contained in the PBX.

Complementing this numerical form of identification with the user's full name allows instant identification, without consulting any tables or organizational charts. Many companies have building and mailstop naming and numbering conventions, which serve much the same purpose in correlating the computer user's name with some concrete location and method of contacting the user.

Identifying network services, like file servers and LaserWriters, with extension numbers aids users as well as network administrators, in that it provides an obvious path for the user to follow if he or she is having trouble with some particular device or service. If, for instance, a user is unable to log into a server because he or she has forgotten his or her password, a telephone extension which will reach the network administrator responsible for the maintenance of that server is handily present right in the name of the device.

If more than one person tries to use the same networked printer, user names are again invaluable. If one user is tying up a LaserWriter with a very long, low-priority document, and another user tries to print to the same printer, they'll be informed of both the name of the first user and the name of the document being printed. In an emergency, a good user-naming scheme would allow the second user to contact the first, and ask to interrupt his/her print job until the second user had gotten whatever needed to be printed out.

As I explained in Chap. 2, network devices find unique identifiers to use as network addresses. The fact that these are assigned dynamically, and are not guaranteed to remain the same from device to device at different times, as well as the fact that randomly assigned numerical identifiers aren't inherently informative, necessitated the creation of Chooser Names, as the Macintosh Name was called under Systems prior to 7.0. If laser printers were identified only by a numerical string, and that string were prone to unexpected changes, it would not be useful, as you wouldn't know where to pick up your finished pages. If, however, each has a textual name assigned by its users, that name can be used by the Chooser to remember what printer you used last, and find it again.

3.5 The Solution

A feeling of exhilaration temporarily overcame Mark upon his realization that by inducing Luis to "share" the hard disk on his Macintosh he'd just acquired nearly thirty megabytes of space to store computer games in, with the added benefit of plausible deniability. At the same time, Mark also realized that other weaker-willed souls might be led astray by the same temptation. While he recognized that file sharing was a useful feature of the Macintosh operating system, indeed one which would prove invaluable to conducting business on a small network, it was also one which could be sorely abused. As a result, he determined to proceed with the addition of more users to his growing network, but to inform them what he regarded to be proper use of the network, as well.

4

LocalTalk Topologies

4.1 The Problem

As Mark added a few more users to his simple network, he began to encounter problems. The first one was cables becoming disconnected when users tripped over them. Later, he began to wonder how to add users in other rooms without stringing cables through doorways, making it impossible to close the doors (and thereby impossible to comply with some fire regulations). Mark decided to investigate the possibility of running network cables inside the walls, like electrical cable, plumbing, and other utilities.

4.2 The Daisy Chain Topology

In Chaps. 2 and 3, we've been working with a simple daisy-chain topology. To review, a daisy-chain network consists of as many LocalTalk connectors as there are devices to connect, modular telephone cables interconnecting each LocalTalk connector, and a quarter-watt, 120-ohm RJ-11-mounted resistor terminating each end of the chain. If the chain is broken at any point, it is divided into two smaller chains, which cannot communicate with each other, and may

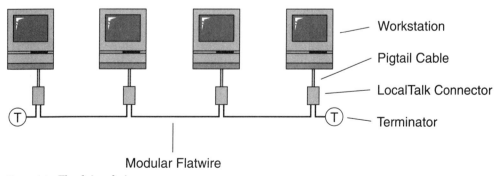

Figure 4.1 The daisy-chain.

be internally unreliable, due to the partial lack of termination at the broken end of each.

As we've seen, daisy chains are inexpensive and easy to construct, but we've been dealing with a few devices in the same room, which is what daisy chains are best suited for. Their weaknesses become more apparent when they're spread over larger areas.

Unlike the walljack and drop cable arrangement that your telephone uses, each adjacent pair of daisy-chained devices are normally connected with a single contiguous, plug-terminated cable, which can become inconvenient and unattractive if it has to be run between rooms. Adding jacks or butt-adapters further decreases the reliability of your network, while adding possible points of failure. The high impedance of 28-gauge modular telephone cable is exacerbated by the fact that the conductors are stranded, rather than solid wire. That is, each of the conductors is made of many tiny strands of wire twisted around each other, rather than the single piece of annealed copper found in each conductor of a twisted-pair cable. Stranded cable can be subjected to much more manipulation and flexion than solid-conductor cable, but at the expense of maximum signal transmission range and other beneficial characteristics. While the jacketing of modular cables is also designed to be more flexible, it's not as resistant to puncture or abrasion as that of twisted-pair cable, dangers which are encountered when wire is pulled through walls.

In addition to being subject to physical maltreatment, daisy-chain networks are particularly vulnerable to two electrical problems, which will be discussed further in the next chapter: impedance mismatches and near-end crosstalk. Impedance mismatches, and the symptom they cause, signal reflection, occur when wires of different diameter or impedance are joined together and a signal is passed through them. Part of the amplitude of the signal, sometimes a large part, is reflected back toward the sender, rather than passing on through the join. Near-end crosstalk is a phenomenon which allows signals to partially cross from the wires they're supposed to be running on to other nearby wires, diminishing their own strength and corrupting the signals on the other wires, as well.

Both Apple and Farallon optimistically predict a 1000-foot maximum network length when using a daisy-chain topology.

4.3   The Trunk Topology

If you think of a daisy-chain network as a "serial" connection between devices, the trunk topology is the equivalent parallel form of connection. More resistant to damage and accidental disablement, and suited to connecting machines located in different rooms, trunks are best suited to networks with a few machines spread over a great linear distance which are not going to require detailed management or the unexpected addition of new devices once the network has been constructed. Trunk networks made of twisted-pair wire cannot be upgraded to use network protocols faster than LocalTalk.

Since a trunk network is parallel, provision can be made in the form of extra wall jacks at the time of construction for more devices than you have at the

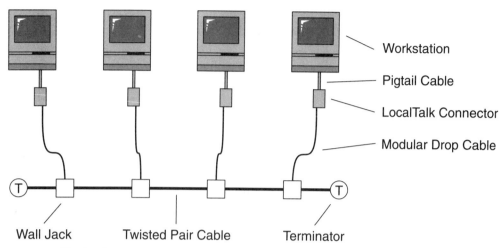

Figure 4.2   The trunk.

time, and LocalTalk connectors added later. Simply put, the fact that a trunk network is parallel, rather than serial, means that if one user removes his/her LocalTalk connector from the network, it doesn't affect anyone else.

Trunk networks consist of a single unbroken length of twisted-pair cable, up to 3,000 feet in length, with wall jacks distributed along its length. The wall jack at each end of the trunk has a terminating resistor across the outside pair of terminals (the screws upon which the black and yellow wires "terminate" or end), while at the jacks in between, the active conductors are stripped and wrapped around the terminals, with care being taken not to break them. When wrapping a conductor around a screw-down terminal like those on most wall jacks, it's important to wrap the conductor clockwise, rather than counter-clockwise, so that the action of tightening the screw will tighten, rather than loosen the connection. The 120-ohm, quarter-watt resistors used in terminating LocalTalk networks can be recognized by their color coding: a gold or silver band, followed by a brown one, a red one, and a second brown one. The first band simply identifies the accuracy with which the resistor complies with its specified resistance: gold indicates ±1 percent, while silver indicates ±5 percent. The other bands are more crucial in identifying the component.

In combination, three factors allow the much longer length of trunk networks. First, since the wire is thicker, 22- or 24-gauge, with solid conductors, it presents much less impedance to the passage of electrical signals than does the 28-gauge stranded wire of which daisy-chain networks are made, so signals travel farther before they dissipate and become unreadable. Second, since the conductor is continuous, rather than being made up of many short segments of wire, each with slightly different electrical characteristics, there are no impedance mismatches which might cause signal reflections. Third, and most important, is the fact that the cable used is twisted-pair, which allows receiving devices to perform accurate signal-to-noise discrimination, since sources of

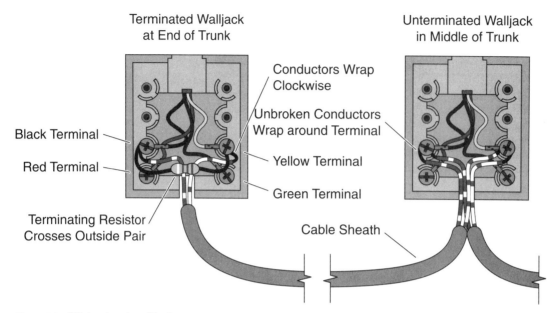

Figure 4.3 Wiring trunk walljacks.

noise are generally equidistant from, and thus affect, both conductors of a twisted pair equally.

Signal reflection and attenuation are the two most important threats to the integrity of most trunk networks. Signal reflection, mentioned above, in the section on daisy chains, is a simple phenomenon, but one which must be dealt with proactively, rather than reactively. At the time you're planning your network, try to minimize the number of joins between wires by routing wire runs in such a way that you can pull long contiguous runs of wire, rather than bringing wire from two locations and joining them on a terminal or punchdown block (a matrix of terminals made to facilitate interconnections). Where joins are necessary, consider soldering the conductors together on a terminal, if the join is to be a permanent one. If you're using existing wiring, try to pick conductors which you can trace for their whole length, and you know to have few joins in them, rather than ones which have ends where you need them, but are in unknown condition between. Longer runs of contiguous cable are nearly always more reliable than short runs with joins in them, so in the installation or choice of wire runs, always keep this possible tradeoff in mind.

Attenuation is the natural degradation of the amplitude of a signal as it passes through a wire. As the amplitude decreases, the difference between 0 and 1 bit becomes less apparent, and network devices are less likely to be able to interpret them correctly. As square digital waveforms dissipate, they lose their definition as well, which makes it more difficult for devices to correctly maintain synchronization with the signal, further impeding its successful interpretation. Although attenuation can become a factor in very long trunk networks, most LocalTalk transceiver vendors rate their hardware for 3000 to 4000 feet, and this is probably conservative. Few trunk networks grow this long, as management of a cable plant of that size usually dictates a star topology.

If your network is well mapped, finding a break in your cabling isn't too hard. Usually breaks are first discovered by a user (Workstation 1) who tries to use some service—a laser printer, for instance—and cannot find it, or gets some kind of error. Workstations with mounted AppleShare volumes which become disconnected will also inform their user immediately. The locations of the user and the missing service are your first two clues.

From a workstation you know to be at one end of the network, in this case the workstation called "Administrator," use a simple network transponder program like Apple's Inter•Poll or Farallon's CheckNet, shown here, to look out at the machines on your network. In order to "see" the machine, it needs to have registered its node name on the network. The Macintosh operating system 7 and later do this for Macintoshes, and printers do it automatically when they're turned on.

Check first to see whether you can see Workstation 3, the machine at the opposite end of the network. If so, your problem isn't a physical one, unless it's intermittent. If you cannot see the machine at the other end of the network,

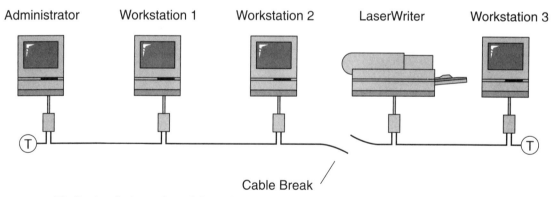

Figure 4.4 Finding breaks in trunks and daisy-chains.

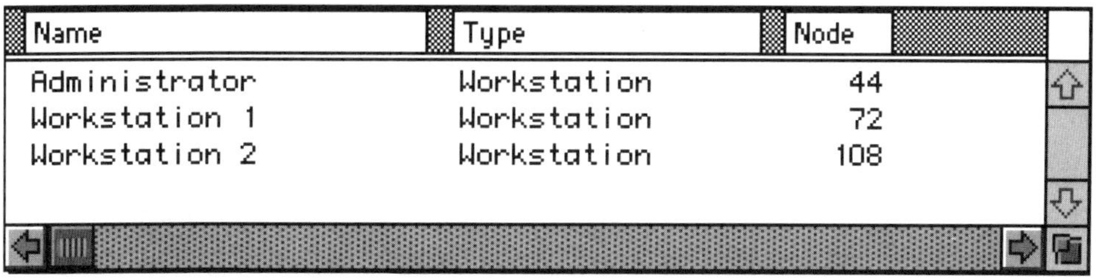

Name	Type	Node
Administrator	Workstation	44
Workstation 1	Workstation	72
Workstation 2	Workstation	108

Figure 4.5 The view from the administrator's workstation.

find the furthest machine you can see, in this case Workstation 2. The break in your network is probably between that device and the LaserWriter on the opposite side of it.

To make absolutely sure, you can look again from Workstation 3, at the opposite end of the network, and see whether you can see all the machines except those you saw before. Here we can see the LaserWriter, which wasn't visible from the other side of the break, and Workstation 3. Adding these to the ones we saw before, we've now accounted for all the devices on our map in Fig. 4.4, we know that there is a break in the network between Workstation 2 and the LaserWriter, and that there are no other breaks. Management techniques and tools will be discussed at greater length in Chap. 12.

Trunk networks typically wind their way through the walls of a building in a serpentine manner, and should be well mapped at the time of installation, since they're otherwise hard to find again, if a need to repair or modify them arises later. This diagram shows a simplified three-node trunk running through typical office space. The trunk begins at a terminated wall jack in office 1, and runs up between the wall studs and over the top of the sheetrock, where it ends above the ceiling tiles. From there it runs over to the corner office, but drops down in a loop to an unterminated jack there, and comes back up again, to end by dropping back down to the terminated jack in office 3.

In trunk networks, labeling of the cable at the point at which it leaves the jack is essential. If testing were to reveal a fault in the wiring between the corner office and office 3, and you opened the jack in the corner office, you would have no means of determining which direction was which, on the cable, if they were not labeled. That is, you'd be looking at a jack with a cable leaving in two directions, but it would be hard to determine which one went to office 3, and which to office 1.

4.4 The Passive Star Topology

The LocalTalk star topologies evolved as Macintosh networks grew through larger office buildings, in response to the problems associated with adds, moves, and changes on daisy-chain and trunk networks. In most modern office buildings, wiring is installed in a manner loosely complying with AT&T's Premises Distribution Specification (or PDS), the Electronic Industries Associ-

Name	Type	Node	
Laser Printer	LaserWriter™	247	⇧
Workstation 3	Workstation	91	
			⇩

Figure 4.6 The view from workstation 3.

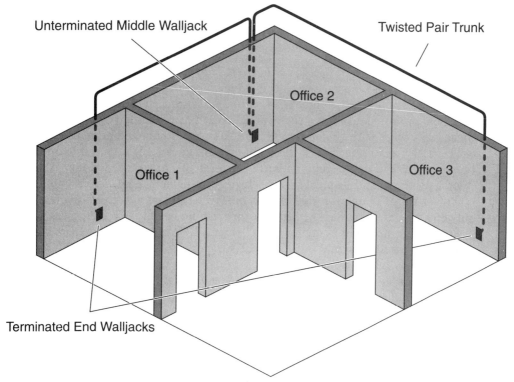

Figure 4.7 Routing a trunk.

ation/Telecommunication Industry Association 568 specification, and the IBM Cabling System specification. Each floor has a central wiring closet which usually adjoins the utility shaft, and may have subsidiary closets closer to the perimeter of the building. This is called the horizontal wiring. The central closets are then connected to each other and to a main closet in the basement by "risers" which are usually just large-diameter pipe sunk through the floor. These constitute vertical wiring. While it may be quite difficult or expensive to install a trunk, many buildings have existing unused horizontal distribution wiring running from central closets to offices, or have conduit through which cable can be easily pulled. These terms will be discussed extensively in the next chapter.

The problem then becomes one of connecting all these "home runs" of wire from individual offices. Unfortunately, the simplest solution is the passive star.

Like trunks, passive stars create a parallel connection between devices. In trunk networks, we have short drop cables connecting individual devices to a long trunk, or bus. In a passive star, we've got long home runs connecting devices to a very short bus. The home runs begin at wall jacks in offices, and run through the walls back to the wiring closet, where they end (or "terminate," this time used in the other sense of the word) on punchdown blocks. The bus in a passive star is formed by crossconnect wire running in vertical loops connecting the rows on which the home runs end.

The main reason for creating a passive star network is monetary. In a prewired building, a passive star can often be put together with minimal outlay of capital and no particular expertise. However, the many reasons for not using passive stars far outweigh this advantage, in nearly all cases.

In addition to the problems of signal attenuation and impedance mismatches, passive stars have three problems that other topologies don't. All of these have to do with the electrical properties of a branched network.

The first problem is that of the 3000-foot distance limit imposed by attenuation. In a trunk or daisy-chain network, it's relatively hard to reach such a length. If, on the other hand, your network is branched, each branch counts toward the 3000-foot total. Thus, in a five-branch passive star, the average branch will be only 600 feet, and on an eight-branch star it would be only 375 feet.

The second problem is one of signal strength. When a device on a trunk or daisy chain sends a signal out its LocalTalk port, the strength of that signal is immediately divided by two, as it has to travel in both directions down the wire to which the device is attached. On a passive star, signals converge on the punchdown block at the center, and are divided by [the number of branches – 1], so on a five-branch star the signal strength would only be at 25 percent after leaving the punchdown block. On an eight-branch star it would be at 14 percent. This effect and the normal effects of attenuation are cumulative.

The third problem is more complicated, and has to do with network termination. On trunks and daisy chains, termination was simple: We put a resistor

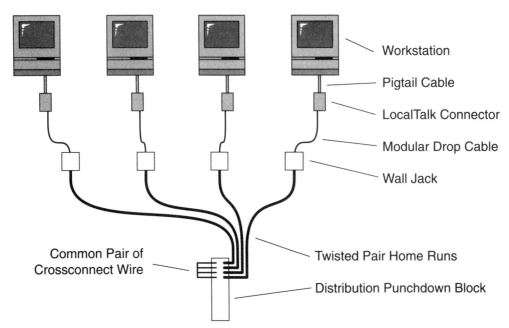

Figure 4.8 The passive star.

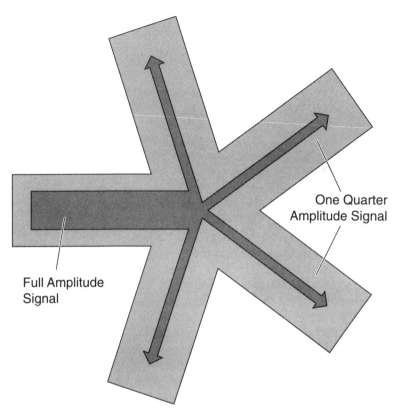

One Quarter
Amplitude Signal

Full Amplitude
Signal

Figure 4.9   Signal strength splitting on passive stars.

across each end, to absorb signals when they got there and prevent them from reflecting back. The resistors had the effect of shorting out the network just a little bit. Since we had two 120-ohm resistors, the total resistance of the network was actually half that. On a five-branch passive star, if we were to terminate all five branches, the resistance would have dropped to 24 ohms, and the network probably wouldn't work. If, on the other hand, we leave several branches completely unterminated, each will generate signal reflections, an electrical problem which plagues many networks and will be discussed in the next chapter.

4.5   Multiport Repeaters

The combination of simplicity of management and cost savings inherent in the star topology and the problems with passive stars proved to be a strong incentive to engineers. The first answer proved to be the multiport repeater, which serves as the hub of an active star.

Instead of connecting the home runs physically with a common bus, like a passive star, a multiport repeater connects them logically, while maintaining each one as a separate physical and electrical network. Each home run then

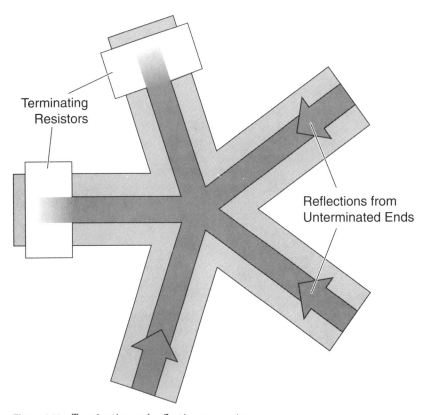

Figure 4.10 Termination and reflection on passive stars.

becomes very simple. Each one consists of a pair of wires with a device at each end. When a device sends a packet, that packet travels down the home run, and is received by the repeater. The repeater, in turn, transmits identical packets back up each of the other home runs, where they are received by the other network devices. Since each home run constitutes a separate physical network and signal attenuation is not cumulative between home runs in an active star, each can take full advantage of the 3000-foot network limit, and we see a further gain in that we now have a potential span, or diameter, of 6000 feet between devices.

While the multiport repeater at the hub of the network may not have any "understanding" of the packets it receives and retransmits, it does more than just serve as an amplifier. It interprets them as digital signals, and creates identical new digital signals on the ports to which the other home runs are attached. Thus, not only does it eliminate the signal strength splitting problem, it also takes care of the degradation of the signal's waveform.

Multiport repeaters are internally terminated and have provision to deal with the reflections of signals that they themselves transmit, so, strictly speaking, no termination is necessary at the workstation end of the home run. While it is sometimes recommended that the wall jacks at the end of active star home

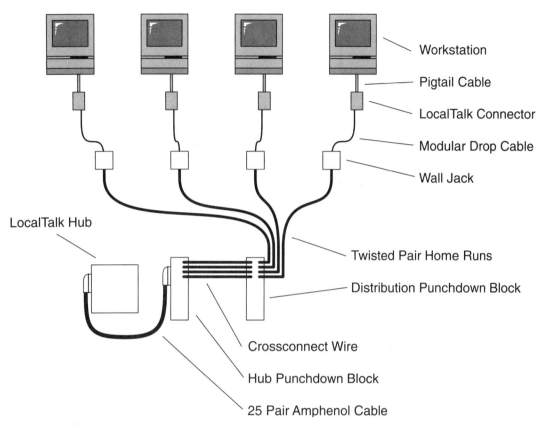

Workstation

Pigtail Cable

LocalTalk Connector

Modular Drop Cable

Wall Jack

LocalTalk Hub

Twisted Pair Home Runs

Distribution Punchdown Block

Crossconnect Wire

Hub Punchdown Block

25 Pair Amphenol Cable

Figure 4.11   The active star.

runs be terminated with a resistor behind the faceplate, as in Fig. 4.3, this greatly complicates the installation and later modification of the network, since no wall jacks should already be wired in that manner, and the resistor would have to be removed before the wall jack could be reused in any other of voice or network capacity. Moreover, placing any kind of electrical component, such as a resistor, inside a jack violates one of the major tenets shared by all the common building wiring specifications, like AT&T's PDS, EIA/TIA 568, and the IBM Cabling System, all mentioned before. The simplest solution is to use the RJ-11-mounted resistors, as used in daisy-chain networks, on the LocalTalk connector of the device at the end of each home run. Thus no modification of properly wired wall jacks should be necessary either before or after their use in an active star network.

As the multiport repeaters which form the hubs of star networks become more complicated, they also provide more management features. Some hubs can identify which user is attached to which port, and thus physically locate the user with respect to a wiring diagram, and thus a building map or blueprint as well. Most collect statistics on the number of packets coming from each port, as well as the percentage of those packets which are outside specifications or damaged. Nearly

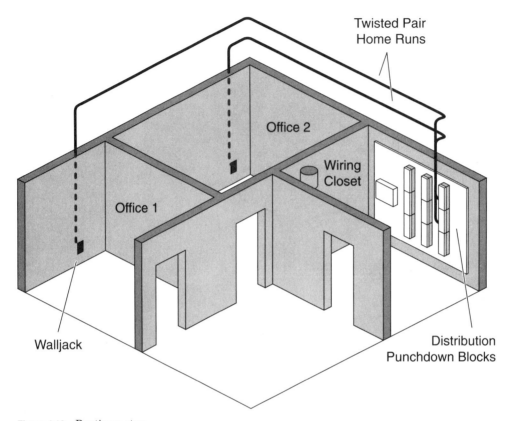

Figure 4.12 Routing a star.

all can automatically isolate ports on which devices are having catastrophic failures, so as to shield the rest of the network from the "fallout" or side effects.

The two main disadvantages of the active star are the cost of the hub and the fact that it constitutes a single point of failure which can affect the whole network. The added expense of the hub, especially when divided by the number of users, is easily offset by the savings comprised by the use of existing, or standardized, building cabling and the gain in managerial functionality. Nevertheless, it can present a barrier to entry on very small networks. Fortunately, the cost of such hubs is continually falling and, at the same time, the low priced hubs are also beneficiaries of new and better management features developed for more expensive devices. The fact that in active star networks many machines are dependent upon the functionality of a single device, the hub, is one that merits serious consideration and planning, but not worry. That hubs are relatively simple devices, and are constructed with but a single purpose, is greatly in their favor. Most hubs will work in nearly any network, right out of the box, with no configuration or special preparation needed, and hub vendors are generally eager to minimize the downtime of customer networks, and thus provide relatively good service and comprehensive warranties. In larger sites, where many hubs are in use, investment in a "spare" hub is nevertheless a reasonable precaution, as is the use of an uninterruptible power supply, to keep networks up and available through power outages and brownouts.

The wiring of buildings for star topologies is very different from that of trunks, and will be covered in the next chapter.

4.6 Switched and Routed Stars

Two newer forms of hub provide more complicated service than simple echoing of packets between their ports. These hubs offer potentially higher performance, but each of them has some drawbacks as well.

Hubs which perform packet switching, instead of repeating receive packets from the devices attached to each port, partially decode the packet address headers, figure out who the packet is addressed to, compare the address to an internal table to determine what port the addressee is located on, and send the packet out only that port. This has two advantages over a regular repeated active star.

First, it's a relatively effective form of security. A lot of information can be gleaned from the data that flows over the networks of most businesses; packet switches greatly reduce the amount of data going over each wire, and guarantee that the only data which does go over each wire is that intended for the machine at the end of it. Thus, to find out someone's e-mail password, or watch them access a database, a malefactor would have to make a physical connection to the home run on which they're located, which in most offices would be fairly conspicuous. Network security issues are further discussed in Chap. 13.

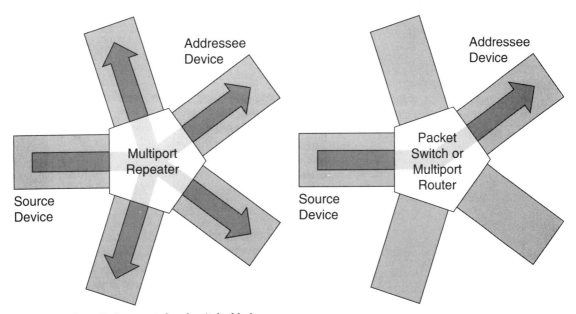

Figure 4.13   Security in repeated and switched hubs.

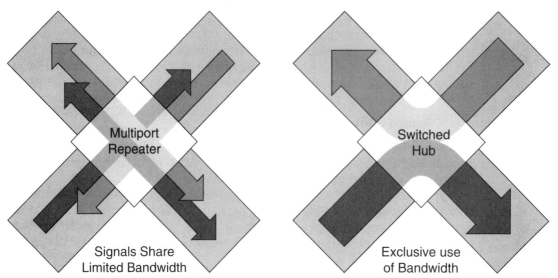

Figure 4.14   Bandwidth allocation in repeated and switched hubs.

Second, and more highly touted by most vendors, packet switches effect an increase in overall network throughput, under many circumstances. Since traffic which isn't broadcast is seen by only one other device, devices which aren't involved in any particular transaction may continue to send packets between each other, utilizing a full 230.4 kilobits per second, provided the processor in the hub has the power to support it. Thus the higher bandwidth advertised is not higher between any two particular devices, but as a sum of all concurrent transactions. In a repeated star, if there were two simultaneous transactions occurring between two different pairs of machines, each would be occurring in 50 percent of the available bandwidth, using a total of 100 percent. In a switched star, however, each could potentially use up to 100 percent of the bandwidth, totaling up to 200 percent.

Multiport routers have much the same functionality as packet-switching hubs, except that they use more accepted methods, are more expensive, and are slower. Instead of making all machines appear to be on the same network but not actually sending each packet to each device, routing hubs make each port a separate network, or "zone," so that devices don't expect to be able to see traffic from other ports. This routing of packets and maintenance of the zones is more time-consuming work than switching, so it forms a slight bottleneck. Aside from these two features, multiport routers and switches share the same advantages.

Multiport switches and routers also have a disadvantage in common. In Chap. two, we observed the packet transactions involved in the printing of a document. Low-level diagnostic techniques like this are invaluable in troubleshooting network faults, and both packet switches and multiport routers make these techniques prohibitively difficult. Since your Macintosh's AppleTalk drivers filter out any packets which aren't either addressed to it or have been broadcast to everyone, tools which allow you to watch packets going by on the network between two other nodes turn the AppleTalk drivers off, and collect and interpret the data that comes in the LocalTalk port themselves. As you can see in Fig. 4.13, if AppleTalk is turned off on your machine, and you aren't directly connected to the same port as is one of the devices you want to monitor, there won't be any traffic on your port at all, much less any from the devices you're interested in. Thus, you have to do all your management from within the wiring closet, and since you have to change the problem's physical environment before you can observe it, you have no means of detecting whether in doing so you're further changed the parameters of the problem in some way as well. Some network software, notably the DataClub AFP server and many networkable computer games, do not work over routers, and would thus also be rendered useless on a routed star, but would be unaffected by a switched one.

4.7 Combination Topologies

Although in a perfect world every network would be constructed exactly to one of the topological models, even the best networks are subject to experimental modification by users and occasional emergency modifications by their network administrators, which put them outside of one of these models. In fact, it's probably fair to say that most networks end up incorporating combinations of the simple topologies at some point.

When users add devices, it's often by daisy chaining them from the LocalTalk connector on the first, or legitimately connected device. On a network which is already a daisy chain, this is perfectly acceptable, so long as they are at one of the two ends, and are careful to reterminate the network. If they're in the middle of an existing daisy chain when they add a device, they will be disrupting service to other users, so this is best done at night, outside of business hours. One danger to which networks populated by presumptuous users sometimes fall prey is users adding devices with common telephone line "splitters" which have one plug and two jacks. Since LocalTalk networks usually use cabling and hardware that are indistinguishable from those used by telephones, many end users assume that they are as topologically flexible. This is not the case. Splitters in effect create passive stars, without any of the benefits of centralized wiring, and with the combined faults of both that and the daisy-chain topology. Splitters can bring even the most robust networks quickly to their knees. On trunk networks, the addition of a few daisy-chained devices shouldn't affect the network terribly adversely, so long as no one tries to terminate them, no more than one or two devices are daisy chained from each legitimate one, and the daisy chains don't extend more than twenty feet or so. Even on the best constructed passive stars, daisy chains are unlikely to ever work well.

Mixing topologies in order to add users to active stars presents something of a dilemma. Many people argue that putting more than one user on each port of a hub makes good economic sense. It usually doesn't present much of a technical difficulty, as nearly any network that works already will continue to work if attached to one port of a hub. Thus you can put a trunk on each port, or daisy chain off the home run, or add one or two more home runs, forming a passive star. Each of these methods is, of course, limited by the constraints normally imposed by the topology you're connecting to the port. The usual argument in favor of adding users is that doing so further amortizes the cost of the hub, which is often the major investment in the network at that point, and it postpones the purchase of the next hub. What this discounts, however, is the loss in value which occurs as soon as you add a second user to any port. Since a large part of what you're paying for in any active hub is the management capabilities, putting additional users on ports is a waste of this investment. When you put a second user on the port, you've lost the absolute diagnostic information available to you before. If garbage or bad packets are coming in off one port, you now no longer know which machine is responsible; you've only narrowed it to a range of possibilities. Also, if the hub shuts the port down to protect the rest of the network, not only the offending device but now any other users on that port have lost access to the rest of the network, and users elsewhere on the net have lost access to services which may be located on that port.

At a higher level, when you've used all the ports on one hub and have decided to add a second or third hub, you need some means of interconnecting them. As with any other topology, you need to be aware of the amount of traffic that's being generated by your users. The twenty-two devices that would fit on two

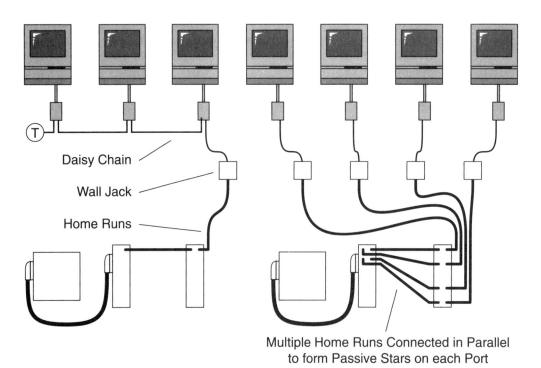

Daisy Chain

Wall Jack

Home Runs

Multiple Home Runs Connected in Parallel
to form Passive Stars on each Port

Figure 4.15   Adding devices to an active star.

twelve-port hubs (leaving one port on each for interconnection to the other) may be as many as you can practically fit on one network without a router, or you may be able to get as many as thirty-three devices onto your net before things become intolerably slow. Hubs don't use external LocalTalk adapters, so you can't daisy chain them per se, but some people put them in trunks, and many people "cascade" them, in a hierarchical arrangement. By cascading multiport repeaters off of a central multiport router or packet switch instead of another repeater, traffic load limitations can be avoided, and more than two or three LocalTalk hubs can be interconnected, potentially as many as the central router or switch has ports. Most networks, however, begin to incorporate faster network systems than LocalTalk by the time they reach that number of users.

Devices called concentrators can be used to aggregate multiple hubs into a single device. They're made by many different vendors, but all provide essentially the same service: They're rackmounts into which cards of a standardized size will fit, each card being either a network hub or some other device. Concentrators provide an internal network which interconnects all the device cards; they generally have a single central power supply, which tends to be a liability since it concentrates a function otherwise shared by multiple devices into a single point of failure.

4.8   The Solution

Of the topologies he investigated, Mark was able to find some fault with each. Daisy chains were clearly not designed for networks of more than a dozen

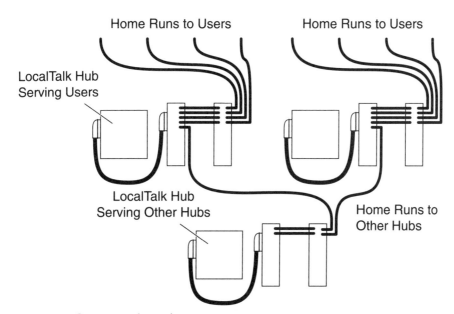

Figure 4.16   Interconnecting active stars.

people. Trunks showed promise, but looked as though they might become too limiting, should his network needs expand to require a larger area of coverage or include more devices. Passive stars appeared to be the root of all evil, and he was determined not to be tempted to sell his soul in exchange for the monetary savings they might afford. All in all, active stars appeared the best choice, despite their relatively high initial per-device cost. Mark resolved to use active star cabling wherever practical, and to temper the costs by occasionally daisy-chaining devices from a single outlet, where one user had more than one device on his or her desk.

Wiring Techniques

5.1 The Problem

Having experimented with small networks of different topologies in his own area of the office for a few weeks, Mark confronted reality and decided he had to figure out how to go about wiring the whole office.

It became obvious to him as a result of his experimentation that active stars were his preferred topology, because of the greater management flexibility that hubs allow. He's heard, as well, that faster networks often use star topologies, and that if he does a good enough job of cabling the building this time, he won't have to do so again if he decides to switch to a higher-performance network in the future.

Thus he resolved to see what's required of building wiring, and whether Luis and he can do it themselves or must find a contractor to perform the work.

5.2 Basic Architecture and Global Decisions

The first step in preparing to build a network in any building is to get a set of blueprints for the building. You may be able to get these from a building manager or whoever is handling the lease of the building, if your company does not own it, the office of the architect who designed the building, or from your city's zoning office or office of city planning.

5.2.1 Planning the installation process

For our examples, we'll use a building with two stories above ground, and a basement.

Next, begin to visualize the set of plans not as separate floors, but as sections through a three-dimensional object, and distinguish the areas of the building which you'll be using for your wiring closets, the points of convergence of the building's telecommunication and network wiring.

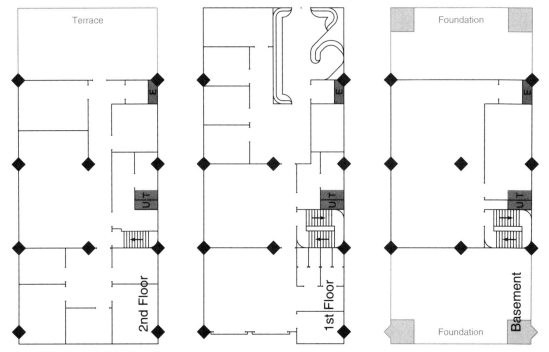

Figure 5.1   Typical office floorplan.

In most buildings which were originally constructed as office space in the last forty years, the wiring closet spaces will have been included in the original design of the building and should be easy to locate. In older buildings, and buildings originally constructed as residences or non-office space, you may have to define your own wiring closets. If you have any choice in the matter, the wiring closets on each floor should be vertically aligned, and they should be as central as possible to the rest of the building, to minimize the length of the horizontal cable runs from each closet to the outlets on its floor.

There are several types of wiring closets, most of which are noted on the plan in Fig. 5.2. On each of the two above-ground floors, where network users will be located, there is a closet marked "IC," which stands for "intermediate closet." These closets serve the floor on which they're located with "horizontal cable" running from the closet to each user work location. There should be one such closet on every floor. In the basement, there's a closet marked "MC," which stands for "main closet."

The main closet ties the intermediate closets together with "vertical cable" in the same way that the intermediate closets tie the workers on their floors together with horizontal cable. Thus, the intermediate closets and the main closet together form the nodes of two levels of a network cabling tree hierarchy. The vertical cable is the first level of branches, the horizontal the second level, and the user work locations form the leaf nodes.

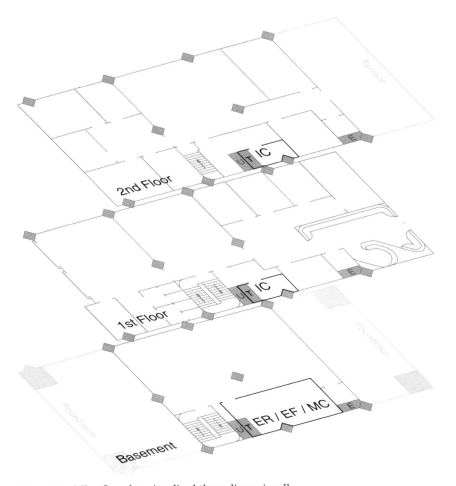

Figure 5.2   Office floorplan visualized three-dimensionally.

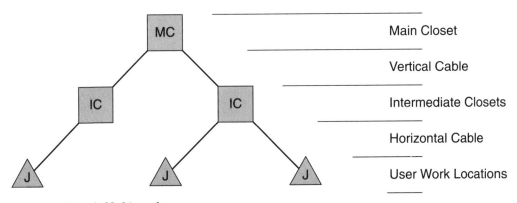

Figure 5.3   Closet/cable hierarchy.

In addition to serving as an MC, the basement room will serve two other functions: entrance facility, or EF, and equipment or computer room, ER. An entrance facility is the location at which external services, like telephone service and wide-area network connections to other buildings, enter your building. A computer room is a secure central location for large computing equipment. In most large businesses in the sixties and seventies, this was a room which contained a single mainframe computer. Now computer rooms more frequently contain microcomputer-based network servers and perhaps a few mid-sized computers running multi-user operating systems like Unix.

Once you've located the wiring closets, walk around the building, blueprints in hand, and look at all the areas people will be working in, finding their boundaries. Practically speaking, each individual office or cubicle-filled area should be treated as one work area. The standard abbreviation for work area is WA.

Look for patterns of use, and try to determine how many jack outlets should be located in each area, and where they should be. You may wish to read the section on work areas, later in this chapter, before deciding upon outlet locations, since most of the various building wiring specifications have something to say about appropriate outlet density and locations. One outlet at each potential desk location is a good rule of thumb. This means two or three outlets in an average office room, and one or two for every cubicle in larger work areas.

Jack outlets are marked on floorplans as triangles. A circle surrounding the triangle indicates that the outlet is floor-mounted, rather than wall-mounted, while the addition of cross-hairs behind the circle indicates that it's ceiling-mounted. A curved arrow leading out of the triangle indicates that the outlet is served by a run of conduit. An arrow on the end of the line means that the conduit is a home run, that it is a direct and contiguous run of conduit back to the

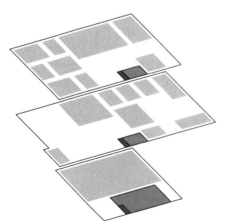

Figure 5.4 Define user work areas.

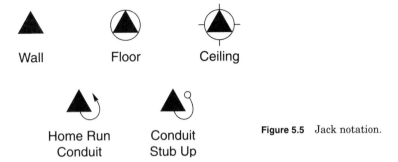

Wall   Floor   Ceiling

Home Run   Conduit
Conduit   Stub Up

Figure 5.5 Jack notation.

wiring closet; an empty circle at the end of the line indicates that the outlet simply has a piece of conduit running up through the wall into the false-ceiling area, but no farther.

When you've decided where each outlet should be located, mark them on a copy of the floorplan.

All the outlets on any floor form a conceptual star, with its center at the wiring closet. Finding a way of organizing and routing the branches of that star, the home runs, is the next step. This is discussed further later in this chapter, in the section on horizontal cabling.

Assuming this building to be one with a suspended-tile ceiling and cable raceways above that, we can use the raceway method. In my experience it's the most common method of building wiring, and in many ways the easiest to perform. This and other methods of cable distribution will be discussed later in this chapter, in the section on horizontal cabling.

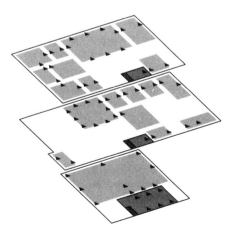

Figure 5.6 Mark outlet locations.

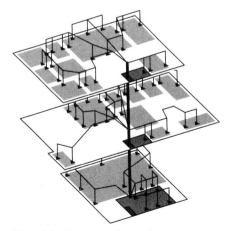

Figure 5.7 Raceway wire routes.

Once you've decided upon locations for the cable runs, calculated the length of cable you'll need, and decided upon the type and number of outlets, you can determine what pair-count (how many pairs of conductors inside the cable) to buy. This should be based upon the number of pairs required to support a single maximally populated outlet location. The wire-pair requirements of various types of jacks will be discussed at length in Sec. 5.6, later in this chapter, and types of cable are discussed in Sec. 5.1.2. Cable will come on 1000-foot or 2500-foot spools. The larger the spool, the less waste you'll have in unusable scrap lengths and the better deal you're likely to get. Beware, though, that the spools become harder to handle as they get larger. Four-pair cable weighs about 20 pounds per thousand feet, but 25-pair cable can weigh over 100 pounds per thousand feet, depending upon the gauge and the amount of insulation. Large pair-count cables, occasionally used in risers and often between buildings, are extremely heavy and require powered handling equipment. For example, 24-gauge 500-pair cable generally weighs about 2500 pounds per kilofoot, while 2100-pair cable of the same gauge weighs about five tons per kilofoot. Obviously, if such cable is to be used in risers, it requires continuous support, since it shouldn't be called upon to support more than a half foot or so of its own weight. When you've reached an acceptable compromise between the number of pairs you need to run, the diameter of cable you're willing to pull, and the size of spool you can handle, and decided what kind of punchdown blocks you want, order your supplies. Generally the one-stop distributors of cable and components are fairly flexible on price, so ordering all your supplies at the same time, from the same distributor, will give you a fair amount of bargaining leverage.

The installation process itself is done in two stages: roughing-in and finish wiring. The roughing-in stage encompasses the building of the wiring closets and the pulling of all your vertical and horizontal cable. The finish wiring stage should basically just involve wire termination: wiring all the outlets, performing cross-connection, and connecting services. If you're trying to figure out what to do when, temporally divide the roughing-in from the finish wiring, and segregate tasks into one of the two categories. If you really can't decide what category to put a task in, use the following criteria: Anything which requires power tools or raises dust is a roughing-in job, and anything that requires a wire stripper or punchdown tool is finish wiring. It's fairly important to keep these two phases separate, because the finish wiring phase typically requires that equipment and wires be exposed, and this could easily lead to their being damaged during some of the tasks involved in the roughing-in phase.

Once the entire cable plant has been installed, terminated, cross-connected, and services brought on-line, the job is completed by testing each home run. If you're going to be providing analog telephone service all the way to the users' work areas, either directly from the telephone company or through your own analog PBX, you can test the quality of the lines using several stages of tests. The first and simplest is to attach a telephone or test set at the jack, take the telephone handset "off-hook," listen for a dial tone, dial one digit to break the dial tone, and listen for any noise or static on the line. If there isn't significant noise, there are further tests which can be performed, each involving services of the telephone company's switch. You may be able to get the phone numbers which access these ports of your switch from your local telephone company's service department. First, there's a so-called "howler" which is a swept-frequency tone generator. It generates a continuous audible tone which sweeps back and forth from low to high frequency. If you call that port and listen to one cycle, you should hear it continuously, without any dropouts. Next, call the dialback port, and hang up. It will call you right back. Listen for the phone to ring, pick up the phone, listen for the connection, and hang up. Last, and also useful when you're trying to figure out what line you're looking at, there's a port which will repeat the phone number you're calling from back to you in a recorded voice.

If you're using a PBX, follow the testing instructions that came with it. These will probably include dialing out on a trunk line and dialing another extension.

To test the network functionality, power up all your hubs and any routers you may have (they'll be discussed further in a later chapter), and attach and boot one LaserWriter or Mac running a Chooser-visible service at the end of the longest cable run in your building. Then walk around to each outlet with a portable Macintosh, connecting it, opening the Chooser to check for the service, and then using Inter•Poll to bounce echo packets off the other device. If you encounter errors, note the number and type of error packets, try again, and then proceed to the next jack, keeping a log of your tests. This form of testing is conceptually identical to the "network break location" testing described in Chap. 4, and similar troubleshooting techniques are discussed in Chap. 12.

5.2.2 Selecting cable

You need to be careful in choosing the type of cable from which to build the *cable plant,* the sum of all the cable at your site, since you should end up with only one type of cable, although perhaps in different pair-counts in different places. The most basic decision to make is the gauge, or diameter, of the conductor. Larger-gauge conductors present less impedance, and thus result in less attenuation of signals and more reliability in long runs of cable. Smaller gauges cost less, are lighter and easier to pull. The two gauges from which you can practically choose are 22 and 24. As with shot, there's an inverse correlation between the number of the gauge and the diameter, larger numbers indicating smaller diameter, and vice versa. Twenty-four-gauge conductors are pretty much standard, but cables made of the thicker 22-gauge cable are widely accepted substitutes, provided they meet all the same specifications for electrical characteristics and durability as their thinner counterparts. Once you've begun installing one gauge, you absolutely cannot change your mind without replacing all your existing cable, since the impedance mismatch created by an interface between the two types of cable is extremely debilitating to high-frequency signals like those used in digital communication.

After you've chosen the gauge you're going to use, your remaining choices have been narrowed. You need to decide upon the grade, or quality level, of the cable you want to use. Ordinary American- and European-manufactured twisted-pair cable which is not otherwise marked generally meets the specifications for the grade-three quality level. This is the lowest-quality cable which is sufficient for use with 10-megabit Ethernet networks and modern digital telephone systems. Two higher grades are available: grade four, which will support 16-megabit Token Ring networks, and grade five, which supports 100-megabit communication, like TPDDI (or Twisted Pair Data Distributed Interface), a standard for 100-megabit networks which is currently under development. Grade-four and -five cables are sometimes called Enhanced Unshielded Twisted Pair, or EUTP, to distinguish them from ordinary grade-three cable. Again, the additional capabilities result in an increased cost per foot of cable. If you choose to use grade-four or grade-five cable in order to provide for conversion to a faster networking system in the future, you need to use higher-quality punchdown blocks and jacks as well. At the time of this writing, a type of punchdown block called "66" style is rated at grade-three and grade-four transmission quality, and only a style called "110" is capable of meeting grade-five specifications. At this time, there are no grade-five jacks available, although many of the better ones meet grade-four specifications. Thus, any networks built today will have to have their jacks replaced before they're likely to accommodate 100-megabit networks with any comfortable tolerance. Quality levels are determined on the basis of threshold performance levels in two criteria: attenuation and near-end crosstalk. Also, each must be within fifteen percent of the standard impedance, 100 ohms, throughout the applicable frequency range. These three are the principal electrical problems which limit all networks, and they'll be further discussed later in this section.

Another important decision that must be made early on in the process is whether or not to pull fiber-optic cable as well as copper. If you do pull fiber, should you try to install jacks and cross-connects, or just leave it in the wall for the time being? FDDI (Fiber Distributed Data Interface, the current standard for 100-megabit fiber-optic networking) cards for the Macintosh are a relatively recent innovation. The field is extremely new, and techniques for terminating and cross-connecting fibers are still very much in flux. It's likely that the ever-growing need for greater network throughput will drive standardization in this area, but given the pace of development thus far, that's still likely to take several years. Although it was far from clear a year ago which size of fiber would be standard, 62.5/125-micron multimode graded index fiber is now commonly recognized as the only viable standard for building cabling, while 10/125 singlemode fiber is now nearly standard for interbuilding use. The 62.5/125 designation is a measurement in microns of the diameter of the core, which carries the signal, and the cladding, which keeps the light contained within the core. Multimode means that the core is thick enough that light rays can enter it without being perfectly aligned with its axis, whereas singlemode fibers must use carefully polarized and aligned light sources. Graded index means that the ratio of refractive to reflective index changes continuously within the fiber, reversing itself from the center to the edge of the core. Since the light is depending upon a high refractive index, or high transparency, to propagate itself, this means it travels most easily at the center of the core. As the refractive index grows smaller and the core becomes more reflective, near its outside edges, the light which strays from the center of the core is reflected back into the center.

In addition to supporting higher speeds, fiber also supports longer distances. Since no uses are currently contemplated which require in-building runs shorter than 3000 feet, fiber home runs can all originate in the main closet, rather than out in the intermediate closets, if that proves organizationally convenient. Since the optical signals don't require a ground for reference, individual fibers are used where an electrical connection would require a pair of conductors. FDDI uses a dual counter-rotating ring topology. In a ring topology, each machine is connected to the machines on either side of it in a kind of daisy chain, but one which forms a complete circle rather than a bus. A dual counter-rotating ring is one which is comprised of two co-spatial rings, connecting machines each having two network interfaces. In addition, it's permissible for some devices to connect to only one of the two rings. Thus for a dual-connect (connected to both rings) FDDI outlet, four fibers are required, one each for signals received from the prior station in the ring and those sent to the next station, for each of the two rings. Thus the minimum foreseeable need is for four fibers at each outlet. You may wish to run more if you want to support multiple workstation or device home runs at each outlet, or feel like looking even further ahead to the needs of fiber-based video teleconferencing and other applications not likely to be in common use before the end of the century.

The main trick to pulling fiber is not bending it too much. The more tightly it's bent, the less light gets through, and the harder it is to interpret the signal at the other end. The rule of thumb in pulling fiber is to never bend it to a radius that's less than ten times the outside diameter of the cable. Thus a standard four-fiber PVC-jacketed indoor-use cable, which has an outside diameter of 0.285 inches, might fail if it were ever bent with a radius of less than about three inches. Such cable is currently available for ten to fifteen times the per-foot cost of similarly jacketed copper cable of the same conductor count.

The testing of installed fiber requires tools which are currently very expensive, and installation requires careful attention to the radii of bends; if cabling contractors who specialize in fiber and already have these tools exist in your area, it's definitely worth checking their rates before trying to pull any fiber yourself. At any rate, be sure to leave many feet of slack in the wall at each end of each run of fiber cable; you don't know how many generations of connectors you may end up needing to terminate it with, over time, but you can bet that each time it happens, you're going to have to trim off the last one, making the cable shorter.

Although it currently appears that FDDI Duplex Media Interface Connectors, or MICs, will become standard for use in work areas, and Straight-Tip Connectors, or STs, are predominant in closet cross-connections, neither offers very high density and neither is trivial to assemble, especially in the field. The density is a problem for two reasons: Since FDDI uses a dual counter-rotating ring topology, some computers connect to just one ring and others connect to both rings to enhance reliability. Unfortunately, two FDDI MICs won't fit through the opening behind a NuBus card. In wiring closets, the space required to patch ST connectors hasn't yet reached a premium but soon will, if the trends that copper wiring followed are any indicator.

One viable compromise would be installing fiber in your vertical runs only. Four to eight fibers between the main closet and each intermediate closet would provide for the interconnection of FDDI-backplane equipped concentrators. A concentrator, as mentioned before, is simply a rackmount with slots into which network hub cards can be placed. The backplane is the tiny internal network which interconnects the back of each of the cards. Thus, fiber could be used to extend this higher-speed backplane throughout your building, at a much lower expense than pulling enough fiber to directly connect workstations.

At any rate, at the time of this writing, I'd say that it's definitely worthwhile to install fiber-optic cable against future need, any time you're already installing copper, but that it's too early to worry about connectorizing the fiber. The price of the fiber itself is unlikely to come down drastically, but connectors may become cheaper, easier to use, and denser.

5.2.3   Selecting punchdown blocks

The type of punchdown block, 66 or 110, is the next major decision. Punchdown blocks, which were mentioned in the chapter on LocalTalk topologies, provide a field of interconnected contacts. These contacts allow long runs of wire to be terminated once, and then interconnected with short lengths of wire, as many times as may be necessary in the life of the building. (In this chapter, we'll be using the word "terminate" almost exclusively in its literal sense, to end a wire at a terminal, rather than to place a resistor across a pair of wires.) The point behind this is that any time a cable has to be reterminated, its end must be trimmed back. Each time this is done, the wire gets shorter. Since each piece of wire is finite in length, one can do this only so many times before the wire becomes too short to reach both its source and its intended destination, and a new wire must be pulled through the walls, floor, or ceiling, an expensive and labor-intensive process. If instead we terminate each cable run only once, on terminals designed to facilitate cross-connection, we can then "patch" between wires to create the paths we desire. The patches are expected to be disposable, and are of negligible cost. When a change must be made, the cable runs are left terminated as they are, the existing cross-connect is thrown away or reused in a shorter incarnation, and a new cross-connect is created to complete the change.

66 and 110 blocks have different sets of strengths and weaknesses which should be considered in choosing which to employ. These qualities will be discussed further in the next section, on building the main wiring closet, but, in summary, 66 blocks are an established first-generation standard, and they're easy to learn to use. 110 blocks are a more recently introduced second-generation product, and they're harder to learn to use if you haven't already learned on 66 blocks, but they offer two advantages: They support digital data rates up to about 100 megabits, and they allow many more wires to be terminated in the same area of backboard.

66 blocks are probably a better choice for a beginning network administrator, especially if it looks like it may be some time before support is required for networks faster than Ethernet, or if you have to rely upon outside contractors to do your wiring. In the long term, however, think of 66 blocks in transitional terms, since their use will eventually wane in favor of 110s.

If you already have some experience with 66 blocks, anticipate the need for higher-speed networking, and are ready to buy the tools and learn to work with 110 blocks yourself, they're undoubtedly a good choice.

5.2.4 Network electrical problems to keep in mind

The fact that the path electrical signals must take between any workstation and the hub that serves it is actually made of several different pieces of wire leads to an electrical problem called signal reflection. Even in the best case, the path will include the jack on the workstation's network adapter, a plug in that jack, a drop cable, another plug, another jack, some horizontal cable, a punch-down terminal, a cross-connect wire, another punchdown terminal, a short wire connecting that to a female Amphenol connector, the connector itself, a male Amphenol connector, a few feet of 25-pair cable, and another pair of Amphenol connectors. Regardless of the care with which each of these components was made, they'll each have a slightly different characteristic impedance, although the plugs are the worst, since their pins are of a different diameter than the wire, and their contacts aren't as good as those on a punch-down block. The net effect is that signal amplitude is lost at each join between two pieces of the conductor path. When an electrical signal encounters a junction between the conductor in which it's traveling and a higher-impedance conductor, part of the signal is reflected back in the form of garbage. This extra noise on the network can garble other oncoming packets, and the strength of the original signal is diminished as well.

A simple model which may aid in thinking about the problem is this: If you take two plexiglass bars, abut them end-to-end, and shine a flashlight into the

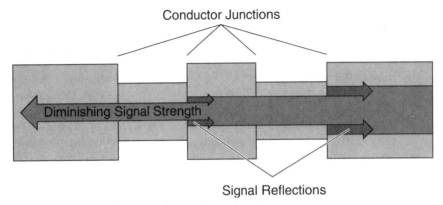

Figure 5.8   Signal reflections and impedance mismatches.

near one, some of the light is going to reflect off the join, rather than passing through to the other side of the far one.

To avoid impedance mismatch problems, limit the number of joins in the end-to-end signal path as much as you possibly can, and make sure that all your cables, including line cords, are of the same gauge.

Another electrical problem which is particularly debilitating to both networks and voice telecommunications is *near-end crosstalk,* or NEXT. Like impedance mismatches, NEXT is particularly a problem in jacks and connectors.

Near-end crosstalk describes the "inductive coupling" of electrical signals from one conductor pair in a jack or cable to another. Inductive coupling basically means that the magnetic fields generated by the flow of electricity on different nearby conductors influence each other. The effects of that influence are seen as changes in the electrical signal on the other conductor, in the form of a signal which incorporates part of the other conductor's. The reason it's called near-end crosstalk, rather than just crosstalk, is that the effects of crosstalk which happens at the near-end, near the transmitter, are much greater than those which occur farther out on the wire. NEXT is greatest where conductors are allowed to run parallel and close together. The twisted pairs of conductors in cable are designed to reduce this by preventing any two conductors from lying precisely parallel to each other, and making sure that, on average, no two conductors are any closer to each other than any other two. If the effects of

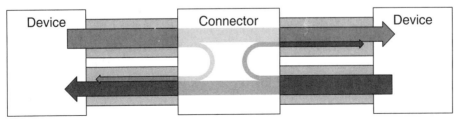

Figure 5.9   Near-end crosstalk.

near-end crosstalk are distributed across two or more conductors, the signal-to-noise discrimination circuitry in the receiving machine can identify and subtract the component of the signal that's an effect of NEXT. Thus, much of the NEXT which will occur in your network will be inside jacks.

To avoid the problems of NEXT, use higher-quality-level cables and connectors. NEXT is strictly regulated by Underwriters Labs and the EIA/TIA, the certification bodies which offer quality-level corroboration.

The third major electrical problem which limits networks is *attenuation*. Attenuation is the natural decrease in amplitude that a signal suffers as it travels through any medium; this is what puts length limits on networks. Two factors make attenuation worse: First and most obvious, the higher the signal's frequency, the more delicate it is, and the more easily susceptible it will prove to be. Second, increased conductor temperature also raises attenuation, to the tune of about one percent for every five and a half degrees Fahrenheit. Although higher-quality cable does make attenuation less of a problem, it's hard to say what the demands of future networking technologies will be. Thus it's still safest to stay within the 300-foot length limits for vertical and horizontal cable, if at all possible.

Until this point, all our diagrams have represented the flow of signals on the network as arrows of varying width, loosely corresponding to average signal voltage, or amplitude. In order to really understand the effects of noise on a digital signal, we're going to have to take a little deeper look into the anatomy of the signals.

In Fig. 5.11, we have one byte, eight bits, traveling down a single conductor (remember, if we look at the signal as an electrical waveform, rather than as an abstraction, we have to consider each conductor of a signal-carrying pair separately). The height of the bar indicates the wave's amplitude, measured against a scale of zero to five volts, at the left. Across the bottom, we can see the amount of time it takes for the bits to pass a given point in the wire. One bit takes about four and one-third thousandths of a second, while the whole byte takes nearly three and a half hundredths. Across the top, the values of each bit are indicated. The manner in which LocalTalk bit encoding is done relies on the receiver being able to determine whether the line voltage level has changed significantly within a bit, or just between bits. When the voltage changes levels in the middle of a bit, and back again at the end, a zero is indicated. If no change is detected until the end of the bit, it's a one.

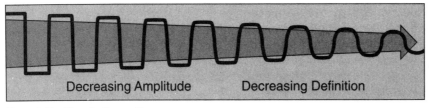

Decreasing Amplitude   Decreasing Definition

Figure 5.10   Signal attenuation.

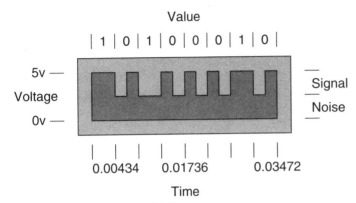

Figure 5.11   One byte on LocalTalk.

As you can see, in Fig. 5.11 the voltage level is going from about 2.5 volts to 5 volts, without ever dropping down to zero. This is the effect of noise, which is an artificial increase in the base amplitude.

When the signal is generated, it's a pretty square wave, and it really is pretty close to zero and five volts. As it travels across the network, the cumulative effect of crosstalk, signal reflection, and attenuation raises the base level of constant garbage, ensuring that the signal never goes quite back down to zero, and the addition of these other waves tends to dull the crisp corners of the original waveform.

Now that we understand the effect of noise on a signal traveling down a single conductor, we have to consider the other conductor of the pair to see the whole effect. The second conductor is carrying a signal which begins as the inverse of that on the first conductor. Thus the peak of a wave on one conductor would temporally correspond with the trough of the associated wave on the other conductor of the pair.

Although it may not at first be apparent, this is the reason for twisted-pair wire. Induced current generated by inductive coupling and NEXT is the single largest contributor to noise on most networks. Since this is an effect generated by a magnetic field, the strength of which drops of as a function of distance, the effect itself is distance-dependent. The farther a wire is from a source of noise, the less it will be affected. Thus, if we twist two conductors around each other,

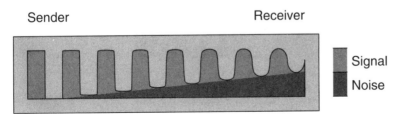

Figure 5.12   Noise entering a signal.

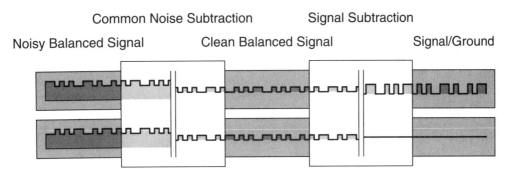

Figure 5.13   Common mode rejection.

they will *on average* be affected equally by all sources of electromagnetic inter-ference, since, on average, they're the same distance from any source.

This is the basis of the signal-to-noise discrimination method that's em-ployed by most network devices. Called "common mode rejection," it depends upon both conductors in a pair being affected by sources of noise roughly equally. Since the signal is "balanced," that is, one conductor is carrying the inverse of the first, when the largest common component of the two signals is found (the "common mode"), it can be subtracted from each, since it is, by defi-nition, noise. This leaves a much weakened, but clean, version of the original signal. The inverse of the signal is then subtracted from the signal, doubling its amplitude and, with luck, further clarifying it. This then becomes a standard digital signal as is used inside an electronic device, where the voltage changes indicating presence or absence of a bit are measured in comparison with a con-stant ground, rather than a second waveform.

5.3 The Main Closet

Wiring closets are where nearly all the work on a network is performed, both during the installation and afterwards. Unlike electrical or other utility clos-ets, they tend to be places where you wind up spending quite a bit of time. I know several network administrators who've moved their offices into their main wiring closet for the sake of convenience.

As explained above, the Main Closet, or MC, is the one to which all cable runs finally lead. It should serve as a center of concentration of as many ser-vices as possible, eliminating, insofar as is practical, the need to venture out to the intermediate closets on other floors. This centralization makes changes much easier and less time-consuming to perform.

In addition to providing final termination points for all vertical cabling, it's likely that the space you designate as your main closet will also serve as entrance facility and equipment room. Thus, provisions for these additional functions should also be made in the planning of the room.

Since it's so important to the network, and it'll be difficult to change after it's been initially set up, it's important to construct all your wiring closets, and especially your main closet, carefully and with provision for future needs and expansion.

5.3.1 Physical arrangement

First, if the locations of your wiring closets are not absolutely dictated to you by the construction of the building you're in, your first concern is to make sure that the rooms you choose are of adequate size. In total, the space you designate for main and intermediate closets should probably amount to between one and two percent of the total area of the building. The amount of backboard space available should be minimally of area equal to a bit less than one percent of the floor area of the building, rounded up to the nearest multiple of 32 square feet, the area of each sheet of plywood used to form the backboard. Thus, in a small office of 5000 square feet, about 50 square feet of space should be allocated for the main closet, equipment room, and entrance facility; a single four-by-eight sheet of plywood attached to the wall will probably provide sufficient backboard area. In a larger building of 50,000 square feet, with five floors and a basement, 500 to 1000 square feet should be divided between the MC/EF/ER and five ICs, one on each floor. Ideally, each of the intermediate closets would be of perhaps 50 to 100 square feet with at least 64 square feet of backboard in each, leaving several hundred square feet of floorspace for the main closet. You may want to allocate a little extra space for the topmost intermediate closet, since it may also end up serving as an AE, or Antenna Entrance, holding equipment related to any antennas or satellite dishes you may locate on your roof. Offices of under 5000 square feet can use wall cabinets, which contain the backboards, but are only two feet deep, with outward-opening or sliding doors which offer unobstructed access to the backboards. Such closets should still be wide enough to accommodate at least two four-by-eight backboard panels. Since backboards cost virtually nothing and aren't particularly difficult to install, there's no particular reason not to cover all four walls of each of your closets, while the closets are still empty and easy to work in.

Backboard panels should be sheets of standard three-quarter-inch or thicker plywood, stood endwise, and mounted with their lower edges a few inches above the floor, level and secured to the studs within the wall, or fastened to concrete with concrete anchors, such that it can securely bear the weight of any equipment or enclosures you may choose to mount on it. The heads of the screws or lag bolts you use to attach it should be countersunk if possible, so as not to impede the placement of punchdown blocks or other equipment over them. If you're mounting the backboards on a standard interior wall, be sure that your screws are seating firmly in either wood or metal studs. Studs should be spaced at sixteen-inch intervals, so once you've found one, you can find the rest more quickly by measuring over sixteen inches horizontally and making a test hole. Don't worry about the test holes—the whole wall will be covered by the backboard anyway. Your screws should form columns following each stud up the wall, and the screws should be spaced vertically six to eight inches apart. If you're mounting the backboards on masonry, use masonry anchors appropriate to the composition of the wall, and rated for an adequate load. This will probably require that you pre-drill the backboard, mark the wall through the holes, and use masonry bits to create the holes in the wall. While this is likely to provide good shear resistance, it may not hold the backboard against the wall absolutely solidly. If you find this to be so, you can cover the back of the backboard with an adhesive compound, reattach it, wait for the adhesive to set, and try again.

Installing backboards, pulling large cable runs, and the like are all activities performed during the roughing-in stage of the installation. You should be sure that none of your network or computer equipment is present at this stage, since the sawdust and masonry dust can easily enter equipment through vents.

EIA/TIA specifications require that no point on a distribution frame or rackmount in either a main or intermediate wiring closet be farther than six feet from a properly grounded 110V AC power outlet. There are to be at least two AC power outlets, and at least two separate AC power circuits. Additional outlets are to be arranged around the perimeter of the room, no farther than six feet apart. Since most distribution frames and rackmounts are six to eight feet tall, the requirement basically dictates one or more outlets at the base of each frame or rack. If this requires the installation of additional power circuits or wiring, remember to try not to create runs of power cable which could end up lying parallel to later telecommunications and network cable runs.

It's recommended that the AC power circuits which supply wiring closets have their breaker boxes located either at the closets being served or in the main closet, rather than elsewhere, with other AC power breakers for the building, both to facilitate easy resetting by network personnel and to prevent their being accidentally turned off when electrical personnel are working on other circuits. When choosing circuit breakers for your network equipment, it may be tempting to select GFCI, or Ground Fault Circuit Interrupt breakers, rather than ordinary ones. Whereas normal circuit breakers are relatively slow to trip, GFCI breakers monitor the difference between a circuit's load and the ground, and trip almost instantaneously upon detection of a short or ground. While this protects people from electrocution, and could potentially save equipment, GFCI breakers are unstable by nature, and are often tripped as a result of sudden changes in loading when computers are turned on or off, and are sometimes even affected by supply-side changes in power level. These features of GFCI breakers would combine to make your power supply eminently safe but utterly unreliable.

If there's a main building grounding electrode, and it's located somewhere other than the main closet, a 0.75-inch conduit should be run to it from the main closet to provide direct access to grounding facilities. If your main closet is also serving as an equipment room, EIA/TIA specifications require a 1.5-inch conduit. All rackmount frames and metal cross-connect frames should be connected to ground, using a wire of adequate gauge.

If you've used any shielded cable in your building, you must determine how you're going to ground the shield. Unfortunately, there are two methods and the various building wiring specifications offer discrepant opinions as to the correct one. The purpose of grounding is to ensure that the electrical potential of the ground on various devices throughout your building is the same, so that differences in ground will not be translated into a flow of DC current across your network, providing an outlet for any current which is induced in the shield as it passes sources of electromagnetic noise. The problem is that any sizable flow of current through the shield will disrupt signals traveling on the wire pairs within the shield, negating any benefits it would otherwise provide. Since different wiring closets will certainly have different ground potentials, despite your best efforts to provide them all with good grounds, grounding a shield at each end (that is, any time it enters a wiring closet) could potentially lead to a constant, if low-voltage, current through the grounds. The alternative most people prefer is to ground shields only at one end, rather than at both ends. This necessitates that some additional care be taken when bonding shields to ground, lest you become confused as to which end of a cable you're dealing with.

Cable shield usually consists of either a sheet of foil wrapped around the conductors or a sleeve braided out of very small bare conductors. Neither type is designed to be terminated on insulation-displacement contact (IDC) terminals of the type which are found on punchdown blocks, so if you're using shielded cable, you should supply each wiring closet with a grounding tower or a block of screw terminals, connected by a single direct heavy wire (10- and 12-gauge are commonly used) to the building's main ground. Grounding towers are the preferred method.

Grounding towers are usually located immediately adjacent the termination point of the cables they serve. They're grounded metal bars with clips bonded to them. First, strip back the cable sheath and shielding as far as needed to

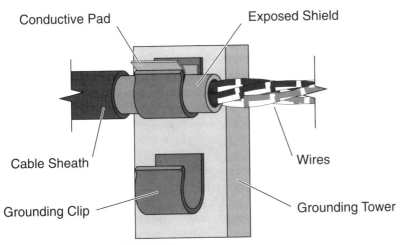

Figure 5.14   Grounding shielded cable.

reach the termination points from the grounding tower, allowing some slack in between. Then strip the outer sheath back to expose an inch or two of the shield. Create a conductive pad by folding a piece of the initially stripped shield over once or twice. Wrap this around the exposed shield from below, and press the whole thing into the clip, using finger pressure only. The purpose of the pad is to ensure a constant connection to ground, while not requiring so tight a fit that the shield could be easily damaged.

Remember that all transformers generate radio-frequency interference. Since transformers are extremely common, care should be taken to locate them as far as possible from cable runs and cross-connect fields in wiring closets. Wherever possible, eliminate or relocate transformers entirely. For instance, the "ballast" in a fluorescent light is a large transformer, which can disrupt nearby high-speed networks. Using incandescent light in wiring closets is therefore a good idea, provided the lights are turned off when not in use, to avoid overheating the closet and placing undue load on any air-conditioning equipment which may be servicing the room.

Not surprisingly, there are specifications related to the lighting as well. The lighting is supposed to provide 50 foot-candles of illumination measured at a point three feet above the floor at the center of the closet, or in the center of each aisle if it's a larger room. It should be controllable via an on/off switch (as opposed to a dimmer switch) adjacent to each entrance to the room. It's important that the power for the lights be drawn from a separate, general-purpose circuit, rather than either of the two dedicated circuits supplying the closet's AC power outlets. It's recommended that an emergency lighting system be provided, illuminating the room and showing the way to the exit, and that consideration be given to backup power sources which provide automatic cutover, maintaining a constant supply of power to networking and telecommunications devices through any power outages which may occur. Unlike workstations, most network devices, like repeater hubs, modems, and routers, draw very little current, and a single uninterruptible power supply unit of moderate capacity should suffice in closets where you don't also have servers to power. UPSes (uninterruptable power supplies) of less than 100kVA capacity may be located in or near the closet, while larger units should be remotely located. If a UPS is to be located in the closet, be sure adequate ventilation is provided as well, in case of battery leakage.

If air-conditioning equipment is used, rather than turning it to a very low temperature setting, which would at first seem to provide the best environment for your equipment, you're better off allowing it to run at a relatively high temperature. While not as good for the equipment and not as comfortable to work in, it's still well within the operating specifications of all the components in your closet, and it puts a much lighter strain on the air-conditioner. The air-conditioner is thus less liable to fail, and when it does fail the temperature change will be much less as the room warms to its natural temperature, putting less thermal expansion stress on components and wire joins.

Temperature and humidity should be regulated to between 65° and 75°, with 30%–55% humidity. Positive atmospheric pressure with respect to the surrounding rooms is desirable, since it will tend to obstruct the entry of airborne contaminants. Again, be careful as to the power source. Don't try to power an air-conditioner from the same circuit that your network equipment or servers are on. Sharing a circuit with the lights, however, wouldn't be particularly detrimental, provided the amperage rating of the circuit is not thereby exceeded.

If there are fire-extinguishing sprinklers in your wiring closets, you should put wire cages on them to prevent them from being triggered accidentally as a result of being bumped or jogged by, for instance, the top of a ladder. Strongly consider alternative fire extinguisher technologies; where legal, Halon is preferred for use in computer and equipment rooms, since it's dielectric, highly effective against the types of fires likely to be encountered in such areas, quick to clean up, and doesn't damage computer equipment at all. In either case, be extremely careful when doing anything in the closet that could trip either heat- or smoke-activated extinguisher systems. Auxiliary hand-held fire extinguisher units should be provided in equipment rooms, located adjacent to each doorway, and clearly marked.

Photocopiers, photostat and photographic processing equipment, and blueprint equipment should all be located away from wiring closets and equipment rooms, since devices of these types emit substantial quantities of particulate contaminants and corrosive vapors which can be damaging to electronic equipment and electrical contacts.

If your main closet is also serving as an entrance facility, keep the needs of service providers in mind. Try to locate the entrance itself in such a way that they won't have to cross any rights-of-way that don't belong to them, and be sure to allocate adequate space immediately inside (within one foot of) the entrance for their demarcation points. If possible, increase security by isolating the main closet and equipment room from the entrance facility with a locking door, while keeping the entrance facility itself easily accessible to utility service personnel. Consider adding a second entrance facility, remote from the first, which can be used as a backup. Accidents which would interrupt services entering through an underground conduit might not affect those provided via aerial drops, and vice versa. All entrance points should slope upward as they enter the building, to slightly impede the flow of water into the building. Only 4-inch conduit should be used to enter the building, as that's what all utilities have standardized on. Be sure that enough conduits exist that they don't become over-filled. Forty percent full is generally considered the most a conduit should be filled, to allow for easy pulling of cable. In a 4-inch conduit, this amounts to about 5 square inches of the total cross-sectional area, which is about 13 square inches. The conduit should be reamed on both ends, so that pulling will not damage cable sheaths.

5.3.2 Backboard layout

The single most important concept to understand before laying out a backboard is that, unlike the real world, where we have four points of the compass, there are only two meaningful directions in building wiring. These directions are *service* and *distribution*. Service is the direction that heads back to the main closet, and within the main closet toward whatever devices are ultimately providing services: network hubs, incoming telephone line demarcs, PBXes, et cetera. Distribution is the direction in which the final user of the services lies, out in the user work area. Just as a vertical line through the center of each demarcation punchdown block separates your premises cable plant from the telephone company's network, so should you be able to draw a single vertical line down the center of each backboard in your building, separating the punchdown blocks on the left, on which service cables terminate, from those on the right, on which distribution cables terminate. This convention greatly simplifies the cross-connection of cable runs, and makes it possible for wiring contractors to walk into closets they've never seen before, and immediately begin to make sense of what they see.

In Fig. 5.15, also showing the relative heights of a person, a backboard, and 66 blocks, we can see the two directions. Here, we've got spaces for forty service blocks and forty distribution blocks. Forty 66 blocks will terminate 1000 pairs, providing service to 240 RJ-45 jacks, since they're normally made to fit six to a block, rather than overlapping some between blocks. To the left of the service blocks is open backboard area, reserved for the mounting of network and telecommunications service devices and demarcation points. If you need to save space, equipment which doesn't need to be physically serviced and can tolerate any higher temperatures that may exist nearer the ceiling can be mounted above the punchdowns.

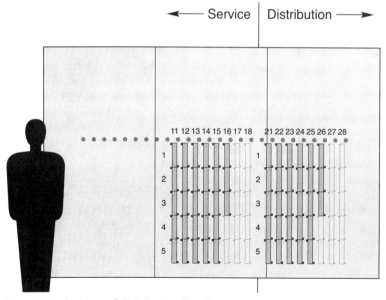

Figure 5.15   Service and distribution directions.

In laying out your backboards, you need to keep a few things in mind. First, that the point of a backboard is to facilitate short and easily understood cross-connections within the flow of the building wiring. Second, that each backboard area should be clearly divided into three areas: one with mounting space for services devices and demarcation points; a second containing service-side punchdown blocks, upon which those services and any other services terminate; and a third containing distribution-side punchdown blocks, upon which cables terminate which either directly or indirectly lead to users' outlets. Although there is no written standard, the three areas are generally laid out in that order, left to right, as illustrated.

Before you can begin laying out your backboard, you must have already decided upon the type of punchdown block you're going to use. Details on punchdown blocks and their mounting requirements are discussed later in this section. Calculate the number of blocks you'll need to support the number of jacks you're planning on installing by dividing the number of pairs provided to each location into the number of pairs supported on each block, multiplying by the number of jacks served by the particular closet, adding whatever you feel is a reasonable number for future expansion, and multiplying by two to provide both service and distribution blocks for each run. This is such a flexible number that it's hard to make any generalized recommendations, but if you're having trouble, simply figure out the largest number of users that could possibly be packed into your building, and assume that each one will need several devices. A very loose average density in office buildings is about one user every 100 square feet, requiring three jacks, split between one or more outlets within that ten-foot-by-ten-foot area.

When you've figured out the number of punchdown blocks you want to install, calculate the backboard area you'll need to do it in, based upon the punchdown block dimensions provided later in this section, or upon your own measurements, and start trying different combinations of rows and columns to see what fits best. Try not to locate any punchdown blocks less than one foot from the floor, or above shoulder height. Remember that you've got to drive a lot of screws into the backboard, and the punchdown tool itself can tire you out if you have to hold it in an uncomfortable position. As well, it's much easier to find rows and columns of terminals on punchdown blocks when they're viewed head-on, rather than from an angle. Keep a low stool or cable spool in the closet to sit on when working on blocks lower on the board.

Be sure to provide for some means of routing cable and cross-connect wire around the columns of punchdown blocks. To keep cross-connect wires neat and orderly, 110 systems use a kind of wire retainer which can be bolted into the column every so often. 66 systems use "mushrooms," which are white plastic spools, screwed into the backboard above and to the right of each column of blocks, over and around which you can bend loops of cross-connect wire. Whatever kind of punchdown block you use, cables which terminate on the blocks in a column should be stapled to the backboard, and run vertically behind and underneath the standoffs brackets for the column they serve.

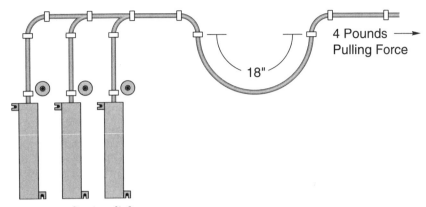

Figure 5.16 Strain relief.

Strain and tension relief are important to consider at the ends of cable runs, where they terminate on punchdown blocks. Eighteen inches of slack is specified, and it should be protected with cable fasteners, such that it takes more than four pounds of pulling force applied to the cable run before the slack is pulled out and a load is put on the terminal itself.

It's important that modular test jacks be supplied both in the Entrance Facility, which is probably located in the Main Closet, and in the intermediate closets, to facilitate the isolation of faults. In residential and light commercial telephone installations, this is usually provided in the form of a "bridge disconnect device" which is simply a wire termination point on the telco side of the demarcation point which divides the telco's wire from yours, with an RJ-11 jack for each line of incoming service. The service is then bridged to the premises side of the demarc with a tiny patch cord, about four inches long. By disconnecting the patch cord, a telephone can be plugged into the telco side of the demarc to determine whether a service discontinuance is caused by a local wiring fault or by the telco. Similar methodology should be employed in the data portion of the cable plant. This may be as simple as providing 258 adapters and modular taps for your punchdown blocks. 258 adapters split a 25-pair RJ-21X, or Amphenol, jack out into six RJ-45 jacks. They're thus useful for direct testing of LocalTalk and Ethernet hubs since, if they themselves are fully functional, they isolate the hub from the premises wiring for diagnostic purposes. Likewise, modular taps like the Siemon Testar adapters, which work with 66-style blocks, fit over four pairs of terminals on the face of a punchdown block, and provide a single RJ-45 jack for testing. AT&T's 1110A1-3 and 1110A1-4 adapters bring, respectively, three and four pairs of a 110 block into an RJ-25 and an RJ-45 jack. These can be used to tap directly into any wire run from any punchdown. If cross-connects are removed, this provides an endpoint for an isolated wire run.

Once you've laid out your backboard on paper and know where everything's going to go, make templates or mark the outlines of punchdown blocks and

components, and begin putting up the mounting screws for the standoff brackets, if you're using 66 blocks. As soon as you've figured out where all the screws
are going to have to go, including ones for areas of the backboard that won't be
used immediately, you can make your life easier by using a spring-loaded cen-
terpunch to start holes at each screw location.

When you're transferring your templates or outlines onto the backboard, it's
handy to have a long level around, to draw horizontal reference lines with. You
can't take it for granted that the edges of the backboard are square or, in older
buildings, that the floor is level. When you get around to installing components
on the backboard, there are six- and eight-inch torpedo levels, and shirt-pocket
sized ones, as well. These are handy to have when installing outlets in work
areas, too.

Different things that you'll be mounting on your backboard will come with
screws, some of which will be Phillips, some standard. You should standardize
on a specific kind of screw to use in wiring closets throughout your building,
probably #2 Phillips, and buy round-headed ¾-inch machine screws of that
type in bulk. That way, you won't have to search for the right screwdriver when
you're working.

Standoff brackets for 66 blocks, which hold them away from the surface of
the backboard and provide clearance for feeder cables, are mounted by placing
one "mounting ear" over the bottom mounting screws, and pivoting the bracket
counterclockwise until it engages the top mounting screw. If you've positioned
the screws carefully, the bracket should need to initially flex slightly, just as it's
being popped over the shaft of the screw, and should then be seated firmly, but
without being flexed any more. As well, you have to start mounting standoff
brackets from the bottom of each column.

When stripping the sheath from cables, always use the rip cord, if you can
find it. It's a fine strand of nylon, which is bundled in the cable with the wire,
immediately adjacent to the sheath. If you pull it back along the wire, it'll cut
through the sheath, just like the plastic strip at the end of a pack of chewing

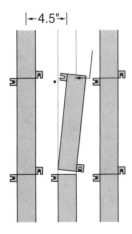

Figure   5.17 Mounting   89D
standoff brackets.

gum. This is preferable to using a sheath-removal tool, since the rip cord exerts only outward force, away from the wires, rather than inward, toward them.

If you can't find the rip cord, or need to open a sheath from the middle of a run of cable for some reason, a useful tool to have in your belt is a seam remover, which can be found in sewing shops. It has a dull flat point, something like a tiny letter opener, with a crescent-shaped blade behind it, such that it can easily be used to slit the sheath of a cable without damaging the conductors inside. I've found that it works better, and allows much more control, than the specialized wiring tools advertised to fill the same need.

5.3.3 Using punchdown blocks

As mentioned before, there are two types of punchdown blocks in common use, and it's well worth the trouble to acquaint yourself with both before deciding which to use.

The older of the two is the 66 block. Including the depth of the standoff bracket which allows rear clearance between the block and the backboard for cables, 66 blocks measure 2.75 inches wide, 10 inches high, and 2.75 inches deep. In addition, clearance for the passage of cross-connect wire is required on each side, and the blocks are thus spaced on 4.5-inch centers on the backboard. Each 66 block provides for the cross-connection of 25 pairs of conductors. This gives a ratio of pairs terminated to square inches of backboard area of 0.55.

66 blocks were originally developed by and for Bell Telephone. They're used currently, and have been for some time in the past, throughout small business and light industrial network and telephone installations. The cost of an aver-

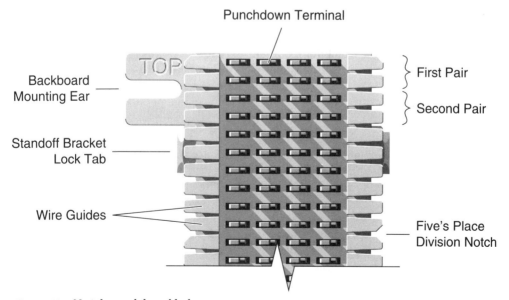

Figure 5.18 66-style punchdown block.

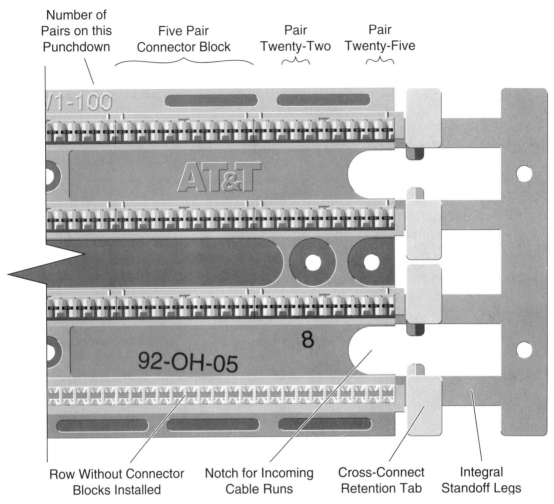

Figure 5.19 110-style punchdown block.

age 66 block, including an "89D" standoff bracket, is in the neighborhood of $9.00, or about $0.36 per pair.

110 blocks cover a larger area, but terminate many more pairs. An average 110 block includes integrated standoff legs and measures 10.75 inches wide, 3.5625 inches high, and 3.25 inches deep. The standoff legs block out the necessary horizontal clearance space on the backboard, so this is an overall measurement. Rather than containing terminals within the punchdown block itself, 110 blocks provide mounting points for add-on "connector blocks" which contain the terminals. 110 blocks of the size described terminate 100 pairs. Larger blocks are available terminating 300 and 900 pairs, and are three- and nine-time multiples of the height of the 100-pair model. In each case, the ratio of pairs terminated to square inches of backboard area is 2.61, or nearly five times that of a 66 block.

110 blocks were originally developed by Western Electric, AT&T's production arm, and have since been promulgated and propagated primarily by AT&T as the cornerstone of their PDS building wiring spec. They're found in most large business installations installed since the mid 1980s. The price of an average 100-pair 110 block, including "C-5" connector blocks and "88A" cross-connect retention clips, is about $32.00, or $0.32 per pair.

The main difference between the 66 and 110 styles is space, not cost. The increase in space efficiency that 110 blocks provide comes at a price, however. As the terminals are much closer together, more care and skill is required to terminate wires. Also, to achieve the higher density, 110 blocks employ a terminal system which makes removal and replacement of cross-connects easy, but re-termination of the ends of incoming cables extremely difficult by comparison.

To understand this problem, some background understanding of the way punchdown blocks work is required. Both 66 and 110 blocks use terminals of a type called IDC, or "Insulation Displacement Contact," mentioned earlier in association with grounding shields, rather than the screw terminals found in most walljacks. Screw terminals require that a wire be manually stripped and shaped, hooked over the terminal post, and the screw tightened—a time-consuming process, and one which is inherently fault-ridden. Errors can be made at nearly any point in the process: in the stripping, when conductors are often nicked and damaged, or the wire is not stripped back far enough; in the shaping, when the hook in the wire can be formed in the wrong direction, too large, too small, or with too much or too little exposed conductor between the end of the insulation and the hook; in the hooking over the terminal post, when the conductor may be inserted between the wrong two washers, or overlapping a washer; and in the tightening, which can be underdone, leaving a loose contact, or overdone, again possibly damaging the conductor. After all that, the conductor end may still need to be trimmed, to avoid shorting against other conductors or terminal posts. This may seem like an exaggeration, since these problems can be anticipated by using a little common sense and the skills are picked up with practice, quickly becoming second nature, but regardless of the amount of practice you get, screw terminals will always be slow and error-prone. IDC terminals are a second-generation terminal, designed to eliminate as many of the faults of screw terminals as possible. Wires need not be trimmed or stripped, and the forming of a hook can be performed sloppily, using only fingers, without fear of threatening the integrity of the connection to be made. The connection is made by pushing the wire between two contacts which are spaced such that the conductor can rest between them, in contact with both, but the insulator is pushed aside. The tool which is used to push the wire, called a punchdown tool, has a small blade on its face, which automatically trims the wire end. Punchdown tools in general, and D-814 impact tools, as the ones used on 66 and some other kinds of blocks are called, use a spring-loaded mechanism much like that in a hand-driven center punch to force the wire between the contacts.

In Fig. 5.20, you can see how the contacts of a 66 block are arranged, and the V-shaped notches into which the wires are pushed. There are two kinds of 66 blocks shown here, common blocks and split blocks. In common blocks, each

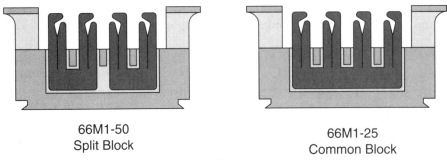

66M1-50
Split Block

66M1-25
Common Block

Figure 5.20   Cross-sections of common and split 66 blocks.

row of terminals is actually a single piece of metal, with four terminals on it, poking up through the front of the punchdown block. (Refer back to Fig. 5.18 for a front view; this is a cross section, looking down from the top.) Thus, when a wire is punched down on any of the terminals in a row, an electrical connection is formed between it and anything else punched down in that row. They're punched down to a common conductor. Split blocks, on the other hand, have two pieces of metal in each row, each with two terminals, and thus are "split" down the middle. To make a connection between wires punched down on opposite sides of the same row, a "bridge clip" must be placed across the two center terminals, connecting them, the two pieces of metal, and, by extension, the two wires which have been punched down on that row. You can easily tell the difference between split and common blocks by wiggling a terminal with your finger; if each of the other three terminals in the row moves, it's a common block. If only the other one on the same side moves, it's split.

Although IDC terminals make quick work of most of the wire-handling bottlenecks that earlier terminals presented, they exacerbate a different one: that of getting the wire onto the correct terminal. The density of screw terminals on the face of an eight-pin telephone jack is approximately 1.8 terminals per square inch. The density on the face of a 66 block is more than eight times that, at sixteen terminals per square inch. The correct terminal must be visually distinguished, and the wire must be successfully positioned over the two contacts of the terminal, prior to punching down. This problem can be partially alleviated by using a permanent felt-tip marker to mark the edges of the wire guides at the top and bottom of each pair, or on horizontal cable termination points, the beginning and end of the wires which terminate each jack. As you may have noticed, the guides are already notched every five pairs, to help with this problem.

To correctly match a wire pair with a pair of terminals, the correct wire pair must be distinguished, as well. Since the color-coding of wire is universal, I'll explain it before proceeding with the punchdown blocks.

Wires are designated using a base-five counting system, in which each value is represented by a color, rather than a numeral character. Thus the lowest-order place, the ones place, contains values equal to decimal one through five, and the next place, the fives place, contains values equal to decimal zero through twenty, or five times zero through five times four. The colors are as follows:

Value	In one's place	Equals decimal	In five's place	Equals decimal
1	Blue (BLU)	1	White (WHT)	0
2	Orange (ORN)	2	Red (RED)	5
3	Green (GRN)	3	Black (BLK)	10
4	Brown (BRN)	4	Yellow (YEL)	15
5	Slate (SLT)	5	Violet (VIO)	20

In a twenty-five-pair cable, each pair is color-coded with alternating stripes of two colors, giving a total of twenty-five possibilities. In addition, since the wires are paired, they must be individually distinguishable, as well. The individual wires of a pair are referred to as "tip" and "ring," derived from old coaxial cable terminology, where one conductor really did form a tip, and the second surrounded it, forming a ring. The tip is the first conductor of any pair, and the one marked primarily with wide bands of the fives place color and secondarily with narrow bands of the ones place color, while the ring conductor is the second of the pair, and features the reverse marking. Tip and ring are sometimes annotated using the characters + and –, respectively, but should never be called "positive" and "negative" to avoid confusion with DC power circuit terminology.

Thus the first twenty-five pairs are marked as follows:

Pair	Tip	Ring
1	WHT-BLU	BLU-WHT
2	WHT-ORN	ORN-WHT
3	WHT-GRN	GRN-WHT
4	WHT-BRN	BRN-WHT
5	WHT-SLT	SLT-WHT
6	RED-BLU	BLU-RED
7	RED-ORN	ORN-RED
8	RED-GRN	GRN-RED
9	RED-BRN	BRN-RED
10	RED-SLT	SLT-RED
11	BLK-BLU	BLU-BLK
12	BLK-ORN	ORN-BLK
13	BLK-GRN	GRN-BLK
14	BLK-BRN	BRN-BLK
15	BLK-SLT	SLT-BLK
16	YEL-BLU	BLU-YEL
17	YEL-ORN	ORN-YEL
18	YEL-GRN	GRN-YEL
19	YEL-BRN	BRN-YEL
20	YEL-SLT	SLT-YEL
21	VIO-BLU	BLU-VIO
22	VIO-ORN	ORN-VIO
23	VIO-GRN	GRN-VIO
24	VIO-BRN	BRN-VIO
25	VIO-SLT	SLT-VIO

In the first pair, WHT-BLU/BLU-WHT, the WHT-BLU conductor is the tip, and should appear at position one on a punchdown block, while the BLU-WHT conductor appears at position two, WHT-ORN at position three, ORN-WHT at position four, et cetera. Notice that all varieties of punchdown block support rows or columns of twenty-five pairs, divided into groups of five pairs. This is to correspond with the wire color-coding scheme.

In cables of more than twenty-five pairs but not more than six hundred, the wires are internally segregated in units of twenty-five pairs, bound with a color-coded string or tape, and the coding repeats from one to twenty-four in the twenty-fives place, providing for twenty-four 25-pair units, or 600 pairs. For example, the YEL-SLT pair under a BLK-GRN binder tape would indicate the 20th pair of the 13th binder unit. Multiplying 13 by 25, we get 325. Add 20, and we find that this is the 345th pair in the cable.

Beyond six hundred, two different "super-unit" binding schemes are employed, one based on super-units composed of fifty pairs, or two binder groups, the other based on hundred-pair conglomerations of four binder groups each. The fifty-pair super-units are color-coded S1 through S39, where the first 600 pairs (S1–S12) are bound under a second-order binder coded WHT, the next 600 (S13–S24) are coded RED, and the last 600 (S25–S36) are coded BLK. Although this could obviously be extended to cover an additional 1200 pairs, hundred-pair super-units are generally used for larger cables. Hundred-pair super-units are numbered S1 through S39, where the first six super-units (S1–S6) are coded WHT, the second six (S7–S12) are coded RED, the third six (S13–S18) are BLK, the fourth six (S17–S24) are YEL, the fifth six (S24–S30) are VIO, the sixth six (S31–S36) are BLU, and the last three (S37–S39) are ORN. Occasionally, cables in the 1500- to 2100-pair range will be grouped in an admixture of fifty- and hundred-pair super-units. These cables should be eschewed when possible, to avoid confusion.

In all cases, color-coded cables are constructed with the lowest-numbered pairs, units, and super-units at the center of the cable, with numbers progressing outward in a spiral.

Although most telephone and network services are not polarity-sensitive within individual pairs, polarity should be maintained nonetheless, to provide for forward compatibility with future services which may not be able to afford such tolerance.

On 66 blocks, the positioning of the wire is aided by guides. First, the two wires of the pair you wish to terminate are bent over a finger, to make hook shapes of them. Next, they're positioned between the wire guides at the edges of the punchdown block, which serve to stabilize them vertically. Then they're positioned horizontally by sliding them inward, over the terminals' hooks, visible in Figs. 5.20 and 5.21. Once there, they're pulled back slightly to engage them with the hooks. Slight tension maintained on the wire pair with one hand will keep them positioned correctly until you can use the punchdown tool to terminate each of them in turn.

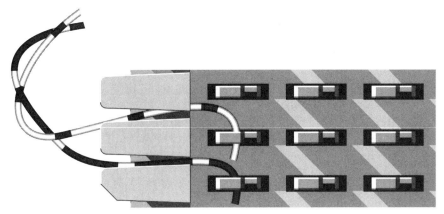

Figure 5.21   Detail of wire positioning on 66 block.

Since each wire guide is associated with a specific row, care must be taken to ensure that wires are placed over the wire guide associated with the row to which they're to be punched down, rather than under it. Also, the hook of the wire must always open downward, because that's the end which will be trimmed off. If the hook opened upward, and you held the punchdown tool right-side-up as well, the main wire would be cut off, and the stub would be punched down to the terminal. Although you'll probably make each of these mistakes (terminating the wire upside down, holding the punchdown tool upside down) once or twice, correct termination procedures quickly become habitual.

To terminate the wire, hold the punchdown tool with the side marked "cut" facing down, since you want the wire cut below the terminal, not above it. On the Harris-Dracon D-814 tool, which is the most prevalent, the cut side is yellow, while the non-cut side is blue. All but the cheapest punchdown tools use keyed bits, so you don't need to worry about getting the bit into the tool right-side-up. Hold the tool firmly and, while holding the wire to be terminated steady with the other hand, place the punchdown bit over the terminal (it should completely surround the terminal and slip on easily), and press firmly, directly forward, to compress and trip the tool, pressing the wire into place, displacing the insulation, and finally cutting the end off. Be sure to always hold the punchdown tool horizontally, so that it does not bend the punchdown terminals.

110 blocks, which are themselves kind of a second-generation punchdown block designed to correct the perceived deficiencies of the 66 style, take the strengths and weaknesses of the 66 block even further. Although the density of terminals on the face of the block is nominally 18 per square inch, or just 12 percent higher than a 66 block, there's much more space between the four rows, so the fifty terminals in each row are spaced correspondingly closer together, only fifteen hundredths of an inch apart, in fact.

Simply fan the wires out in the correct order, and rest them in their proper notches. It's a bit easier to find the right places to punch down wires on a 110 than a 66 block, since both the 110 block and the connector blocks are color-coded. On the block, before connector blocks have been punched down, the fives place colors are marked, so there are five groups of five pairs, colored white, red, blue (substituting for black), yellow, and violet. Each pair on the connector blocks is individually color-coded with the one's place colors—blue, orange, green, brown, and slate. Since wires being terminated on a 110 block need not be hooked over, even less time is spent preparing the wire. Notice the difference between the horizontal spaces between the punchdown rows. Some spaces end with notches, while others run the full width of the block, and have cross-connect retainers at their ends. The notch is to allow the ends of cable runs to be drawn up from the standoff space below the block, while the retainers are to hold cross-connect wire in place. Thus the rows alternate, cable, cross-connect, cable, cross-connect, and so on. This is necessary to allow both cables and cross-connects access to each punchdown row. Unlike 66 blocks, 110 blocks use two planes of terminals. The rear plane is for the cable runs, and the front plane for cross-connects. This is the main method by which the higher density is achieved. As stated before, it also makes it difficult to move terminated cable runs, since they're in the rear plane. In Fig. 5.22, the top right-most connector block is terminating both a five-pair cable run and a full complement of cross-connect wires. This was achieved by first laying the conductors from the cable run out on the row without the block, and using the punchdown tool to seat

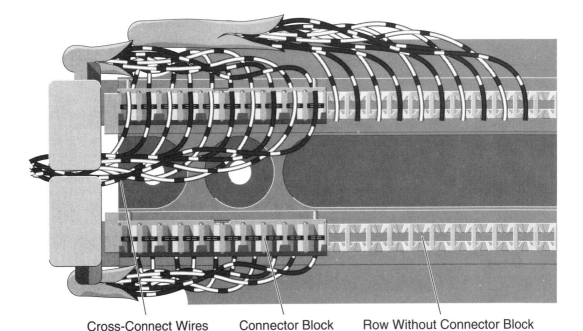

Cross-Connect Wires   Connector Block   Row Without Connector Block

Figure 5.22   Detail of wire positioning on 110 block.

them on the row and trim them flush. A connector block is then seated over them, and punched down, displacing the insulation and making contact between the conductors and its terminals. Although a D-814-type punchdown tool can only terminate a single conductor on a 110 block at a time with the bits currently available, as many as ten wires can be terminated simultaneously with a 788 J1 punchdown tool, designed specifically for 110 blocks.

The dual-plane nature of the 110 block system is more clearly evident in a horizontal cross section. In Fig. 5.23, you can see the wire positioning guides which are molded into the plastic of the block itself, and onto which cable runs are punched down. They don't actually meet a terminal at that point, though; the first punch simply snugs them into the guides, and trims off the excess wire. The IDC terminals are located within the connector blocks, which are then placed over the wire positioning guides and wire ends. When the punchdown tool presses the connector block down, the IDCs on the bottom of the connector block contact the wires. Cross-connect wires are then punched down on the top of the connector block.

There's an evolutionary trend apparent in 110 blocks: the newer style is faster to use, if you've got the practice, sharp eye, and steady hand to use them;

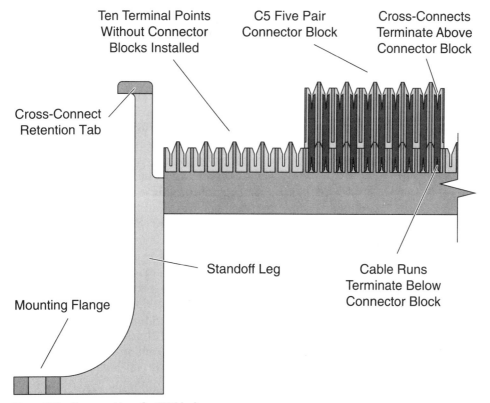

Figure 5.23   Cross section of a 110 block.

otherwise, you may get frustrated trying to learn on them. They cost about the same as 66 blocks, use much less backboard space, and will support higher-speed networks in the future. On the other hand, they aren't yet a universal standard by any means and even many telecommunications and network wiring professionals don't yet have any experience with them, or possess the specialized tools to work with them.

5.4 Vertical Cable

Vertical, or backbone, cable connects the main closet with each of the intermediate closets. At the point at which it enters the main closet, your vertical cable should contain one conductor for every pin in every jack in your building, although it's not directly tied to any of them. This is likely to be an extremely thick cable bundle, and this is the reason for the vertical alignment of the wiring closets. The slots and sleeves of the wiring closets should provide an easy method of passing the bundle vertically to each closet, without requiring that it be bent or even that it touch anything else during the pulling process. To this end, the ceiling of the top intermediate closet often features a solidly mounted screw-eye or pulley above the slot or sleeve, so that vertical cable can simply be hoisted up from the main closet.

The section on horizontal cable will describe the process of pre-fabricating a wiring harness to simplify the pulling process, but this is probably the first place you should try it, since it's by far the simplest and easiest to measure.

Be careful, when pulling cable, never to exceed about 25 pounds of pulling force. Although the actual breaking tension of the conductors is much higher, the thin copper conductors can easily be stretched, making them more brittle, and changing their impedance and other electrical characteristics. The insulation and jacketing materials used on wire and cable provide no strain-relief at all, as you can see by removing some from a piece of wire and stretching it by hand. Thus the entire pulling force is borne by the conductor itself.

Cable brittleness is also adversely affected by tight bends and low temperatures. Never pull cable at below-freezing temperatures, unless you're using cable specially designed for low-temperature installation, some of which can withstand being pulled at temperatures as low as −40° Fahrenheit. Also, as in wiring closets, no cable should be bent with an inside radius of less than one inch. Staples or other cable fasteners should be used to ensure that this won't change, and to relieve the bend of any tension or strain.

If you anticipate very different uses for different vertical cables, you may wish to think about purchasing shielded cables, to help prevent interference between them, since they'll be running parallel and in fairly close proximity to each other for some distance. Although LocalTalk, Ethernet, and Token Ring networks aren't terribly affected by the 40-volt current in ringing telephone lines and the power circuits of ISDN service, it's easily conceivable that future network services might not be so tolerant. A rule of thumb to apply to the use of shielded cable is that maximum distances should be lessened by a quarter to a third, since it shields against NEXT (Near-End Crosstalk) between cables but tends to intensify the other electrical problems associated with cable runs. Thus, shielded cable would probably best be used where the vertical cable run is of 200 feet or less in length. Fortunately, this should be the case in all but the tallest buildings. If you do this, remember to ground the shield, in the manner described earlier.

As mentioned before, all electrical wires act as antennas, generating magnetic fields in the space around themselves, regardless of any plastic insulation. The magnetic fields of nearby conductors interact, creating an "inductive coupling" whereby some of the signal strength from each conductor is passed to the other. Since telecommunications and network applications normally use signals of five volts or lesser amplitude, they don't affect each other greatly, even within bundled cables. When they pass near a 110-volt or 220-volt AC power cable, however, the problem becomes much greater; as it does, the nearer, or more closely parallel, the conductors run. Thus it's important to choose cable runs which are as remote as possible from any vertical AC power distribution cables.

It's imperative that all cables be marked at each end, and at regular intervals along their lengths. Ideally, the markings should be only a few feet apart, and each should consist of the cable number, the location on the cable in feet from the service end, and the total length of the cable. This applies not only to vertical cables, but to horizontal cabling as well. This is better done with the cables laid out flat than while they're being unrolled from a spool, since the possibility of cumulative error in measurement is greater if you perform a large number of small measurements as the cable is being pulled. Time-Domain Reflectometers, or TDRs, are popular but expensive tools for measuring the length of cables and the distance to faults in the cable. Although they can be used to check for the existence of faults in cables which are still on-reel, they should not be used to check the distance to those faults, or the length of cables which are coiled, especially ones tightly coiled, as on a spool, since this coiling produces an electrical effect called interwinding capacitance, which can affect the TDRs' readings by 10 percent or more.

Figure 5.24 Cable marking.

After the cable has been installed, it may still develop faults, and that's when the cable length markings come in handy. You can use a TDR to test the cable from each end, locate the fault within the cable, check your records to see exactly where the cable runs (in vertical wiring you should be able to skip this step), and go find the cable. By examining the markings, you can find the spot on the cable which is having the problem, and you can look for causes. Perhaps the cable has become crimped by something that it's wedged into, or something's fallen on it. Perhaps a conductor inside simply cracked, as a result of forces put on it while it was being pulled. Cables can also be damaged subsequent to pulling, by entirely unrelated activities—nails being blindly driven into walls to hang pictures, for instance. In any case, without the cable markings, the TDR would be of no use.

Avoid joining wire in the middle of runs if at all possible. Most current services like LocalTalk, 10Base-T Ethernet, and 16-megabit Token Ring will withstand the impedance mismatch of a join, but there's no way of predicting the sensitivity of devices using network systems which haven't yet been finalized. Since your longest expanses of cable shouldn't be over 300 feet and most cable is available in 1000-foot lengths, there's really little need for joins. If it does become necessary for some reason, solder the join. Field soldering is fairly easy: Use staples or other cable anchors to fix the ends of the wires to be joined so that stress cannot be transferred to or through the soldered joint, twist the wires to be joined about each other, and wrap a short length of flux around the join. Heat the whole join with a cordless soldering iron or butane lighter, until the flux melts around the join.

5.5   Intermediate Closets

The intermediate closets, which serve each floor, are extremely similar in nature and design to the main closet, save that they tend to be single-purpose and much simpler. Like main closets, they need at least two walls covered with backboards, and should provide both service- and distribution-side punchdown blocks. In the intermediate closets, however, home runs from outlets in the users' work areas terminate on the distribution blocks and, with one exception, vertical cable from the main closet terminates on the service blocks. The exception is that some services, especially distance-sensitive network services, are provided at least in part from within the intermediate closets. Specifically, this means multiport repeaters serving users on that floor. These in turn cascade back down their own home runs, in vertical cable, and attach to ports on other multiport repeaters in the main closet.

As in the main closet, install jacks with home runs near any devices which support out-of-band management signaling. In the case of Farallon StarControllers, this allows you to create runs through the vertical cable back to StarControllers and a management station in the main closet.

If you anticipate the need for ring or bus topologies in the future, it is allowable, although nonstandard, to run cable between the intermediate closets, so long as the full and normal complement of vertical cable returns to the main closet as well, and all other requirements are met. Bus and ring topologies should then be constructed out of horizontal home runs by cross-connecting in the wiring closet.

5.5.1 Firestopping

One of the main concerns in complying with building codes and local regulations is maintaining the integrity of the fire barriers that have been designed into your building. Typically, these include each structural floor/ceiling slab, all supporting walls, and any stairwell shafts. Whenever you run cable through a firewall, you're penetrating it, creating a point at which fire could pass between fire zones. This is dealt with by "firestopping" the points of penetration. Firestopping is the stopping-up of such holes with mechanical blocks, putties, cements, and ceramic fibers which are designed to block the passage of fire and heat, and withstanding the pressure of a firehose without losing those properties.

Although there are many hundreds of different firestopping products available, the majority fall into one of four categories: mechanical, putty, cementitious, or fiber pillows.

Mechanical firestops are simply frames which fit into the hole through the firewall, and a set of fireproof blocks and shims which you pack the hole with once the cable has been passed through. They're the easiest to use, once they've been installed, and probably the most reliable, but they're by far the hardest to initially install.

Putties can be used either alone or in conjunction with pillows, as illustrated in Fig. 5.25. They're probably the most commonly employed firestopping measure. The putty is simply packed into the hole, around the cables, and removed again when necessary.

Cementitious products come in the form of a cement-like powder which is mixed with water, poured, and allowed to set. These are generally considered inconvenient, since they're not reenterable; if you do re-enter, you have to make a new one. Also, they can crack if the penetrating item undergoes thermal expansion.

Fiber pillows are typically called "mineral wool" or "ceramic fiber" pillows. They're filled with fibers which are normally somewhat flexible and compressible, but expand and harden when heated. Such pillows are especially useful during construction, or in areas which need to be re-entered frequently. They can be used alone, or in conjunction with putties, for longer-term applications.

Firestopping products are rated either F or T, depending upon their performance. F-rated firestop systems prevent the passage of flame to, or sympathetic ignition on, the side opposite the fire, and they can withstand the pressure of water from a firehose. T-rated firestops perform the same, but also limit the temperature on the opposite side to a 325° rise above ambient. Some firestopping materials are also approved for other uses, such as environmental protection seals in industrial applications.

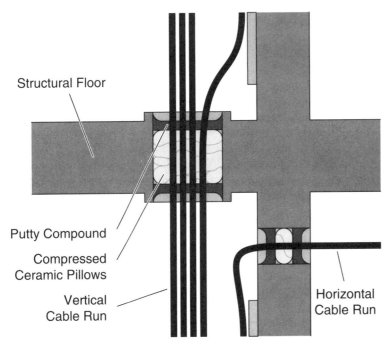

Structural Floor

Putty Compound

Compressed
Ceramic Pillows

Vertical
Cable Run

Horizontal
Cable Run

Figure 5.25   Firestopping.

5.6 Horizontal Cable

Horizontal cable connects each outlet in the user work areas to the intermediate closet on the same floor. It's usually of smaller pair-count than vertical cable, but should be otherwise identical wire, of the same gauge, number of twists per foot, and electrical characteristics.

5.6.1 Wiring methods

There are a number of different general methodologies that have been devised for getting cables from wiring closets to user work areas, or, in techie talk, horizontal cable distribution. For the most part, the one you choose will depend largely upon the construction of the building you're installing in, and the locations and accessibility of the work areas. It's likely that you'll end up mixing at least two of the methods mentioned here, and there's absolutely nothing wrong with doing so, provided that you and whomever else will be responsible for maintaining the cable are fully acquainted with the peculiarities of each of the methods you choose to employ. Some of the methods are infrequently used, and I'll just touch on those briefly, but a few—the raceway, conduit, and poke-through methods in particular—tend to cover the majority of the cable in any installation.

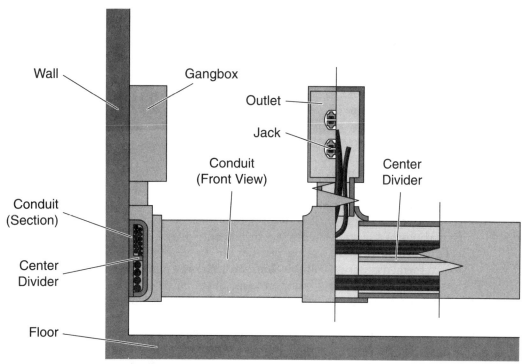

Figure 5.26 A baseboard conduit system.

5.6.1.1 Baseboard method.
The baseboard method depends on the use of baseboard-shaped conduit, which runs through the building, hugging the walls at floor level. The vendors of baseboard conduit tend to supply integrated systems of gangboxes, faceplates, and jacks.

The components tend to be made of slightly flexible plastic, in either white, beige, or electrical ivory. The conduit usually comes in boxes of ten-foot sections, which can be trimmed to length with a hacksaw. The conduit is usually adhesive-backed, and can be stuck directly to most walls without much surface preparation, since it doesn't weigh much. Gangboxes use a variety of mounting methods, and all other adapters—T-connectors, end caps, and corners—usually just snap on and off over the conduit. Most of the larger sizes of conduit have one or more internal dividers of some kind, which are sometimes tinned to act as a partial shield between the two sides. In any case, this is useful if you have to run AC power at the same time as network and telecommunications cable.

The big trick to installing conduit is correctly estimating the number of each kind of component you'll need, and the number of pieces of conduit, since it's usually fairly expensive. The best way to estimate is to survey an entire floor or regular subdivision of your building, and determine exactly how many you'll need for that floor, then prorate that out to cover the whole building, and add whatever margin of error you think you can afford to pay for.

Baseboard conduit isn't as attractive as concealed wiring, and it's more vulnerable to tampering, accidental damage during normal office activities, and electromagnetic interference from office equipment in the work area, but it can be invaluable in buildings with thick stone or masonry walls, or when speed is of much greater importance than other factors. It's inappropriate in large rooms, since it can only serve locations at the walls, and it's extremely bad in damp areas, since it offers little or no moisture protection. The baseboard method is also occasionally referred to as the perimeter pathway method, or the moulding raceway method.

5.6.1.2 Cell floor method. The cell floor method is dependent upon the existence of a cellular concrete floor in your building. Such floors are laid in three stages: first, a flat layer of concrete, then a layer of corrugated steel, and then another layer of concrete. The space between the first layer of concrete and the corrugations of the steel sheeting remains empty, and can be used to pull cable through, provided there are perpendicular "trenches" at each end. There are also pre-formed concrete cellular floors, which are single blocks of concrete containing molded cylindrical ducts in two-, four-, or six-inch diameters. The cell floor method and the underfloor duct method are very similar.

5.6.1.3 Conduit method. The conduit method can be implemented fully, using home runs of conduit running all the way from each outlet gangbox back to the wiring closet, or it can be implemented partially, as "stubs" extending upward from the gangboxes above the top edge of nonstructural walls and the cable run, then carried back to the wiring closet on a raceway, in a plenum, or by some other method. Except in some cases when conduit is installed at the time of a building's construction, it's nearly always run above a suspended-tile ceiling.

The point behind conduit is that it can follow a complex path and it simplifies the pulling process, since pulling no longer has to occur in straight lines. Instead, a fish tape is fed in one end of a section of conduit, and pushed through to the other side. There, it's attached to the wire bundle it's going to pull, and the whole thing is retracted back to where the tape was inserted. The advantage is that the tape need not be guided, and the conduit can go around corners, avoiding obstacles which would otherwise need to be circumvented each time cable was pulled.

The two types of conduit that could be easily used to house communications wire are EMT and PVC. EMT (extruded metal tube) is thinwall metal conduit, while PVC is polyvinyl chloride plastic. Of these, EMT is preferable, since it can be grounded, and will then act as a shield from EM interference. There are other types of conduit, which are inappropriate for various reasons. These include IMC (or intermediate metal conduit), rigid metal conduit, and Romex, which is a spring-like flexible metal conduit.

Conduit is basically a very thin metal pipe that's smooth on the inside. In pulling cable through it, you're dependent upon the inside diameter remaining the same, and there not being rough junctions upon which a pulled cable could catch. If you decide to install conduit, most of the work you do will be with the basic goal of making it easier to pull cable through it. When you cut the conduit, using a hacksaw, you must also use a round file to deburr the end of the cut, and taper it inward slightly. Make sure you cut as nearly perpendicular to the axis of the conduit as possible, so that the piece you're cutting will butt up cleanly against the next piece in the run.

Conduit is bent, using a tool which supports the walls of the conduit, so that they can't spread out, allowing the inside of the curve to collapse outward. Thus the same inside diameter is maintained through the turn, lessening the friction you'll feel while pulling. The tools which are used to bend conduit generally only come in one or two radii for any particular diameter of conduit, but be sure that the one you get provides a bend radius that's at least ten times the inside diameter of the conduit.

Regardless of how carefully you work with the conduit, you'll need to install junction boxes or pulling elbows periodically, on all but the shortest runs. The main criterion which is used in deciding where to place a box or elbow is the number of turns the conduit has taken since the last one, since they're what cause most of the friction. The method of calculating is simple: Count the number of degrees of turns the conduit takes, and don't allow it to go past 180° before adding another junction or elbow. You should also install a new junction box if you've laid 100 feet since the previous one, even if it's been perfectly straight.

When locating junction boxes, think about the use that the space you're over will see in the future. Try to locate them over hallways or open areas, rather than within offices, so you'll be able to get a ladder in to work on the cable run, and won't have to stand on anyone's desk. If you have to locate one above a solid ceiling rather than a suspended-tile one, try to do it near an access panel.

If you use conduit on the exterior of a building, be sure to put in artificial low-points, just as you'd put drip-loops into cable, and drill a drain-hole at the lowest point. If you're in an area that freezes in winter, this is especially impor-

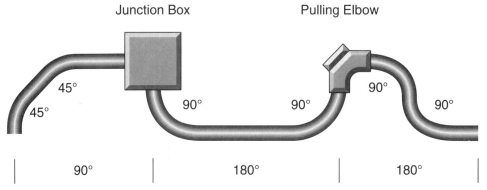

Figure 5.27   Conduit 180° rule.

tant, since water trapped in conduit can freeze and damage either the conduit or the cable when it expands.

When choosing a conduit size, calculate the combined cross-sectional area of the cable bundle you intend to pull, and compare it to the cross-sectional area of the conduit. Your conduit should never be more than 30 percent full, or you'll begin having trouble pulling cable through. Conduit is available in quarter-inch increments from 0.5 inches to 1.5 inches, and half-inch increments from there up to four inches.

As with cable runs, conduit runs should be clearly labeled at both ends: in the work area, and in the closet. Remember to leave a length of pull-cord or fish tape in any conduit runs you lay.

The advantage of conduit is that it greatly simplifies the pulling process, especially for fiber-optic cable. The cost is all up-front, in that it's much harder to install a single run of conduit than to install a single run of wire. Conduit is best used where you foresee a need to pull cable again in the future, outlet locations are unchanging over time, or you need to provide extra protection to your cable runs.

5.6.1.4 Overfloor duct method. Overfloor ducts are simply pieces of extruded plastic or rubber which form a "speed bump" with a hollow center through which cable can be run. This is a really bad idea for all but the least permanent installations, and a suspended overhead cable run of some type is probably preferable even for most temporary installations. Most building wiring specifications explicitly forbid the use of any overfloor ducts for signaling cable distribution.

5.6.1.5 Plenum method. The plenum method utilizes existing ducts associated with central heating and air-conditioning systems. Most already use some sort of vertical-and-horizontal distribution system similar to that used by the cable plant, and most also have convenient access hatches.

The main problem with using air plenums for cable distribution is that the normal polyvinyl chloride jacketing used on telecommunications cable produces toxic fumes when it burns, and for this reason it's a violation of fire codes to locate it in air ducts. This spurred the development of plenum cable, which uses a fire-resistant teflon jacket, and is legal for use in plenums. Unfortunately, plenum jacketing approximately doubles the per-foot cost of most cable.

The decision as to whether to use plenums for cable distribution should be largely based upon the convenience of air plenums to the areas to which you need to pull cable. If they provide a short route, there are adequate access points to pull the cable, and you can afford the increased cable cost, it's probably a good bet.

5.6.1.6 Poke-through method. The poke-through method is a fairly clean way of locating floor-mounted outlets out in the middle of rooms which don't have structural or utility pillars. It requires a suspended-tile ceiling on the floor below, however.

Horizontal distribution cable is routed down through the wiring closet's slot or sleeve, to the false ceiling area of the floor below, as you can see in the cross-sectional side view in Fig. 5.28. From there, it's distributed in raceways or conduit to the outlet location, where it passes back up through a hole, and into the floor-mounted outlet above.

As the public utilities always like to remind us, "always call before you drill." In this case, it's especially important, because many modern office buildings use pre-stressed concrete slabs for structural floors. These are basically concrete blocks containing high-tension steel frames, which lend considerable strength and load-bearing capacity to the concrete slab by holding it together. If you drill through one of the metal elements, or even through a particularly vulnerable area of the compressed concrete, you could substantially weaken the floor.

Contact the office of the building's architect, if you think the floor might be of this type. If the floor was a pre-manufactured slab, chances are it will be fairly easy to determine from specifications the safe areas to drill. If that doesn't work, the floor can be x-rayed before drilling.

When you're ready to drill, first check from below, at the location you think corresponds with the jack location above, to make sure the area is clear of obstructions. Then go back upstairs and drill a guide hole down from the jack location. Check again from below to make sure it's coming out about where you thought it would, and then drill the final hole. Since the floor is a fire barrier, the hole must be firestopped as soon as you've pulled the cable through.

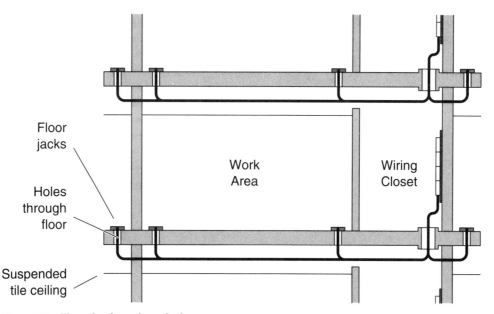

Floor
jacks

Holes
through
floor

Work
Area

Wiring
Closet

Suspended
tile ceiling

Figure 5.28   The poke-through method.

The poke-through method is fairly easy, inexpensive, and has a certain elegant simplicity that makes it attractive, provided there aren't problems drilling through the floor. Since it's mainly useful for floor-jacks, which aren't themselves terribly desirable under most circumstances, it's of limited utility as a general-purpose cable distribution method, but it complements conduit and raceway installations well. Be sure, however, to document these runs carefully, because they'll be inherently harder to trace later, since they pass up and down through the floor.

As you can see in Fig. 5.28, there's no suspended ceiling in the wiring closet. Since suspended ceilings serve no purpose other than to conceal the utilities which are being provided from the closet, they're of no function in the closet itself, and would merely get in the way. The minimum clear height at any point in a wiring closet is ideally at least eight feet unobstructed, and the actual structural ceiling should be higher.

5.6.1.7 Raceway method. The raceway method is probably the easiest and most common horizontal cable distribution method is use today. Like conduit, it depends upon a suspended-tile ceiling for concealment. Raceways are basically just troughs, in which cable can be laid. There are quite a few varieties, with solid or ventilated bottom trays and sides, and tops which are either open or covered by hinged panels. Raceways with ventilated bottoms are often called ladder trays, since they resemble small ladders, suspended horizontally. Race-

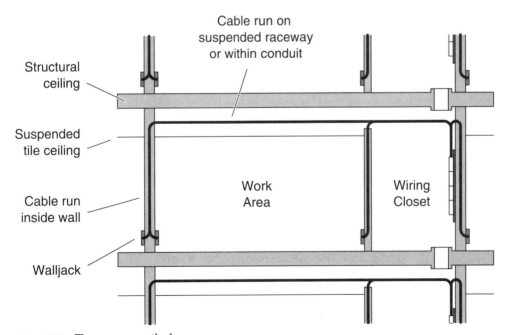

Figure 5.29 The raceway method.

ways with hinged tops, and solid sides and bottom, usually fitted with knock-outs for cable entry, are sometimes called wireways.

Cable raceways can be supported in one of three ways: by cantilevering them from a wall or pillar; by resting them on a trapeze, which is itself suspended by two rods from the structural ceiling; or with individual rods attached to the structural ceiling. In any case, the tray should be provided with one foot of clear space above, and supported at least every five feet, within two feet of each side of any junction or fitting.

If the raceway is made of metal, it should be bonded to ground at the wiring closet. If it's carrying AC power as well as network cable, it should be provided with a shielding barrier running longitudinally down the middle of each section, to separate the two types of cable.

If holes are cut through firewalls to allow passage for raceways, they should be firestopped as soon as installation is complete. Raceways are generally inexpensive and not terribly difficult to install. They're not quite as easy to use as conduit, but they're much more flexible in the long term. They're a very practical solution to most run-of-the-mill building cabling problems.

5.6.1.8 Raised floor method. Raised floors are the computer-nerd's version of suspended ceilings. Used primarily in computer rooms, raised floors use pillars to support large floor tiles, which can be raised to access the wiring space below. Raised floors generally provide between one and two and a half feet of vertical clearance for massive quantities of cable.

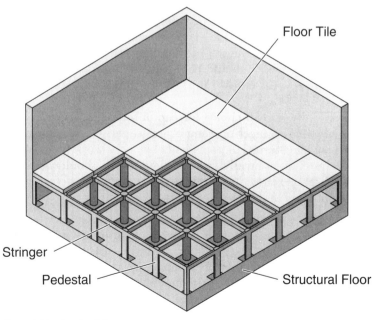

Figure 5.30 A raised floor.

The main problem with raised floors is that the tiles have to be taken up any time you want to make a change. Some types, called cornerlock tiles, are attached with bolts at each corner to the tops of the supporting pedestals, while others simply rest on the stringers. In either case, the tiles are lifted out with big rubber suction cups. Obviously, no equipment can be on top of that tile when you want to lift it out.

If you're having a raised floor installed in a room which wasn't originally designed with that in mind, there are several considerations which should be taken into account. Rooms designed for raised floors have "depressed slabs" or structural floors sunken by a similar amount, so that the final raised floor is level with the floors in the rest of the building. If you don't have this advantage, you'll have to install stairs or ramps up to the raised level, which will make it more difficult to move equipment in and out of the room. If you're in an earthquake-prone area, be sure that the system you employ includes stringers, which cross-brace the tops of the pedestals and provide support all the way around the edge of each tile. Make sure all metal parts of the raised floor and support structure be well bonded to ground.

Floor outlets can either be pedestal-mounted, and extend through a hole in the tile above, or they can be mounted on the tile. Although the latter is easier to install, you have to provide some means of disconnecting the wires from the back of the outlet each time you want to move the tile more than the eighteen inches your cable slack will allow. In either case, make sure that you know approximately where all the equipment will be located in the room before you start placing outlets, because you want the outlets to be proximal to equipment, not walkways.

Ideally, one or more large-diameter conduit runs should connect the underfloor area of any raised floor room to the wiring closet associated with that floor. Raised floors for computer or equipment rooms should have a minimum vertical clearance of one foot, which should be adequate to provide minimum crossing distance from any sources of EM interference that might also be running in the underfloor space.

Raised floors are generally a good choice for computer rooms, which often require huge masses of cable connecting computers to peripherals, terminal servers to telephone lines, et cetera. They're a bad choice for work areas, since they're quite expensive and structurally inconvenient. They should never be used in wiring closets, because they don't provide nearly enough accessibility for the constant cable changes that occur in closets.

5.6.1.9 Undercarpet method.   Where there is no practical alternative, wire can be run underneath office carpeting. The problems with this are obvious, mostly to do with the virtual two-dimensionality of the space between the carpet and the floor: first, it's difficult to make cables thin enough that they don't create a significant bump in the carpet, attracting extra friction from things passing over. Second, it's impossible to maintain minimum crossing distances between telecommunications and network cable, and other sources of EM interference, since they're essentially all running in the same plane.

The first problem is largely dealt with by using cable which maintains the individual twisted pairs, but lay them side-by-side, rather than in a round bundle. This creates a double-thick ribbon cable. The second problem is dealt with in two ways: by limiting the length of undercarpet cable runs as much as possible, preferably to less than thirty feet; and by requiring that any telecommunications and network cable which must cross other cable underneath the carpet do so at a perpendicular angle to it, and be entirely perpendicular within six inches of each side of the other cable, as shown in Fig. 5.31. Don't route your network wiring such that it crosses AC power cable at or near a join, junction, or splice in the AC power cable.

Undercarpet cable should come with a junction box for connecting the service end of the undercarpet run to the distribution end of the normal home run. You must use this, rather than attempting to create splices, for the same reason that you use punchdown blocks in a wiring closet: to allow later modification without pulling new cable. Don't try to mix-and-match components from undercarpet wiring systems offered by different vendors unless both vendors claim interoperability, as this may lead to insufficient tolerances between components, or other conditions which may promote increased wear on the system.

When undercarpet AC power cable is installed, carpet squares are required. These are simply pieces of carpet cut into squares, on the order of two feet on a side, which can be laid down just like tiles, but pulled up again to expose the cable beneath. They can be useful, as they allow access to cable underneath without requiring the removal of all the furniture from a room to roll back a full-sized carpet. Even if you won't be sharing any space with AC power cable, you may wish to try using carpet squares.

When undercarpet cable is used, the junction boxes may be installed during the roughing-in, but the cable itself should not be run until the last stages of finish wiring, so as to avoid exposing it to damage from construction traffic.

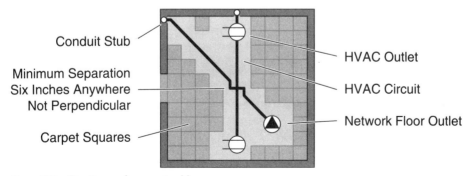

Figure 5.31   Routing undercarpet cable.

If you're thinking of installing undercarpet cable, there are two requisite qualities you should look for in the room that you're cabling: level, continuous, hard floors, which will support the cable well, and not offer many edges against which the cable could be pressed; and a dry environment, where the cable won't be subject to liquid spills, especially solvents which could damage the cable sheath and wire insulation.

5.6.1.10 Underfloor duct method. Some buildings with concrete floors have systems of cable distribution ducts installed in the floor at the time the concrete is being poured. Such systems provide regularly spaced floor outlets across large, open floor areas. As with the poke-through method, the main liability of this method is that it only provides floor outlets, and must in most instances be combined with another method to allow an entire building to be equipped with outlets.

Underfloor duct systems generally contain two kinds of ducts: feeder or header ducts, which run perpendicularly at one or both ends of a room; and distribution ducts, which cross the span of the room every five or six feet, and which provide floor outlet access at regular intervals. These two types of ducts can exist on the same plane, or they may exist in two planes, with feeder ducts lying slightly below distribution ones. Flushducts, which require the least depth, are pre-fabricated metal or plastic duct systems which are laid into the wet concrete such that their top surface is flush with the surface of the concrete. In any case, hand holes, which are like miniature manholes, should be located at each intersection between a feeder and a distribution duct, to facili-

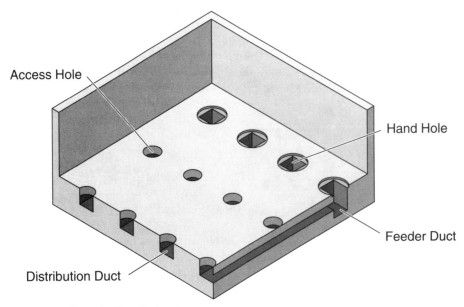

Figure 5.32 An underfloor duct system.

tate cable pulling. Feeder ducts should all be provided with underfloor conduit home runs to the appropriate wiring closet.

Like raceways and baseboard conduit, many underfloor ducts contain longitudinal dividers, to separate different types of cable.

5.6.1.11 Weathermaster method. A method not so much of distributing cable, but of locating intermediate closets in buildings which have no space for them, the weathermaster method, when used, is often used in conjunction with plenum cable distribution. The idea is to install both vertical and horizontal cable runs in air ducts, and locate your backboards in the required clearance space surrounding heating and air-conditioning units on different floors. Obviously, this is a technique of last resort.

5.6.1.12 Zone method. The zone method is also not exactly a means of distributing cable. The zone method is an alternative to the creation of complicated wiring harnesses, which will be discussed later in this section. It works in small buildings in which no cable run is particularly near its length limit.

Basically, you define wiring "zones" which may loosely correspond with your defined work areas, and calculate the distance to the center of each zone, and add to that the distance from the center of the zone to the most distant outlet. Cut all the cables for that zone to that total length, tie the bundle together from the wiring closet out to the point at which it hits the center of the zone, and leave all the ends free from that point on. Take the harness to the center of the zone, and pull the service end back to the wiring closet, leaving all the distribution ends radiating from the center of the zone. Take each one, pull it to its outlet, cut off the excess, and record the finished length of that run.

This method is quite wasteful of cable, which is bad for two reasons: First, the cable costs money and the scraps you end up with won't be long enough to use elsewhere; second, the longer your cable runs, the more attenuation you'll have in your network.

The zone method does speed up cable pulling a bit, so that's what you're buying for the extra money and attenuation. The zone method shouldn't be used when any cable runs are near their maximum length, since it increases the length of nearly all of the runs.

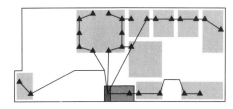

Standard Wiring Harnesses

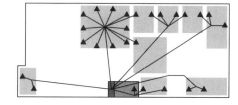

Zone-Style Wiring Harnesses

Figure 5.33 Zone method wiring harness.

5.6.2 Making wiring harnesses

Regardless of the wiring method you decide to use, it's important to learn to make building wiring harnesses that use cable efficiently, are easy to pull, and reduce the amount of work per run as much as possible. Building wiring harnesses are much like the wiring harnesses in cars, scaled up. In fact, they tend to be even simpler, since all the wires are coterminous at one end.

For an example, let's go back to the first floor of the floorplan we looked at in the beginning of this chapter. In Fig. 5.34, one basic set of home runs and the jacks they serve are highlighted. We're going to do this as a suspended ceiling raceway pull, but it would work very similarly with most other methods. The first step is to figure out how long the runs are going to be. Don't try to do this by measuring on the blueprint.

Although measuring distances through rooms can give fairly accurate results, you should visually inspect the space the cable is actually going to be pulled through prior to the pull; if you're doing that, it's not much more trouble to actually pull a pull-cord through the longest home run to check your mea-

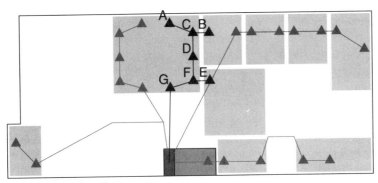

Figure 5.34 Runs to be served by one harness.

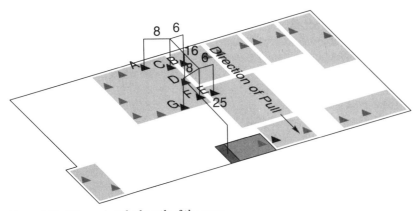

Figure 5.35 Measuring the length of the runs.

surements. Unless there are specific obstacles to be avoided, all the drops from the wiring harness in the ceiling should be the same, and we're using 10 feet as that measurement here.

Once you've got all the distances noted, calculate the length of each home run. Be sure to include the drop back down the wall on both ends, and the eighteen inches of required slack on each end (noted in Fig. 5.36 as three feet added to the service end of the harness). After that, you should probably add some extra slack, relative to the length of the run, to take care of anything unexpected, or errors in your measurements. Ten percent extra slack should be enough; if you've measured and inspected the run carefully, you probably won't need much of it, but it's better to throw away a few feet of extra slack than a whole run that's been cut too short.

This results in the following lengths for each run:

Run	Length (feet)	Plus 10% slack
A	80	88
B	78	86
C	72	79
D	64	70
E	62	68
F	56	62
G	48	53

When you've figured that out, and you're sure it's right (check against the pull-cord from the longest run, if you did that), go ahead and cut the cables to length. Be sure to unroll the cable from the spool, suspending the spool so it can turn, or rolling it along the ground to unroll the cable (rather than setting it flat on its side, and uncoiling the cable from the top, since doing so puts lots of kinks into the cable and the wires inside). When you've got the cables cut,

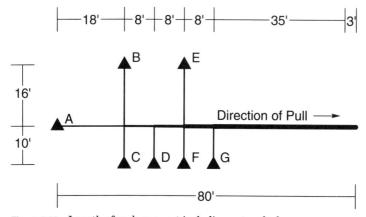

Figure 5.36 Length of each run, not including extra slack.

line them up at one end, and begin marking the cable number and the distance from the service end, every few feet, just as you did with your vertical cables.

Before you can start binding them together into a harness, you have to figure out at what point each cable should depart from the harness. If you look back at the axonometric floorplan, you can see that each run has at least the last eleven and a half (ten plus eighteen inches slack) feet unbound from the rest of the runs, to descend through the wall to the jack it serves. Two runs, B and E, need six additional feet to reach the point at which they descend to reach the jack. Thus cable A will serve as our reference, since it's the longest, and the others will be included in the wiring harness from the point indicated below:

Run	Free of harness	Plus 10% slack	Subtract from cable length	Round to . . .
B	17.5	19	67	67
C	11.5	12.5	66.5	67
D	11.5	12.5	57.5	57
E	17.5	19	49	49
F	11.5	12.5	49.5	49
G	11.5	12.5	40.5	40

Thus you can see that cables B and C enter the harness at the same point, as do E and F, just as it appeared they should in Fig. 5.36.

When making the harness, fix the cables together with cable ties. Cable ties are the thin plastic strips with a ratcheting mechanism at one end, such that the tail of the tie can be inserted in the ratchet and tightened, but not loosened again. Be sure to leave the cable ties fairly loose, because the positions of the cables need to change slightly, relative to each other, as the cable is being pulled, to accommodate the difference between the inside and outside bend radius of the bundle. You can, however, use a piece of electrical tape to fix the tie with respect to one of the cables in the bundle. Don't attempt to affix the loose cable ends to the harness, even just for the duration of the pull, since they'll be on the trailing end of the harness as it's pulled, and it would impede a later step.

When the harness is fully assembled, take it to the most distant jack location (labeled "A" in Fig. 5.36), and begin pulling it through the raceway toward the wiring closet. You can make this easier by laying pull-cords or lengths of fish tape in the raceway at strategic locations, such that you can simply attach one to the front of the harness, pull the harness some distance, detach the cord or tape, attach the next one, and continue. It probably won't go quite that smoothly at first, but with a little practice your cable-pulling technique will become more sure and fast.

In this example, of course, we've come nowhere near the length limits imposed upon cable runs, but you're likely to in a few runs in any building. Different specifications vary by a few feet in one direction or other, but all are in basic agreement that no single run from an outlet to a closet, or between two closets, should exceed 300 feet of actual cable footage. The EIA/TIA spec allows 295 feet, but allows a combination of up to 20 feet of cross-connection in the main closet and intermediate closet, and up to 10 feet of line cord in the work area, beyond the jack.

5.6.3   General horizontal wiring techniques

Pulling cable, as mentioned above, is generally accomplished by running a nylon pull-cord or spring-steel fish tape through a path you wish cable to follow, from the end opposite where the cable currently is. Attaching its end to the cable, and pulling the cable back to the origin of the cord or tape, a cable bundle is progressively pulled from the end of a run to the wiring closet.

There are a number of ways to attach the end of the cord or tape to the cable bundle. Usually the end of the cable is available, and it's most convenient to attach to that. If you're using a cord, strip back the sheath four to six inches, and join the cord to the wire bunch using a square knot. If you're using a tape, use the wires to form a lark's-head knot through the loop at the end of the tape. When you've formed the knot, wrap the whole join with electrical tape, beginning at least four inches behind the forward edge of the cable sheath, and proceeding forward to a point several inches beyond the knot, lapping each successive row of tape over the leading edge of the previous one, and stretching the tape tight on every turn but the last few. This creates a smooth front for the bundle, with no forward-facing edges which can get caught on anything as the cable is being pulled.

The two main problems in binding the cable to a cord or tape are in making a knot with as small a cross-sectional area as possible, and in making sure that pulling tension is conveyed to the whole cable, not just some components of it.

For instance, attaching the cord or tape to just the cable sheath would simply stretch the sheath out until it broke, without moving the wires at all. Con-

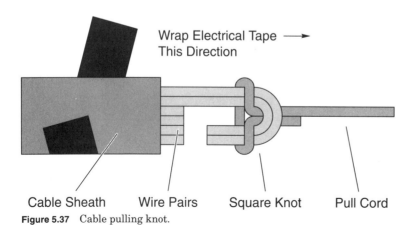

Wrap Electrical Tape ⟶
This Direction

Cable Sheath   Wire Pairs   Square Knot   Pull Cord

Figure 5.37   Cable pulling knot.

versely, just pulling the wires, without the electrical tape binding the sheath onto the knot, would pull the wires out of the sheath, leaving it behind. The problem with reducing the size of the knot is that the only way to do it is to leave something out of the knot. The sheath, as I just said, is always left out of the knot, so that's a start. If you still need to make the knot smaller, you can include only half of the wires, as illustrated in Fig. 5.37, and trim the others back behind the knot. If you do this, however, you must be sure that you select one wire from each pair, so that you don't just pull some of the wires out of the cable, leaving the rest where they started. A better, if more time-consuming, way of making the knot smaller is to strip the sheath back farther, perhaps eight to ten inches, and trim most of the wires back at random lengths, such that they form a rough cone. Separate this into three approximately equal-sized cones, and braid them together. Knot the end of the braid through the pull-cord or fish tape. This way, as tension is applied to the ones actually in the knot, they bind harder against those not included in the knot, pulling the braid tight.

There are pulling "baskets" commercially available which work on the same principle. Designed to be attached to the end of a fish tape, they're basically just open- or closed-ended tubes, loosely woven out of steel wire. When the end that's attached to the fish tape is pulled, the whole contraption tightens down on the cable, gripping it firmly. These are particularly useful when you need to pull on the middle of an expanse of cable, and don't have access to either end of it, since there are "offset eye" baskets which open down the side. You join the two sides together around the cable and lace them together with a steel wire closure.

When you pull your horizontal cable, be sure to pull a few pull-cords, along with the cable bundle, so that you don't have to do as much work to pull additional cable in the future. If you use one of the pull-cords later, be sure to use it to pull another, given adequate space.

You can use any nylon cord that's of adequate strength, and not too stretchy, for pull-cord. Fish tapes are just spring steel wires that have been flattened into a tape, and have one end bent into a hook or an eye. They usually come in long lengths on a winder, but this can be heavy and difficult to handle. One alternative is to buy replacement tape packages, and cut the tapes inside to various lengths so you'll have one of approximately the right length for any job. Fish tapes are desirable since you can push them through conduit or ducts, or over raceways, as well as pulling with them. Pull-cords generally have to be laid in at the time the run is installed, or pushed through with a tape.

When you need to pull cable through partially obstructed vertical segments in your horizontal wiring, for instance from a ceiling area down to a wall-mounted outlet, and you have access to the top of the run, you can use a ball-chain to get a pull-cord through. Find the heaviest ball-chain you can, probably about three-sixteenths of an inch in diameter, and attach two or three feet of it to the end of your pull-cord. Lower the ball-chain in from the top of the run, and jiggle it a bit, if necessary. Since the balls are round and heavy, and roll around easily, it'll tend to find openings and drop through.

Use particular care when pulling cable through studs and joists, especially metal ones, or through any tight holes. It's very easy for friction applied to the cable sheath to cause the sheath to begin to stretch at the pulled end and simultaneously bunch up behind the tight spot. Once this happens, getting the sheath smoothed out again is a time-consuming task. Worse yet, if the sheath bunches up, it can be abraded much more easily, exposing the wires inside to damage during the pull. Although both PVC and Teflon jackets are fairly slippery, vaseline-like cable-pulling lubricant is available for use in particularly tight spots. Alternatively, if you have time, short conduit sleeves can be pushed through the holes, and deburred and reamed at each end.

If you need to make an opening in a wall—to install a wall outlet, for instance—or to pass a cable though, try not to use a drill to make the first hole. If there are any wires inside the wall at that point, they'll wrap around the bit of a drill and be destroyed. This is the unpleasant way to locate AC power circuits. Instead, use a hammer and chisel, or just push a screwdriver through, if you're dealing with drywall. Once you've got a hole, you can take a piece of wire, bend it into an L-shape, stick it into the hole, and rotate it to find any obstructions.

If you do need to drill, there are drills made specifically for use during cable installation. They're quite long, and have a little hold near the end, through which you can pass a wire, to pull back through the hole once it's drilled. When you drill, use your arms to push the drill, rather than pushing with your body weight, since that'll allow you to feel the moment the tip of the drill breaks through the other side of whatever you're drilling. When you feel that happen, stop the drill immediately, and push it forward, feeling around for obstacles and obstructions, until you encounter the next surface you need to drill through, most likely the opposite side of the wall. Only then should you start the drill turning again. If you grind the tips of the bits to a more acute angle, you'll be able to feel a little more easily when the drill starts to break through the other side of whatever you're drilling.

There are two ways of using staples to support and fix the position of cable. First, and most obvious, is to use either a T-25 or T-75 staple gun, holding it parallel to and over the cable, so that the cable rests entirely within the channel in the face of the stapler, applying a staple which surrounds the cable and ties it directly to the surface it's traveling over. The second method is to use a pair of T-25 staples, fired perpendicular to the run of cable, and just underneath it pass a cable tie through them, using the cable tie to bind the cable in place. This latter method is used primarily when a need to modify the cable run by adding or replacing cables can be foreseen, or when a bundle of cables needs to be held. In either case, the cable should be supported every six to eight inches, and within two inches of the beginning and end of any bend.

In routing horizontal cable, you may find it expedient to pass the cable along the exterior of the building, and re-enter at an otherwise difficult-to-reach spot. While this is routinely done, keep in mind that there are good reasons to avoid it, if at all possible: First, it's a security risk, since it allows physical

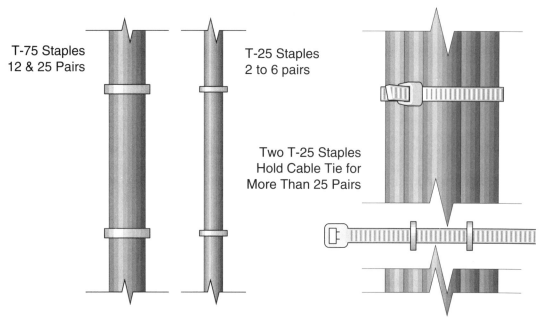

T-75 Staples
12 & 25 Pairs

T-25 Staples
2 to 6 pairs

Two T-25 Staples
Hold Cable Tie for
More Than 25 Pairs

Figure 5.38 Stapling methods.

access to the network from outside the building; second, it decreases the integrity of an outside wall, and can let moisture into the building; third, it's something of an eyesore.

If you do decide it's necessary, there are a few things to keep in mind, all having to do with maintaining the weatherproofing of the outside wall. Drill the guide hole from the inside out, so that it'll be in the right place on the inside, but drill the final hole from the outside in if it appears at all likely that the exterior surface could be prone to cracking or splintering. In either case, angle the hole downward as it goes out, so as to avoid moisture seeping in. Use a drill that's only slightly larger than the nominal outside diameter of the cable that you need to pass through the hole. Make sure there's a drip-loop in the cable immediately outside the wall, so that water will tend to run down the cable away from the hole, rather than toward it. Lastly, seal the hole from both sides with a caulk or sealant which is formulated for use with whatever the interior and exterior surfaces are made of.

Although it doesn't usually pose too great a problem when simply passing a cable perpendicularly through an external wall, avoid routing cable within exterior walls, since they're very likely to contain insulation. Most insulation is of the fiberglass baffle type, which wraps itself around drill bits and itches for days if you get any on your skin.

On horizontal cable runs which are particularly crucial, or which you fear may be damaged somehow, consider running a second cable, using an alternate

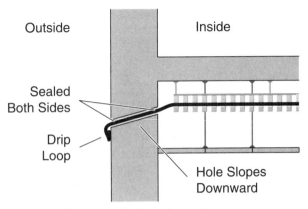

Figure 5.39   Routing cable through outside walls.

route. The cable need not terminate on a jack, but just be left within the wall at the outlet location. That way, if you do detect a wiring fault at some later time, you can simply cut service over to the alternate cable, without having to pull new cable first.

Another consideration in routing cable is proximity to sources of electromagnetic interference. As stated earlier, running parallel to cable which is carrying any significant current is an extremely bad idea, since it intensifies the inductive coupling effect. There are, however, established guidelines for "crossing distances," or the minimum distance that network and telecommunications cable should pass perpendicular to other types of cabling. The guidelines are as follows:

Current source	Crossing distance
Lightning system wire	6 feet
Any uninsulated wire	5 feet
AC power over 300 volts, w/o conduit	5 feet
Transformer lead to neon sign	6 inches
Radio and TV antenna leads	4 inches
AC power under 300 volts, w/o conduit	2 inches
Low-voltage signal and control	none
Anything with grounded shield or conduit	none

Where these tolerances cannot be achieved, it's recommended that you install additional shielding between the conductors.

Again, it's important that no parallel conductor wires, like the Quad cable which telephone companies used in residential and some business installations prior to the introduction of ISDN, be used in the horizontal wiring, as it would preclude the offering of vital services to users. This is particularly important to note when using undercarpet wire, which often sacrifices twists in exchange for some lessening of thickness. Remember that parallel conductors act as antennas and promote inductive coupling of signals between what should be separate pairs.

5.7 Work Areas

EIA/TIA specifications require that no unbroken wall space (that is, space between doors, or from a door to a corner) of greater than twelve feet in length be without a jack, and that no point in any room be farther than twenty-five feet from a jack. Regardless of the size of the room, the minimum service to be supplied to any work area is one outlet with two jacks in it.

Anticipated jack locations to which cable has been pulled, but no jacks have actually been installed, should be fixed with a junction box and a blank faceplate, marked on the outside with the work area and outlet number.

Careful consideration should be given to security concerns before any jacks are located in inherently insecure locations, like unlocked maintenance areas, bathrooms, and outdoors. Further discussion is devoted to physical security issues in Chap. 14.

Regardless of the mounting method, EIA/TIA specs require that outlets extend not more than 2¼ inches from the surface on which they're mounted. Most pre-manufactured outlet and gangbox assemblies comply with this standard.

5.7.1 Wiring jacks

When trimming excess cable off a run you've pulled, be sure to leave at least eighteen inches of slack. You can remove the cable sheath from the last three to six inches of the cable, and you shouldn't strip more than a half-inch of insulation from the ends of the conductors.

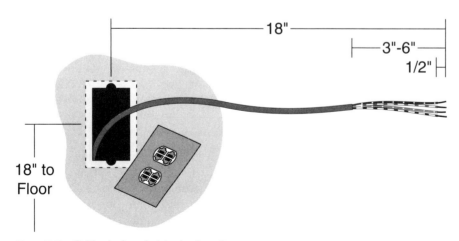

Figure 5.40 Cable slack and stripping lengths.

The reasoning behind these specifications is as follows: Less than eighteen inches of slack may make it hard for later installers to reuse the cable, if a different kind of jack proves to be necessary, for instance. You shouldn't remove more of the sheath than you need to, because the sheath helps preserve the pair-twisting of the conductors inside, which helps keep interference under control. Stripping more than a half-inch of insulation from the conductors will leave excess bare wire beyond the screw terminals that the wires wrap around, which can short against other conductors, or to a ground, like a junction box the jack may be in, so stripping less means less trimming later. In wall jack installations, the slack cable may be pushed back inside the wall, and there's usually somewhere similar to push, or coil up, the extra cable in other types of installations. Any unused pairs from the cable should be wrapped around the cable sheath, rather than trimmed back, so that the sheath won't have to be split further to access them later. Their ends shouldn't be stripped at this time, so that the insulation can protect the conductor ends.

The correct matching of conductors to corresponding pins in jacks is crucial, as failure to do so is utterly debilitating, and can be tedious and time-consuming to diagnose. You're only likely to have to deal with two kinds of jack: USOC-standard RJ-series modular six- and eight-position jacks. There are two other kinds of jacks in common use, both variations on the standard RJ-14. Jacks and plugs are sometimes referred to by number of pin positions and the number of those which actually terminate conductors.

Positions	Conductors	USOC code
6	2	RJ-11C
6	4	RJ-14C
6	6	RJ-25C
8	8	RJ-45

Although it's likely that any six-position jacks you use will be RJ-14, or four-conductor, rather than two- or six-conductor, all three varieties use the same color-coding and notation. RJ-45 eight-position jacks are not an extension of the six-position jacks, however, and use an entirely different conductor-to-pin assignment, and a different method of dividing pins into pairs.

In Fig. 5.41, you can see the relationship between the individual pins of the jack, and the wire pairs that feed into them. On the left, the six-position jack uses the first three pairs of a normal four-pair cable. Pair one, WHT/BLU-BLU/WHT, is the inside pair on pins three and four. WHT/BLU, the tip conductor, goes to pin four, while BLU/WHT, the ring conductor, goes to pin three. Pair two, WHT/ORN-ORN/WHT, which would be the outside pair on an RJ-14 jack, has its tip on pin two, and ring on pin five. Pair three, WHT/GRN-GRN/WHT, has its tip on pin one, and ring on pin six.

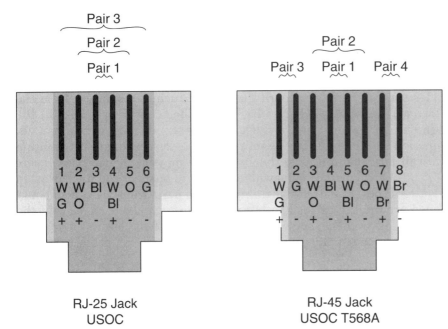

Figure 5.41 Jack pin assignments.

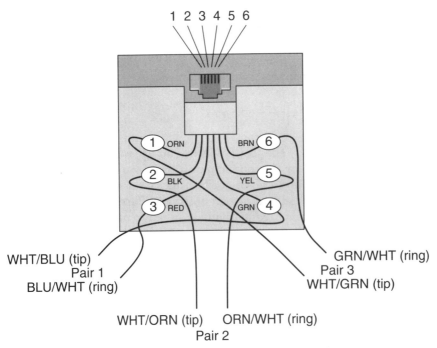

Figure 5.42 RJ-25 conductors.

When you're actually terminating wires on jacks, take care to avoid becoming confused by the wire colors inside the jacks, which are color-coded the same as modular flatwire and bear no relation to the standard base-five coding.

RJ-45 jacks maintain the same arrangement of the first two pairs, using the same pin positions and polarity, but place the third and fourth pair outboard of the first two, to either side, rather than nested concentrically, as before.

In Fig. 5.43, pins one and two form pair three, and pins seven and eight form pair four. In each case, the first of the two pins is the tip, and the second the ring.

When you're wiring jacks, especially with wire from a large pair-count cable, it's sometimes easy to get wires tangled up or confused, or to lose one of the two wires of a pair. Locking surgical forceps are a great aid in wiring jacks, because you can use them to hold wires that you've sorted out. They're inexpensive, and sold by many tool companies.

Although jacks which use 66- and 110-type punchdown terminals are available, and are very fast to work with, they're relatively expensive. The lowest common denominator in jack termination is the screw terminal. Better screw terminals use a short screw which accepts either Phillips #2 or $\frac{1}{32} \times \frac{1}{4}$ standard screwdrivers and has two washers.

When using a screw terminal, first prep the wire end by stripping about ½ inch of insulation and bending the end around into a hook shape, either with your fingers, or around one jaw of a pair of needlenose pliers. It's very important that the wire bend in a clockwise direction, when viewed from above. This

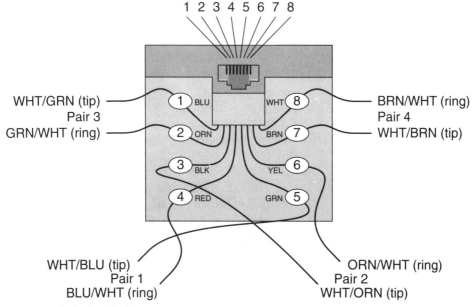

Figure 5.43   RJ-45 conductors.

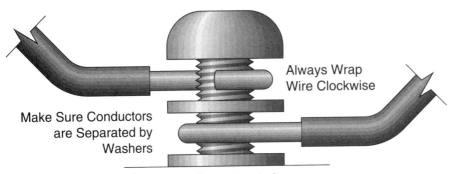

Always Wrap
Wire Clockwise

Make Sure Conductors
are Separated by
Washers

Figure 5.44 Wrapping conductors around screw terminals.

is so that it will tighten itself, rather than working itself loose, when the terminal screw is turned clockwise. Next, bend the wire up, perpendicular to the plane of the hook, so you can get the end around the terminal without getting caught on other wires and terminals. Hook the wire around the terminal in such a way that there's a washer between it and the other wire that's terminated on the same screw. This is to prevent one wire from cutting through the other when the terminal is tightened. Turn the screw down firmly, but without applying a lot of pressure, and examine the terminal area to see whether any uninsulated conductors are protruding beyond the head of the screw and the washers. If so, use a pair of dikes, or diagonal cutters, to trim them off.

5.7.2 Line cords

Line cords, also frequently called drop cables, are the short cables terminated with modular plugs which are used to connect users' devices, like computers and telephones, to the outlets in their work area.

Try to use twisted pair line cords, preferably made with the same kind of cable that's been used for the vertical and horizontal wiring. Maintain the color-coding scheme, use the correct pairs for the correct pins on each end, and remember that line cords terminated with eight-position plugs should maintain polarity, while ones using the RJ11/14/25 six-position connector should reverse it. If your cords are made from flatwire, this is easy to check. When laid flat, cords which maintain polarity will have one plug right-side-up, the other upside-down. If the cord reverses polarity, both plugs will be either right-side-up or upside-down. Although an effort has been made by standards bodies to make the polarity-sensitivity of services which use six-position connectors non-critical, eight-position line cords absolutely must maintain polarity, since the two outside pairs would otherwise be reversed.

Quad and flatwire line cords are allowed under EIA/TIA 568 only if each one is of eighteen inches or less in length, but that concession is tempered by a strong contraindication.

In true building wiring, unlike the trunk network diagrammed in the previous chapter, no termination or other devices are allowed within the jack.

Baluns, transceivers, adapters, terminating resistors, and splitters must always be placed external to the jack. This is to make the jacks "clean" for all uses. If devices were allowed inside jacks, they would almost certainly preclude the use of the jack for some as-yet-unseen future application, and then every single jack would have to be opened and modified, or even replaced. This is a monumental task on any network, and almost unthinkable on very large ones. For LocalTalk users, this shouldn't prove to be much of a problem. Star-Connector-type PhoneNet connectors are internally terminated, while the full-size ones come with plug-mounted resistors. LocalTalk connectors require an RJ-14 line cord, while standard telephone desk sets require an RJ-11 or 14. If you want to use RJ-45 jacks exclusively throughout your installation, as many people do, this leaves you with several options.

The simplest is to use ordinary flatwire RJ-14 line cords, plugging them into the RJ-45 jacks. This will work, but may squash pins one and eight in the jack if the jack is physically manipulated too many times, requiring that the jack be repaired or replaced before being used in an eight-pin application. Alternatively, line cords can be bought or manufactured with RJ-45 plugs on one end, and RJ-14s on the other, or you can use external adapters at the jack, with an RJ-45 plug and an RJ-14 jack, and then use the standard RJ-14 line cord from there.

Hand-held crimping tools, which look much like large nutcrackers, are used for field termination of line cords. Modular plugs are available loose, in large bags, and line cord can be of the same type as your horizontal wiring, or it can come from bulk spools of modular flatwire, if you're making cables for telephones or less sensitive applications. First, the external sheath is stripped from the cable, exposing the individual insulated wires. These are fanned out in the correct order, by color code, inserted into a funnel-like set of guides in the back of the plug, and pushed forward until they stop. Working the handle of the crimper depresses the die, which forces the sharp blades on the inside ends of the plug's contacts to pierce the insulation of the conductors below them. At the same time, the cord restraining tab is bent down, to crimp and hold the outer sheath of the line cord in place. Although I've illustrated an RJ-14 plug with modular flatwire in Fig. 5.45, the technique is identical for solid-conductor RJ-45 line cord termination, save that there are different types of modular plugs for solid and stranded-conductor wire, and you should be sure you're using the correct type, as neither contacts the wrong kind of wire very securely.

You should be cautioned that hand-crimped line cords are nearly invariably of lower electrical quality than those mass-produced by machine, due to the variable conditions under which the crimping occurs. The only real reason to perform hand-crimping is to create custom-length cords on the spot, if no manufactured ones are available. If you do find it necessary to crimp your own line cords, be sure to test the crimping tools you have with the plug blanks you plan to use, as there are often slight mismatches which create even less reliable terminations. When possible, use plug blanks sold by the maker of the crimping tool you use.

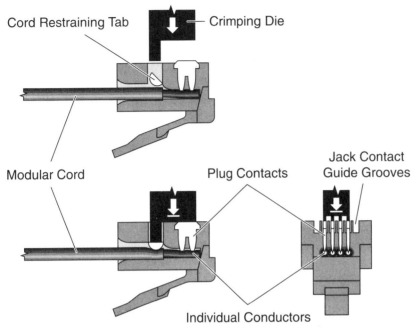

Figure 5.45   Crimping an RJ-14 modular connector.

5.8   Documentation and Recordkeeping

The point of all the marking of cable ends during the installation is to facilitate recordkeeping which, in turn, facilitates the diagnosis of problems and greatly simplifies adds, moves, and changes.

Most likely the best way of maintaining these records is in the form of a computerized database, which can be accessed from any of the wiring closets, either from permanently installed workstations there, from text-based terminals, from portable computers connected temporarily, or by launching a database client on a server or other computer which already resides in the closet. If the database of cabling records is to be of any utility, it must be both complete and up-to-date. This means that when initially created, the choice of the fields of the database must be very carefully considered.

The cable plant should be considered as a huge set of home run pairs, and each home run pair should be individually documented. Starting from a pair of pins on the jack, backtrack toward the service that's being provided, noting every conductor or terminal passed through along the way. In this case, the jack is one of several residing in an outlet, which is in a user work area connected to its floor's intermediate closet by one or more pairs within a horizontal cable. When the cable reaches the intermediate closet, it terminates on pins of a distribution-side punchdown block, which should be numerically located by row and block. These are cross-connected to pins of a service-side punchdown, which should be similarly documented. This punchdown is the terminus for pairs traveling on a vertical cable. If the site is large enough, the cable may contain a multiple of 25 pairs, in which case the binder group of 25 within the cable must be recorded as well. These pairs terminate on a distribution-side block in the building's main closet, and are cross-connected to service blocks which, in turn, are receiving services which must be identified and numbered.

In Fig. 5.46, we've documented sixteen points. With this information, an administrator can find the individual pairs associated with a particular user at any point at which they appear, and will know where they're going, where they've come from, and what service should be traveling on them. The only additional piece of information that's occasionally included is a short textual or graphical description of the location of the jack within the work area. When in textual form, this might be something like "7 ft. from W end of N wall, up 18 in." In graphical form, it's usually marked with a triangle in a square marked with north-south-east-west directions, and meant to symbolize any room.

Pins on 66-style punchdown blocks can be uniquely identified by a punchdown block number, a column number (one through four) and a pair number (one through twenty-five). Pins on 110s should be identified by column from the left on the backboard, row down from the top, and pair on the row.

A standard method of numbering jacks within each outlet should be devised, and faceplates should be numbered, prior to installation. This helps avoid confusion among installers, administrators, and users alike. Since your outlets may end up looking different, and containing different kinds of jacks, it's good to use a simple left-to-right, top-to-bottom numbering scheme.

Each time a home run is added, disabled, or rerouted, it's imperative that the records be updated immediately, both to avoid the possibility of the person making the change postponing, and then forgetting, to document it, and so that

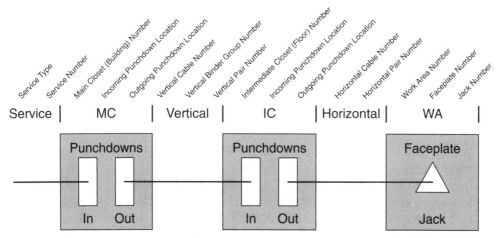

Figure 5.46   Cable plant datapoints.

other installers or administrators who may be working on other parts of the cable plant will have-up-to-date information and won't try to use the same pairs for some other purpose.

A computerized database serves both of these ends: It makes instant updates easier to make and propagate to other installers or administrators; and it can be sorted and searched on any of its fields, whereas finding the record for a specific set of punchdown pins, for example, in paper documentation may be difficult or time-consuming. Whether the documentation is kept in electronic or paper form, it's imperative that there be only a single authoritative record, which can be used to resolve discrepancies. In either case, pairs which are to be worked on should be "logged out" or "locked out" of the record in some way while work is underway, so that conflicting changes will not be made simultaneously, creating a new discrepancy. Moreover, a record of the previous state of any change must be maintained, so that it can be reverted to, if necessary, to resolve any new problems that appear after a change. As well, installers should record their own names, those of the companies they work for if they aren't in-house employees, the time the wire pairs were originally logged out, the time the change was recorded, and a short textual description of the purpose of the change and the authority which ordered the change performed. If an interdepartmental chargeback is to be made for the change, that should probably be explicitly recorded at the time of the change, as well.

In addition to documenting the paths that home runs take, you may want to maintain a set of maps of your wiring closets, diagramming the locations of different kinds of punchdown blocks, equipment, distribution frames, outlets, and the like. This should be keyed to a list of the devices, with descriptions of the function and appearance of each device, so that people unfamiliar with a particular closet can acquaint themselves with its workings, or can be talked through procedures over the telephone, with a common point of reference for describing features of the closet. Like the wire database, these should be available at each wiring closet, and they should be updated at the time of any change, using an authoritative master copy to resolve discrepancies. Unlike the wire database, however, these shouldn't change very frequently, so it may be more convenient to maintain them in paper form, in binders. Just be sure to version-number and date each copy, so that superseded copies can be easily detected and destroyed.

5.9 The Solution

After procuring and thoroughly examining all the building wiring specification documents he can find, Mark decides that, with the help of his assistant Luis, he should be able to install a cable plant in American Grommet's building that will satisfy the requirements of AT&T's Premises Distribution System spec, the IBM Cabling System spec, and EIA/TIA 568. With the money he's calculated that they'll save by performing the suspended raceway installation themselves, they can afford to hire a contractor to pull four-conductor fiber-optic cable, which Mark plans to leave, unterminated in the wall, for future use.

The cable plant itself will be of 24-gauge grade five unshielded twisted pair, with twelve pairs to each faceplate. The faceplates will contain three RJ-45 jacks, one carrying telephone on the inside pair and LocalTalk network service on pair two, one reserved for a faster future network, and the third reserved for future digital telephone service. A blank spot will be left on each faceplate for the future installation of an FDDI jack for the fiber-optic cable.

Mark decides to use 110-style blocks, even though he's got adequate space to use 66 blocks, because he tried both during the course of his investigation, and found himself able to use the 110s without much difficulty, and doesn't want to have to change the type of blocks later. He also purchased and tested a wide variety of different wall jacks, and borrowed electronic testing equipment from a friend to test the electrical characteristics of each. He settled on one which had good performance characteristics, but was also part of a system of modular components, including gangbox, faceplate, and interchangeable jack modules.

6

The Dedicated Server

6.1 The Problem

As the number of people on the network and the amount of business being conducted across it both began to increase, Mark was faced with a new problem: scaling services to meet users' needs. Although scaling printing services simply meant adding new LaserWriters to the network, file sharing quickly became a problem, as people began to rely upon it to distribute data to coworkers. Users began to come to him, complaining that they needed to retrieve a file from a machine which had been shut down by its user, and users complained that the file-sharing software was slowing down their machines so much that they were having a hard time getting any work done.

Realizing that this must be a common problem in networks the size of his, Mark determined to find the accepted solutions to data sharing problems, and implement the appropriate ones.

6.2 Hardware Selection

As the number of computers on a network begins to grow, point-to-point services like personal file sharing become insufficient for business needs. A faster, more reliable method of providing services is called for. The answer has proven to be dedicated servers. Dedicated servers are machines which simply provide services to the users of other machines, and are not themselves used by any single user. Since they don't have to provide much foreground processor time for a single user, they're free to dedicate a lot of background processor time to requests for service received over the network. Since the cost of the single machine is amortized over the number of people using the services it provides, it can be a surprisingly economical way of enhancing the network. The weights associated with the value of increased server performance versus that of increased client performance vary by site and by application; finding the point at which any process bottlenecks is difficult, but the reward is increased return on capital investment, in the form of faster response and higher reliability in network services and the flow of business that depends upon them.

6.2.1 Platform selection

The choice of a server machine is constrained on the low end by a need to meet some basic performance and expandability criteria. First, you probably want a machine with NuBus expansion slots, for future network and communications upgrades. Second, machines with processors prior to the Motorola 68030 are difficult to run in 32-bit clean mode, and thus may be inappropriate for use with future software; furthermore, they may not provide adequate performance for a multiuser machine. Third, eight megabytes of RAM is a practical minimum for server processes to run in. Fourth, you're likely to need a forty-megabyte or larger boot disk, in addition to the one you intend to use for file serving. Interestingly, a screen may not be necessary; once configuration is complete, a screen is rarely needed, and there are means of managing so-called "headless servers" across a network, which will be discussed further in Chap. 12.

Beyond providing the minimum requirements necessary to any given service, additional improvements to server machines fall primarily into one of two categories: performance and reliability.

6.2.2 Bottlenecks and performance

Raising the level of performance of a server machine is almost never as simple as using a processor with a higher clock speed. Determining bottleneck points and the relative effectiveness of different improvements is crucial. In order to find and eliminate bottlenecks, gaining a low-level understanding of the problem at hand is the first step. To provide examples, let's consider two servers with very different bottlenecks: one serving a database to a large workgroup, the other serving large multimedia files to a small workgroup.

In the first case, a query is generated by a user. An application turns mouse-clicks and typed entries into a request, and sends a packet. The limitation here is one of user speed. The packet crosses the network to the server. Since the packet is very small, the time involved is negligible, even if there are many users sending such packets. At the server, the query is queued, and dealt with as soon as the processor can get to it. This is entirely server-processor dependent. When it's our query's turn, the processor begins searching the database files, correlating information, and narrowing the response. Since the database is kept on disk, this is going to take a while, regardless of the speed of the processor, the network, or the client. Meanwhile, the processor may be managing the incoming and outgoing queues.

When the disk reads are done, and a result is found, the result is packetized and returned to the originator of the query, across the network. If the query was badly phrased, and resulted in a large answer, this may take a while, but the client software may be able to begin putting the response on-screen as soon as the first few packets come in, and it's certainly not going to take as long as it'll take the user to read or skim over. Thus the bottlenecks here are, in order of greatest to least importance: the server's hard disk access time and throughput, the server's processor speed, the network speed, and the client machine speed. Interestingly, this situation would respond very well to investment, since this order is exactly opposite the order of the relative expense of upgrading each of these components. A faster hard disk or disk array, and perhaps a NuBus SCSI accelerator card, would probably cost somewhere between $1000 and $6000; buying a new server machine might be in the $5000 to $8000 range; upgrading the speed of your entire network could cost many hundreds of dollars per user; and upgrading the client machines would cost thousands of dollars per user.

In the second case, a user drags a large file, perhaps a QuickTime movie or a digitized sound, from a file server window onto a local hard disk icon, causing the Finder to send a request for a file transfer to the mounted AppleShare file server. The server responds quickly to this simple request, finds the file in its directory structure, locates it on disk, and begins feeding it out onto the network, a packet at a time. The receiving machine simply puts up a dialog box saying "now copying" and doesn't really have to deal much with user requests for the next few minutes. The bottleneck here isn't on the user machine, which can't do anything to speed up the transfer. It isn't really on the server machine in this instance, either, because although it may have taken several hundredths, or perhaps even tenths of a second to locate the file, move the hard disk's read head to the right position, and begin reading, and it may not be able to transfer data off the hard disk at more than a few megabytes per second, the LocalTalk network itself is unlikely to support a transfer rate greater than one megabyte per *minute*. Thus the primary bottleneck here is the network. Upgrading an AppleTalk network from a LocalTalk medium to an Ethernet cabling system is the subject of Chap. 9. Secondary bottlenecks are disk transfer rate and server processor speed, but these are a distant second and third, even if several users were to begin transferring files simultaneously. Again, though, the relative costs of the bottlenecks line up favorably: Since we posited only a small number of users, the prospect of investing a few hundred dollars apiece on an upgraded network needn't be too daunting. Since the files are large ones, the hard disk is likely to already be a large one. As large hard disks are, for the most part, also already fairly fast, upgrading the disk is likely to produce a small incremental gain, and will certainly be very expensive. Upgrading the processor might price out about the same as upgrading the disk in this case, but to even less effect. Upgrading the user machines would be absolutely ineffective.

6.2.3 Fault tolerance and redundancy

The second type of upgrade to a server machine encompasses measures intended to increase the reliability of the machine. Reliability in a server is fairly easily defined in a single word: uptime. All foreseeable events which could bring the server down, or keep it down when it crashes, should be at least considered, if not provided for in advance. Ironically, this leads to a design goal in servers which is usually more associated with physical machinery than with computers: fault tolerance, or the ability to keep operating effectively in the presence of what would be otherwise debilitating impairments. This objective should be kept in mind even when deciding which model of Macintosh to use for a server. Different models have features which may make them more susceptible to failure than others. For instance, a model with parity-checking RAM would be inappropriate, since upon detecting a corrupted bit in RAM, it restarts the computer, interrupting any server processes which may have been occurring. Servers are generally left running continuously for days at a time, and the passage of fast particles and rays through the RAM causes bits to flip. This is to be expected, and will eventually, if left long enough, lead to a crash. But for the machine itself to restart each time this begins to occur would make for an excessively unreliable server.

One of the first and easiest measures to take is installing an uninterruptable power supply, or UPS. UPSes are large lead-acid or gel-cell battery packs, much like car batteries, which automatically feed power to your server and associated devices in the event of a power surge, brown-out, or failure. Since many client processes load immediately at startup, while server processes often take longer to launch, if a client machine and a server machine are booted simultaneously, as would occur after a power outage, the client machine would be unable to find any network services, and would not provide the user with helpful error messages. If, on the other hand, the services were maintained throughout the outage, they will be present when the clients come back up. When routers, devices which connect separate networks together, are discussed in Chap. 9, you'll see why avoiding power outages to such services becomes critical as your network grows.

Beyond maintaining power to the server, you should think about providing redundancy for critical components. In practice, this means the hard drives. The best way of accomplishing this is to "mirror" your server's hard drives onto similar drives which are used as up-to-the-minute backups. Mirroring is accomplished with the installation of a NuBus card equipped with a second SCSI bus, and an Extension to direct SCSI writes to both SCSI busses. Thus you can configure your server with two identical chains of hard drives and, when a failure occurs, the backup drive will seamlessly take the place of the failed one and an alarm will be triggered to notify you of the failure. In a more complicated system called RAID (Redundant Array of Inexpensive Disks), if any disk fails, checksums on the others can be used to temporarily operate in its absence, and to restore the data from it onto a replacement disk, when one becomes available. The replacement can even be performed as a "hot swap" without shutting down the server. RAID arrays with this functionality require three or more disks with a single controller, and tend to cost two or three times what the disks alone would.

As a more general approach to redundancy, think about what a failure of any one, or any combination of components on your server, would mean, and devise contingency plans for such occasions. If the Macintosh has a hardware failure, do you have either enough spare parts to get it running again (this would mean stocking a power supply, full motherboard, fan, and floppy drive, in addition to whatever provisions you've made for the hard drives), or another machine that can be pressed into service while the server's be replaced or repaired? Do you have a full set of spare cables, terminators, and the like, in case one is damaged? Do you have both off-site and on-site backups of all your server software, so that the boot drive can be recreated, or corrupted files and applications replaced?

Only by thinking in such seemingly pessimistic terms, or by blind luck, can you reasonably expect to keep a server running satisfactorily in the long term. Remember that computers aren't entirely solid-state, and they aren't entirely digital. Just like any piece of machinery, they require constant maintenance if they're to operate continuously and consistently.

6.3 File Services

The type of service which first springs to mind when many people think of a dedicated server is file serving. Dedicated file serving has advantages and drawbacks unlike those of the point-to-point file sharing that we experimented with in Chap. 3. It's available to users on a more constant basis than services which are dependent upon another user's machine, and the performance is not dependent upon someone else's whim, either. On the other hand, using it to transfer a file from one user's machine to that of another user is indirect, since the file must be placed in a folder on the server which the user of the destination machine is allowed to access, and the other user must then mount the file server as well, transfer the file to his or her own machine, and delete the copy on the server. Where it excels is in storage of data for group access. Files which need to be accessed and updated by all members of a workgroup can reside on a file server and be kept constantly up-to-date.

6.3.1 Configuring AppleShare 3.0

Apple's dedicated file-serving software is called AppleShare File Server. Version 3.0 can currently be run on all Macintosh models other than the Mac Portable (the 1989-vintage suitcase-sized portable Macintosh). To install AppleShare File Server 3.0, first insert the Server Installer disk into the machine you want to make a file server. By default, the installer script installs the file server, a print server (which will be discussed in the next section), and file-sharing client software. It will place the AppleShare File Server, AppleShare Print Server, and AppleShare Admin applications and IWEm Print Server document in the root level of the System Folder, place the File Server Extension and AppleShare Chooser Extension in the Extensions folder, and force a restart of the computer. Subsequent to this restart, System 7 File Sharing will no longer be possible on this machine. AppleShare supersedes File Sharing.

Unlike previous versions of the AppleShare File Server, most of the functionality of version 3.0 is contained in the System Extension, rather than in the application. The extension takes approximately 170K of RAM when the server isn't running, and a variable amount, greater than 700K, when it is running, depending upon the size of the directory structure that's being served. The main advantage of this scheme is that under System 7, extensions can allocate memory dynamically. That is, unlike applications, which run in a memory partition of basically fixed size, extensions can request more memory from the System, subsequent to the time they're launched. Thus, if your AppleShare server is quietly serving an 80-megabyte hard drive, and you insert a 650-megabyte optical cartridge, the server process can requisition additional memory from the System, which can, in turn, enlarge its own heap into the Finder's freespace.

Once you've booted, open the System Folder and launch AppleShare Admin. AppleShare Admin will examine the attached drives, and then ask that the server be named and assigned a password. After you provide these, it will assign preliminary access privileges and create preferences files. Next, it will bring up the user and group lists, empty except for the special users Adminis-

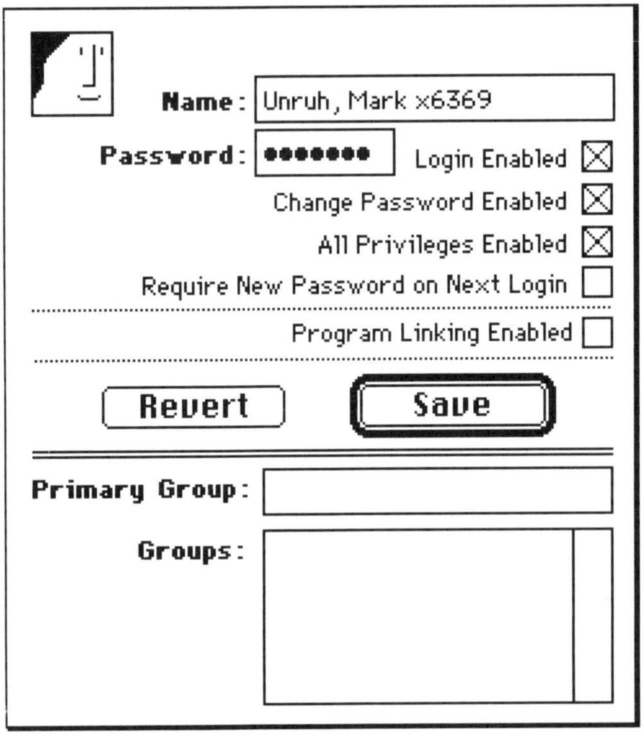

Figure 6.1   AppleShare user configuration window.

trator and <Any User>, and it will prompt you to define a real name and a password for the Administrator account.

The <Any User> account corresponds with the "guest" login option in the AppleShare client Chooser Extension. The guest account has, by definition, no user name other than <Any User>, and no password. Thus it can simply be enabled or disabled, depending upon the level of security you wish to enforce. As a general policy, it's better in the long run not to try to let legitimate users log in through the <Any User> account, but to define accounts for each one, instead, and disable <Any User>.

To create additional user accounts, select "Create User . . ." from the "Users" menu, and fill in the name and password field as you did for the Administrator account. This time, however, make sure that the "All Privileges Enabled" box is not checked, since this is what defines a user as a file server administrator, and gives him or her access to other users' private folders. Also consider checking the "Require New Password on Next Login" box, which will do just that, so that you won't know the user's password anymore.

Notice the difference between the four possible varieties of user icon (Fig. 6.2). At top, the <Any User> account has a dotted outline, indicating that login privileges have been disabled by unchecking the "Login Enabled" box, at the top of the configuration window for that user. Second is an Administrator account which has been disabled. Third is a normal user icon, enabled, and with no Administrator privileges. At the bottom is the icon for a normal, enabled Administrator account.

Next, create a group. To do so, select "Create Group . . ." from the "Groups" menu, and fill in the group name. One way of adding a user to a group is to drag the small icon associated with the user entry from the User List window to the Members field of the target Group window. As you get more users and groups, though, you may want to use a complementary process, upon the creation of new users: Open the user configuration window, and drag a group icon into the "Primary Group" field.

This is the group to which the user can most easily grant access to folders he or she has created. Additional groups, folders assigned to which this user will be allowed to open, can be dragged into the "Groups" field, lower in the window.

6.3.2   Arranging a server volume

Once you've gotten the users and groups defined, it's time to think about how you want to arrange your server volume. First of all, it's dangerous to serve

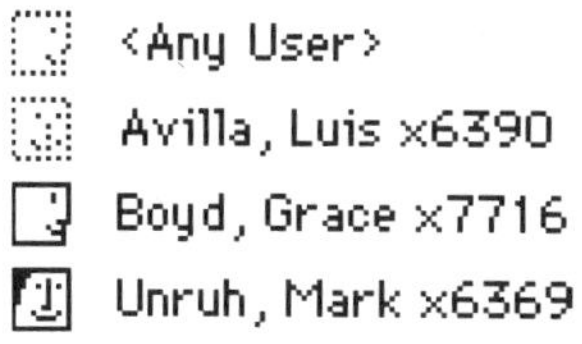

    <Any User>

    Avilla, Luis x6390

    Boyd, Grace x7716

    Unruh, Mark x6369

Figure 6.2   AppleShare user icons.

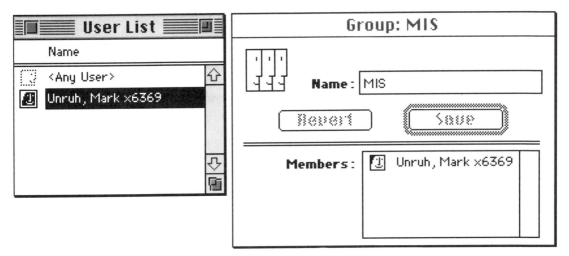

Figure 6.3 AppleShare group membership definition.

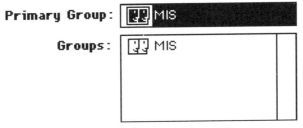

Figure 6.4 AppleShare primary group definition.

space from your server's boot drive because, unless you partition the drive beforehand, you have no way to prevent users from filling all available freespace. If they do so, and then someone tries to save an open document which has become larger since last saved, or an automated process like an electronic mail server running on the same machine needs to write a file to disk, you're going to have a big problem, and many of your services will break. That being the case, let's assume we've got two hard drives on our server: a small boot drive, in the 40-megabyte range, and a larger drive which will hold user files, of several hundred megabyte capacity. On this second drive, begin laying out a folder hierarchy. For a number of reasons, you may wish to make the root level of your server volume one level deeper than that of the drive it's being served from. First, the root level of the drive then provides a convenient and entirely hidden place to stash things which you haven't yet assigned access privileges to, or need to store temporarily. Second, if it becomes necessary to move the server to another disk, it makes the task slightly easier.

You may want to consider serving CD-ROMs, if any are available containing large amounts of data or software your users are likely to need, since they're much cheaper than an equivalent amount of hard disk space. CD-ROMs are, as the name implies, read-only, which eliminates many of the administrative hassles associated with assigning access privileges. CD-ROM drives do have unfortunately slow access and transfer times, in comparison with hard drives, but this won't slow other operations occurring on the server. Finder interaction can be greatly speeded by using a utility like SpeedyCD, which creates a duplicate of the CD's desktop file on the server's hard disk, which not only allows faster read times, and thus faster navigation through the folders of the disk, but allows directory modifications as well, like the creation, deletion, movement, and renaming of folders. With the addition of one or more CD changers, a single server can publish many CD-ROMs. Currently, all changers are based on the Pioneer mechanism, which holds six disks in a removable magazine. Access times are significantly increased when disks must be swapped into and out of the magazine, but the drives are relatively inexpensive, in the $1000 range. Six CDs can hold over three and a half gigabytes of information, so the tradeoff may be an advantageous one, if you have more than just a couple CDs your users would like to access, and doubt that more than one user would be accessing the CDs in a single drive at any given time.

At the root level of the served volume, it's probably best to have a small number of clearly labeled folders. Custom icons, if carefully chosen, can provide useful visual differentiation between folders. Remember that the icons assigned to folders are contained in invisible files named "Icon" inside the folder; if access privileges for the folder do not allow everyone to see the files within it, an icon cannot be assigned to it. It's important that the folder locations and view methods be established carefully, since it'll soon be too late to change them. Users quickly become used to clicking on folders by location, rather than actually distinguishing the folder they want by reading the name of each. If you shuffle the folders, they'll end up wasting a lot of time in confusion, opening the wrong folders.

In Fig. 6.5, I've delineated five categories into which I think (speaking as the network administrator of this hypothetical site) all my users' files can be organized. In an Applications folder, major applications will be found. A Utilities folder provides a repository for utility-type applications which aren't used in the daily course of business, like Disk First Aid or Apple File Exchange. A Documents folder is provided for company or department-wide documents, like electronic letterhead, fax cover sheets, reports, and the like. A Disk Images folder will contain disk image files for creating installation disk sets for commonly used software. Last, the Drop Folders folder is where users will have folders of their own to store things and be able to drop things in other users' folders.

Within each of these five "primary" folders, there will be additional "secondary" or sub-folders. In the Applications, Utilities, and Disk Images folders, the secondary folders will probably carry the names of the vendors of the software you use. In the Documents folder, secondary folders might be used to differentiate letterhead from marketing literature, or blank expense account

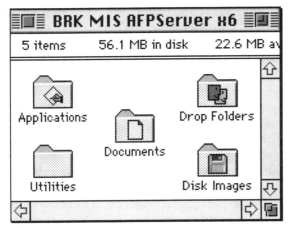

Figure 6.5   Root level of a hypothetical AppleShare server.

forms from price lists. Inside the Disk Images and Applications folders there might be a tertiary layer of folders, as well, named after individual applications. Thus the path to one disk image of the System 7.1 Installer would be BRK MIS AFPServer x6369:Disk Images:Apple Computer:System 7.1:Install 1, and the path to a Microsoft Word glossary file would be BRK MIS AFPServer x6369:Applications:Microsoft:Word 5.0:Standard Glossary.

The most interesting secondary-level folders, however, are the drop folders. Drop folders are ones which are "world writeable"; that is, anyone can modify the contents, but the folders cannot be opened by anyone other than their owner. Thus they provide a sort of electronic "in box." Drop folders can be configured either for individual or group ownership.

On any AppleTalk File Protocol-compliant server, there are three relationships that a user can have with a directory—owner, group, or everyone—and there are three privileges which can be allowed: see folders, see files, and make changes. Thus, for every folder, there's a matrix of nine privilege assignments, and an owner and a group must be specified for any folder which has owner and group-dependent privileges. At the time the server is being created, these privileges are assigned by selecting "Access Information . . ." from the "Privileges" menu of AppleShare Admin.

The folder/file selection list at the left is used to navigate to the folder you wish to define access privileges for. Later, the owners of individual folders can change privileges using the "Sharing . . ." item of the "File" menu of their own Finders.

In Fig. 6.7, we've defined a folder owned by Mark Unruh, our network administrator, and the default owner of all folders on the server. No group has been defined, because this is to be an individual drop folder, and other people in his group, the MIS department, are intended to have the same privileges as everyone else. Mark, the owner, has full privileges: He can see both any folders and any files within this folder, and he can make changes within this folder, such as creating new folders or documents, deleting folders and documents, and renaming things. In short, within this folder, he can do just about anything he could on his local machine. Other users, however, can simply make changes; they can't see either the files or the folders within Mark's folder. The Finder is smart enough to know that if they aren't allowed to see anything in a folder, it shouldn't even allow them to open it. Thus they can drop something in from the outside, but they can't see in or take anything out.

Creating a group drop folder is simply a matter of adding a group to the User/Group field, and assigning folder and file viewing privileges to the

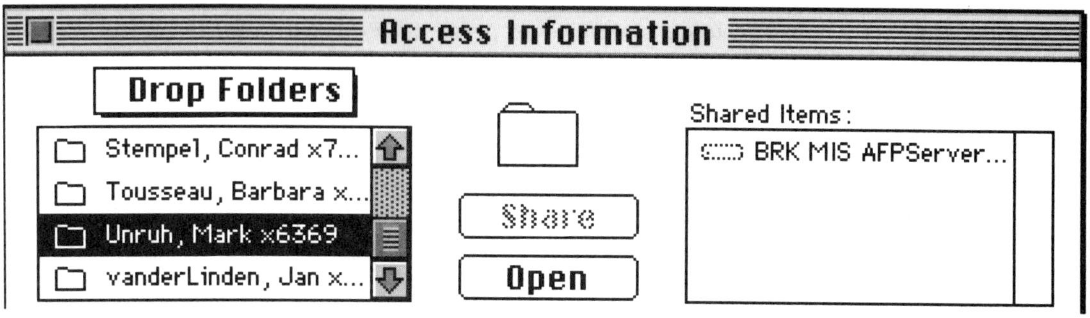

Figure 6.6 AppleShare Admin access information window.

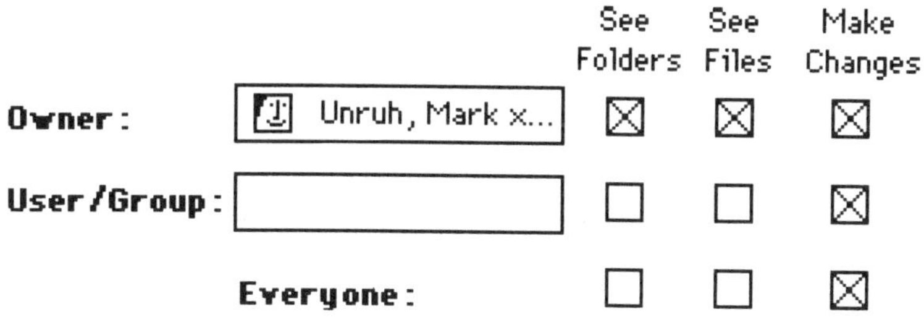

Figure 6.7 AppleShare individual drop folder privilege matrix.

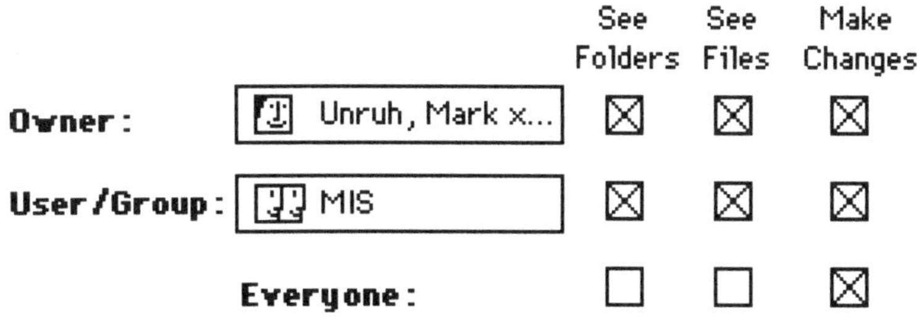

Figure 6.8 AppleShare group drop folder privilege matrix.

group. The owner of the folder need not be a member of the group; it can remain the network administrator. This doesn't change the access privileges that the group has with respect to the folder, but it does insure that a user who's been defined as owner can't redefine the privileges to exclude the rest of the group.

In addition to the normal folder icon, there are three icons which the Finder uses to represent different privilege levels. A strap around a folder indicates that privileges to open that folder have not been conferred upon you, either as a member of any particular group, or as a member of the meta-group "everyone." The folder in Fig. 6.9 named "None" is of this type. The addition of a small arrow, pointing downward, denotes a drop folder. You still may not open the folder, but you may put things into it. You can open any folder which does not have a strap, and folders which you personally own are marked with a black tab at the top, like the one named "Own".

Even though you may open a folder, the actions you may perform when inside it may still be limited. When this is the case, small icons appear in the upper left-hand corner of open windows, defining the limits that have been placed on your actions.

Three icons exist, forming five possible combinations (Fig. 6.10). From left to right, in the top row, the icons indicate that "see folders" has not been allowed; that "see files" has not been allowed; and that "make changes" has not been allowed. Combinations of "make changes" and either of the other two are possible, as well, as shown in the second row. As was mentioned previously, folders in which you can see neither files nor folders cannot be opened in the first place, so no sixth icon combination is necessary.

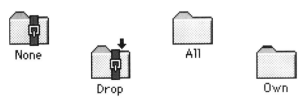

Figure 6.9 Special AppleShare folder icons.

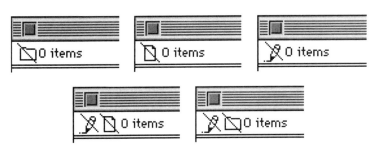

Figure 6.10 Action-limit indicator icons.

A fourth icon is used to indicate an entirely locked volume, such as a CD ROM. It's the same icon which indicates a locked floppy disk or other volume on a local machine, but on an AppleShare volume, it always appears in conjunction with the "make changes" disallowed icon. In addition, it can appear with the "see files" or "see folders" privilege disallowal icons. Notice in Fig. 6.11 that the number of items is updated as well, to reflect only the number that are actually visible.

In Fig. 6.12, both group and individual folders are shown. The group folders have been named such that they appear at the top of the list, by adding a non-printing character with a low ASCII value to the beginning of the name. This is the method used by a lot of manufacturers of System Extensions, who wish

Figure 6.11   Locked volume indicator icon.

Figure 6.12   Drop folders.

theirs to be the first to load at boot time, and the names can be copied in the finder from such files. Alternatively, names beginning with spaces will also be displayed at the top of a list.

The software within the Applications folder is another special case. Most of it is likely to be commercial software, use of which is limited by a user license. Such licenses will be discussed further in Chap. 14, but in summary, you may wish to allow only a fixed number of users to concurrently run a piece of software, and you may wish to "copy protect" it, so that users cannot make copies of the software. Keep in mind that since this requires that the software be run from the server volume, rather than a local hard disk, it will degrade both server and network performance.

In Fig. 6.13, we've selected a copy of Microsoft Word on the server, entered the number of licenses we possess—ten—and copy-protected it, so that users cannot make copies outside of this license. Also, the application is locked, so that permanent changes to it cannot be saved by users.

The last step in configuring your AppleShare server is to set the server preferences, by selecting "File Server Preferences . . ." from the "Server" menu. In this window, you can set many of the operating parameters of the server. First, it's where you change the name and administration password for the server.

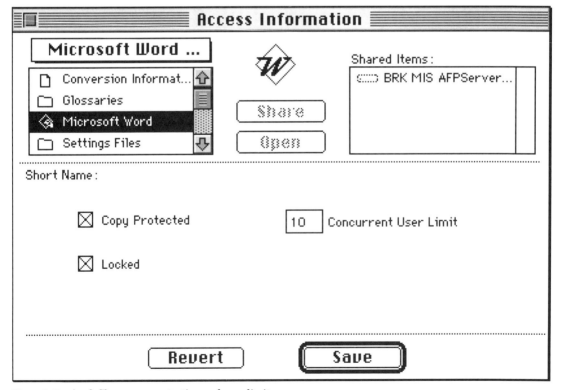

Figure 6.13   AppleShare copy protection and user limits.

Second, it allows some password security measures to be specified: minimum length (between one and eight characters), length of time until the server forces each user to change passwords, a number of unsuccessful login attempts before access to the account is automatically suspended, and whether or not you will allow users to set their machines to perform automatic logins without requiring them to enter their password. Be warned that the failed login threshold can invalidate the administration password, as well as other passwords, potentially a very serious problem.

When you've gotten your AppleShare server volume configured as you want it, go back to the System Folder, make an alias of the AppleShare File Server application, and put it in the Startup Items folder, if you want AppleShare to be launched automatically at boot time in the future. Then go back to the Access Information window, select the folder which is the root level of your server volume, and press the "Share" button.

6.3.3 Alternative file servers

Although AppleShare is the most widely used file server for the Macintosh, there are other servers available, both hardware- and software-based, which use either the same AFP protocols as AppleShare or other, proprietary protocols.

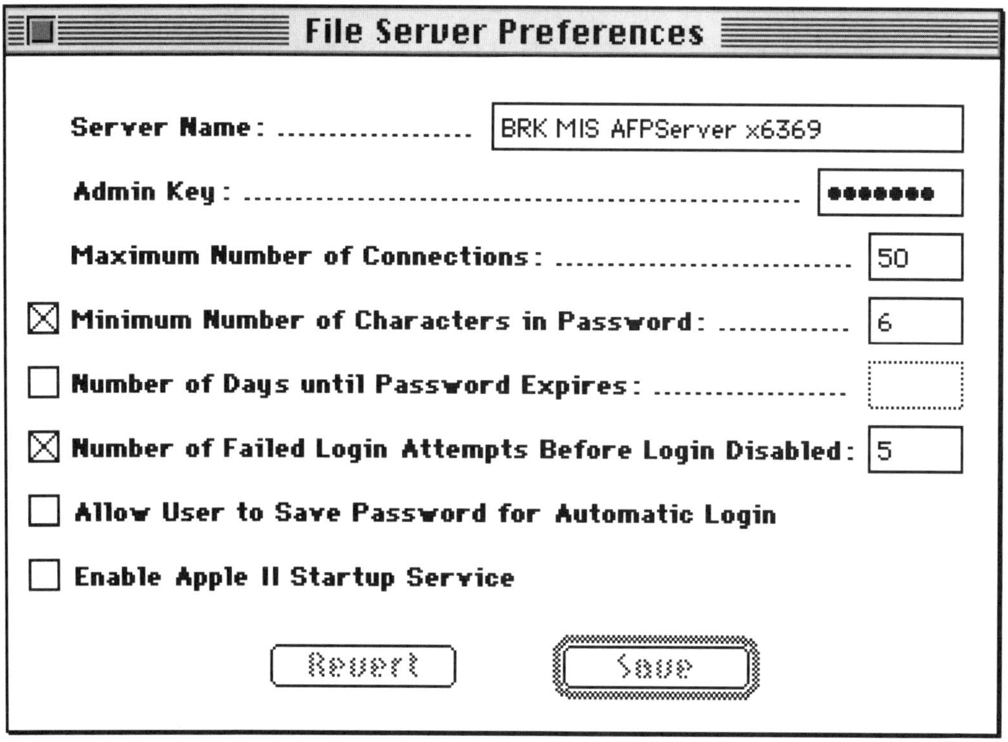

Figure 6.14 AppleShare server preferences window.

The two foremost software alternatives are TOPS and DataClub. TOPS is a rather venerable piece of software which actually predated AppleShare, and thus, unfortunately, the AppleTalk Filing Protocol as well. It's not really a file server technology, as it's used point-to-point, and now competes more directly with the personal file sharing that Apple has included in system software subsequent to System 7; it's still fairly widely used, however, and supports DOS and Windows, as well as Sun's windowing interface for their Unix computers. As TOPS isn't a dedicated server technology, I won't dwell on it here. DataClub is a kind of hybrid between point-to-point and client-server models. DataClub "virtual servers" are created by one or more machines running background server processes. Instead of each appearing as a separate file server in the Chooser, however, all the server machines in one zone form a single AFP volume. Since it's AFP compatible, no special software is needed to be a client. The advantage is greater performance scalability; the drawbacks are the necessity of all server machines being powered on simultaneously to make the full server accessible, and the background processor time required on the servers, which are also presumably being employed as user workstations.

There are four general categories of alternative hardware AFP server: proprietary platforms, Intel 80×86 platforms with proprietary software, Unix platforms with proprietary software, and Unix platforms with nonproprietary software. Proprietary platforms, usually hard-drive or PC-clone-sized boxes with SCSI and LocalTalk or Ethernet connectors on the back, have acquired a bad reputation, as historically they've been flawed and badly supported by their developers. They require remote Macintosh management front ends, which attempt to emulate the look and feel of AppleShare Admin. Performance has usually been comparable to a midline Macintosh platform running AppleShare, with price about half that. Software has been written to make AFP servers of Intel 80286 and 80386-based PC computers, and traditionally these have been marketed as bundles, including both hardware and software. The more recent of these support Macintosh-formatted SCSI drives, Ethernet and LocalTalk, and perform as well as or better than the fastest Macintosh platforms running AppleShare, at about half to two-thirds the price. Again, they're usually managed remotely, from a Macintosh. One of the most common non-Macintosh-based AFP servers is the Novell Macintosh NetWare-Loadable Module, or "Mac NLM." It's a software "translator" which runs on a Novell NetWare file server, and converts NetWare calls to AFP calls, and vice versa, appearing on AppleTalk as a normal AFP server. There are AFP server software packages available to run under the Unix operating system, as well. The most common proprietary implementation is one called uShare, which is bundled with several vendors' (notably the Sony News server) Unix platform servers. That and several other packages are available stand-alone to be compiled on existing Unix hosts as well. The most common nonproprietary Unix-based AFP server, CAP, or Columbia AppleTalk Package, is publicly distributable, unsupported software written at Columbia University. It's widely used by other universities, since it's free, and the hundreds of hours spent compiling and configuring it don't count, since that's done by grad students. For-profit organizations without sources of free labor, however, might be happier in the long run sticking to supported software.

6.4 Print Services

The one printing-related service that a central server can provide to users is spooling. When users turn on "background printing" in the Chooser, the operating system begins spooling print jobs onto the user's own machine and printing them in the background. While this does immediately return control of the machine to the user, printing the document takes a fixed amount of processor time. If the printing process is forced to operate in the background, it gets a smaller slice of the available processor time, and consequently takes longer, in real time, to complete. In a foreground-printing situation, the printer serves as the bottleneck in the printing process. It requests packets, buffers them, deals with them, and repeats, while the user's machine waits to send it more data. In a background-printing situation, the printer is just as slow, but the user's machine becomes the bottleneck. The printer asks for packets, but now has to wait for the user's machine to send them, gets them, buffers them, processes them, and repeats.

Centralized spooling can help this, by eliminating the printer-caused delays. When a centralized print spooler is used, the user's machine is free to send the print job as fast as it's able. The spooler then takes care of the actual transaction with the printer and, since it may be spooling jobs to several different printers simultaneously, as well as performing other server functions, it's not inconvenienced by the delays imposed by the printer.

The performance advantage can be substantial, particularly when printing large, simple documents. In the testing associated with the writing of this chapter, I measured spooling rates of 40 pages (or 25,000 words) per minute, printing text from Microsoft Word, between two Macintosh IIs. By contrast, few laser printers print at rates greater than eight pages per minute, and many print at or near six pages per minute. The rate at which they can accept new pages and new print jobs is likely to be lower still.

In addition, the central spooling point provides a log of the documents that have been printed and printer errors that have occurred. As a document log, it can be used for accounting or load-balancing purposes, since it shows the time jobs were started, the number of pages, how long they took to complete, and who sent them. As an error log it can be useful in troubleshooting and diagnosing recurring printing problems.

There are, however, two drawbacks associated with centralized print spooling. First, it doubles the network overhead associated with each print job; second, it precludes the use of third-party Laser Prep files.

Compare the flow of traffic in a direct-printing situation, illustrated in Fig. 6.15, to that of a print job in a spooled environment, in Fig. 6.16.

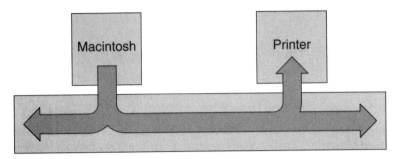

Figure 6.15   Normal printing traffic flow.

In Fig. 6.15, traffic flows in bursts across the network, primarily from the Macintosh to the printer. In a LocalTalk environment, three such print jobs could be reasonably expected to coexist without greatly hampering each other.

In a spooled environment, however, there are two streams of traffic: a shorter, extremely bandwidth-intensive one from the Macintosh to the spooler, and the ordinary bursty one from the spooler, now printing the document, to the printer itself. Over the span of the whole print job, twice as much traffic has been generated. Thus the network can become the bottleneck when multiple print jobs are spooled simultaneously. Many, many print jobs would have to be spooled concurrently to negate the time advantage to the user, but this heavy use of the network will increase the amount of time it takes for the first page of any particular print job to actually come out of the printer, and it has a negative impact on other services coexisting on the same LocalTalk segment.

The other difficulty that's sometimes encountered by spooler users is that the spooler always uses Apple's Laser Prep file to initialize the printers it's spooling to. Thus, if you're using PageMaker, or some other application which uses its own Laser Prep (in this case called "Aldus Prep"), you'll encounter PostScript errors unless you tell the software that you want it to use the Apple prep file. In PageMaker, this can result in changes of word- and letterspacing, and thus in line breaks and wrapping, as well.

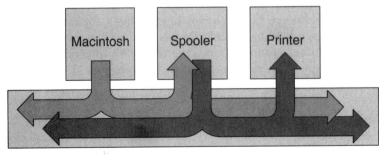

Figure 6.16   Spooled printing traffic flow.

Centralized print spooling is a tradeoff. It provides users with an incredible increase in perceived performance, it makes more efficient management and troubleshooting possible, but it's a minor liability to other services on large LocalTalk networks. It would pose a particular liability on LocalTalk networks which use packet-switched hubs, and should be avoided in such situations, as it concentrates traffic on individual ports, creating new bottlenecks.

Centralized print spooling is probably best suited to smaller LocalTalk work groups which are either independent or indirectly connected to a larger network via a router, a traffic filtering device which will be discussed in Chap. 8.

6.4.1 Configuring AppleShare Print Server

Although there are other centralized print spooling applications on the market, AppleShare Print Server is included in the AppleShare 3.0 package, and works well for most applications.

Upon first being launched, AppleShare Print Server presents a dialog allowing selection of printers to be spooled to, much like a Chooser. When you select one, an options configuration dialog is presented.

In Fig. 6.17, we've selected a LaserWriter called "Backbone LaserWriter x4527" and created a spooler called "MIS LaserWriter x1209," but allowed bypassing. That is, not only the name of the spooler will appear in users' Choosers, but the name of the original printer, as well. We now have the

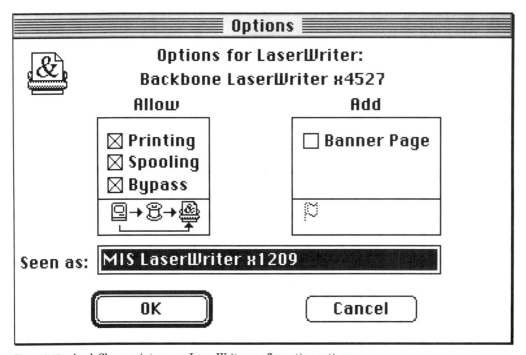

Figure 6.17 AppleShare print server LaserWriter configuration options.

appearance of two separate printers. Also, we've specified that no *banner page* will be printed. A banner page is an extra sheet at the beginning of each print job labeling it with the sender's name and the name of the document. The spooler will still print a banner page for jobs which result in errors, rather than printed pages. The only indication to the user that the MIS LaserWriter is a spooler is that instead of the status message "The LaserWriter is printing your document," the spooler will send the status message "The spooler is spooling your document."

As documents begin to flow into the queue for each printer, a list will be built in the queue window, displaying the status of each job. At the far left of Fig. 6.18 is an iconic representation of the state of the job: moving from Macintosh to spool, sitting in the spool, or moving from the spool to the printer. In the next column is the name of the document being printed, and the next contains the Owner Name of the machine the job is being sent by. The fourth and fifth columns show the time at which the job began to spool, and the sixth column shows the number of output pages the job will be.

As print jobs are completed, and move off the top of the queue window, they're recorded in the log window (Fig. 6.19), along with events like printer initializations. The first column indicates whether the print job was completed, canceled, or resulted in an error. The second and third columns contain the document and sender's names. The fourth and fifth columns contain the start and finish times for each job, and the final column shows how many pages were actually printed.

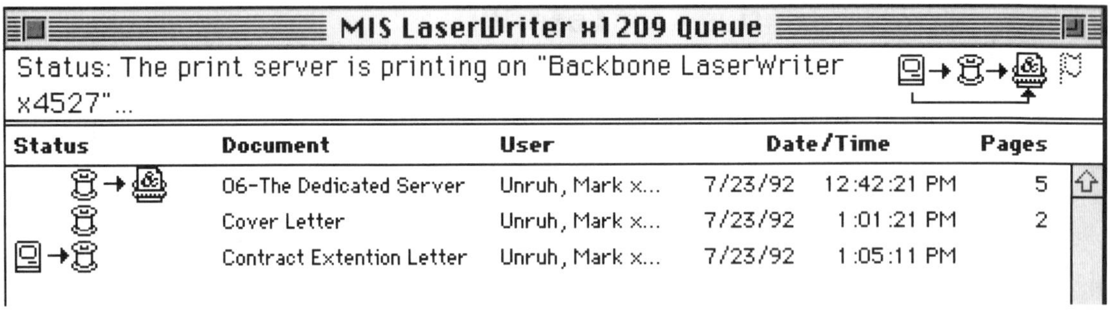

Status	Document	User	Date/Time		Pages
	06-The Dedicated Server	Unruh, Mark x...	7/23/92	12:42:21 PM	5
	Cover Letter	Unruh, Mark x...	7/23/92	1:01:21 PM	2
	Contract Extention Letter	Unruh, Mark x...	7/23/92	1:05:11 PM	

MIS LaserWriter x1209 Queue — Status: The print server is printing on "Backbone LaserWriter x4527"...

Figure 6.18   AppleShare print server printer queue.

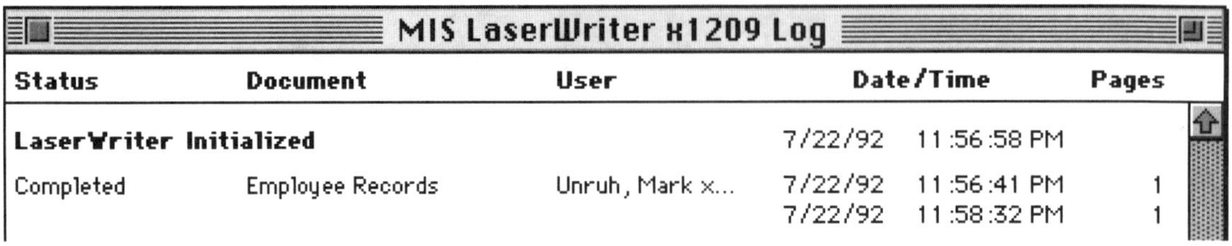

Status	Document	User	Date/Time		Pages
LaserWriter Initialized			7/22/92	11:56:58 PM	
Completed	Employee Records	Unruh, Mark x...	7/22/92	11:56:41 PM	1
			7/22/92	11:58:32 PM	1

MIS LaserWriter x1209 Log

Figure 6.19   AppleShare print server printer log.

6.5 Mail Services

Electronic mail, the exchange of memos and documents across the network, rather than on paper, is the second most heavily used network service, in most offices, after printing and before file sharing. Electronic mail, or "e-mail," tends to be more free-form than paper mail, as it can be addressed to many people, either directly or in groups, and can contain enclosures of any sort of computer document. Most e-mail packages support carbon copies and even blind carbon copies, recipients who aren't visible in the address lists that the other recipients see.

There are three main models for e-mail: peer-to-peer, client-server, and store-and-forward. The models correspond with efficiency breakpoints based on number of users. That is, peer-to-peer mail systems are, for the most part, only useful with an extremely small number of users, while client-server systems are useful in large workgroups and small sites, and store-and-forward capabilities are necessary at large sites, or when connections between multiple sites are needed.

In a peer-to-peer system, mail is exchanged directly between the sockets established by the e-mail applications on two different users' machines. This means that in order to exchange mail, both machines must simultaneously be turned on, both must be running the e-mail software, and both must be visible to each other on the network. While these may not sound like great impediments, when, in a small office, is a user most likely to e-mail someone? When they aren't there—exactly the same time their machine is most likely to be turned off. Unless each peer keeps its own address list, which cannot be authenticated in any way, messages cannot even be addressed to machines which aren't visible on the network. The practical limit of a peer-to-peer system is somewhere in the low tens of users.

In a client-server system, clients send their mail to a central server, which forwards it on to its destination as soon as is feasible. The server also maintains an authoritative user list, which is used both as an address book and as a means of authenticating users, in conjunction with a password. It greatly reduces the burden on the clients, as they no longer have to maintain contact with more than one other machine. In addition, it can allow users to connect even when away from the office, by using modems, a technique which will be discussed further in the next chapter. A single dedicated server, with proper resources, can handle a number of users somewhere in the mid-hundreds, with several tens of users connected at any particular time.

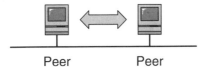

Peer   Peer

Figure 6.20 Peer-to-peer e-mail.

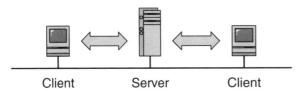

Figure 6.21   Client-server e-mail.

Store-and-forward is simply a logical extension of the client-server system. Multiple servers each have their own group of users; when a user associated with one server wants to send mail to a user associated with another server, the mail is exchanged between the two servers. The servers all work in unison to keep address lists coordinated. Since the connection between servers is hidden from the user, it can be accomplished in any number of ways, in addition to across an existing network. Many store-and-forward links are established on an as-needed basis using modems and telephone lines between sites. Store-and-forward systems are capable of growing to support thousands of users.

We'll be looking at two e-mail packages, both of which support client-server and store-and-forward methods. In this chapter, we'll cover configuring them to provide client-server mail services, and the "gateways" which connect servers to form store-and-forward systems will be covered in the following chapter.

6.5.1   Configuring Microsoft Mail 3.0

The first of the two packages is Microsoft Mail, or MS Mail, as it's more commonly called. Installing the server is trivial. Simply put the "Server and Utilities" disk in the machine you want to make a server of, drag the "Microsoft Mail Server" extension into the System Folder, and reboot.

Nearly all the management of an MS Mail server is done from a client, while logged in to the server administration account. Installing the client software on at least one machine is the next step. To do so, insert the "Macintosh Workstation Version" disk and run the installer. It will install a Desk Accessory and a Chooser Extension. Restart the client machine and open the Chooser. Select the MS Mail icon, and highlight the server when it appears in the list to the right. It will appear with a default name, until you have a chance to rename it. Close the Chooser, and open the Microsoft Mail Desk Accessory. You'll be prompted for a name and password. The initial name and password

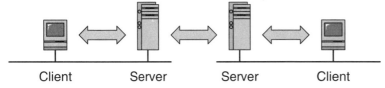

Figure 6.22   Store-and-forward e-mail.

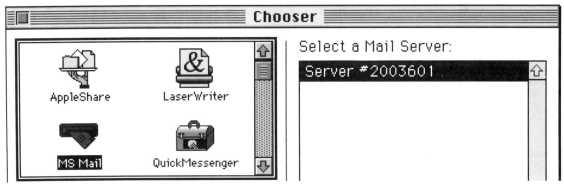

Figure 6.23 MS Mail chooser extension.

which must be used to access the server are "Network Manager" and "mail". The password "mail" must be in all lowercase letters, as MS Mail uses case-sensitive passwords.

Once you're logged in, select "Server Users/Groups . . ." from the "Mail" menu. Here, you can add new users and modify or delete existing ones. We'll add a few and then change the name of the Network Manager account. It's extremely important that even if you don't change the name, you do change the password on this account immediately. Otherwise, any user could log in as a mail administrator, and change others' accounts.

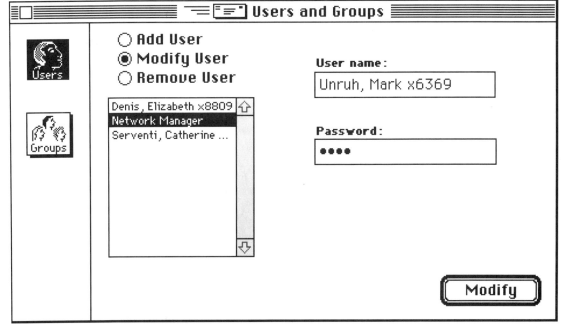

Figure 6.24 MS Mail user definition.

Clicking on the "Groups" button allows you to create and manage groups of users. A group is a single address that functions as a mailing list. That is, if you send a piece of mail to a group, everyone defined as being in the group will receive a copy. Click on the "Address Groups" button to select the users you wish to include in each group.

If you want users to be logged in to the server automatically when they start their machines, so that they can be notified of mail arrival, open the Chooser again, select the MS Mail Extension, and press the "Set Up" button.

By checking the "Sign in to Mail automatically" box, you specify that the MS Mail client software should open a connection to the server ("log in") as soon as the machine is turned on. Although it may be much easier for some users, having the software remember your password for future logins is a security breach, in that anyone who turns on the machine will be able to read that user's mail, and send mail as though they were that user. Consider that trade-off carefully before using the "Password entered by system" option.

When users create mail, they should now be presented with a dialog much like the one you used as administrator to add users to groups, that they can use to add addresses to the "to:", "cc:", and "bcc:" lists for the message.

When a piece of mail is sent, files can be enclosed with the message, a copy of the message can be retained by the sender, and a return receipt can be requested. A return receipt is a message that the server sends to the sender of another piece of mail, to notify the sender that the recipient has actually opened, and presumably read, the message. It's something like sending a reg-

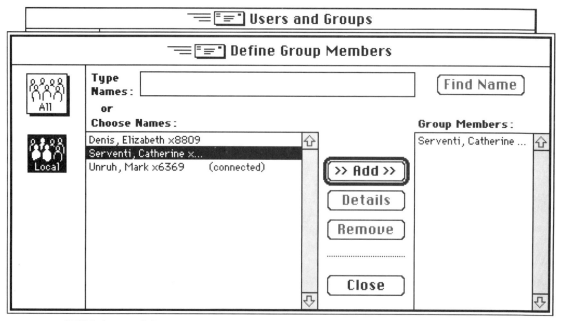

Figure 6.25   MS Mail group definition.

Figure 6.26   MS Mail login preferences.

istered letter, but since it's a feature of most e-mail systems, it's more commonly used in e-mail than in the paper-mail world.

When the mail is received, it can be dealt with in a number of ways, as indicated by the buttons along the bottom of the form (Fig. 6.27). *Reply,* obviously, sets up a form for you to enter a message in, pre-addressed to the sender of this message. *Forward* allows you to forward the message you've received on to other users. *Print* simply prints a copy of the message on the currently selected printer. *Move* allows you to file away incoming messages on your own machine. *Delete* removes the message permanently. Until you file or delete a message, it's still actually resident on the server, and you're just reading a copy of it on your screen. Thus users must eventually file or delete any message, or a backlog of read messages will start to fill the server's hard disk. This is one of the traditional problems associated with client-server mail systems.

6.5.2   Configuring QuickMail 2.5

QuickMail, the most widely used Macintosh e-mail package (actually both QuickMail and Microsoft Mail support DOS and Windows clients, as well), also uses a System Extension to provide server functionality. QuickMail currently ships on a set of seven disks, including server, Macintosh client, DOS client, and remote Macintosh client software. The disk Install 1 contains installation scripts for all the Macintosh software. Insert it into the machine you wish to become the server, and launch the "Server Install" script.

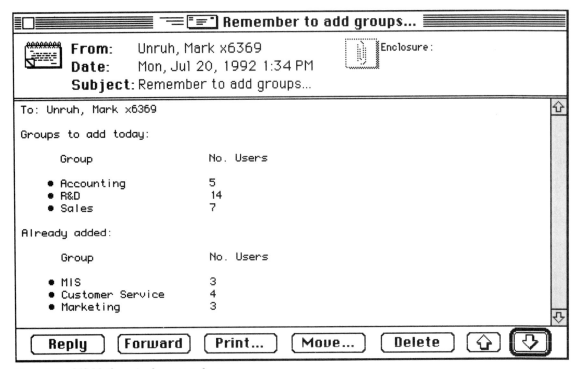

Figure 6.27   MS Mail received message form.

It will install QM Server, the server Extension; NameServer, which provides directory assistance; QM Administrator, the application for configuring the server; and an assortment of communications tools used in performing store-and-forward operations. When the installation is finished, the script will require you to restart.

Once the computer has restarted, open the System Folder, find QM Administrator, and launch it. Select "New Mailcenter . . ." from the "File" menu.

The pop-up menu should have "Online" selected. In QuickMail parlance, an online mailcenter is one which interacts with client software, rather than one which deals with other e-mail servers or information services.

Press the "Custodian" button, and enter the name and password of the person who will be the e-mail administrator.

A dialog identical in appearance will be used to define all the users of online mailcenters. You can now begin adding those users by selecting "Create . . ." from the "Users" menu, and filling in the fields of the form. The <Return> and <Tab> keys move the text-insertion point to the next field, while the <Enter> key adds the user to the database, and clears the form for the next entry.

Next, insert the Install 1 disk into your first client machine, and run the "Workstation Install" script. It will install a QuickMail System Extension and Desk Accessory, as well as some associated utilities. When it's finished, restart the client machine.

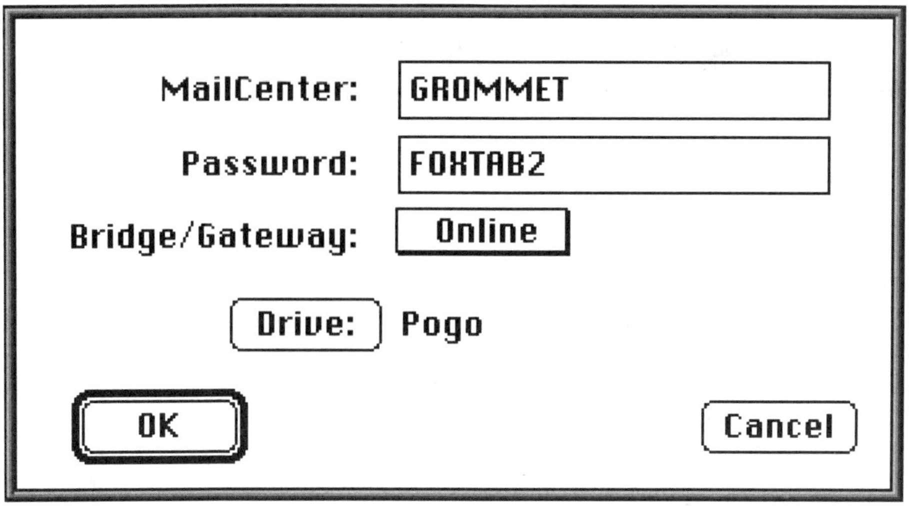

Figure 6.28 QuickMail mailcenter creation dialog.

Upon restarting, you should be presented with a QuickMail login dialog like the one in Fig. 6.30. Press the "MailCenter" button, select the name of the mailcenter you defined, and press the "OK" button. Press the "Name" button, select your name, and press the "OK" button. Type your password and press the "Connect" button.

You'll be prompted to select a nameserver, which will be, by default, "White Pages."

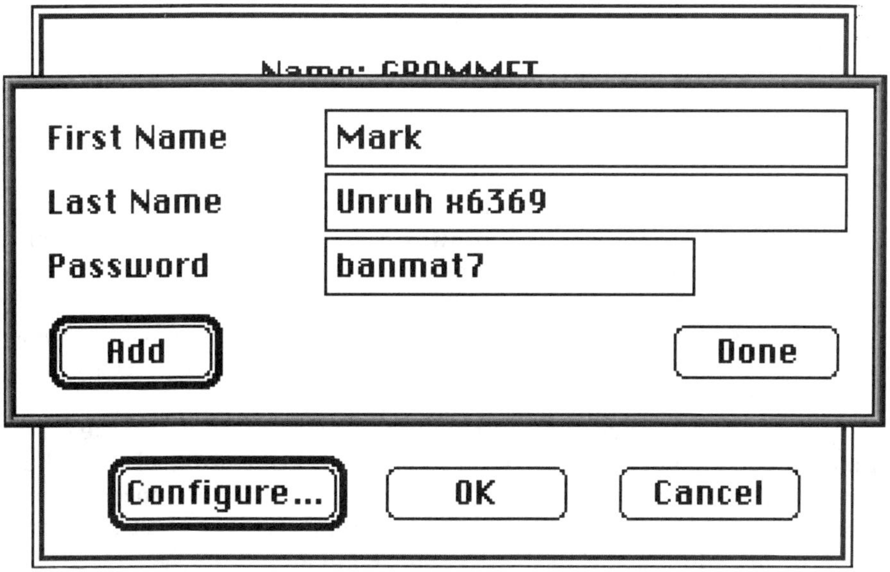

Figure 6.29 QuickMail user creation dialog.

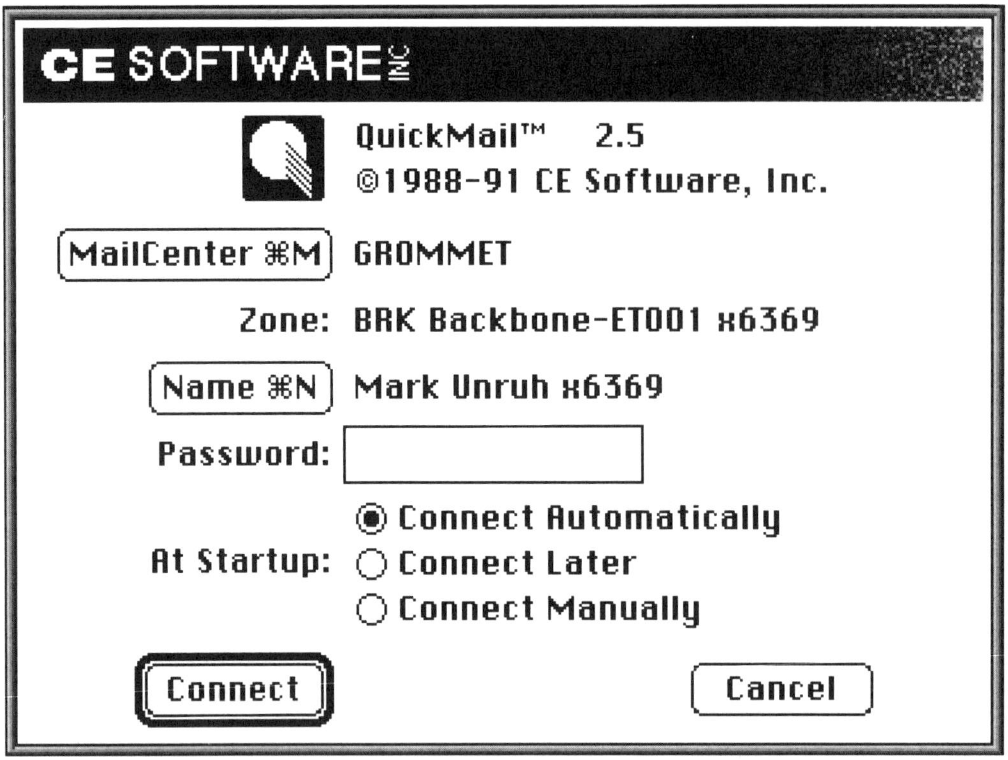

Figure 6.30 QuickMail login dialog.

Once you log in, you can press the "New" button for a pop-up menu of forms. Select one, fill it out, and press the <Enter> key, or press the addressing bar at the top of the form. This will bring up a list of addressees. Select an addressee, and send the message.

Again, there's a range of things you can do with a received message. From left to right across the button bar at the top of the form (Fig. 6.31), you can file your message away in a folder on your local machine, you can print it, you can save it to a text file, you can throw it away, you can retrieve any files which may have been enclosed with it, you can retrieve a clipboard (if the sender pasted something in), you can listen to enclosed voice-mail, you can see whether a return receipt was requested, you can forward the message to someone else, or you can reply to the originator of the message, the person you got it from, or everyone who's seen it.

The QuickMail server process is in the form of a Control Panel on the server machine. At some point, you may wish to open the Control Panel and adjust the amount of memory allocated to the server process, if performance begins to seem sluggish with several users logged on. Here, the server is set to allocate sufficient memory for itself that it can handle eight simultaneous transactions with users while maintaining decent performance on most machines.

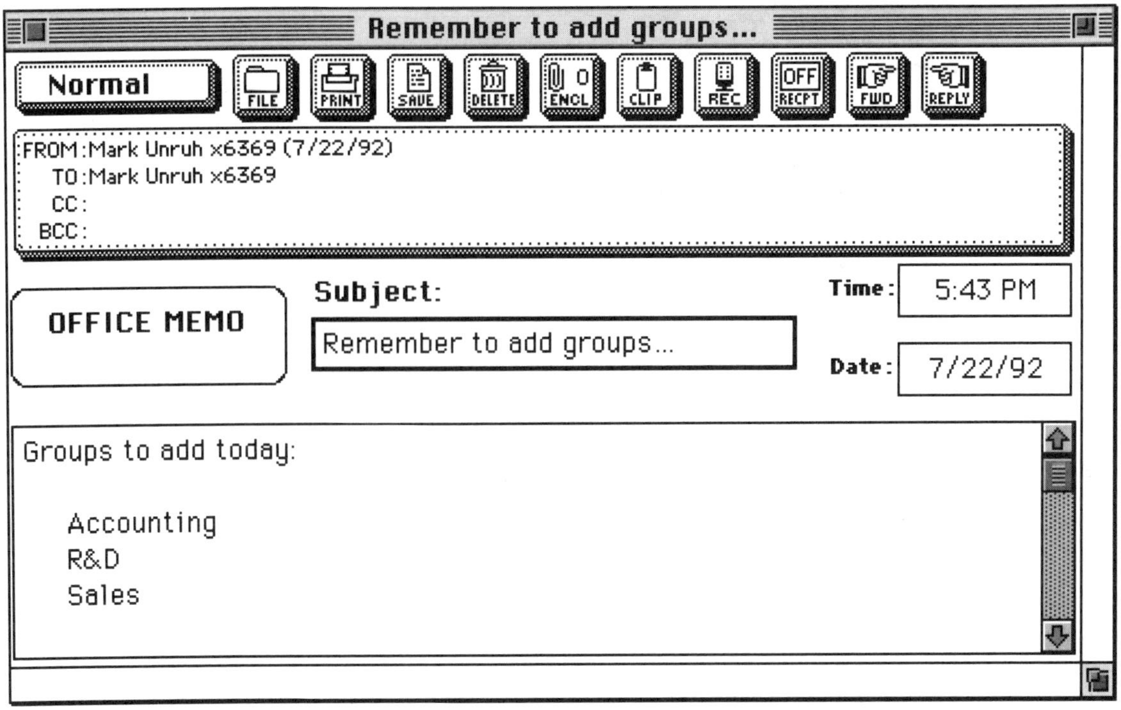

Figure 6.31 QuickMail received message.

All in all, the two e-mail packages are more alike than not. From a network administrator's point of view, the main difference lies in the method of administration. If you prefer logging in from a client machine and doing remote administration, MS Mail may be the way to go. If you prefer using a full-blown application running on the server itself, QuickMail provides that.

From a user's point of view, the two packages are fairly similar. MS Mail has a slightly more standard interface, and so may be marginally easier to learn to use.

6.6 Database Services

In many businesses, flexible access to large amounts of information is of crucial importance. That's why computerized spreadsheets won instant and nearly universal popularity when they were introduced in the late 1970s. Today, much more powerful data correlation and retrieval services are available. In many ways superseding the "flatfile" spreadsheets, multiuser databases can take the same information, and serve it up in any number of different presentation formats, in response to queries which can often take very complicated forms. Moreover, the information in these databases can be simultaneously input, modified, and accessed by many users, each operating across the network from their own machine.

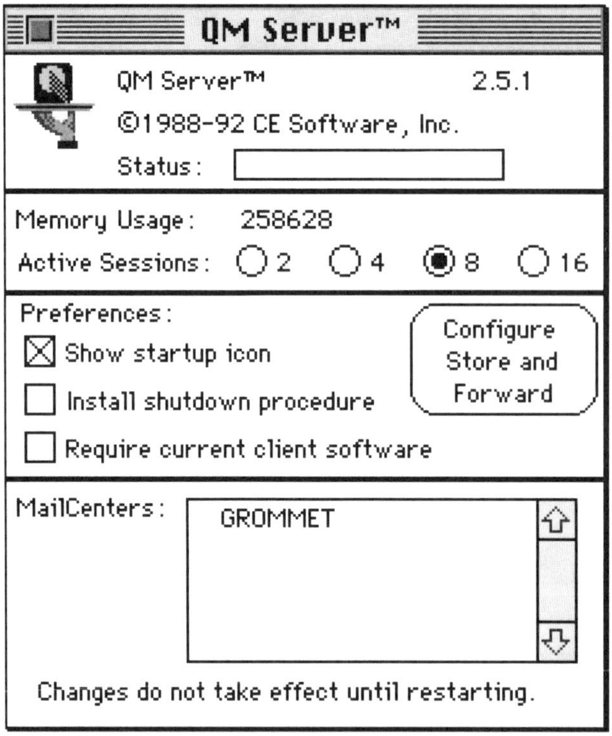

Figure 6.32 QuickMail server control panel.

In this example, we'll set up a database of employee records, using File-Maker, and access it across the network.

After copying the FileMaker application onto one of your server's drives, and presumably creating a folder for it, launch the application and create a new database file. If you expect the file to grow a lot, you may want to locate it in an unshared area of one of your data drives, rather than on the boot drive, where it could encroach upon the freespace necessary to the operation of the server processes. When you create the new database, FileMaker will first ask you to define the fields of the file.

Defining a field mostly just means assigning it a name (for reference), and a type (that is, what format of data it will contain). Beyond that, fields can be prefilled with a constant, and constraints can be placed upon the data the field will accept.

In Fig. 6.34, we're creating a list of possible values for the "City" field. To get to this dialog, press the "Options . . ." button in the field definition dialog, and the "Edit Values . . ." button in the entry options dialog visible in the background.

Next, by switching into the "Layout" mode from the "Select" menu, we can begin arranging the fields into the report format we want. This is accomplished

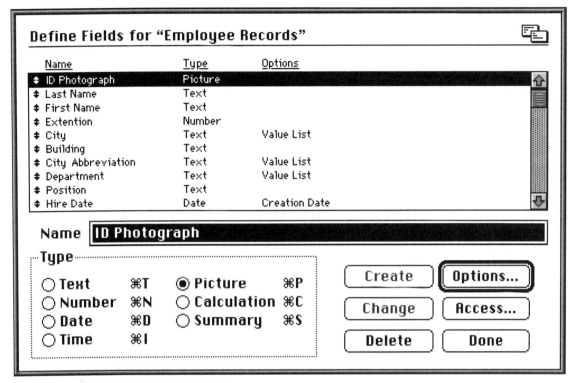

Figure 6.33   FileMaker field definition.

by simply dragging field, text, and graphic objects around, much like in a drawing program. One important thing to keep in mind is that there are at least three areas of the layout, each with different properties. The header, where we've placed the titles, will be printed at the top of each page of the report. The body, where we've placed the fields, will be filled in with data, and replicated as many times as is necessary to display the data. The footer field will be printed at the bottom of each page, and is useful for things like page numbers or dates, which can be inserted using the "Paste Special" item from the "Edit" menu. The size, typeface, and color of each text and data item can be individually chosen from the "Format" menu, as can some of the behavioral characteristics of the fields.

After selecting the "City" field in Fig. 6.36 (notice the black handles at the corners of the field), by selecting "Field Format . . ." from the "Format" menu, we can specify that the City field in this report layout be filled in from a pop-up list, rather than by typing. This makes the list of values we entered earlier easily accessible to whomever has to do the data entry.

To perform data entry, switch to "Browse" mode from the "Select" menu, and type <Command>-N to create a new record. The tab key moves the text-insertion point to the next field, and where fields have associated lists, like the

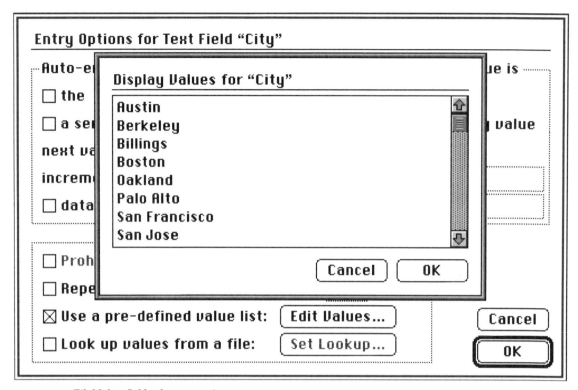

Figure 6.34 FileMaker field value constraints.

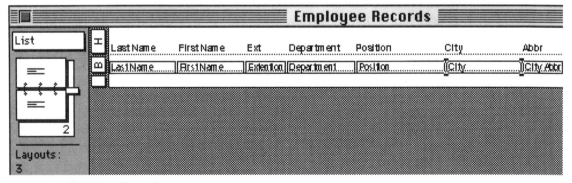

Figure 6.35 FileMaker Report Layout.

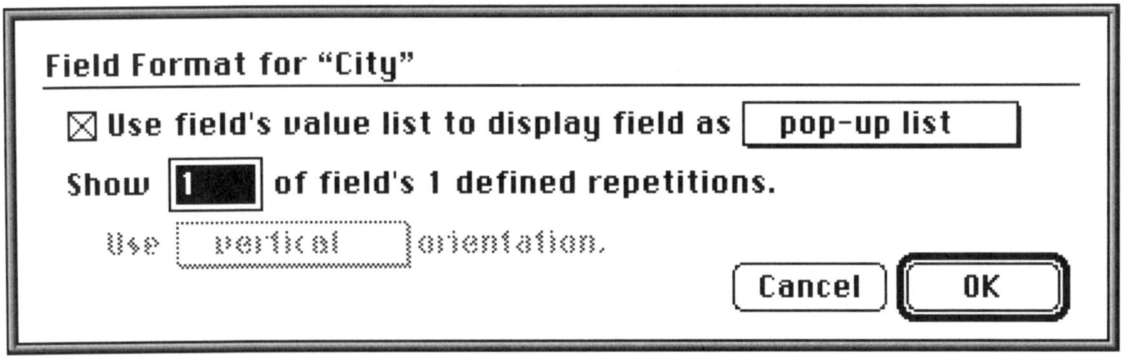

Field Format for "City"

☒ Use field's value list to display field as [**pop-up list**]

Show [**1**] of field's 1 defined repetitions.

Use [vertical] orientation.

[Cancel] [**OK**]

Figure 6.36 FileMaker field formatting.

City field in Fig. 6.37, the keyboard can be used to select an item from the list, either by typing letters from its name, or by use of the arrow keys.

Now that a data-entry style layout is working, you may want to define some data output-oriented forms. This "Yearbook" form, for example, contains only the ID Photograph, Last and First name, Extension, Position, and Department fields, and is organized to print in two columns of five on standard paper. New forms are created by selecting "New Layout . . ." from the "Edit" menu, while in Layout mode.

The last step in creating a database file is to assign access privileges. Passwords and groups are defined in the submenus of the "Access Privileges" menu of the "File" menu. In this instance, a master password has been defined, dog-cow4, which allows access to the whole database; a second password has been defined which allows only browsing and printing; while a third, patfor3, allows creation and editing of records, but not the deletion of existing records, nor the layout of new forms.

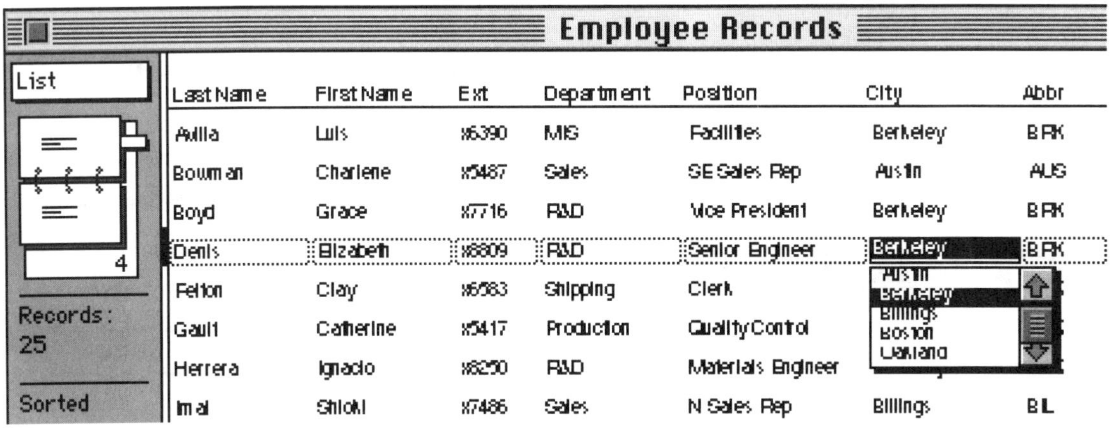

Employee Records

	Last Name	First Name	Ext	Department	Position	City	Abbr
List	Avilla	Luis	x6390	MIS	Facilities	Berkeley	BRK
	Bowman	Charlene	x5487	Sales	SE Sales Rep	Austin	AUS
	Boyd	Grace	x7716	R&D	Vice President	Berkeley	BRK
4	Denis	Elizabeth	x8809	R&D	Senior Engineer	Berkeley	BRK
	Felton	Clay	x6683	Shipping	Clerk	Austin Berkeley	
Records: 25	Gault	Catherine	x5417	Production	Quality Control	Billings Boston	
	Herrera	Ignacio	x8250	R&D	Materials Engineer	Oakland	
Sorted	Imai	Shioki	x7486	Sales	N Sales Rep	Billings	BL

Figure 6.37 FileMaker data entry.

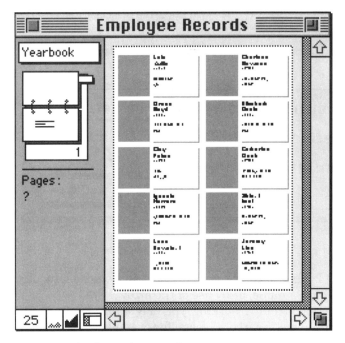

Figure 6.38   An alternative report layout.

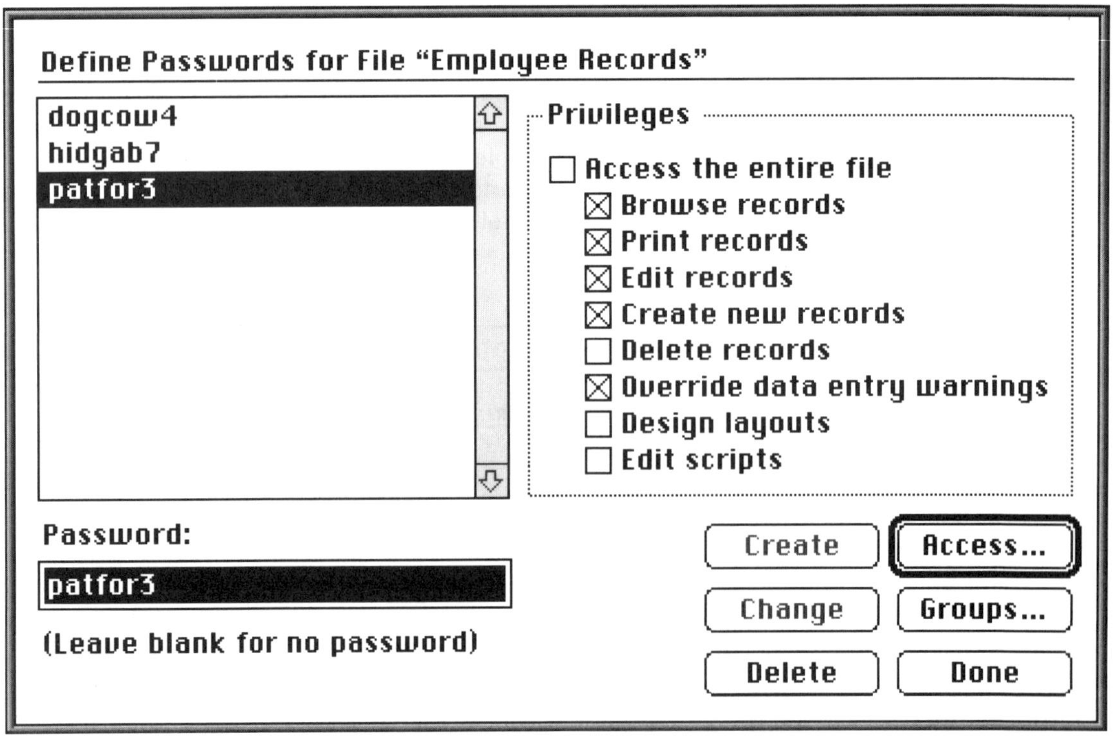

Define Passwords for File "Employee Records"

dogcow4
hidgab7
patfor3

Privileges

☐ **Access the entire file**
   ☒ **Browse records**
   ☒ **Print records**
   ☒ **Edit records**
   ☒ **Create new records**
   ☐ **Delete records**
   ☒ **Override data entry warnings**
   ☐ **Design layouts**
   ☐ **Edit scripts**

Password:

patfor3

(Leave blank for no password)

[**Create**]   [**Access...**]

[**Change**]   [**Groups...**]

[**Delete**]   [**Done**]

Figure 6.39   Password/privilege definition.

In the privilege overview, dialog groups are associated with passwords and access to specific fields. In Fig. 6.40, the group Entry has been associated with the password patfor3 (as well as the master password, by default), and can access all the existing form layouts, all the fields except Hire Date, which can only be viewed, and Salary, which is invisible.

Now that the database has been created, simply make sure that the "Exclusive" item in the File menu is unchecked, so as to allow remote access to the database, and place an alias to the file (not the application) in the server's Startup Items folder, so that the database will be made available to network users whenever the server is booted. One problem with FileMaker is that if any password protection is employed, a password must be entered at the server before the database will be served. Even if the null password is assigned to browse only, with no field visibility, someone must still dismiss the dialog box that FileMaker puts up at launch time. One means of dealing with this problem is to use a macro package like QuickKeys to launch the FileMaker document and dismiss the password dialog, all in a single sequence.

From any other copy of FileMaker on your network, you should now be able to press the "Network" button in the open database file dialog, and select any database that's open on the server machine. If the network or server are very

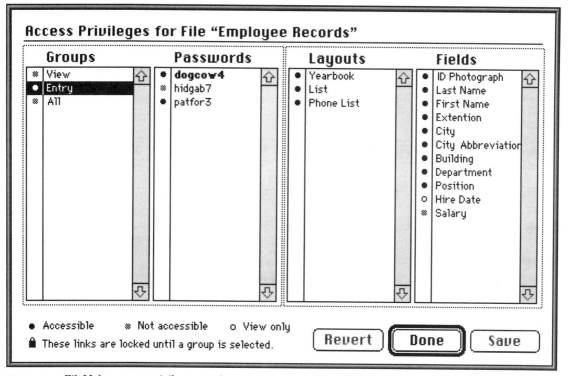

Figure 6.40 FileMaker access privilege overview.

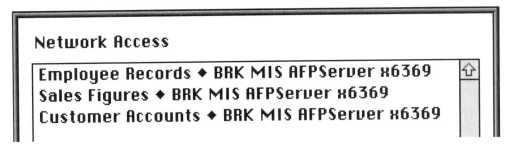

Figure 6.41   FileMaker network access dialog.

busy, and you receive no response, try holding down the Option key as you click on the Network button, to increase the NBP lookup timeout that File-Maker uses.

Once it's opened, it should behave just as a local database would. It can be queried by selecting "Find" from the "Select" menu, and specifying the parameters of the query you want to issue. The simple query defined in Fig. 6.42, for instance, would return a list of all the employees in the Production and Shipping departments.

6.7   The Solution

Having investigated central file, print, mail, and database serving, Mark decided that he needed to implement each service to some degree. Central file serving he embraced wholeheartedly, since it eliminated in one stroke many of the users' problems which had prompted his inquiry into centralized ser-

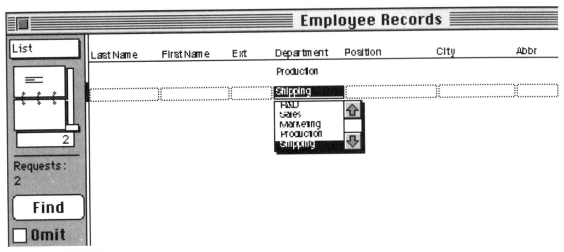

Figure 6.42   FileMaker query.

vices. Print serving, he concluded, was probably a necessary evil, since it organized the printing process, allowed accounting and tracking of the costs involved, and would provide useful clues to the appropriate times and locations for new LaserWriters. Mark decided to take a cautious approach with electronic mail. Since it was not a service already in use to some degree, like file sharing and print serving, there was little pent-up demand for it. Faced with two seemingly similar choices of product, he decided to implement both, to a limited degree, and on a provisional basis. If one or both of the e-mail packages became popular, his doubts would be answered, and if not, little lost. Mark had planned to implement a database, for the use of his assistant and himself, in tracking cable plant and network managerial changes. He determined to proceed with that, and offer database services on a department-by-department basis once he'd acquired a thorough understanding of the issues involved.

7

Electronic Mail Gateways

7.1 The Problem

Since he'd set up electronic mail servers and gotten them working together, Mark's users had quickly adopted it as a means of communication. It had in fact functionally taken the place of the water cooler, serving as a locus for the exchange of bawdy jokes and office gossip between employees. A few had actually used it to send memos and exchange data pertinent to American Grommet's business, so it was serving its intended purpose, as well.

Mark, however, was sure there was more to life than sending e-mail down the hall. While installing the local area network e-mail software, he'd seen mention of "e-mail gateways" in the manuals. E-mail gateways appeared to extend the reach of the local area e-mail server in delivering mail, and he decided to investigate the possibilities further.

7.2 QuickMail Gateways

Of the two e-mail systems discussed in the previous chapter, QuickMail is provided with more plentiful gateways. Many are actually included with the product.

Gateways all provide some form of translation service, and they can typically be divided into three categories: ones which translate e-mail between formats or protocols used by different e-mail systems on the same network; ones which connect your local e-mail system to an external mail delivery service, often called an "online service"; and ones which provide some method of transporting messages between e-mail servers, other than across a local area network.

Under QuickMail, all processes are treated equally as gateways, even the "online mailcenters" like the one we configured in the previous chapter. Thus the initial configuration of a gateway should be familiar. QM Administrator must be running at all times you want gateways to function.

The QM Administrator application serves as the center of each QuickMail server which uses gateways. It receives messages from each mailcenter, finds the mailcenter which contains the destination address, and forwards the message to that mailcenter. QM Server processes can, obviously, communicate with each other across a network without need of gateways, just as they communicate with their clients. To pass messages to and from QuickMail servers which aren't accessible through the network, or to other types of services, they must communicate through QM Administrator, just as any other mailcenter would. In Fig. 7.1, clients served by the center QuickMail server can communicate with clients of the server on the left because they're on the same network, and their respective server processes can exchange the mail directly. They can communicate with users of the server on the right via a gateway.

When gateways have been installed, the QM Administrator application window displays them in a scrolling field of its main window, with status information for each one. It's important that QM Administrator have both sufficient

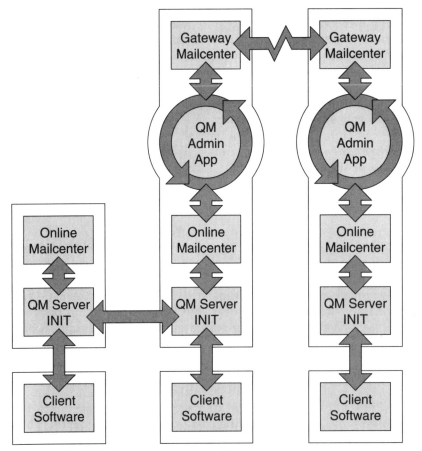

Figure 7.1   QuickMail's message-passing architecture.

memory and disk space to operate in. Both free disk space and available memory are displayed near the top of the window. A good rule of thumb is that 50–100 kilobytes of memory be allocated for each gateway running. Like any other application, the memory allocation is set in the "Get Info" window for the application in the Finder, and must be set while the application isn't running. Disk space requires more individual attention. Try to keep your mail server running from a boot disk which doesn't have other file-generating processes on it, and no users saving data onto it. Keep track of the amount of disk space mail is using, and chart it over time. You should be able to spot any trends readily, and anticipate any disk space shortages well before they occur. If any mail server does run out of room, it will stop accepting new incoming messages.

7.2.1   LAN and WAN mail protocol conversion gateways

Third-party QuickMail gateways are available to connect QuickMail to many other e-mail systems including, among others, the following; cc:Mail, a package used primarily on PCs running DOS and Windows; Digital Equipment's DECNet Mail and VMS Mail, used on and between Digital Equipment VAX computers running the VMS operating System; Hewlett-Packard's DeskMate Mail; Novell's MHS, or Message Handling System; Microsoft Mail, the other major Macintosh e-mail system; Banyan's VINES; X.400, an e-mail standard which was originally designed to facilitate communication on large networks, but is variously judged to be far ahead of its time, or to have missed the bus entirely; and lastly, SMTP, or Simple Mail Transport Protocol, the Unix e-mail

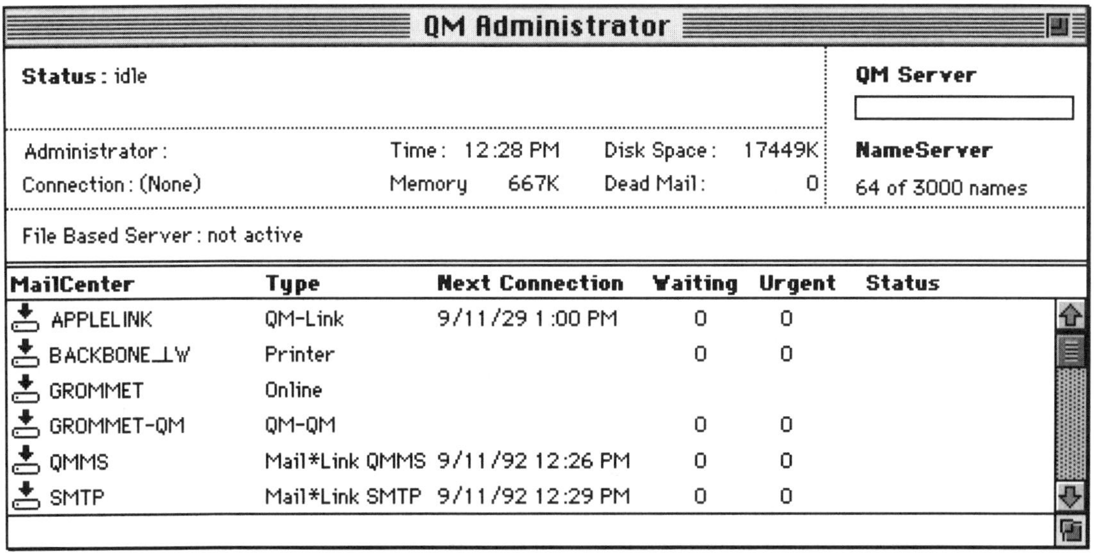

```
╔═══════════════════════ QM Administrator ═══════════════════════╗
║ Status : idle                                    │ QM Server        ║
║                                                  │ ┌──────────────┐ ║
║                                                  │ └──────────────┘ ║
║ Administrator :          Time : 12:28 PM   Disk Space : 17449K │ NameServer   ║
║ Connection : (None)      Memory   667K     Dead Mail :     0   │ 64 of 3000 names ║
║ File Based Server : not active                                   ║
╠═════════════════════════════════════════════════════════════════╣
║ MailCenter      Type         Next Connection   Waiting  Urgent  Status ║
║ APPLELINK       QM-Link      9/11/29 1:00 PM      0       0             ║
║ BACKBONE_LW     Printer                          0       0             ║
║ GROMMET         Online                                                 ║
║ GROMMET-QM      QM-QM                             0       0             ║
║ QMMS            Mail*Link QMMS 9/11/92 12:26 PM   0       0             ║
║ SMTP            Mail*Link SMTP 9/11/92 12:29 PM   0       0             ║
╚═════════════════════════════════════════════════════════════════╝
```

Figure 7.2   QM Administrator application.

protocol, and the acknowledged standard at large sites. The installation of a QuickMail-to-SMTP gateway will be demonstrated in Chap. 11.

7.2.2 Online service connection gateways

Gateways are also available to connect QuickMail to commercial e-mail delivery services. As these services were an already-working method of transporting mail across the country or even around the world at the time QuickMail was first released, these gateways were initially a very high priority, and most of them are included in the QuickMail package. Unlike the gateways described above, which simply translate high-level protocols on a pre-existing network connection, these gateways all require that the server be equipped with a modem of some kind and an outgoing telephone line. The modem is used to call out to a service's POP ("Point-Of-Presence," meaning a destination modem which is attached to the service to which you're connecting).

Probably the most widely used gateway is one connecting QuickMail to AppleLink, a service Apple has contracted with General Electric Information Systems, or GEISCo, to provide to their own employees, third-party software and hardware vendors, and Macintosh users. Although it's by no means the least expensive online service, it has a good reputation for reliability, and is widely used by Macintosh-oriented companies. At the time of this writing, Apple is moving AppleLink over to America Online, also a well-respected online-service provider.

The first step in installing any QuickMail gateway is to drag the gateway icon into the "QA" folder within the server's System Folder.

Once a gateway has been placed in the QA folder, it becomes available in the QM Administrator application. To create a new gateway, select "New MailCenter . . ." from the "File" menu. In QuickMail terminology, any gateway, or even any group of users served by the same server process, is called a "mailcenter." Mailcenters should be named in a way that will be easy for users to find and identify in a list, and they should be named from the "outward looking" point of view, rather than the reverse. Thus the mailcenter which connects our server to AppleLink should probably be called "APPLELINK" rather than "GROMMET." Assign a password to the mailcenter and select the type of gateway you want to use from the pop-up list.

You'll next be prompted to choose a custodian for the gateway. This person can be selected from any of the online users, and will receive logs, error messages, and any mail for which an address cannot be resolved. You can change the default "send log every 1 days" to a larger number if you don't feel like being buried under a heap of e-mail statistics. On your own machine, you should probably create a system for yourself whereby you archive each log file received, so that you can refer back to historical ones in the event of a problem.

Next, press the "Configure . . ." button. This will bring you to a configuration dialog that's specialized for the AppleLink gateway. Nearly every gateway has one configuration dialog which is unique to it in some way. In the case of the

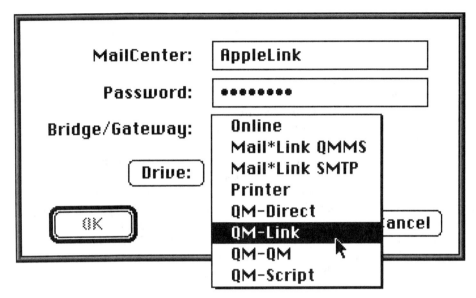

Figure 7.3 Creating a QuickMail-to-AppleLink gateway.

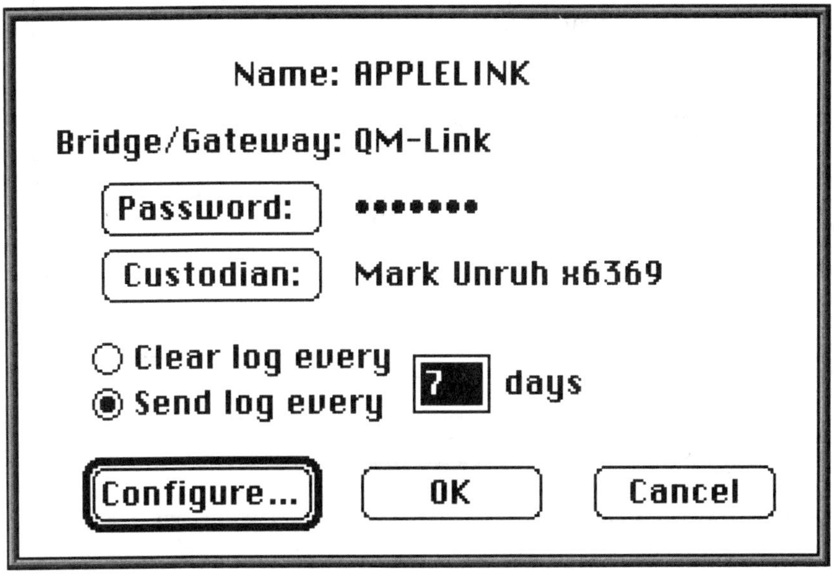

MailCenter: AppleLink

Password: ••••••••

Bridge/Gateway: Online
Mail*Link QMMS
Mail*Link SMTP
Printer
QM-Direct
QM-Link
QM-QM
QM-Script

Drive:

OK   Cancel

Name: APPLELINK

Bridge/Gateway: QM-Link

Password: •••••••

Custodian: Mark Unruh x6369

○ Clear log every
◉ Send log every   7   days

Configure...   OK   Cancel

Figure 7.4 QuickMail gateway custodian assignment.

AppleLink gateway, this dialog allows the pairing of AppleLink account names with QuickMail account names. You needn't have an AppleLink account for each person; many companies have only one account shared by all their users. If you do have more than one account, however, be sure to enter the information for the "default" account first. This is the account through which all mail from people who don't have AppleLink accounts of their own will be sent. If you have a general, company-wide account, it should most likely be the first entered. Accounts are entered by pressing the "Create" button and filling out the fields of the dialog which that calls up.

When the account names have been entered, select the level of detail you want the log to contain. When you're first starting out, you may want to set it to "debugging" level, which will include diagnostic information on failed connections. Later, since this will most likely generate bigger log files than you want to deal with, you can set the logging level back down to "all activity" or "mail exchanged." Next, select "Script . . ." from the "QM-Link" menu, and find the "AppleLink.Script" file in your QA folder. If the "display connection" box is checked, a dialog box will be brought up when a modem connection is initiated

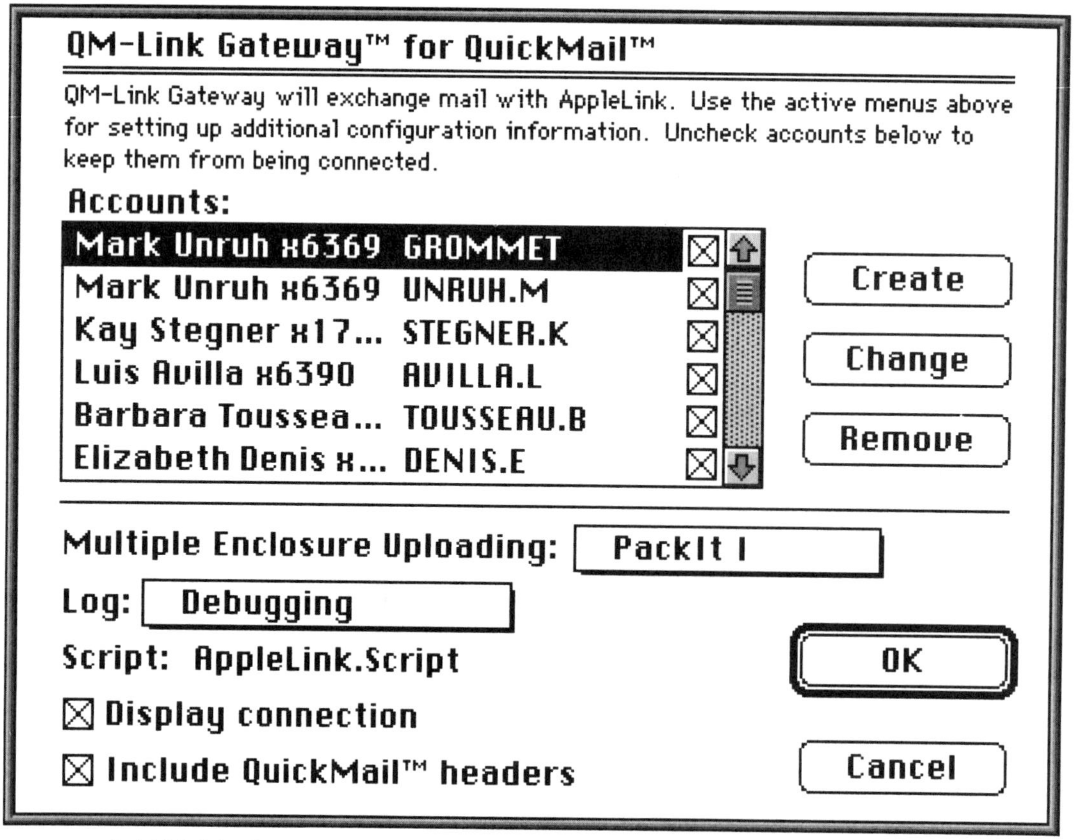

Figure 7.5   QuickMail AppleLink account configuration dialog.

with the AppleLink host, and you can watch the login procedure. This is a diagnostic feature used for troubleshooting malfunctioning connections. The "include QuickMail headers" check box enables the inclusion of a short header at the top of each outgoing message, which can be interpreted by a QuickMail server at another site, if the other site is also using a QuickMail-to-AppleLink gateway to handle their AppleLink traffic.

The most important information in this header is the destination address, followed by the sender's address. If you were to send a piece of QuickMail to someone named "Jay Heller" at AppleLink account "MCCALL.ASSOC," and you knew that a QuickMail gateway was handling the account at the other end, but that Jay was not the only person using that account, the header would be useful to you. In this case, the first two lines of the message would read:

```
Attn: Jay Heller
SentBy: Mark Unruh x6369
```

The third line would be blank, and the message would begin on the fourth line. Without this clue as to the identity of the recipient, the gateway on the other end would have to give up and send the mail to its custodian, who would have to try to figure out who it was for, and forward it manually. A great deal of the traffic on AppleLink now contains these headers, even if it's not sent by someone using a QuickMail gateway.

The next step in configuring the QuickMail gateway is to select "Preferences . . ." from the "QM-Link" menu. The ensuing dialog will prompt you for two pieces of information: the "System," which should read "APPLE," and the "Service," which will depend upon what kind of AppleLink account you have, and will be documented in information from AppleLink. It will also present you with check boxes, allowing you to enable and disable various services. The most important of these is the disallowal of the sending of mail by people who don't have their own AppleLink accounts. This disables the multiple outgoing user special function of the first account on the list.

Next, select "Connect Times . . ." from the "QM-Link" menu (Fig. 7.6). This dialog is common to all gateways, and controls the frequency with which the gateway is activated by the QM Administrator application. When the gateway is not active, messages sent to it are collected at the server, and wait for it to become active. The first check box allows the setting of a threshold number of outgoing messages which should force QM Administrator to activate the gateway, which will then proceed to process them. The second check box allows the setting of a separate threshold, presumably lower, for messages assigned an "urgent" priority. Although this is probably a good idea, all users consider their own outgoing mail urgent, so the threshold should be set with discretion if it's used.

This takes care of outgoing mail, but the service has no way of contacting your QuickMail server when you have incoming mail; you have to call it periodically to find out. To do so, check the third box, and set an interval, start and end time,

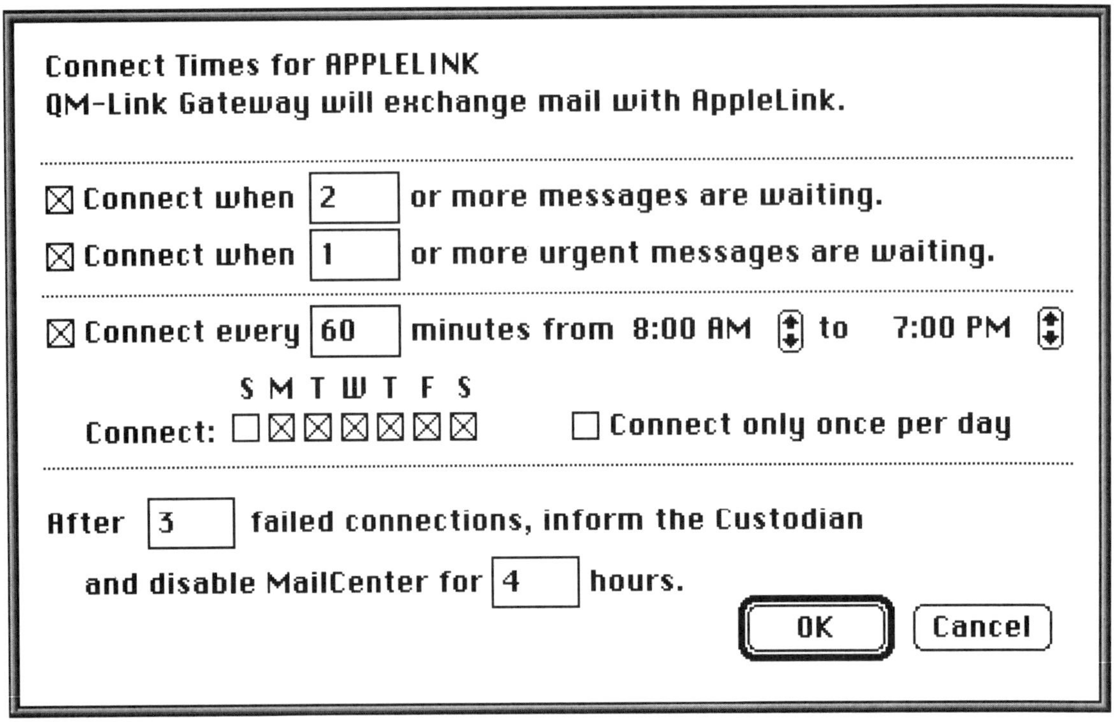

Connect Times for APPLELINK
QM-Link Gateway will exchange mail with AppleLink.

⊠ Connect when [2   ] or more messages are waiting.
⊠ Connect when [1   ] or more urgent messages are waiting.

⊠ Connect every [60   ] minutes from 8:00 AM [⬍] to   7:00 PM [⬍]

        S M T W T F S
Connect: □ ⊠ ⊠ ⊠ ⊠ ⊠ ⊠   □ Connect only once per day

After [3   ] failed connections, inform the Custodian

and disable MailCenter for [4   ] hours.

[OK   ]   [Cancel]

Figure 7.6   QuickMail connect times dialog.

and what days of the week on which you want connections to occur. In this example, the gateway is configured for fairly heavy incoming traffic, checking every hour on the hour, eleven times each day, six days a week. If set this high, you might not want to also connect on outgoing mail, saving it for delivery at the scheduled connection times. Fewer connections reduces the fees charged by AppleLink, while more frequent connections results in speedier mail delivery.

Last, you need to specify behavior under error conditions. If the gateway fails to connect to AppleLink several consecutive times it's activated, this is indicative of a major failure of some kind. You can set a failure threshold beyond which you're notified, and the gateway is temporarily disabled. This temporary disabling is also primarily to save you from running up large charges in the event of a malfunction. You may want to consider setting the delay before reactivation to a high enough number that it'll delay until after you arrive at work in the morning, if it fails during the night. The down side of this is that if the cause of the failure is temporary, it may go away before you return, and cause you unnecessary diagnostic headaches, while still not delivering mail in the interim.

Once you've set the connection times, you need to tell the gateway how to deal with the modem. Using QuickMail, this is done with the Communications ToolBox, a standard communications configuration interface. This is done in a dialog opened using the "Connection . . ." item in the "Settings" menu.

The dialog which appears at first (Fig. 7.7) may not look like this, but it will once you select "Apple Modem Tool" from the pop-up menu at the top of the window. Make sure that the "Dial phone number" radio button is highlighted, rather than the "Answer phone" one, and insert the phone number of your local AppleLink point-of-presence. If you check the "redial" button, remember that the number of times you indicate will be multiplicative with the number of times set in the threshold at the bottom of the "connection times" configuration dialog. Set tone or pulse dialing, and select the modem type which most closely matches yours from the pop-up menu at the bottom of the window. By checking "NO CARRIER," you can force QuickMail to hang up the phone if the connection is lost, rather than simply staying off-hook. This is a good idea. "Display Modem Monitor Window" tells the Comm Tool-Box to bring up a dialog in which it displays communications to and from the modem. This is much like the "display connection" option in the AppleLink main configuration window, but helps to debug modem problems, rather than AppleLink problems. Last, set the baud rate to the lower of the highest common speed supported by your modem and the modem at the AppleLink POP, and select the port to which your modem is connected from the list at the bottom of the window.

Lastly, add to the gateway's user list the names and AppleLink addresses of people with whom you think your users will want to communicate, in exactly

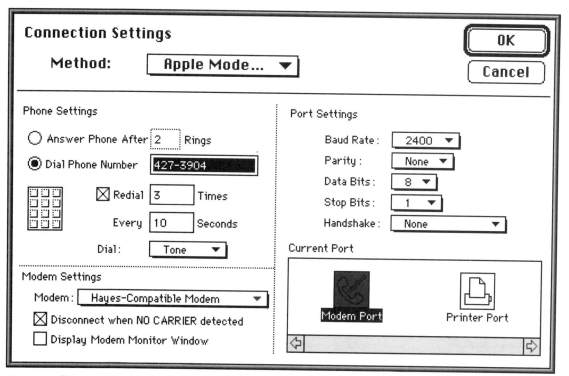

Figure 7.7 Communications ToolBox modem tool configuration.

the same way that you added your own users to the online mailcenter, by selecting "Create . . ." from the "User" menu. The only difference is that gateway users need an address, as well as a name. Here, the address is the destination AppleLink address. On AppleLink, you can add supplementary routing information to the address by appending it after a backslash (\). Only the "ODAY" address is really necessary in the address field.

In addition to user addresses, there are two special addresses used by the AppleLink gateway. One allows users to change their account information, while the other is used for performing AppleLink address lookups. By sending a special included form to account "User ID Search," users can request that the gateway do an address search on any text string they provide, and return a list of all matching addresses.

A QuickMail gateway very similar to the AppleLink one exists for an online service called CONNECT, which was quite popular at the time QuickMail was released, but has since fallen somewhat into disuse. America Online, a third graphically interfaced online service, has no currently supported QuickMail gateway.

QuickMail gateways to several other, primarily text-based, services like CompuServe, GEISCo's GEnie, MCI Mail, and SprintMail, are all handled through a generic text gateway, which uses a connection script to control communications between the gateway and the foreign mail host.

7.2.3 Other connection methods

The third variety of gateway exists primarily to convert messages to a different transport medium, rather than a different protocol. Some of these use different media to transport mail to and from other QuickMail servers, while others have other kinds of final terminals entirely.

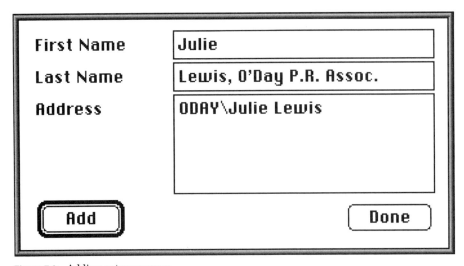

Figure 7.8 Adding gateway users.

In the former category, gateways are available to connect QuickMail servers to other, remote, QuickMail servers via modems and regular telephone lines, via switched 56kbps synchronous data lines, and via X.25 packet-switched networks. Two different modem connection gateways are included in the Quick-Mail package. One, the "QM-Direct" gateway, is used for connecting to exactly one other site, which has a known list of users. The other, "QM-QM," is newer and more flexible, allowing communication with any number of other QM-QM sites, and gleaning addresses from incoming mail.

The second category, gateways which convert QuickMail messages for final delivery over a different medium, includes gateways which allow e-mail to be directed to Telex addresses, other people's fax machines, alphanumeric pagers, exported to database files, or sent to regular networked or non-networked printers.

The printer gateway is included in the QuickMail package. It has fairly flexible configuration options, and can be used to print outgoing correspondence directly, if restraint is used in the choice of message form used with it. Different letterhead graphics can be specified for the address, first, and additional pages. One drawback is that the Printer gateway can print only to the printer that's currently selected in the Chooser of the machine on which the gateway resides. Thus, if gateways are desired for multiple printers, other machines must run QM Administrator with separate gateways.

7.3   Microsoft Mail Gateways

Microsoft Mail, while much easier for users to learn to operate, is in some ways less intuitive to administrate, and has a smaller number of available gateways.

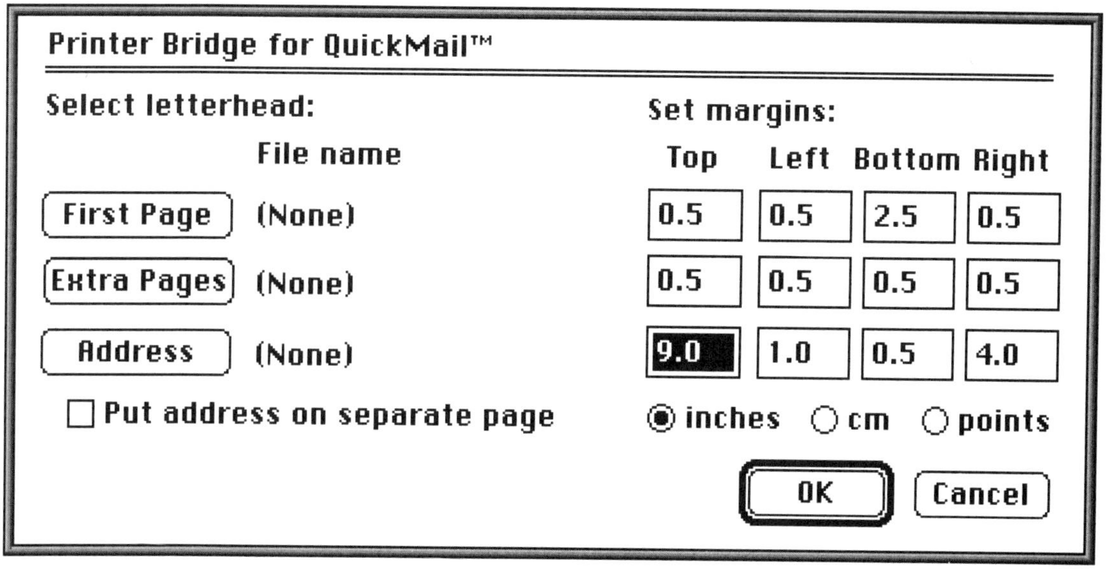

Printer Bridge for QuickMail™

Select letterhead: **Set margins:**

	File name		Top	Left	Bottom	Right
First Page	(None)		0.5	0.5	2.5	0.5
Extra Pages	(None)		0.5	0.5	0.5	0.5
Address	(None)		9.0	1.0	0.5	4.0

☐ Put address on separate page   ◉ inches   ○ cm   ○ points

[OK]   [Cancel]

Figure 7.9   QuickMail printer gateway configuration dialog.

Unlike QuickMail, no application need be run on the server machine to activate the gateways. Instead, the gateways are activated by a Chooser Extension, called "MS Mail GW." Where QuickMail uses a Control Panel server to deal with client software across the network, Microsoft Mail uses a System Extension.

Where QM Administrator served as the message-directing authority in the QuickMail system, its Microsoft Mail analog, the MS Mail GW rdev (Chooser extension) is in some ways more subservient to the local server process. Again, servers can exchange mail with each other, as well as with clients. Microsoft Mail servers can initiate their own remote network connections to the networks on which other servers reside, by telling the Server Connection application to initiate an AppleTalk Remote Access connection to the remote network. (AppleTalk Remote Access will be discussed in Chap. 10.) Once it sees the

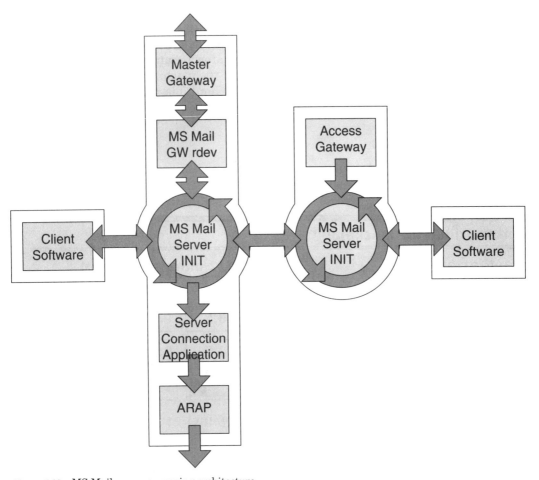

Figure 7.10   MS Mail message-passing architecture.

remote server through this temporary network connection, it exchanges mail with it, just as it would with any local server.

The only other major architectural difference is that MS Mail uses "Access Gateways" to allow users on one server to send mail through gateways which are associated with a different server process. These access gateways are very much like aliases. They essentially stand in for the real gateway, supplying the local server with the address list from the real or "master" gateway. Once the mail has been addressed, the access gateway is no longer needed, and the mail is sent to the server which handles the master gateway.

If you've got a running MS Mail server, gateway installation is fairly simple. The first step is to drop the MS Mail GW extension into the Extensions folder in your System Folder, and restart the server machine. Once it's restarted, open the Chooser, select the MS Mail GW icon, and select the server's name from the list. Then log in as network manager from the client software, and run the Gateway Installer application.

Within the Gateway Installer application, select "Install Gateway . . ." from the "Gateway" menu, and you'll be prompted to find the gateway you want to install. This can be done either from client software installed on the server machine, or across the network.

7.3.1   LAN and WAN mail protocol conversion gateways

Like QuickMail, MS Mail offers gateway connectivity to Digital's DECNet Mail and VMSmail, Novell's MHS, X.400, and SMTP. There's also the MS Mail com-

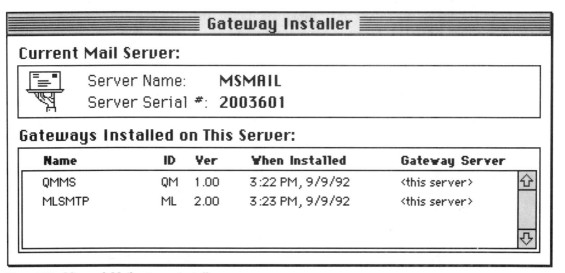

Figure 7.11   Microsoft Mail gateway installer.

ponent of the MS Mail-to-QuickMail gateway, which we'll use to demonstrate MS Mail gateway configuration.

StarNine's QMMS Microsoft Mail-to-QuickMail gateway is about as complicated as e-mail gateways get, but provides a good model for understanding the conceptual framework within which they operate.

The successful transfer of a piece of mail from a Microsoft Mail user to a QuickMail user, or vice versa, requires that the mail be handed off seven times from software process to process. First, the user creates the message, using MS Mail client software. The client software must pass the mail to the user's server. The server, recognizing the mail as being addressed to a destination that isn't local, passes it to the MS Mail GW extension. The GW extension determines which gateway should handle delivery, and passes it to the MS Mail QMMS gateway. That gateway finds its QuickMail counterpart, and passes the mail to it. The QuickMail QMMS gateway passes the mail up to the QuickMail Administrator application, which queries the mailcenters until it finds one, the online mailcenter, which serves the addressee. It passes the mail to the online mailcenter, which is the front-end to the QM Server Control Panel. The server then notifies the addressee, if that user is logged in, or stores the mail for future delivery. When the addressee finally opens the mail, it's passed a final time, from the QuickMail server to the QuickMail client software.

It's a complicated process, but not difficult to understand if one examines it on a step-by-step basis. If any one of the seven hand-offs fail, the mail will not be delivered. Some failures may generate error messages, which can be used to diagnose the point of failure, while other pieces of mail will simply disappear, as though into an electronic black hole. The logging functions of the gateways are also invaluable diagnostic tools, and should always be set to as detailed a logging level as possible during the configuration and testing phases of installation.

Getting the basic e-mail functionality set up in the last chapter took care of the connections between server and client processes, each of which constitutes

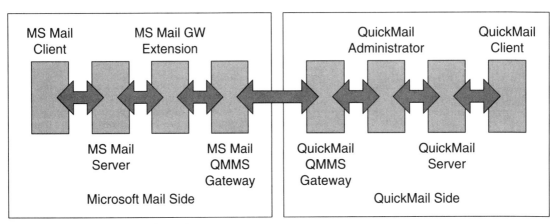

Figure 7.12   QMMS gateway schematic.

one hand-off on the end of this long connection: one and seven, in order. If you've already gotten any other QuickMail gateways working, you also know the Administrator application can pass mail back and forth to the online mail-center, which is connection six. If you selected the MS Mail server in the MS Mail WW Chooser extension, and have any other MS Mail gateways running, you've demonstrated the functionality of connection two. This leaves the installation of the two complementary gateways, and the bringing up of connections three (from MS Mail GW to the MS QMMS), four (between the two sides), and five (from the QM QMMS to QuickMail Administrator).

Once you've used the Gateway Installer to copy the gateway code onto the server machine, select the "Connect Times . . ." item from the "Gateway" sub-menu of the "Mail" menu of the client software. Select the "At the times selected" radio button, and check the "Connect immediately when there is out-going mail" box. This will allow the MS Mail gateway to connect to its Quick-Mail gateway counterpart any time it has mail to deliver.

Next, select the "Recipients . . ." item from the "Gateway" submenu, and begin adding the names of the QuickMail users, where the Alias field contains their names as they will appear to MS Mail users, and the E-Mail Address field contains their QuickMail address, followed by a period, and the name of the online mailcenter which serves them. When the QuickMail address itself contains a period, the whole address should be enclosed in quotes, then followed by a period outside the quotes, and the mailcenter name.

Obviously, MS Mail aliases can be created for users at QuickMail mailcenters which aren't of the "online" type. Thus this same system could be used to provide MS Mail users access to gateway services which aren't available directly under Microsoft Mail, or have not been installed under MS Mail. Thus, for example, the address we entered in the QuickMail AppleLink gateway in Fig. 7.13 would be reached from the MS Mail side of this gateway at

```
"Julie Lewis, O'Day P.R. Assoc.".APPLELINK
```

or simply

```
ODAY\Julie Lewis.APPLELINK
```

which doesn't contain any periods and thus requires no quotation marks. This isn't a great example, since there's a perfectly good MS Mail-to-AppleLink gateway available, but you get the idea. The same method could be used to reach someone on CompuServe or print something out through a printer gateway.

The remaining steps in configuring this connection are all on the QuickMail side and basically mirror these. First, install the gateway in the QA folder. Next, create a new mailcenter in QM Administrator. Then add your MS Mail users' names into the QuickMail gateway and try sending a test message through.

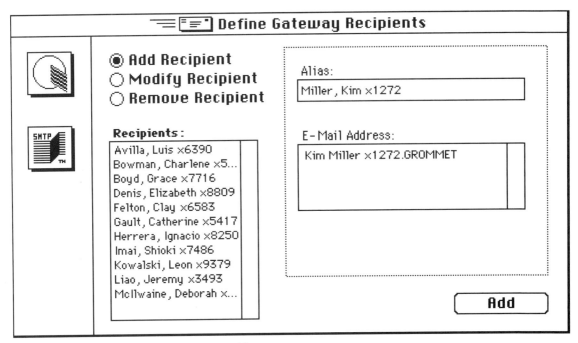

Figure 7.13   Defining Microsoft Mail gateway addresses.

7.3.2   Online service connection gateways

As mentioned, Microsoft Mail also sports an AppleLink gateway. There's also an MCI Mail gateway. Each is configured by following basically the same steps that were required in installing the MS Mail half of the QMMS gateway. The other half of each of those gateways is a part of each of the respective online services, and the middle connection between the two is in the form of a dialup connection between two modems.

7.3.3   Other connection methods

A couple of different methods of connecting MS Mail servers on different networks have been developed. Beside the traditional server-gateway-modem-modem-gateway-server connection, as used by QuickMail, Microsoft Mail offers a connection to Farallon's Liaison half-router, which allows two whole remote networks to be connected temporarily over telephone lines, so that the servers can behave as though they resided on the same network and transfer mail directly without using gateways.

An MS Mail fax gateway is also available, so that faxes can be composed using the MS Mail client software, and sent to the recipient's fax machine by a gateway on a machine with a faxmodem. One great advantage of fax and printer gateways is that addresses appear the same as any other to the user, so a single message could be sent to several users, one via a fax gateway, one on a paper memo, and one using electronic mail, all with only a single action by the sender. Before the advent of e-mail, the delivery of each of these messages would have required special and separate attention on the part of the sender.

7.4   The Solution

After configuring several gateways for both his QuickMail and Microsoft Mail systems, Mark found that he quite enjoyed the added abilities these gave his e-mail system. Users quickly began to discover ways of routing e-mail through the external gateways to business partners at other companies, and many added their electronic mail addresses to their business cards.

The choice Mark had anticipated between QuickMail and MS Mail had never forced itself upon him, as there were users of each who, although far from satisfied with the system they themselves were using, vastly preferred it to the other, and derided those users who had made the opposite choice. The use of gateways to transfer mail back and forth made the differences between the capabilities of the two systems transparent to users, and so each user was able to select an e-mail system solely on the basis of which interface they preferred using. Many of the less technical users gravitated to the easy, intuitive MS Mail interface, while most of the computer nerds opted for the broader range of options afforded by QuickMail's interface.

As use of the initially installed gateways became routine, Mark began to experiment with more complicated interaction between gateways, setting up a data-entry system using custom-designed order forms, which were automatically imported into a FileMaker database and printed out in the form of packing slips and shipping labels on a printer gateway in the shipping department. At the end of each week, the database would export a series of sales summaries, which were automatically mailed to the appropriate managers. Although the system was complicated and Mark wasn't entirely confident that he'd want to base so-called "mission-critical" operations on it, he was impressed with the flexibility that the gateways and features of different e-mail systems offered, particularly when used in combination.

8

Zones, Routing, and Ethernet

8.1 The Problem

After bringing the new file and e-mail servers online, Mark noticed that network performance had degraded terribly. This was obviously due to the increased load of traffic between workstations and servers, but knowledge of the cause did not immediately lead to any obvious solution, other than unplugging the servers. Too late for that, unfortunately; users had already come to depend upon them.

In the continued development of most any network, there comes a point at which LocalTalk cannot be made to perform adequately, or cannot provide some needed service, and must be replaced with a faster networking system. Correctly identifying this point is important, since converting too early can be an unnecessary waste and can distort the relative attractiveness and practicality of some paths of expansion, while converting too late requires extraordinary and expensive measures to prolong the life of the LocalTalk network beyond the point at which it should reasonably be abandoned.

Mark set himself to the task of investigating the possible upgrade paths upon which he might take the network.

8.2 Partitioning

The first step in increasing network performance is partitioning the network into separate "zones." Traffic does not pass between zones unless it's addressed to a node in a zone other than its own. Devices which partition networks in this fashion are called routers.

These zones appear as a list in the Chooser (Fig. 8.1). Services now appear in only one zone, which you must select from the list of "Apple Talk Zones" in the lower left-hand corner. Just as Apple Talk devices have both NBP names and node numbers, Apple Talk zones are defined by their names, but have an underlying structure of "net numbers" or numerical addresses. Zone names

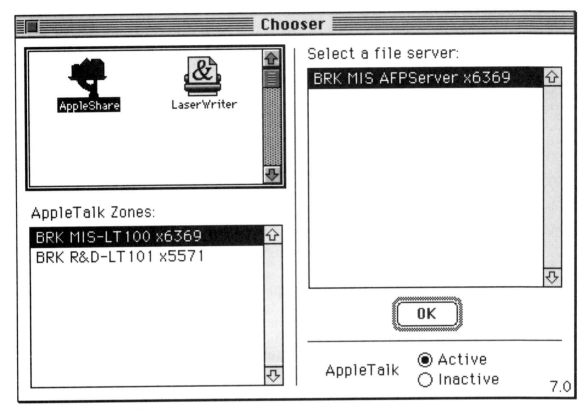

Figure 8.1   The Chooser showing zones.

and net numbers are not, however, simply two expressions of the same thing. Multiple nets may be contained in a single zone, and under network systems other than LocalTalk, multiple zones may be associated with multiple nets, without corresponding directly with any of them. This issue will be dealt with later in the chapter.

Saying that routers partition networks can, at first, be somewhat misleading. A network must be separated into two, and the router then sits between them, acting as a kind of Maxwell's Demon, sorting packets. Devices which perform routing can be extremely simple. All they know, and all they need to know, is what's on each side of them, where sides are represented by ports, or network connections on the router. By comparing the destination address of each packet with the port on which the packet was received, it determines whether or not the packet needs to be forwarded on to the other side.

The node addresses are now composed not only of a node number, but a net number as well. It's important to distinguish between nets and zones, as mentioned above; the distinction will be reviewed in more detail later in this chapter, in the section on Ethernet. The address is usually expressed with a decimal,

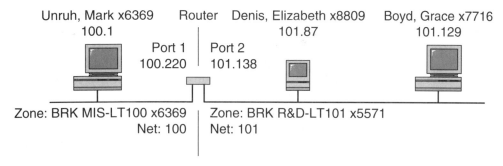

Figure 8.2 Partitioning action of a router.

thus the address of the machine "Serventi, Catherine ×8724" is no longer just 87, it's 101.87, since 101 is the number of the net that it's attached to.

If a process on that machine were to send a packet to one on the machine "Boyd, Grace ×7716," the packet would be examined and discarded by the router, since the destination address was on the same net that's attached to the port of the router on which the packet arrived. Since the router is the last device on that net, the packet goes no further, and Mark's Macintosh, which is on another net, doesn't see it at all. Since this is a baseband network, and machines can't send packets when other machines are already transmitting, this filtering effect increases apparent network throughput. In this instance, there's no reason why Mark couldn't be transmitting at the same time as one of the machines on the other side of the router.

As another example, let's take a packet from Mark's machine to Grace's. Grace's address is 101.129, a fact Mark's machine is presumably already aware of. The packet leaves his machine with that address in the Datagram Delivery Protocol header, but the address of the router in the Link Access Protocol header. The router receives it, determines that the destination address net number is not the same as the net to which the receiving port is attached, and consults its routing table. A routing table contains a list of all the nets the router knows about, and which side of the router each one is on.

In the case of the router above, the routing table is as follows:

Network range	Distance	Port	Next IR	Entry state
100	0	1	0	Good
101	0	2	0	Good

The packet is addressed to a node on net 101, so the router jumps to that line of the table and finds that net 101 is one that's directly attached to it (distance 0 hops, or "no routers away"), and that it's attached to port 2. With this information, it can take the packet and retransmit it out port 2 to the addressee.

Traffic which passes through the router defeats the increased efficiency that the router buys you, though, so it's extremely important to make a good decision about where to locate your routers. If you partition clients from their servers, for instance, all the network's traffic will still be flowing between the two groups, only it will now have to flow through the router, which takes time, since the router has to keep looking things up in its table.

Figure 8.3 illustrates a common misuse of routers. In this example, a packet from 100.1, Mark, to 102.28 must pass through an intervening net, 101, which is thus tied up with traffic unnecessarily. Here, a new routing table entry must be made for the newly attached net, 102:

Network range	Distance	Port	Next IR	Entry state
100	0	1	0	Good
101	0	2	0	Good
102	1	2	205	Good

Router A, when it received the packet mentioned above, would jump to the third line of its table, beginning with the net number of the addressee. Upon finding that the distance to net 102 is one hop, or one router away, it knows that it'll have to pay attention to the "Next IR" entry. It sees that net 102 is on its port 2 side, and that the next router in the path to net 102 is at address 205. It forwards the packet to 101.205, where the next router has to deal with it. Meanwhile, 101.87, a workstation, can't send a packet, because its section of the network is serving as a highway for packets that are bound elsewhere.

A second problem quickly emerges if this daisy-chain-like strategy of router positioning is carried any further than two routers.

In Fig. 8.4, the fourth network is only accessible through two other networks. Not only does this tie up both of them, traffic-wise, it also means the packet has to do three hops, or pass through three routers, greatly increasing the time it'll take to get to its destination, and increasing the round-trip time

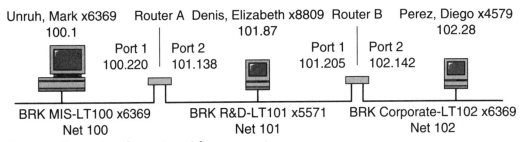

Figure 8.3 Two routers, three nets, serial arrangement.

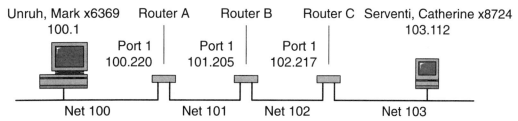

Figure 8.4 Three routers, four nets, serial arrangement.

(the time it takes to send a message to another computer, and get a reply back) twice as much. Here, router A's table would look like this:

Network range	Distance	Port	Next IR	Entry state
100	0	1	0	Good
101	0	2	0	Good
102	1	2	205	Good
103	2	2	205	Good

As you can see, the growth of the hop count is now growing in a linear progression, tied to the number of nets, which is in turn tied to the number of machines. If you were to try to use machines on a network constructed this way, you'd quickly appreciate the degree to which this is a really bad idea. Aside from which, hop counts over 15 are considered errors, and this puts a theoretical limit on your network of between 150 and 300 nodes, which isn't too big. The correct way of adding networks is more like a trunk than a daisy chain. It's often called a backbone.

In Fig. 8.5, users are only located on nets 100, 101, 102, and 103, while net 1 is empty, or contains servers. Traffic from net 100 to net 103 passes through net 1, but doesn't affect nets 101 or 102. That alleviates the first problem. We can examine the solution to the second problem, the hop count, by looking at the new routing table for the first router:

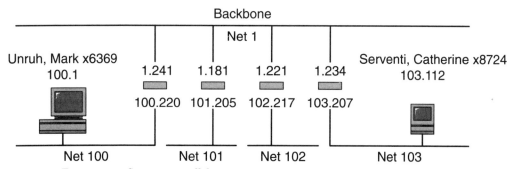

Figure 8.5 Four routers, five nets, parallel arrangement.

Network range	Distance	Port	Next IR	Entry state
1	0	2	0	Good
100	0	1	0	Good
101	1	2	181	Good
102	1	2	221	Good
103	1	2	234	Good

Arranging your routers in this parallel manner makes the distance from any router to any other net attached to the same backbone one hop, and from any "leaf" network to any other two hops. The hop count is no longer a function of the number of nets.

Having taken a look at how routers operate internally, let's now turn to the ways in which they deal with the rest of the devices on the network.

Aside from the routine packets being forwarded through them, the remaining traffic to and from routers is largely in the form of RTMP, or Routing Table Management Protocol packets. There are four varieties of RTMP packets, of which RTMP Data packets are the most common.

RTMP Data packets are used to send routing table entries in a standard form. Every router on a network broadcasts an RTMP Data packet, containing routing table entries it knows about, every ten seconds, out each of its ports. Since this is a broadcast packet, all nodes on that net that feel like paying attention can use the data. For the most part, this means other routers, which integrate the route data into their own routing tables.

In the preceding example, when the router on net 100 received an RTMP Data packet from the router on net 103, the data would appear as follows:

AppleTalk Header

AppleTalk Destination:	1.255	ELAP Broadcast
AppleTalk Source:	1.234	

Short DDP Header—Datagram Delivery Protocol

Dest. Socket:	1	RTMP Socket
Source Socket:	1	RTMP Socket
DDP Type:	1	RTMP Data

RTMP Header—Routing Table Maintenance Protocol

Router's Net:	1
Router's Node ID:	234

RTMP Data

RTMP Tuple #1

Range Start:	1	
Range Flag:	%100	Extended
Distance:	0	
Range End:	1	

RTMP Tuple #2

    Network Number: 100

    Range Flag: %000   Nonextended

    Distance: 1

RTMP Tuple #3

    Network Number: 101

    Range Flag: %000   Nonextended

    Distance: 1

RTMP Tuple #4

    Network Number: 102

    Range Flag: %000   Nonextended

    Distance: 1

RTMP Tuple #5

    Network Number: 103

    Range Flag: %000   Nonextended

    Distance: 0

When the router on net 100 receives this, it immediately adds one to the hop count for each "tuple" or record, because the other router is, itself, one hop away. After doing so, it compares the resultant hop counts with the ones for the same nets in its own routing table. If any of the newly received records have an equal or lesser hop count, they replace the old records in the router's table. Thus the two tables compare as follows:

Net	Existing entries	New entries	< or =?
1	0	1	no
100	0	2	no
101	1	2	no
102	1	2	no
103	1	1	yes

Thus only the last entry, for net 103, is updated. If an entry is not updated in a sufficiently long time, twenty seconds, its status is declared "bad"; it's no longer propagated to other routers, and is eventually purged from the table entirely. That's about all the information routers need to exchange with each other.

If you examine the RTMP packet above, you'll notice that the tuple for net 1, the backbone, is different from the others, containing an "extended" flag, and a "range end=1" value. This net 1 is running on a different kind of medium from the others, which are using LocalTalk. Net 1 is running on Ethernet, an alternative kind of network which will be explained shortly. What concerns us here is the significance of the term "extended." An extended net is a network segment which can contain more than one net number and more than one zone name. In this case, the range start is 1 and the range end is 1, so the network would be called net 1, or net 1-1. We could, however, have a net 11-40, containing ten different net numbers, associated with three or four different zones. In this case, since there's no physical correspondence between devices connected to the network segment and the nets and zones associated with the segment, each device must randomly choose a net number from the range available, and will first appear in the "default zone," one to which devices are initially assigned the first time they boot on the network segment.

The reason for extended networks is two-fold. First, providing a range of net numbers allows the 254-node limit imposed by eight-bit AppleTalk node numbers to be exceeded on a single physical segment, in 254-node increments, one increment per net number. Second, providing multiple zone names allows the use of "multicasts" rather than broadcasts on these heavily populated segments. A multicast is similar to a broadcast, but it's paid attention to by some, but not all, of the nodes which it passes. On extended networks, the multicast addresses are calculated from the zone names, so all devices within any particular zone will see zone multicasts, while devices on the same segment, even using the same net number, will not.

For Macintoshes, the world is a substantially different place if a router exists. The router acts as a sort of proxy in many actions, in particular broadcasts and transmissions to other nets, and the Macintosh must know that its own address is in two parts, both net and node number, rather than just node number. In order for this to work, however, the Macintosh must always know whether it's in the presence of a router and, if so, at what address that router can be reached.

Figure 8.6 is an illustration of the packets that are exchanged between a booting node on a network and that network's router. You may wish to compare this to the similar example in Chap. 2. The first 640 packets are the same LAP Enquiries, used to verify the free status of the hinted node number. Following that, however, you may recall that there were two RTMP packets which went unanswered in Chap. 2 because we had no router on the net at that point. The packets are RTMP Request packets and, if there is a router, it's likely that the first one will be answered. The answer is in the form of an RTMP Response packet, which is much like an RTMP data packet, but contains only the header, not the tuples. That's okay, though, because the "RTMP Stub" socket that the booting node opens to listen for the response can only interpret the header, anyway. What it extracts from the header are the net number and the router's node number. The net number is stored, because this is the first part of the booting machine's address. The router's net number is used to proceed with the NBP registration, this time sending the router NBP Broadcast Request packets and letting it do the broadcasting. You'll notice that the zone field of the NBP Request tuple contains only the asterisk, meaning "this zone." When the router performs the broadcast, it fills in the zone name. Responses, if any, go directly to the booting node, bypassing the router.

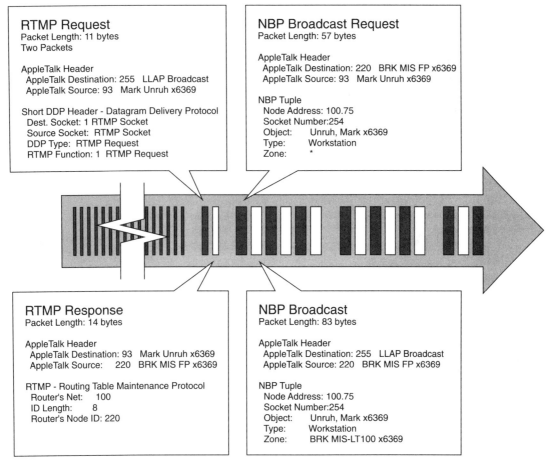

RTMP Request
Packet Length: 11 bytes
Two Packets

AppleTalk Header
  AppleTalk Destination: 255   LLAP Broadcast
  AppleTalk Source: 93   Mark Unruh x6369

Short DDP Header - Datagram Delivery Protocol
  Dest. Socket: 1 RTMP Socket
  Source Socket: RTMP Socket
  DDP Type: RTMP Request
  RTMP Function: 1 RTMP Request

NBP Broadcast Request
Packet Length: 57 bytes

AppleTalk Header
  AppleTalk Destination: 220   BRK MIS FP x6369
  AppleTalk Source: 93   Mark Unruh x6369

NBP Tuple
  Node Address: 100.75
  Socket Number:254
  Object: Unruh, Mark x6369
  Type: Workstation
  Zone: *

RTMP Response
Packet Length: 14 bytes

AppleTalk Header
  AppleTalk Destination: 93   Mark Unruh x6369
  AppleTalk Source: 220   BRK MIS FP x6369

RTMP - Routing Table Maintenance Protocol
  Router's Net: 100
  ID Length: 8
  Router's Node ID: 220

NBP Broadcast
Packet Length: 83 bytes

AppleTalk Header
  AppleTalk Destination: 255   LLAP Broadcast
  AppleTalk Source: 220   BRK MIS FP x6369

NBP Tuple
  Node Address: 100.75
  Socket Number:254
  Object: Unruh, Mark x6369
  Type: Workstation
  Zone: BRK MIS-LT100 x6369

Figure 8.6   Starting up in the presence of a router.

The existence of the RTMP Stub socket on nonrouter nodes also ensures that they'll respond correctly, at no disadvantage, if a router comes online on their net after they've booted without one. The RTMP Stub always listens for RTMP data packets, which are broadcast, as well as RTMP Response packets, which are directed, and only issued after a request. By doing so, they're able to glean the address of the local router which has most recently proved its existence. This variable, the most recent router to have issued an RTMP packet, is called "A Router." On a net like 100, 101, 102, or 103, which has only one local router, A Router will be a fixed value. On net 1, however, there are four routers. A device on net one could have four possible values in A Router, and most likely would have each of the four, over the course of the ten-second RTMP cycle.

Chooser operation is also affected by the presence of a router. As you saw at the beginning of this chapter, the Chooser window itself is modified and displays a list of zones, with the current zone highlighted by default.

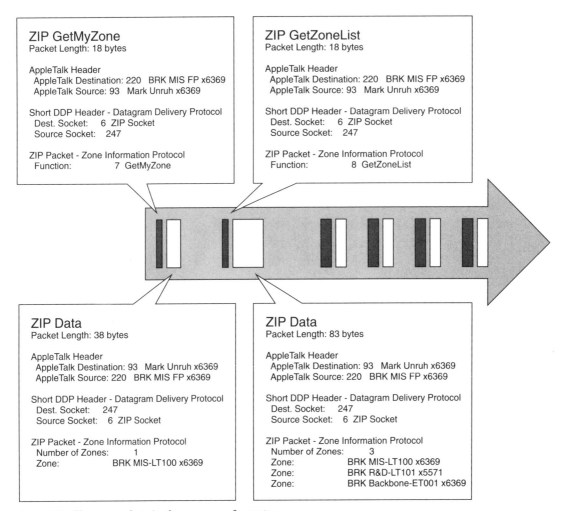

Figure 8.7 Chooser packets in the presence of a router.

When the Chooser is opened, if A Router has been initialized, a ZIP, or Zone Information Protocol "GetMyZone" packet, is sent to A Router. That router responds with a ZIP Data packet, containing the name of the current zone. Next, the node with the Chooser open sends the same router a ZIP GetZoneList packet, and the router responds with another ZIP Data packet, this one containing the entire zone list. On large networks, this list may exceed the size limits of a single packet, and indeed this problem commonly occurs with RTMP packets, as well. When this happens, the data is split into multiple packets, each otherwise identical. The receiving node writes the current zone into the zone list scrolling list, highlights it, and then writes in the rest of the zone list below it.

8.3 Analyzing Traffic Flow Patterns

Now let's take a more in-depth look at the traffic situation. Let's define the word "congested" to mean the most traffic a net can stand without users being adversely affected. How this would relate to actual percentage of bandwidth being used would depend upon user expectations, what kinds of software were in use, and many other factors, so the use of a qualitative term helps us simplify the problem.

Ideally, each net would be running at exactly 100 percent congestion rate all the time, because this would be indicative of maximal resource utilization (much different, as I said, from 100 percent network bandwidth utilization, which would mean complete gridlock). Of that traffic, a large part would be bound for other nodes within the same net, if the network was well designed, while a portion of it would be bound for each of the other extant nets with users on them. Let's ignore for now the possibility of servers on the backbone net. Let's assume that 40 percent of the traffic on the net is bound for other nodes on the same net, 10 percent is bound for each of the other three user nets, and another 10 percent is coming from each of the other three networks.

If you count up the traffic, 30 percent from each of four nets, that's 120 percent, meaning that our backbone net is operating 20 percent above congestion level. Adding a fifth net would bring us up to 40 percent × 5, or 200 percent of congestion level. The solution that evolved to this problem is to provide a backbone that's more congestion-resistant. That means choosing routers which support LocalTalk on one side and a faster type of network on the other side. For the faster network, we've basically got three choices: Token Ring, FDDI, or Ethernet.

Token Ring is a kind of network used by IBM's workstations and larger machines. It runs at 16 megabits per second, which is seventy times faster

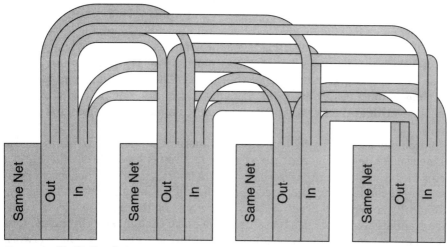

Figure 8.8 Traffic flow between nets.

than LocalTalk. It's well supported on the Macintosh; network adapter cards are available from quite a few different vendors, and Apple and other vendors have developed Macintosh client software interfaces for all the standard facilities of Token Ring networks. Unfortunately, it's also costly and complicated to install, and unsupported on a lot of other computer platforms. Because of this, it doesn't see much use outside those companies which have been committed to buying IBM systems for a long time. Token Ring uses a single fixed topology called, unsurprisingly, a token ring. Token ring-topology networks have daisy-chain-like connections between devices, which form a ring instead of a bus. A token is passed from machine to machine, with data following it. The token is reset when it arrives at the data's destination, or comes back to the sender undelivered.

FDDI, or Fiber Distributed Data Interface, and it's twisted-pair analog TPDDI, are 100-megabit network systems. Running 400 times as fast as LocalTalk, and costing about fifty times as much to install, they are at this point overkill for general use. Costs will fall over the next few years, though, and they are both strong candidates for preeminence in the next generation of networking standards, so it's worth watching with an eye to the future. FDDI and TPDDI use a dual counter-rotating token ring topology which, as touched upon in Chap. 5, is basically what it sounds like: two token rings, superimposed, with the tokens traveling in opposite directions. Stations can connect to one or both of the rings, providing an excellent fail-safe mechanism. If a node or cable segment fails, the dual-connected nodes on either side of the break divert the streams of traffic from each ring endpoint into the end of the other ring, such that the remainder of one ring is used to patch the remainder of the other, creating one viable ring out of two broken ones.

The practical successor to LocalTalk is Ethernet. Ethernet is a 10-megabit (nominally 40 times faster than LocalTalk) network system which can use one of three different topologies which closely mirror LocalTalk ones. Ethernet adapters for Macintoshes are inexpensive, and Apple includes built-in Ethernet support on some models of Macintosh and LaserWriter, just as it does with LocalTalk. The competition between vendors of hubs has reduced the per-port price of Ethernet hubs to a lower point than that of LocalTalk ones. At the time of this writing, star-topology Ethernet networks cost between two and three times what LocalTalk would. This price has fallen by half each year for the past several, and may well fall by that much again before it begins to flatten out.

The problem with utilizing this 40-times increase in bandwidth is in device bottlenecks. While it's theoretically possible to pump 10 megabits, or one and a quarter megabytes of data per second out a network adapter, it doesn't happen in real-world conditions. The perceived performance increase in file transfers, the generally recognized practical test, is likely to be three to fivefold. For network administrators, this is a blessing in disguise, though, since it means that eight to twelve times as many people can be simultaneously accessing network services before your congestion point is reached. Substituting an Ethernet backbone for the LocalTalk one in the example above reduces the backbone traffic from 120 percent of congestion level to 3 percent, presuming the congestion level to be the same proportion of the saturation level under Ethernet as under LocalTalk.

8.4   Deciding When to Make the Switch

Armed with this knowledge, you need to decide how and when to convert your network from LocalTalk to Ethernet.

The work and expense of switching from one network system, like LocalTalk, to another, like Ethernet, can be likened to paying off a mortgage; it can be done in one of two ways. You can perform the conversion over a long period of time, at relatively high total expense, but without spending too much time or money at any one point. Alternatively, you can do it all at once, pulling a few all-nighters, and spending quite a bit of money all at the same time.

Alternatively, an analogy can be drawn between the reorganization of a network for the purposes of enlarging throughput and the elimination of bottlenecks and the restructuring of business processes for similar purposes. Like TQM, a gradual conversion featuring a period of parallel systems is an evolutionary reorganization. The alternative, a quick and total replacement of the previous system is, like BPE, a revolutionary reorganization.

The advantages of the gradual method are easy reversibility at any point, no real hardship at any point, and an increase in the perceived justifiability of the expense. Reversibility is easy if proper documentation is practiced, because this method never requires multiple simultaneous changes be made to the network; thus, at any step, you can point to the change that created a new problem. If you follow this course, you're unlikely to have to spend more than a couple of thousand dollars at any given time, that being about the most a router can be expected to cost, and you'll never have any job more difficult than configuring such a router. During a prolonged conversion, direct Ethernet connections become a prize for users, and the perceived value of those connections is inflated; thus it's relatively easy to use network user demands as justification for continued spending on the conversion, and users will themselves find reasons that they "must" be given faster connections. On the other hand, taking the long view, this is a much more costly means of conversion, both in terms of work hours and dollars invested. Over the course of the conversion, the routers required may add as much as 50 percent to the total expense.

The abrupt method, which involves giving all users faster network connections simultaneously and forgoing a transition period in which two network systems operate side-by-side, requires much more stamina and determination. It is, however, much cheaper in the long run, especially if performed when the price of faster networking technology has already plateaued, or is near doing so. In addition, when you've completed the change, you'll find that the workhours involved are only a small fraction of those required for a gradual conversion. You'll encounter problems which must be worked through without benefit of a background state against which they can be measured. It'll be very difficult to determine what the source of problems is, since all the involved components will be new, and you're unlikely to have much prior experience with any of them.

Perhaps the worst problem, however, is not a technical one: There's little reassurance that the time you've chosen to perform the conversion is correct. It's hard to tell when network adapter prices will level off; since there are no users with faster connections initially, there will be little demand, and once the conversion has been completed few people will remember how much slower the older system was. All this compounds the problem of justifying a large one-time expense.

In either case, the longer you wait to convert, the more money you'll spend trying to stave off the collapse of the older network system. The tradeoff here is between the increasing expense of maintaining the old network in a state that'll support user demands, and the decreasing purchase price of a new network. The longer you wait, the more you'll spend each month on the old network, but the lower the price of a new one will be.

All the discussion of routers in this chapter so far has been predicated on a situation in which a network administrator is gradually converting a Local-Talk network to an Ethernet one. I've done so because this is the most common approach, although certainly not by design. First, we had one big LocalTalk zone, which was getting unwieldy. Then we installed a LocalTalk-to-LocalTalk router to partition it into two zones, restoring some of its previous performance. When this too got bogged down, we added a second router, but this was an even shorter-lived stopgap measure. The next step was to purchase LocalTalk-to-Ethernet routers for each zone, and move the management station and the most generally accessed servers out onto the Ethernet zone, by installing Ethernet network cards in them. Smaller servers and laser printers remained in the LocalTalk zones with all the users. As the company continues to grow, more routers must be purchased, even if some users are being moved onto Ethernet. Eventually, the rate at which users are moved onto Ethernet will surpass the rate at which new employees must be connected to the network, and routers can be eventually retired.

At this point in the conversion, as foresightful readers will have guessed, it's time to start again, since the Ethernet network will be becoming slower and will eventually begin to stagnate, with the addition of all the new users. Some users will probably be demanding connections faster than Ethernet can provide before you've even finished moving the laser printers, always the last to be converted, off LocalTalk.

It's this last problem, being constantly tied up with the upgrading process, that provides the strongest incentive to perform a quick, one-shot changeover. This leaves you time until the next upgrade to spend improving higher-level services, which are what really increase user efficiency; follow the market for faster network systems, so you'll have some foreknowledge of the next step you'll be taking; or even spend some accrued vacation time.

8.5 Conversion Skills

There are two basic skills to be mastered in upgrading networks: router configuration and network adapter installation. Although there are many different brands of router, and many different kinds of Ethernet adapter device, we'll just deal with a few characteristic ones, since the differences are minor.

8.5.1 Router configuration

The basic task which must be performed in setting up a router is the configuration of its seed information. That is, the information which it's to already know at the time it's attached to the network and started. This information relates to the characteristics of the AppleTalk networks on each of its ports.

For each of its ports, the router must know whether the network segment to be connected will be operating in extended or nonextended mode. If extended, it must be informed of the length of the range of net numbers to be attached and the start net number, and the names of one or more zones to associate with those nets. If nonextended, it simply needs to know one net number and one zone name.

It is of absolutely paramount concern that there be complete agreement between the seed information of different routers attached to the same network segment. In the previous Fig. 8.5, if different routers had different spellings for the name of the zone associated with net 1, the zone names will flicker in and out of people's Chooser zone lists, and it'll be very difficult, if not impossible, to reach devices on that network segment.

8.5.1.1 Configuring a FastPath.

For our first example, we'll configure a Fast-Path router, one of the two most commonly used LocalTalk-to-Ethernet routers, to connect net 100 to net 1, the backbone. Routers should *always* be initially configured offline. That is, they should be attached only to the machine that's being used to configure them, not to the rest of the network, even indirectly. Nearly all routers are shipped from the factory with routing turned off, and nearly all routers only NBP-register a port on their LocalTalk side; the FastPath is no exception. This requires us to connect a Macintosh with NetManager, the FastPath configuration software, to the FastPath's LocalTalk port. For testing purposes, a single Ethernet-equipped Macintosh should probably be attached to the Ethernet port, as well.

Once the management software has been launched, and the router selected and opened, the fields dealing with LocalTalk configuration can be filled. The FastPath's available options are aimed primarily at limiting the visibility of devices on the Ethernet side, to protect them from users within the LocalTalk net. These are rarely used outside of educational labs.

The LocalTalk configuration finished, we can proceed to configuring the Ethernet port (Fig. 8.10).

The Ethernet port is configured in much the same way that the LocalTalk one was, except that it's an extended network, so a whole list of zone names

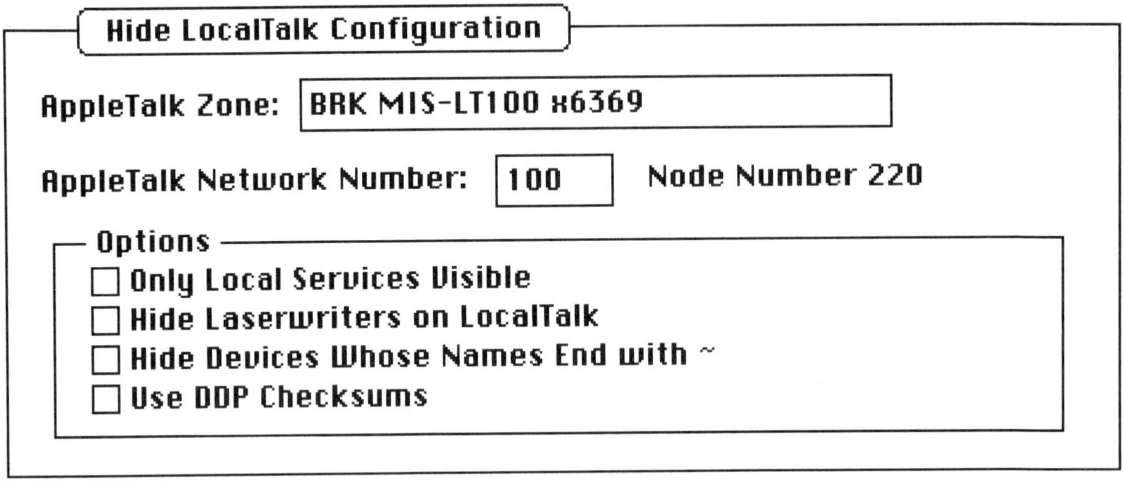

Hide LocalTalk Configuration

AppleTalk Zone: BRK MIS-LT100 ×6369

AppleTalk Network Number: 100   Node Number 220

Options

☐ Only Local Services Visible
☐ Hide Laserwriters on LocalTalk
☐ Hide Devices Whose Names End with ~
☐ Use DDP Checksums

Figure 8.9   FastPath LocalTalk port configuration.

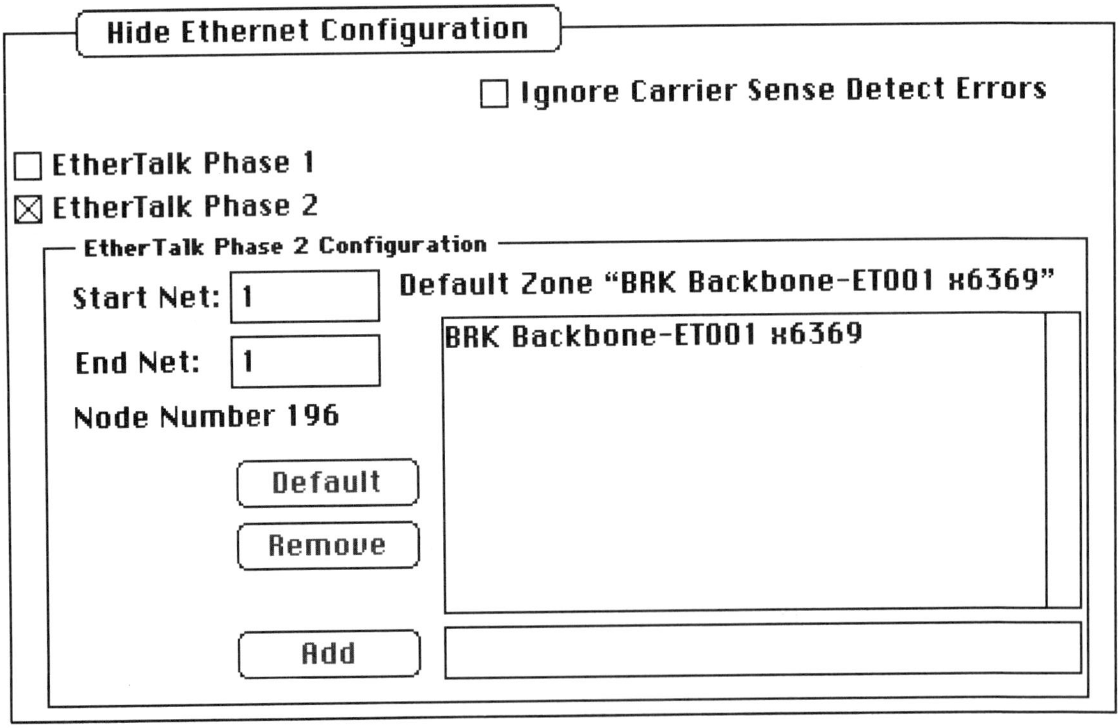

Hide Ethernet Configuration

☐ Ignore Carrier Sense Detect Errors

☐ EtherTalk Phase 1
☒ EtherTalk Phase 2

EtherTalk Phase 2 Configuration

Start Net: 1   Default Zone "BRK Backbone-ET001 ×6369"

BRK Backbone-ET001 ×6369

End Net: 1

Node Number 196

[Default]

[Remove]

[Add]

Figure 8.10   FastPath Ethernet port configuration.

and a range of net numbers can be entered, if use warrants such configuration. Be sure to check "EtherTalk Phase 2." EtherTalk is Apple's name for the AppleTalk protocol, running on Ethernet, just as LocalTalk is Apple's name for AppleTalk running on LocalTalk. Makes sense, right? Well, maybe. Phase 1 is an antiquated version of EtherTalk which did not support extended network segments. It was superseded by Phase 2 in 1989, but some of the largest pre-existing EtherTalk installations didn't complete the switch-over for quite some time, because of the hassle of upgrading so many users' EtherTalk driver software to the new version. Apple has promised that there will never be a "Phase 3," but that's less reassuring than it might at first seem, since many people perceive problems which have not yet been dealt with in Phase 2. In any case, upgrading would not be nearly so painful now, as there are a number of management utilities specifically designed to facilitate the distribution and installation of software on large numbers of user machines. The Phase 1 checkbox was included in the FastPath configuration software so that those sites which had not yet finished upgrading could continue to support both protocols, side-by-side, on the same networks. Routers operating in this manner are called "transition routers" and are widely abhorred, for good reason.

8.5.1.2 Configuring a GatorBox. The other very commonly used LocalTalk-to-Ethernet router is the GatorBox. Although all routers are defined by their function, and are therefore similar at some level, the GatorBox is usually characterized by comparison with the FastPath as emphasizing features, rather than performance. Those additional features will be discussed further in Chap. 12.

We'll configure this GatorBox to act as the router between the backbone and LocalTalk net 101. Again, the router should be configured offline, beginning with a single Mac attached to its LocalTalk port running GatorKeeper, the GatorBox configuration software. Test the router's configuration by attaching another Mac to its Ethernet port, and only then turn it off, put into place on the existing net, and restart it. GatorBox port configuration is accomplished primarily all within one simple dialog. Near the top, the LocalTalk net number and zone name fields should be filled.

One feature the GatorBox offers is a configuration option which changes the router's behavior, upon the discovery of a discrepancy between its seed information and the information that other routers, already running at the time it's booted, are using. By selecting "Seed Port" from the pop-up menu, you're telling it to behave in the same manner as a FastPath: If a discrepancy is detected, it will continue trying to propagate the information with which it was originally seeded. If "Soft Seed Port" is selected, the router will propagate its seed information, but if it detects a conflict, it will adopt the new information in favor of the information it was originally seeded with. Soft-seeding can be a mixed blessing, in that it lessens the danger of a router which is brought up late, with incorrect information, propagating incorrect information through the network. On the other hand, if routers are soft-seeded, it means that it's

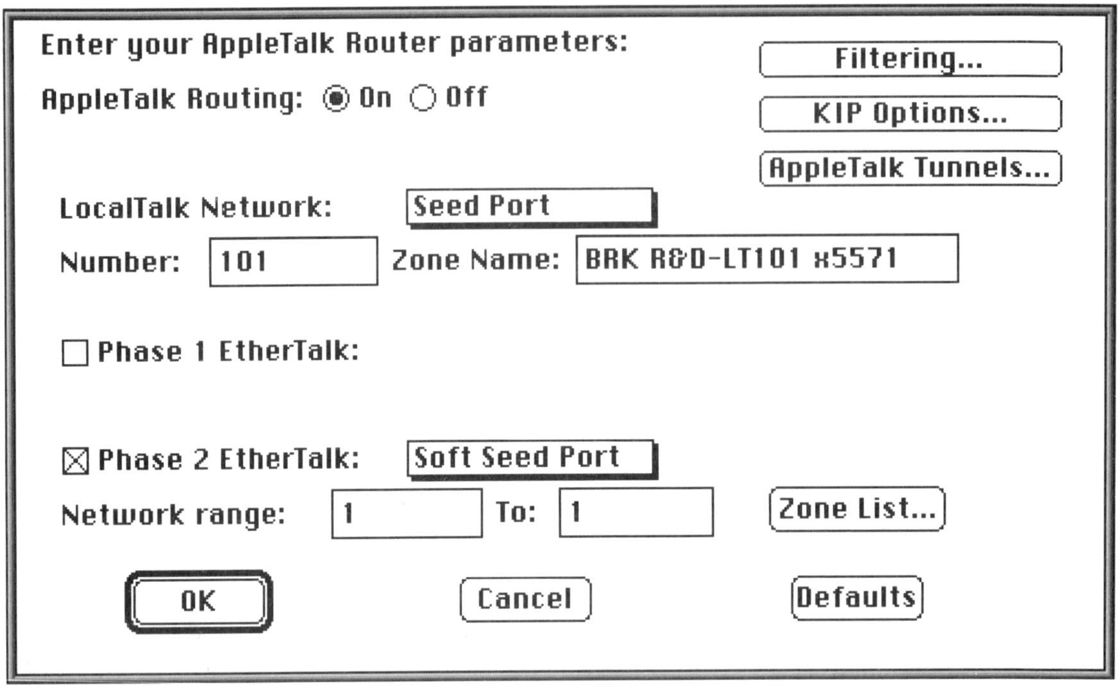

Enter your AppleTalk Router parameters:

AppleTalk Routing: ◉ On ○ Off

[Filtering...]

[KIP Options...]

[AppleTalk Tunnels...]

LocalTalk Network: | Seed Port |

Number: | 101 | Zone Name: | BRK R&D-LT101 ×5571 |

☐ Phase 1 EtherTalk:

☒ Phase 2 EtherTalk: | Soft Seed Port |

Network range: | 1 | To: | 1 | [Zone List...]

[OK]   [Cancel]   [Defaults]

Figure 8.11   GatorBox port configuration.

hard to use them to correct bad information that's already being propagated by previously booted routers. It's definitely good to have the option of soft-seeding routers, whether you choose to do so or not. Ports can also be set to "non-seed." If they're set this way, they need not be given any information at all; when they're booted, they'll begin trying to acquire information from other routers' RTMP packets, and they'll bring the port online once they've formed a complete picture of the net on the other side.

Ethernet configuration is simple, following the same pattern that we've established with the configuration of the other ports. The zone list is entered in a subsidiary window, which is called up by pressing the "Zone List . . ." button.

8.5.1.3 Configuring a promiscuous router. Promiscuous routers, or LAP-level bridges, as they're sometimes called, don't have routing tables and don't use RTMP packets. Often used to attach laser printers to an Ethernet network, they support either a single LocalTalk device or a very small fixed number of them. They operate by accepting all the packets from the LocalTalk side, converting them from LocalTalk to EtherTalk format, and retransmitting them on the Ethernet side without performing any filtering or rejection; thus, they're called "promiscuous." They do take note of the node numbers which the devices on their LocalTalk side acquire, however, and perform filtering in the other direction, passing only packets addressed to those nodes from their Ethernet side to their LocalTalk side.

Since they need no seed information, promiscuous routers usually need no configuration whatsoever. Take them out of the box, and plug them into your network. The only instance in which they might need configuration is if they offer additional features of some kind. For instance, a common feature allows the LocalTalk devices to be placed in a zone other than the default zone on the Ethernet side. This requires software configuration, done across the network, from either side.

8.5.2   Workstation configuration

Putting Macintoshes on Ethernet is a trivial process. Some Macintoshes and LaserWriters have built-in, or "on-board" Ethernet hardware, which has an AAUI, or "Apple Attachment Unit Interface" connector. Such machines need only a small adapter to be connected. The installation process for an AAUI adapter exactly parallels that of a PhoneNet LocalTalk connector. Some other Macintoshes require NuBus cards, which are easily installed, taking perhaps two minutes apiece, and costing little more than the AAUI adapters. Models which support neither NuBus nor AAUI, currently including the "compact" Macintoshes, the Portable and PowerBooks, the LC and the IIsi, require one of a number of different connection methods. Inexpensive non-NuBus internal Ethernet cards are available for the SE, SE/30, LC, and IIsi. The IIsi can also use NuBus cards if it's provided with an adapter, which is unfortunately costly. These specialized cards generally take a bit longer to install, three to four minutes for the IIsi and LC, and twelve to fifteen minutes for the Compact models. The Macintosh Plus, Classic, Portable, and PowerBooks require external Ethernet adapter boxes which connect through the SCSI port, like hard disks. These are fairly expensive, and the degree of performance that they're able to provide has been the subject of some controversy, although that may stem more from the models of Macintosh they're commonly attached to than any inherent problem with the adapters themselves. Because of the way many Ethernet adapters other than NuBus and AAUI types work, they're inappropriate for use in electronic mail servers. This is the result of a conflict between the cards and the e-mail server software, both of which have to use the same mechanism to acquire a "slice of time" from the processor on a regular basis. Occasionally the two processes "collide," crashing both. The frequency with which this happens is dependent upon how heavily each process is being used. Unfortunately, heavy use of these two processes tends to be simultaneous.

Once the adapter has been installed, driver software must be installed. If the adapter was made by a third party and isn't Apple "register compatible" (identical in function), it'll have come with a software installation disk, which you should use. Otherwise, use the Apple System software installer or the Apple Network Software installer to install Ethernet drivers, and update your version of AppleTalk to the latest one, if necessary. When the installation is complete, restart the machine.

When you return to the Finder, you should find that you have a new Control Panel in your machine. The Network control panel is used to switch between

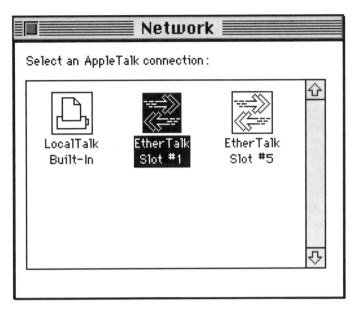

Figure 8.12   The Network control panel.

different physical network connections installed in your computer. In Fig. 8.12, two NuBus Ethernet cards have been installed, and the Apple drivers are in use. The two instances of the driver software have labeled themselves according to the NuBus slot number of the card they're associated with, so that they can be differentiated by the user. To complete the switch-over, select the Ethernet driver icon, rather than the LocalTalk one, which should be selected when you first open the Network Control Panel. Close the panel, and the change should be complete. You can open the Chooser and check which zone is highlighted at the top of the zone list, to be sure that the change has taken effect.

8.6   The Solution

Cognizant of the cost benefits of a speedy transition from LocalTalk to Ethernet, but still leery of risking the cost of an all-encompassing transition, Mark decides to scrape together what funds he can to upgrade as many machines as possible to Ethernet by installing adapters in NuBus and AAUI Macintoshes. The printers and the rest of the users will be placed behind routers, for the time being.

9

Ethernet Topologies

9.1 The Problem

Having decided to upgrade many of his network's machines to Ethernet connections, Mark was surprised to find an almost infinite array of products, nearly identical in appearance, each touted with a different set of extravagant claims.

Wary of being sold a solution to a problem he couldn't verify he had, Mark decided to first investigate all the different types of Ethernet networks, to provide himself with some background with which to evaluate the assertions made by different vendors.

9.2 Thick Ethernet

The first cabling scheme over which Ethernet protocols were run was 10Base-5, which is now called "thick" Ethernet or simply ThickNet. Ethernet cable names were originally assigned using the pattern XBand-Y, where X was the data rate in megabits, Band was either base or broad, and Y was the approximate maximum length of a cable segment in hundreds of meters. Thus 10Base-5 is a standard 10-megabit Ethernet network running on a heavy coaxial cable, which will carry a signal about 1600 feet. We've discussed the meaning of the term *baseband,* defining it as a type of network in which only one device can transmit at a time. *Broadband* networks allow multiple devices to transmit simultaneously on different frequencies. Thick Ethernet networks are trunks, much like LocalTalk trunks, except that they require a little more equipment to plug into.

ThickNet cable is typically four-tenths of an inch in diameter, extremely stiff, and typically colored bright yellow. The cable is named RG-8, to distinguish it from other similar types of cable which meet different specifications. Like cable-television cable, ThickNet cable is coaxial. That is, one of the two conductors inside, the "tip," is an ordinary wire, while the second conductor, the "ring," appears more like a braided shield, surrounding the tip conductor

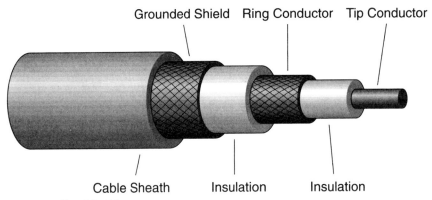

Figure 9.1   Coaxial cable.

and sharing a common axis with it. Surrounding both of these is the shield, which serves to protect the two conductors from interference. As discussed in the previous chapter, you should bond the shield of any shielded cable you use to ground, preferably at only one end. In any case, you should use a multimeter to check for current flowing through the ground; current in the shield itself is one of the few things that can disrupt a signal on coaxial cable.

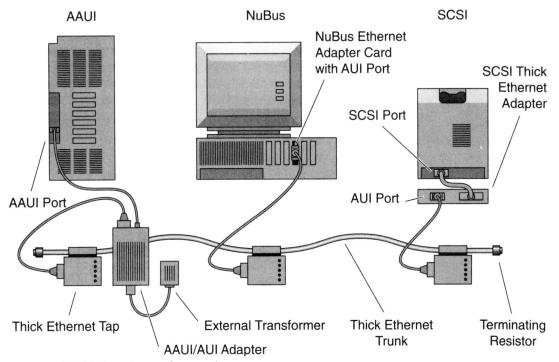

Figure 9.2   Thick Ethernet network connections.

As noted at the end of the previous chapter, different kinds of Macintoshes require different varieties of network adapter device. The common denominator in ThickNet networks is that each must attach to a tap, or transceiver box. These transceiver boxes are very standardized, and all tend to feature the same set of indicator lights, the same size box, and the same connector. Into that connector, called an AUI, or Attachment Unit Interface, plugs a drop cable, terminated with a male AUI connector at each end. The other end of that cable plugs into an AUI connector on the Ethernet interface of the device you're trying to attach to the network.

If you've got a Macintosh with built-in Ethernet, that may not be as simple as it at first appears. Apple decided to use a nonstandard connector, which they dubbed an "AAUI," or Apple Attachment Unit Interface, which doesn't supply sufficient power to run a ThickNet transceiver. Thus, an AAUI-to-AUI adapter is needed, and the adapter must have an external power supply. The transceiver taps the Ethernet trunk, the drop cable connects it to the adapter, the adapter has a cable running to a transformer (which must be plugged into an AC power supply), and another cable running back to the AAUI port on the Macintosh. Needless to say, each of these devices costs money, so you may wish to install a NuBus card in the machine anyway, since they're somewhat simpler to connect to Ethernet.

If you use a NuBus card, the AUI connector is on the back of the NuBus card. A drop cable connects it directly to the transceiver. This is the simplest, least expensive way of connecting to a ThickNet network. Most Ethernet cards have an AUI connector in addition to one of the other two styles of connector, so the same card can serve different functions at different points in its life.

If you've got a Macintosh without expansion card capability, an external SCSI Ethernet adapter box must be purchased. Like a hard drive, it attaches to the SCSI port via a SCSI cable. It also has an AUI connector on the back, so the drop cable should connect that to the transceiver box.

Thick Ethernet cable is almost never installed anymore. It's usually just found in existing installations that were cabled in the late seventies and early eighties. New ThickNet cable costs about four times as much as Thin Ethernet cable, and twelve times as much as two twisted-pair UTP, on a per-foot basis. In addition, the difficulty of handling and pulling the cable drives installation costs up enormously, and the expense of the transceiver boxes mounts quickly, as well. The only real advantage ThickNet can offer is longer transmission distances, a benefit which has been rendered relatively paltry by the development of fiber-optic networking technologies.

9.3   Thin Ethernet

The next cabling scheme developed was 10Base-2, "thin" Ethernet, or simply ThinNet. Like ThickNet, ThinNet supports ten-megabit baseband communication. Since it's a thinner cable, and uses a more daisy-chain-like topology, it only supports a maximum network length of about 600 feet, though. ThinNet networks are, however, much less expensive and much simpler to connect to, as they require no transceiver. The cable is also much more flexible than Thick-Net, so it can be pulled through horizontal cable runs, where ThickNet has to be installed almost like conduit.

ThinNet cable is two-tenths of an inch in diameter, and usually black or blue in color. The specific name of the cable is RG-58U. Since there are several other types of cable which are very similar in appearance and name, but of very different impedances, it's important to be careful when purchasing ThinNet cable.

All ThinNet cables terminate in a male "BNC" connector at each end. These connectors are barrel-shaped, with two bayonets, making their operation somewhat similar to the attachment and detachment of a camera lens. Network devices and adapters all have female connectors, but since the network must have a terminating resistor at each end, no cable end can actually attach directly to a device. Instead, devices are installed using T-connectors, which have two female connectors on their longitudinal axis and one male connector on the perpendicular axis. The male connector attaches to the device, while the cables to the next devices to either side attach to the two female connectors. At each end of the network, the open end of the T-connector is terminated with a 50-ohm resistor mounted in a male BNC connector.

The exception to the rule is the Apple AUI ThinNet adapter, which is its own T-connector, with two female BNC connectors and an AAUI plug on a pigtail. Unfortunately, it's also internally terminated. Although this may at first seem

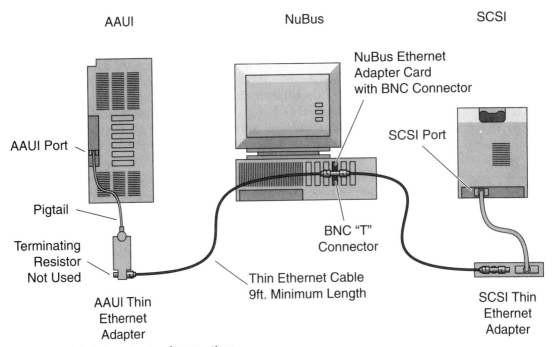

Figure 9.3 Thin Ethernet network connections.

convenient, it makes it incompatible with AMP's FastTap building wiring components, which are the most commonly used and best integrated system of ThinNet cabling components. The AAUI adapter can be treated in all ways like a PhoneNet connector in a daisy chain, except that it never needs a terminating resistor. Again, if the situation warrants it, a machine with an AAUI port can instead use a NuBus Ethernet card to connect to the network, although this doesn't present as much of a cost savings as the ThickNet case did.

The usual approach to connecting a device to a ThinNet network is to install, in the device to be connected, an Ethernet Adapter card with a BNC connector on it. Get one length of ThinNet cable and a T-connector. Attach the T-connector to the back of the Ethernet card, attach the cable to one side of the T-connector, and put the whole thing into the middle of the chain somewhere. Like LocalTalk daisy-chaining, it's really very simple. One thing to keep in mind, however, if you're crimping your own cables, is that each piece of cable must be at least nine feet in length. Lesser distances between fittings can create interference patterns in the signal, since that's near the wavelength of the signal.

If the device you wish to connect has only a SCSI port, a SCSI Ethernet adapter will again be required. As most such boxes support both BNC and AUI connections, it may be necessary to configure DIP switches to indicate which port you want to use.

Thin Ethernet is now installed primarily only inside rooms, in much the same situations LocalTalk daisy chains would be used. It is, however, a fairly robust medium, provided its length limits aren't exceeded, and can be very inexpensive if the cost of installation is not high, since it requires no other components. It costs about one-quarter as much as ThickNet, and three times as much as twisted-pair, per foot.

9.4   10Base-T Ethernet

The form of Ethernet cabling now prevalent is 10Base-T, which uses a star topology constructed of twisted-pair wire. It can easily replace or overlay existing active-star LocalTalk networks, running on the same kinds of wire and jacks. Unlike LocalTalk, it requires an RJ-45 jack, on which the transmit + signal is carried on pin 3 of the second pair, transmit − on pin 6, receive + on pin one of the third pair, and receive − on pin two of the third pair.

10Base-T Ethernet can run over any grade three or higher-quality unshielded twisted-pair wire of 24- or 22-gauge, for distances of up to approximately 300 feet. It's a strict active-star topology; only one device can be connected to any port of a hub, and thus only home runs are allowed. Twisted-pair cable and the wiring requirements of Ethernet-compatible star topology networks were discussed in detail in Chap. 5. The installation of user and network devices was not detailed, however.

Attaching an AAUI-equipped Macintosh to a 10Base-T network requires an AAUI-to-10Base-T adapter, similar in size to the ThinNet adapter. A twisted-pair line cord or drop cable connects the RJ-45 jack on the adapter to that in the service jack. From there, the signal travels over the building's horizontal cable to a multiport repeater in the IC, from there to a similar repeater in the MC, from which it's retransmitted back to all the other ICs and, through them, to all the other nodes on the Ethernet network.

Connecting a NuBus Macintosh requires a 10Base-T NuBus card, which will have an RJ-45 jack on it. The line cord simply runs between that and the service jack. Connecting a device which has no RJ-45 but does have an AUI isn't terribly difficult, requiring a MAU, or Medium Attachment Unit, to adapt the AUI's signal to one appropriate for a 10Base-T network. Of course, external SCSI 10Base-T Ethernet adapter boxes are available as well.

Many 10Base-T hubs have an AUI connector on their "cascade" port, the port used to connect them to other hubs higher in the network hierarchy. Since hub and client 10Base-T implementations are different, this cascade port is a client port, while all the other ports on the hub are hub ports. Only client ports can

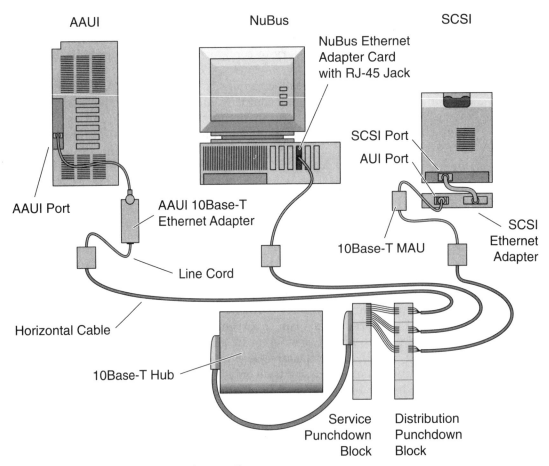

Figure 9.4 10Base-T Ethernet network connections.

connect to hub ports, and vice versa. Two 10Base-T user machines cannot connect to one another without a hub in-between.

9.5 FOIRL

FOIRL (pronounced "foy-ril") stands for Fiber-Optic Inter-Repeater Link. It's not a network cabling system or topology; it's just an alternative way of connecting existing Ethernet network segments together over somewhat longer distances than would otherwise be possible.

Repeaters can be used in any of the above topologies and cabling systems to extend the length of the network, but a limit is placed upon the maximum time it can take a signal to be propagated between the two farthest points on the network. This constraint is imposed by one of the limitations of the CSMA/CD baseband traffic control protocol, discussed earlier. CSMA/CD, to review, stands for Carrier Sense Multiple Access/Collision Detection. It allows multiple machines simultaneous access to the same wire, with the provision that they must "sense carrier," or wait until no one else is transmitting before they do so themselves, and they must be able to detect when packets have collided, so that they can resend. The two major problems with this protocol are as follows: If two machines sense carrier at precisely the same moment, both may begin transmitting simultaneously. This is a statistically remote possibility, but one which becomes more likely the more machines are attached to a single unrouted Ethernet network. The second problem occurs when a machine at one end of the network senses carrier and begins to transmit, and another machine subsequently senses carrier, because the transmitted signal has not yet reached it. This "widens the window" of temporal possibility of the first problem. The longer the network, the longer it takes for an electrical signal to propagate through its length; the more repeaters intervene between the distant ends, the greater the induced delay, as well. Thus copper networks are limited to about 2500 meters in total

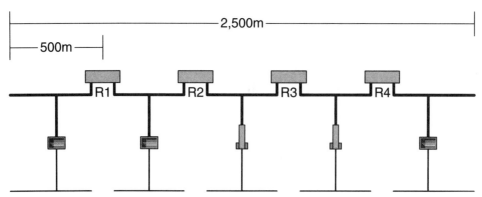

Figure 9.5 Ethernet length and repeater limits.

end-to-end length, with a maximum of four repeaters in that distance. This works out perfectly for five ThickNet segments, and ThinNet and 10Base-T fit easily inside the length limits.

FOIRL allows the distance between two of the repeaters to be extended to bridge a larger geographical distance, nominally 1000 meters, or approximately 3300 feet. It does not, however, allow devices to be connected to the fiber segment of the network.

The maximum overall length of the network should remain the same, 2500 meters, and both of the repeaters attached to the FOIRL link count toward the four-repeater limit, but the FOIRL link may be up to 1000 meters without violating specifications. Provided that the total length of the network remains under 2500 meters, many people have successfully exceeded the 1000-meter limit with one or more FOIRL segments.

In practical terms, the most common use of FOIRL repeaters is to connect the vertical cable in two different buildings located within a half-mile or so of each other. Here, two devices on the same floor of the same building need only pass through one 10Base-T repeater hub. Two devices on different floors of the same building pass through three repeaters: the one on their own floor, the one in the main closet, and the one on the destination floor. Devices in different buildings pass through four repeaters: their floor, their MC, the opposite MC, and the opposite floor's IC.

The problem with this is that the scheme pictured has already consumed all four allowed repeaters, so there's no way to add more buildings. Two is the maximum that can be connected this way. To go beyond two, Ethernet-to-Ethernet routers are required. Like LocalTalk-to-Ethernet routers, these routers filter traffic and retransmit as a node. It's the difference between the manner in which the two types of devices retransmit traffic that allows routers to be used in extending networks where repeaters won't work. Both types of devices induce some delay in the time it takes for the signal to reach its destination, but the repeater does so without providing its own implementation of

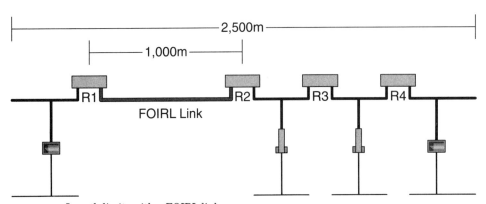

Figure 9.6   Length limits with a FOIRL link.

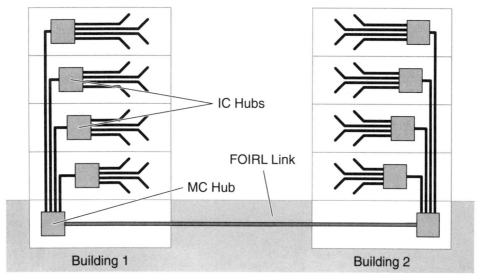

IC Hubs

FOIRL Link

MC Hub

Building 1   Building 2

Figure 9.7   FOIRL linking two buildings.

CSMA/CD, whereas the router acts like any other node and waits until the network is clear before sending. So although the router induces a greater, and less predictable, amount of delay, it does not add to the carrier sensing problem, and can therefore be used to connect two Ethernet segments which each already contain four repeaters. Many of the larger Ethernet-to-Ethernet routers are rack-mounted, like hub concentrators, and can accept additional cards to add more ports, so one router can act as the center of a kind of macroscopic star connecting the main closets of different buildings in a campus or businesspark situation.

9.6   The Solution

After reading up on the history of Ethernet networks, Mark decided that he wanted to use primarily 10Base-T Ethernet, running over his existing cable plant, with a bit of ThinNet for use in the equipment room and main closet, where the advantages of greater simplicity and quicker reconfiguration weighed more heavily. Since he found that NuBus cards which support both ThinNet and 10Base-T cost little more than ones supporting only a single standard, he decided to purchase those in large quantity.

Next, he surveyed network administrators at other nearby Macintosh-using sites, and listened to their stories of Ethernet upgrades. Based upon their horror stories, he chose the vendor who seemed to have perpetrated the fewest of the evils he'd heard cataloged, and called their technical support hotline to discuss his specific needs. He managed thereby to put together a list of part numbers and quantities of each that he'd need, and began shopping around for the best price he could find. Since Ethernet adapters tend to be warranted by the vendor rather than a dealer, price was the only discriminating factor he could see, once he'd decided upon a specific model of card. By spending long and tedious hours calling all the advertisers in the backs of the Macintosh weekly and monthlies, he finally found the lowest price and placed his order. After having diligently shopped for the best price on Ethernet adapters, he decided to splurge and simply order premade line cords, rather than buying a crimping die, a spool of cable, and a continuity tester.

Chapter
10

Auxiliary Services

10.1 The Problem

As American Grommet's daily business gradually came to depend more heavily upon electronic mail and file services, the need to interconnect different offices began to surpass the practical limits of e-mail gateways. Mark began to look for methods of permanently interconnecting American Grommet's two main offices, and to provide some limited level of service to the remote regional sales representatives.

At the same time, it became clear that several other services would have to be provided centrally to ensure reliability, amortize costs among a greater number of users, and facilitate management.

10.2 Network Services

In addition to the simple file and e-mail services, there exist other, less readily classifiable network services. Some of these are of similar importance, although their various natures tend to make them less widely used. Among these, we'll take a brief look at four: network backup, modem serving, fax serving, and time serving.

10.2.1 Network backup

One of the first services to be centralized at many sites is backup. Backing up is the copying of all files, important files, or recently changed files to a remote storage device to safeguard the data against accident.

One of the first, and certainly the most widely used, products which perform this service is Retrospect Remote. A central application runs and resides on a backup server, which should also have one or more very large mass-storage devices attached. Client extensions reside on other machines on the network. At specified times, the application contacts a client on some machine, and requests a catalog of the contents of the machine's hard disks. It parses these, following whatever set of rules you specify, and requests that the files be transferred across the network to it. It writes the files to the storage device, and proceeds to the next scheduled backup. Many options are available at each juncture of the process.

The first step is configuring the client software. Fortunately this can be done centrally, from the server. Serial numbers are entered, and the clients are cataloged in a list. The status of each client can be checked, as shown in Fig. 10.1.

Next, a backup file should be created for each machine you wish to back up. You should exercise caution in your selection of the storage device on which to locate these backup files. If it were your desire to back up each machine at your company once per week, you would need to be able to backup 20 percent of the machines in any given night. (Backup is a time-consuming process, so it's nearly universally performed at night, while users are at home asleep, out on the town living it up, or doing whatever they do when they aren't in the office.) Divide the number of megabytes of disk space to be backed up by the number of storage devices you wish to operate, and you'll have a fair indication of the size of volume you need to back up to. For instance, in a company with 75 employees, each with one 100-megabyte hard disk, the most you'd need to backup is 15×100 megabytes, or 1.5 gigabytes per night. 1.5 gigabytes can easily fit on a single DAT tape cartridge, onto three 5.25-inch magneto-optical cartridges (650 megabytes each), or onto a single, very large hard disk. This last option is not a terribly viable one due to the expense of large hard drives, and the fact that you'd need another one for each night of the week, you'd then need several more sets, to store away.

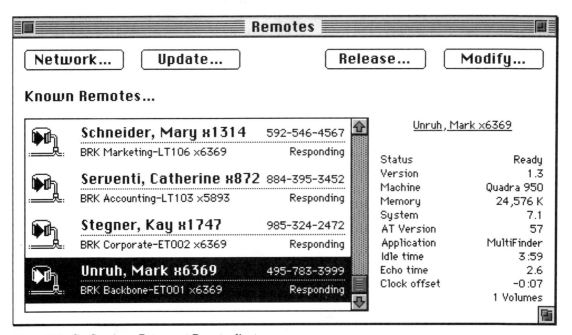

Figure 10.1   Configuring a Retrospect Remote client.

Removable media like the magneto-optical cartridges (something like a cross between a floppy disk and a compact disc) and the DAT tape (a small digital cassette tape mostly used for high-quality sound recording) are preferable, because they concentrate the expense of the storage in a drive mechanism, while lowering the cost of storage media as much as possible by divorcing it from the drive mechanism. Of the two, the magneto-optical cartridges are much more reliable, for a number of reasons. Magneto-optical recording technology requires both heat and a magnetic field to read from or write to the disk platter. Thus, stray magnetic fields cannot damage the information on stored backup sets, a major concern. DAT tapes suffer from this problem, as well as the fact that their videocassette-like recording mechanism and high data density don't result in reliable recordings of data in the first place. Unfortunately, using magneto-optical cartridges is on the order of eight times as expensive, and you'll need to either get up twice in the middle of the night to change cartridges, buy three drive mechanisms for your backup server or, most likely, buy what's called a "jukebox." Jukeboxes operate on magneto-optical cartridges in exactly the same way they do on 45-rpm records, swapping them in and out as they're called for. Many jukeboxes can hold up to twelve cartridges, for a total of nearly eight gigabytes, or enough space to accommodate the backups for each machine at our hypothetical 75-employee company.

Each Retrospect backup file contains both the information related to the client computer that it's associated with, and the data from that computer's hard drives. In the top bar of the window shown in Fig. 10.2, the "source" and "archive" buttons lead to the configuration windows involved in initially creat-

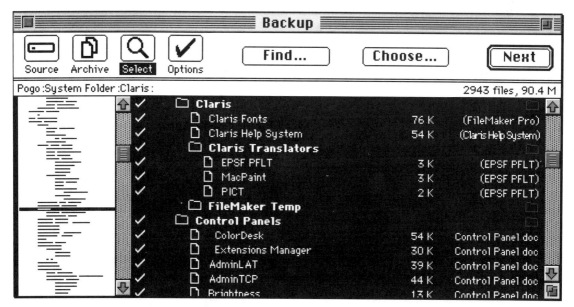

Figure 10.2   Selecting files for remote backup.

ing such a file. The configuration window shown here allows the selection of files from a client machine's hard drive. Here, we've simply selected "all." We could just as easily have asked it to select only those files modified in the last week, or files created by a specific application, or everything outside of the system folder, or everything that isn't an application. In addition, these criteria may be combined to form very powerful selection mechanisms. Most likely, you'll wish to perform an initial backup of the entire drive, and then perform a number of so-called "incremental" backups of changed data, until the medium you're backing up to becomes full.

For instance, let's take one employee. His 100-megabyte hard disk is 80 percent full. The first full backup thus consumes 80 of our budgeted 100 megabytes. The next week, he's modified a number of files, these totaling 5 megabytes in size. These files are backed up again, bringing us up to 85 megabytes used on the backup medium. The following two weeks, he modifies the same, or similar files again, totaling about 5 additional megabytes each week. Thus, at the end of the month, we've used 95 megabytes, and have "snapshots" of the state of the user's disk from one point at each week of the month. At this point, the backup medium should probably be put in dead storage at some other location, stored in a safe-deposit box or something similar, and a new backup begun for the next month. If the media were never recycled, and magneto-optical cartridges were used, this strategy might be expected to cost our 75-employee company about $1000 each month. More likely, however, is that the media would be recycled on an annual basis, so the level of investment would reach $12,000 over the course of the first year, and then only increase if a disk failed or a backup set were saved for more than a year. If tapes were used, the cost would be about $140 each month, and it would probably not be worthwhile to recycle the media, as that would aggravate the tendency to failure, and the monetary incentive wouldn't be tempting enough.

Once the backup files have been created for each machine, you need to decide when each should occur, and schedule them accordingly. Try performing a few backups and see how long they take. Remember that the length of time it takes to back up a given amount of data may change radically, depending upon whether the client is on Ethernet or LocalTalk, whether there are any intervening routers, and whether any other network activity (such as a second concurrent backup being handled by another server) is happening in any of the same network segments.

To schedule backup times, select the "Calendar . . ." item from the "Config" menu. Select machine names from the list at right, and click either on days of the month on which you wish backups to occur, or on the weekdays at the top of the calendar, if you want them to occur on the same day each week. Click in the "Cycle Run" box to indicate that backup is to occur on each specified day of every month, rather than just in the specified month. The options in the lower right control the behavior of the server. If "Install INIT" is checked, the server will install an extension in the System Folder, which will launch the application each time it's time to backup someone's disk, if the application isn't already running. Shutdown alert presents an alert dialog if you try to shut the server down immediately before backups are scheduled to begin.

Remember that each scheduled client must be turned on and connected to the network, as well. Dantz's client software helps in that respect, taking over from the Shutdown Manager part of the Mac's operating system when the Mac is shut down, and giving the user the option of suspending the shutdown until after the backup has been completed. In this way, even if users do forgetfully shut down their machines at the end of the day, the backup is still likely to occur, if the user doesn't explicitly decide to prevent it.

In this instance, as in many questions of server management, a macro package, like QuickKeys, can be invaluable in automating the launching or shutting-down of applications. For instance, you could shut down a file server in the middle of the night, giving any late-night users a little bit of advance warning, and then launch Retrospect, converting the file server into a backup server, and at the same time ensuring that there wouldn't be any extra traffic generated by AFP transactions on that network segment.

10.2.2 Modem serving

Another service that's best centralized, again for the purpose of consolidating the purchase of hardware and sharing it as efficiently as is possible between

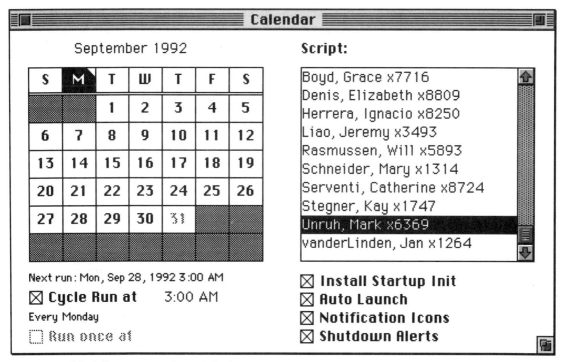

Figure 10.3 Scheduling automated remote backups.

occasional users, is modem access to outside telephone lines. In most companies it's prohibitively expensive to provide each user with a dedicated data line and personal modem. Where this is attempted, the cost of high-quality modems often dictates that slower or lower-quality modems be used instead. In no company, however, would all employees require simultaneous use of outgoing telecommunications channels. Thus this situation is, on the face of it, an ideal one to convert to a centralized client-server model. The number of telephone lines can be greatly reduced, and the number of modems can be reduced, while the quality and speed of each remaining one are raised, so as to utilize the telephone line with maximal efficiency. Maintenance is centralized as well.

There are both hardware and software products which provide modem-serving functionality. The software products tend to require a significant amount of processor time on a host Macintosh, however, and if they're serving more than two modems, additional serial-port cards, as well. Hardware solutions have proven, over time, to be more effective. Shiva, the major vendor of modem-serving hardware, has a number of products which perform this function; some contain integrated modems, but these are generally to be avoided, as they leave no room for the use of higher-quality modems, and are not as cost-effective as separately purchased components. Their two remaining products are the TeleBridge, which serves one LocalTalk-connected modem, and the EtherGate, which serves two Ethernet-connected modems. Here, we'll run through the configuration and use of a TeleBridge.

Once the device has been connected to the network, and a modem attached, Shiva's Internet Manager software is used to configure the device. When you've located the TeleBridge on the network, double-clicking on it will display the configuration dialog shown in Fig. 10.4. Many of the configuration options visible here are associated with dial-in, rather than dial-out; that will be discussed later in this chapter. The pertinent options include the dial-in password, which will be requested of callers before they're connected to the network; dial-in access options, either all zones or the local zone only; and the modem type.

The modem type must be specified because different configuration strings are necessary to initialize different models of modem for use with the TeleBridge. New strings bay be added to those available, or existing ones modified, by using the "Shiva Modems" application.

Once the TeleBridge has been configured, client software must be installed on any machines which wish to use the modem attached to it. This client software consists of two components, a TeleBridge driver, which appears in the Chooser, and a control panel called "Shiva Config." The TeleBridge you wish to use must be selected in the Chooser. If more than one TeleBridge exists in one zone, they form a *pool,* such that if a user selects one of them, and it's busy when the user tries to access it, the user will be served by the next available one, transparently.

The Shiva Config process runs in the background on each client machine, watching for telecommunications applications to try to access a serial port. When one does, the stream of data is diverted out the network connection,

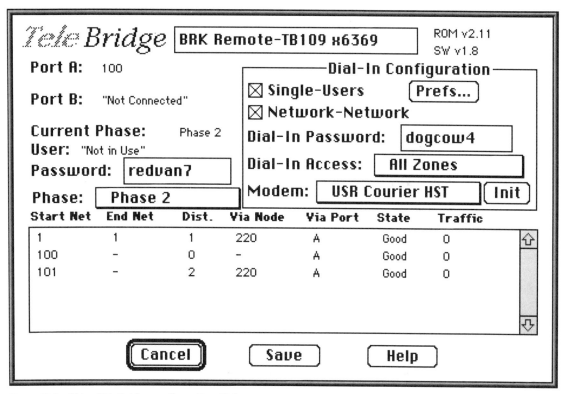

Tele Bridge | BRK Remote-TB109 x6369 | ROM v2.11
SW v1.8

Port A: 100

Port B: "Not Connected"

Current Phase: Phase 2

User: "Not in Use"

Password: reduan7

Phase: Phase 2

┌─── Dial-In Configuration ───
☒ **Single-Users**   (Prefs...)
☒ **Network-Network**
Dial-In Password: dogcow4
Dial-In Access: All Zones
Modem: USR Courier HST (Init)

Start Net	End Net	Dist.	Via Node	Via Port	State	Traffic
1	1	1	220	A	Good	0
100	–	0	–	A	Good	0
101	–	2	220	A	Good	0

(Cancel)   (Save)   (Help)

Figure 10.4 Shiva TeleBridge configuration dialog.

addressed to the TeleBridge, which passes it on to the modem. The modem's responses are then passed back from the TeleBridge to the Shiva client software, which passes them back to the telecom application. This process is called *spoofing,* since the client software and the TeleBridge are working together to fool the telecom application into believing that the modem is directly connected.

In the control panel, several parameters may be configured. First, the type of modem-serving device must be set—in this case, to TeleBridge. Next, the port which you wish to be spoofed must be set. Since this software has not yet been updated to Communications ToolBox awareness, it can only spoof the two existing serial ports, and can't be directly accessed through the Communications Resource Manager component of the Communications ToolBox.

10.2.3 Network fax

There are several methods of sharing faxmodems between multiple computers on a network. One, mentioned previously in Chap. 7, is to use an e-mail gateway, through which electronic mail is faxed to addressees. A second method is to share the faxmodem directly, as though it were attached to each of the client machines, just like a served modem. Unfortunately, Shiva devices don't facili-

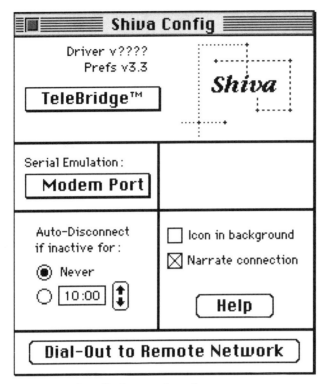

Figure 10.5   Shiva Config control panel.

tate the sharing of faxmodems in fax mode, since the timing requirements of faxmodems are extremely exacting, and faxes cannot be sent across a network in real time. Instead, outgoing faxes generally must be transferred across the network and spooled on a device to which the faxmodem is directly serially connected. Thus, most of the extant fax server products are software designed to be run on a Macintosh. One particularly notable class of exceptions are those with PostScript interpreters, which function more like LaserWriters. Documents are printed to them just as though they really were laser printers, but using a special print driver on the client machine. The PostScript is interpreted, and rastered into memory at 220 dpi, rather than 300, and sent as fax data, rather than imaged on paper.

10.2.4   Network time

One central service provided by many networks, especially ones which contain Unix workstations and larger computers, is time synchronization. There are few software processes that absolutely require accurate time, but some network services can be disrupted by extreme differences between clients and servers; file creation and modification dates are rendered meaningless if there exist any major discrepancies between machines on your network. As well, any time-based macros or scripted actions which require coordination between multiple machines on the network require synchronization of the clocks on those machines.

To fill this need, a number of time synchronization packages have come onto the market. Most are very small and inexpensive, and provide about the same basic services. When a machine is booted up, the client process searches the network for a server which advertises itself as being in possession of accurate time, receives the time from the server, sets the clock on the client machine to match, and purges itself from memory.

This better-than-average time synchronization client provides several features not found in some other packages. Instead of using a proprietary protocol, it uses NTP, or Network Time Protocol, a standard time synchronization protocol developed for TCP/IP networks. Thus this client software is interoperable with Unix hosts which provide NTP services, and the server Control Panel packaged with this software can provide time services to Unix clients, as well. In addition, it's sensitive to time zone and daylight savings issues, which become crucial in networks that span more than one time zone. Lastly, it can either set the time at every boot time, or it can set the time at some specific time of day, for machines which aren't regularly rebooted.

When you've managed to synchronize the times on the machines on your network to a common time, the next step is to synchronize them to a time that's close to correct, in an absolute sense.

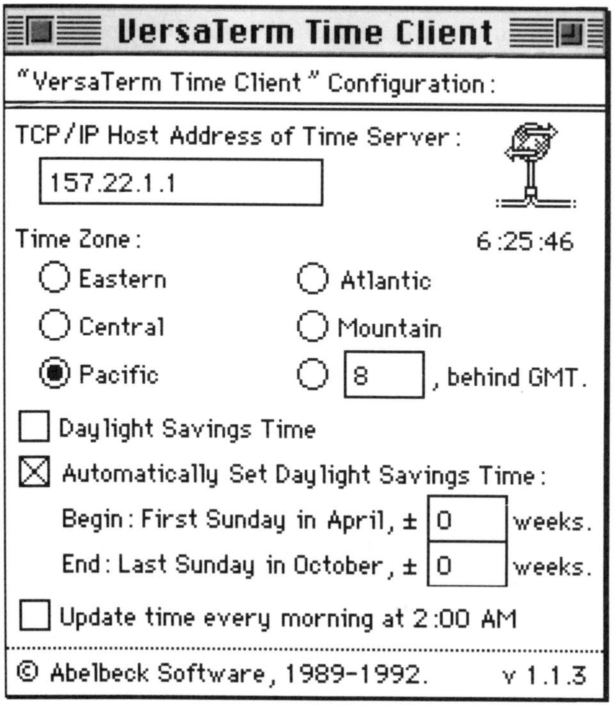

Figure 10.6 A time synchronization control panel.

The mechanisms from which accurate time is usually taken are called atomic clocks. Instead of being based upon electrical or mechanical workings, they're based upon the rate of atomic decay of a radioactive element, usually cesium. Atomic clocks tend to have a serial interface through which they broadcast a stream of data, much like the service that many telephone companies provide. Although many atomic clocks are maintained by private companies, many governments and standards bodies maintain publicly accessible ones as well. In the United States, two of the most widely used atomic clocks are those kept by NIST, the National Institute of Standards, in Boulder, Colorado, and that kept by the Department of the Navy, in Bethesda, Maryland. Macintosh applications which are designed to call one of these clocks and synchronize their host's time to it are commonly available in the public domain, or as shareware. Some of the better ones can maintain logs of the amount of correction required at each call, and interpolate therefrom, eventually maintaining much improved accuracy on the Macintosh host through periodic advance or retardation of the computer's clock.

10.3   Wide-Area Services

As computers become ever smaller and more portable, there is an increasing emphasis on allowing users to connect to the network and access services, even if they're away from the office. The medium by which this is achieved is, perforce, that which is the fastest universally available to your users, regardless of location. Although different schemes using satellite connections, pagers, cellular telephones, and other high-tech media provide appeal due to either portability or high bandwidth, they tend to be expensive and impractical to maintain. The "greatest common factor" which tends to be most commonly used is the ordinary telephone, and this is likely to remain the case until digital telephone service is in common use.

This determined, the next question is how best to use the limited bandwidth that POTS (Plain Old Telephone Service) lines provide. This can be addressed in two ways: by optimizing the bit rate and throughput achieved over the line, and by filtering what you send over the line to the bare minimum that proves necessary.

The first method simply requires a high-quality, high-speed modem. The speed is relatively easily judged, as there are a series of protocols defined for interoperability between high-speed modems, just as there are protocols used between networked computers. Like network protocols, different asynchronous data protocols used by modems each support a different maximum bit rate. A number of 2400bps data protocols are in use, and all are, for the most part, supported by all modems. 2400bps is not, however, a very satisfying rate of network communication. Keep in mind that transferring a file over a pair of modems will take much longer if the file transfer is being mediated by network protocols, which are optimized for higher-speed, multiple-access networks. The file transfer protocols you've probably used between modems, like

Xmodem, Ymodem, Kermit, and the like, are optimized in very different ways to provide for the constraints, and take advantage of the opportunities, of modem telecommunications. When connecting to a network over telephone lines, both sets of protocols will be used, leaving even less room for the actual data. 9600bps, or 9.6kbps, is generally acknowledged to be the slowest practical data rate for dial-up network communications.

The standard protocol for 9.6kbps telecommunications is called V.32, or "vee-dot-thirty-two." The next faster standard is V.32*bis,* which runs at 14.4kbps. A third and even faster version of this standard is, at the time of this writing, undergoing the lengthy ratification process. Although this provisional standard is currently referred to as "V.*fast,*" it's more likely to be ratified as "V.32*ter.*" (In telecom standards lingo, *bis* means "second try" while *ter* means "third time's the charm.") The V.32 standards are usually found in association with a set of data compression and error correction protocols, either Microcom Network Protocols 1-5, V.42*bis,* or both. These protocols provide two functions: They perform mathematical compression on the data as it's streaming into the modem, allowing a higher bit rate between the modem and the sending device than that flowing between the two modems; and they provide error correction in the form of accuracy checks on the data that's been sent. Since these accuracy checks further reduce the number of bits available for real data, error correction is usually found in conjunction with data compression, so the net effect is better in both ways: Erroneous data is not tolerated between the modems, and the net throughput is still higher than it would be otherwise.

As we saw in Chap. 8, the standard way of reducing traffic on a network segment is to use a router to separate it from the source of the traffic. This technique is adapted to telecommunications use by makers of half-routers. An advantage of this method is that there really is no difference between this network connection and a router, so it's an all-purpose solution. Apple has defined a special protocol to connect a single remote machine to a network, which performs more filtering than even a router would, and can thus provide an even more efficient network channel. This solution maximizes the throughput by reducing the breadth of possible application. A third, more general solution, is to avoid using network protocols and carry only one kind of traffic. This is the approach taken by several single-purpose products, particularly some electronic-mail servers.

10.3.1 AppleTalk remote access protocol

Apple's software which implements their dial-in protocol is called AppleTalk Remote Access, or ARA, while the protocol itself is called AppleTalk Remote Access Protocol, or ARAP. The ARA software serves as both remote client and host/server, and comes in several pieces. The two most important are the Remote Access Setup Control Panel and the Remote Access application. Due to the complexity of the ARA installation process, the Installer application must be used. ARA requires extensive modifications to the System file itself, which should not be attempted with ResEdit.

The Control Panel interface facilitates the selection of a modem CCL, or Command and Control Language script, which ARA will use to initialize the modem and send it commands. It also allows you to turn the modem's speaker on and off, and to select the serial port that your modem will be attached to.

In the lower half of the window, (Fig. 10.7), the behavior of the server process is specified. If the "Answer calls" box is checked, ARA will reserve the selected serial port for its own use, and attempt to answer any incoming calls that appear on it. If left unchecked, the server process will not be active. "Maximum connection time" allows the amount of time a remote client may be logged on to be limited. In addition, callers may be granted access to services resident on the ARA server Macintosh itself, or to the entire network, and any services visible to the server machine.

Once ARA has been installed, the Users & Groups Control Panel should display additional options for each defined user, appended to the bottom of the window (Fig. 10.8). Two options appear: allowing connections and specifying that a callback be made. If callback is checked, when a user calls in, ARA will determine who they are, hang up on them, and call back at that number. Thus, this feature is useful only when users call from a single predefined location, or are using variable call-forwarding. There are two reasons for using callback: security and expense. The implications of callback security are discussed at length in Chap. 13. Callback can be used as a cost-limiting measure if your

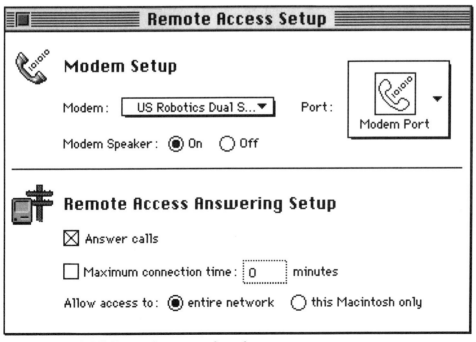

Figure 10.7 AppleTalk Remote Access control panel.

company has arranged for discounted calling rates from your central location, or if you wish to simplify the billing of remote calls to the company, rather than the users.

Once you've configured the Control Panel for the type of modem you're using, on both a server and a client machine, and you've allowed dial-in for one user in the Users & Groups file on the server machine, you're ready to make a connection. When you launch the Remote Access application, you'll see a connection document like the one in Fig. 10.9. Fill in the name field with the name of the user you allowed connections for on the server, fill in the password for that user, and fill in the phone number of the line to which your server's modem is attached. The "remind me of my connection" option posts a periodic reminder to your screen, which if unanswered will disconnect you from the server. This is to avoid both inadvertent expenditure on unused telephone connections and tying up the server with idle connections.

After these fields are filled out, you can initiate the connection by pressing the "Connect" button. If you've elected to display the status window, it will

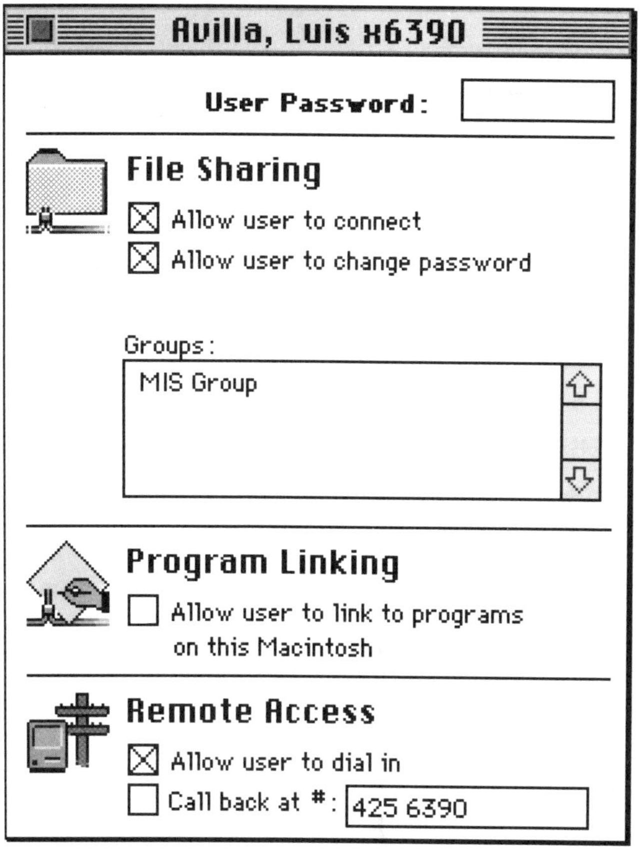

Figure 10.8   Users & Groups configuration window with ARA.

reflect the progress of the connection as it's brought up, and will thereafter display information related to the status of the connection, as shown in Fig. 10.10.

ARA also provides logging of both client and server activity. Actions performed in a server capacity are denoted by a blue bullet to the left of the date (Fig. 10.11), while client actions have no such bullet. Incoming and outgoing calls, connections, and disconnections are all logged.

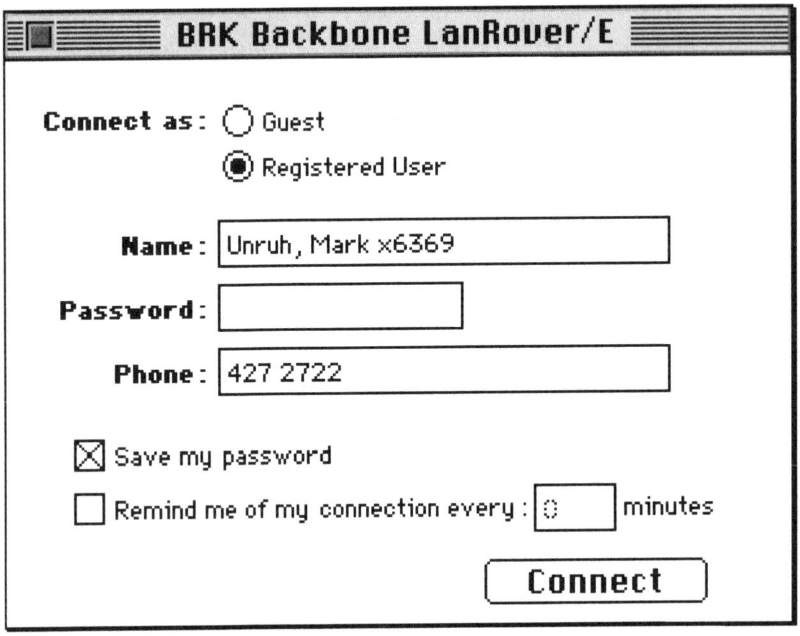

Figure 10.9   AppleTalk remote access client settings configuration.

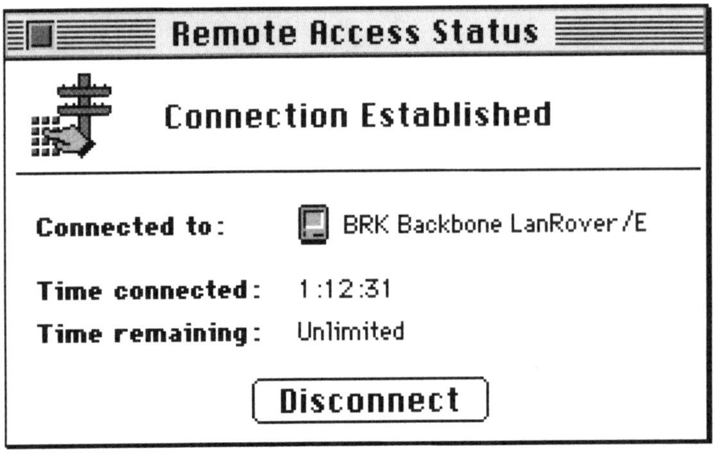

Figure 10.10   AppleTalk Remote Access Status window.

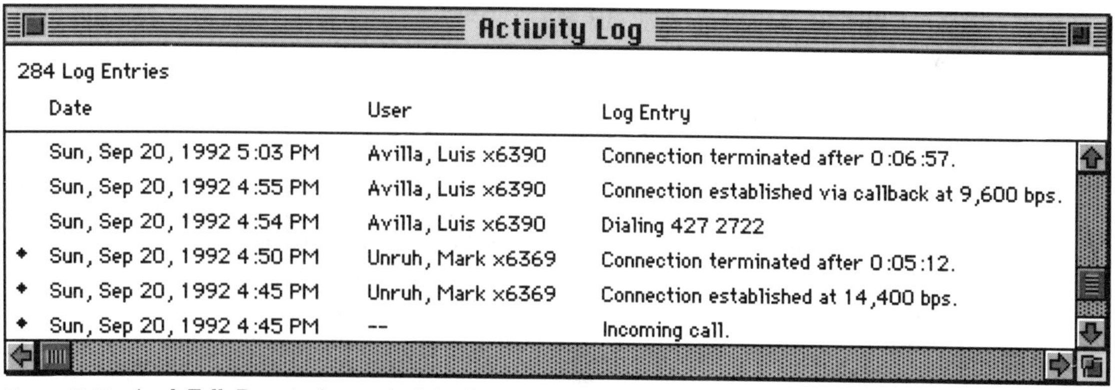

Figure 10.11   AppleTalk Remote Access Activity Log.

ARAP increases the efficiency of dialup connections in one major way: When a client connects, it takes a "snapshot" of the network and zone lists, using ZIP queries to a local router, and passes that information to the ARAP client, kind of like a big RTMP packet. Thereafter, the server filters out all RTMP packets and doesn't send them across the link. On the client end, ARAP caches the net and zone information, and traps for any ZIP queries generated locally. When it sees one, it fills the request with information from its cache, and the request never passes over the connection.

On the server end, a "proxy node" or "forwarding node" number is registered by the server on behalf of the client. The client appears to the rest of the network to be directly connected.

There are several other files associated with Apple's ARA software. One, called "Remote Only," is an adev, or "AppleTalk Device" file, which will appear in your Networks control panel. If it's selected prior to initiating an ARAP client session, devices and zones on the network to which you're locally attached will not be visible during the connection. The purpose of this option is to allow connection to remote networks which contain zone names, and perhaps even device names, which duplicate those in use locally. If such duplication occurs, a remote device may not be accessible at all, while devices in a remote zone will appear in the identically named local zone.

Another associated file is an extension called Remote Access Aliases. This file allows the use of aliases to remote files to initiate an ARAP connection to the network on which the files are located, prior to AppleShare's attempt to mount the AFP server upon which they reside. If a connection is desired to the same network all the time a machine is turned on, such an alias can be put into the Startup Items folder of the machine in question, and a connection will be initiated each time the machine is started. Closing a connection initiated via an alias may be accomplished by opening the Remote Access application, or by shutting down the client machine.

A final associated file is the Serial Port Arbitrator. When used on an ARA server machine, this extension should warn you upon any attempt by another application to use a serial port that ARA is listening for calls on, and ask you whether you wish it to relinquish control of the port to the new application. If a call is actually in progress, it will simply report that the port is in use, and will try not to relinquish it to the new application. The Serial Port Arbitrator works with some, but certainly not all, telecommunications applications.

Since ARA presents an obvious security problem, in that any user with a telephone line can set up their own ARA server, perhaps without even assigning a password, Apple has devised a rather complicated patch. It's in the form of a HyperCard stack available from APDA, a direct-sales branch of Apple. The stack prompts you for the password you wish to require of users, and returns to you a string beginning with the words SecurityZone_ and concluding with a long string of numbers, an encrypted version of the password. This string should be added to the zone list of one router on your network. Whenever a user attempts to start an ARA server process, the ARA software will perform a zone lookup; if a zone with a name beginning with the SecurityZone_ string is found, the user will be asked for a password. The user's response will be encrypted with the same algorithm used by the HyperCard stack, and if the resultant string matches the suffix of the zone name, the user is allowed to proceed.

10.3.2 Half-routers

If the single-user dial-in that ARAP provides isn't adequate for your needs, devices called "half-routers" allow full, transparent network connections over telephone and dedicated data lines. ARAP might be insufficient for a number of reasons: You might wish to do network management from home, requiring the ability to capture RTMP packets; or you might wish to connect two or more whole networks in different buildings, cities, or even countries, allowing all the devices on each network to see all the devices on every other network. These networks of networks are usually referred to as WANs, or Wide Area Networks.

There are two basic methods of interconnecting the LANs which make up a WAN. Asynchronous communication, the first method, involves standard, or analog, modems and ordinary telephone lines. Currently, the highest throughput you can expect over the long term on such a connection is about 20–25 kbaud, or less than one-tenth the speed of LocalTalk. Synchronous, or fully digital communication, comes in many more varieties, and tends to be much more expensive, both in terms of hardware investment and monthly service rates. The lowest common denominator in digital telephone service is 64kbps, often called a "DSO," or "digital signal zero." Different service packages offer different numbers of 64kbps channels. One of the most basic differentiating factors between different types of digital service is whether they're dialable or dedicated. Dialable services act much like standard telephone lines, in that you enter some kind of dialing code or sequence to initiate a connection to another subscriber site, and are billed using a combination of a monthly base rate and a per-call charge. Dedicated services are permanently connected and off-hook to a single fixed remote location, and are billed at a flat monthly rate.

The most common dialable services are ISDN, or Integrated Services Digital Network, and Switched-56. ISDN is generally available with two 64kbps circuit-switched channels and one 16kbps packet-switched channel which is also used for out-of-band signaling, while Switched-56 has a single 64kbps circuit-switched channel, out of which 8kbps is taken for in-band signaling to the central-office switch, leaving 56kbps for subscriber data. Long-distance ISDN connections (ones between sites served by different telephone company central offices) are also often limited to 56kbps, for the same reason, since many telephone carriers have not yet adopted out-of-band signaling methods for long-distance or "Inter-LATA" routed calls.

Dedicated digital services are very standardized, and are nearly always either 64kbps or 1.44 megabits, which is called "T1."

Digital services also require devices similar in some ways to modems to adapt the "terminal equipment" (or router) in this case to the protocols used by the digital service. These are often called "terminal adapters." Some terminal adapters support one or more forms of dialable service, some support 64kbps or T1 dedicated service, and some support both dialable and dedicated service.

The devices which the terminal adapters connect are called half-routers. A half-router is, quite literally, functionally equivalent to one half of a router. Thus two of them may act in unison as though they were one complete router. What's useful about this is that the two halves may be geographically remote, connected by a telecommunication connection of one of the types described above.

AppleTalk half-routers, used to interconnect LANs, are made by a number of different vendors. Several are AppleTalk specific, perhaps supporting a few other protocols, while other more expensive devices support AppleTalk among many other protocols. In the following example, we'll use a Shiva TeleBridge, shown earlier providing modem-pool services, as a LocalTalk half-router, using a modem and ordinary telephone line. The same device could support a synchronous connection, and Shiva's EtherGate, a higher-end model, supports two simultaneous connections to an Ethernet segment.

If you'll refer back to Fig. 10.4, you'll see a "Network-to-Network" configuration area, which is set to allow remote networks to see all zones on the local network, and to require a password of the person initiating the connection. The device is set to use Phase 2 protocols. Near the bottom, a routing table displays the known networks on the local network. If a remote network were connected at the time this table were viewed, its networks would appear as well, all connected to port B, which corresponds to Port A on the remote network's Tele-Bridge, or A or B on a remote EtherGate.

The Shiva Config control panel will be used to initiate the connection. Open the control panel and press the "Dial Out to Remote Network" button at the bottom. The dialog thus called up allows you to select a local TeleBridge to use, and a network to contact. Simply press the "Connect" button to initiate the connection, and be prepared to enter the password for the remote network. New networks can be added to the list by pressing the "New" button and adding a name and telephone number for their TeleBridge or EtherGate.

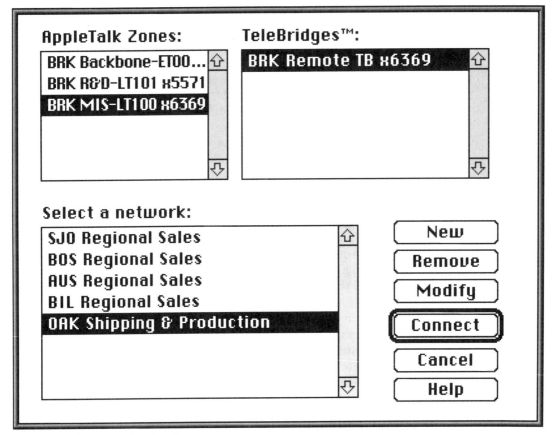

Figure 10.12   Shiva remote network connection dialog.

The user interfaces associated with other vendors' products feature the same basic elements, and most vendors use some form of standalone application, control panel, or desk accessory on a local machine.

10.3.3   E-mail dial-in

Some electronic mail systems, QuickMail for instance, provide for network-independent or "out-of-band" remote dial-in. This alleviates the bandwidth problem in a different way, by lowering the number of protocols wrapped around the data. Instead of a telecom data protocol, an error-correction proto-col, a multitude of network protocols, and the application's own protocol, here we only have the data, error correction, and application protocols, eliminating the bandwidth-hogging network protocol stack. In QuickMail's case, a BBS-like textual interface can even be substituted for the application protocol inter-face, if the remote client wants to use a terminal emulator, rather than the QuickMail Remote software, to access the server. This, however, is probably very slightly less efficient, since whole text strings must be sent to the user, rather than short symbolic codes to the client application.

In any case, these remote e-mail access systems tend to require a dedicated modem and telephone line for the server (often the same that's used for gateways) and a modem and client software or terminal emulator at the client end.

10.4   The Solution

Mark resolved to take the simplest and most direct approaches to backup, modem, fax, and time serving, but to try to cover all bases with dial-in access.

He configured several of his AppleShare servers to convert themselves to back up servers during the wee hours, and back up the clients on their local nets. He appreciated the potential cost savings DAT tape could offer, but preferred to put his trust in the higher reliability of magneto-optical cartridges, and so purchased several optical drives and planned the future purchase of a small jukebox for his most central server.

Always conscious of the impact new devices constitute on the traffic levels of each zone, and hoping to minimize the impact of the modem-serving process, Mark located one TeleBridge in each of the LocalTalk zones on his network. As well, he attached two EtherGates to his Ethernet backbone, intending that they be used for dial-out, network-to-network connections to other American Grommet offices, and for his own troubleshooting dial-in use.

Mark replaced a few of the modems on his e-mail servers with faxmodems, installed fax gateways on the affected machines, and purchased a single combined faxmodem/PostScript laser printer/plain-paper receive fax machine for his backbone.

He attached an old low-speed modem to one of his AppleShare servers, and installed software configured to set the local clock against an atomic clock, once each week. He also installed a time server extension on this machine, and timed clients on all his users' machines and the other servers, effectively synchronizing the entire local network to a single time base.

Last, he installed several ARAP hardware servers on the network's Ethernet backbone. Each server was connected to multiple V.32*bis* modems, and he purchased a pair of provisional V.*fast* modems, as well, to test the effect of their increased performance. He purchased the SecurityZones stack, and configured one of his backbone routers with a SecurityZone zone name, to prevent users from accidentally or unthinkingly turning their machines into ARA servers. Satisfied that he'd pretty thoroughly investigated the range of services that he could supply over AppleTalk, using Macintoshes, Mark began to think about the options that other computing platforms could provide.

11

Taking Advantage of Unix

11.1   The Problem

Having exhaustively examined the services that Macintoshes could provide for his network, Mark decided to look further afield. American Grommet's network had become pretty self-sufficient, but with the exception of the e-mail gateways he'd installed, it was still an island, without connectivity to the rest of the world. Moreover, many people had begun to ask for various services Mark hadn't heard of before, which he found could only be provided by computers running Unix, a different operating system.

11.2   Unix and the Internet Protocols

Unix is the name of a "portable" operating system, which was originally developed by engineers at AT&T Bell Labs at the end of the 1960s. When used in this sense, "portable" means that the source code which defines software can be moved between different makes and models of computer, and compiled to run on any of them. The Unix operating system has been ported to many different hardware platforms, and provides functionally identical operation on each of them. Unix has become something of a standard at universities around the world, because it provides interoperability between the often wide-ranging assortment of computers found in academic environments. The affinity that many graduates have for Unix, and software development under Unix, has furthered its standardization throughout business and industry. There are currently two "flavors" of Unix, one developed by AT&T Bell Labs, called System V, the other developed by the University of California at Berkeley, called BSD. The differences are primarily in the methods of maintaining the directory structure; those differences are transparent to users. There are, however, slightly different utilities which ship with each version. BSD is much more widely used in the United States, while System V is more common overseas. Although Unix is most commonly used on larger computers, many implementations of Unix are available for Macintoshes and other workstations and microcomputers. In the examples in this chapter, we'll be using A/UX, the version of Unix developed and distributed by Apple Computer. A/UX supplies both BSD and System V utilities, but uses the BSD file structure.

One of the keys to the interoperability between different hardware platforms which Unix makes possible is its set of networking protocols. These standard protocols form the point of interaction between different computers; identical implementations of the protocols, as well as the fact that Unix machines are nearly universally standardized on Ethernet hardware, allow them to communicate freely, despite differences at other levels. Like AppleTalk, the Internet protocol family uses a logical bus, and uses CSMA/CD, Carrier Sense Multiple Access/Collision Detection, flow control methodology. The Internet protocol family, or TCP/IP, as it's commonly called, even contains many specific protocols which parallel those in AppleTalk.

The Internet protocol family includes IP, or Internet Protocol, which provides a transport layer; ICMP, or Internet Control Message Protocol, which provides for flow control and echoing; TCP, or Transmission Control Protocol, which provides reliable flow-controlled byte-stream communication; and UDP, or User Datagram Protocol, which provides connectionless communication. IP is analogous to DDP under AppleTalk, ICMP provides a superset of the features of AEP, TCP is similar in many ways to ADSP, and UDP is much like ATP. On top of UDP and TCP, other higher-level protocols are built. NFS, or Network File System, is much like a simpler version of AFP. SMTP, or Simple Mail Transport Protocol, is a standardized protocol used by different kinds of software to deliver electronic mail. FTP and TFTP, File Transfer Protocol and Trivial File Transfer Protocol, allow real-time peer-to-peer file transfer, in much the same manner that Farallon's Timbuktu offers over AppleTalk. Like AppleTalk's Link Access Protocols, every IP packet includes an eight-bit "protocol" field, which identifies what specific higher-level protocol the packet is using. ICMP packets are indicated by a value of 1, TCP by 6, and UDP by 11.

11.2.1 TCP/IP addressing

The single largest difference between the way TCP/IP and AppleTalk work is in their methods of addressing. While AppleTalk uses dynamically assigned numerical addresses for each host, TCP/IP addresses are statically assigned. Static addressing makes a difference in the way management is performed, and in the amount of management and recordkeeping that must be allowed for. Before bringing up a new TCP/IP device on a network, an address must be selected for it by a network administrator. In order for the device to be able to successfully communicate with other devices and avoid disrupting existing traffic, the address must be unique. On a small network, this doesn't constitute a serious problem, but since many of the world's TCP/IP networks are interconnected, forming a global "Internet," the address must be unique not only to the local network, but to all other interconnected networks as well. Since the number of bits used to specify the address of an IP device is limited, specifically thirty-two bits, or four octets or bytes, there are about four billion possible addresses. Although this is a large number, it is finite, and most sites prefer to use contiguous ranges of addresses, which requires that extras be blocked out for future use. The task of assigning address ranges is handled by the Network Information Center, or InterNIC. The InterNIC isn't a fixed group, per se; it's a service contracted for by the U.S. Government, and administered by the National Science Foundation. Regardless of who's contracted to provide the services, the InterNIC can be reached at the electronic mail address info@ internic.net. Addresses of this type will be explained later in this chapter. Since it's usually a laborious and time-consuming process to change the address of a networked device after its initial configuration, and networks using addresses which haven't been officially allocated to them cannot be connected to the Internet, it's worth taking the time to request an address range from the InterNIC well before you're faced with the task of configuring TCP/IP devices.

The most common representation of IP addresses is in "dotted decimal" format, which is formed by converting the four octets of the address into decimal numbers, separated by periods. Thus the address of the Unix machine we'll be using in our examples, 10011011000101100000000100000001, would normally be written as 157.22.1.1, although the hexadecimal, or base-16 form, $9B160101, is used occasionally. The relative frequency of use of these different forms is very much the same as under AppleTalk: Decimal notation is used nearly always, hex is used occasionally by programmers, and the binary is usually only found in raw, uninterpreted captured packets.

The conversion between number systems is fairly simple. While the decimal system assigns a multiplier of ten to each successive place, the binary system uses twos, and the hexadecimal system uses sixteens. When converting from binary to decimal, divide the string into eight-bit bytes, and add up the places in each byte, the first from the right being ones, the second from the right twos, the third fours, and so on, until you reach the eighth place, 128s; you should have a decimal number somewhere between zero and 255. Then proceed to the next byte. Conversion from binary to hexadecimal is slightly more difficult, since neither system is absolutely familiar to us. The hexadecimal system, or simply "hex," uses the digits $0–$9 as they're used in decimal, and then continues on with $A representing a single digit with a value of ten, $B for 11, $C for twelve, and so on, up to $F, which is equivalent to 15. Hexadecimal values are nearly always annotated as such, either by prefixing with "$" or "0x" or suffixing with the word "(hex)," to avoid confusion with decimal number strings. To convert from binary, divide the binary string into four-bit segments, compute the value of the first segment, write it as a hex digit, and repeat with the next segment until you're done.

The InterNIC can assign one of three different *classes* of address range, designated A, B, and C. Class A address ranges are generally only assigned to branches of the federal government and the military, and to extremely large-

128 64 32 16 8 4 2 1	128 64 32 16 8 4 2 1	128 64 32 16 8 4 2 1	128 64 32 16 8 4 2 1	
1,0,0,1,1,0,1,1	0,0,0,1,0,1,1,0	0,0,0,0,0,0,0,1	0,0,0,0,0,0,0,1	Binary
157	22	1	1	Decimal

8 4 2 1	8 4 2 1	8 4 2 1	8 4 2 1	8 4 2 1	8 4 2 1	8 4 2 1	8 4 2 1	
1,0,0,1	1,0,1,1	0,0,0,1	0,1,1,0	0,0,0,0	0,0,0,1	0,0,0,0	0,0,0,1	Binary
$9	$B	$1	$6	$0	$1	$0	$1	Hexadecimal

Figure 11.1 Conversion of binary addresses to decimal and hexadecimal.

scale networks consisting of many universities or corporations. All class A address ranges begin with a single "0" bit, have seven identifying bits, and leave 24 bits free for the user to assign to different machines. Since there are only seven bits which uniquely identify these address ranges, there can be only 128 of them. The 24 bits of user address allow class A networks to contain up to 16.7 million individually addressable IP devices. Because class A address ranges begin with a leading 0, they can easily be identified in dotted decimal notation, because the first place is between one and 126.

Class B addresses are generally assigned to large universities and corporations. Like class A address ranges, class B ranges begin with an identifying string, in this case "10", or two bits. This is followed by fourteen identifying bits and sixteen user bits. The fourteen identifying bits provide for up to 16,384 class B networks. The sixteen user bits allow each of these networks to contain up to 65,534 individual IP devices, and the leading 10 locates the first place of all class B addresses in the 128–191 range.

Class C address ranges are usually assigned to small and medium-sized companies and institutions. Class C address ranges begin with the string "110", followed by 21 identifying bits, and eight user bits. Thus there can be more than two million class C networks, each containing up to 254 individual IP devices, and they can be recognized by a number between 192 and 223 in the first place of their address. The number of possible devices may be somewhat

Class A Network: Advanced Research Projects Agency Network

0,0,0,0,1,0,1,0	0,0,0,0,0,0,0,0	0,0,0,0,0,0,0,0	0,0,0,0,0,0,0,0
0	Network (7)	Local (24 bits)	
10	0	0	0

Class B Network: University of California, Berkeley

1,0,0,0,0,0,0,0	0,0,1,0,0,0,0,0	0,0,0,0,0,0,0,0	0,0,0,0,0,0,0,0
1 0	Network (14 bits)	Local (16 bits)	
128	32	0	0

Class C Network: University of California, San Francisco

1,1,0,0,0,1,0,1	0,0,1,1,0,0,0,1	0,0,0,0,0,0,0,0	0,0,0,0,0,0,0,0
1 1 0	Network (21 bits)		Local (8 bits)
192	5	49	0

Figure 11.2 Class A, B, and C address ranges.

smaller than you would initially assume since, as under AppleTalk, the number 255 ($FF) is reserved for broadcast addresses, and 0 ($00) is reserved as the identity set. That is, any instance of 255 in an address is interpreted to mean "any," while 0 is interpreted to mean "this."

Since our example network has been assigned the address range 157.22.0.0, we know it to be a class B address range, which could potentially include up to 64,516, or 254^2 devices.

Since a single large flat address space can become difficult and inefficient to navigate, we know that our network will be routed, and we can anticipate that we most likely won't need to put more than, say, 254 IP devices on any single segment of it; we will most likely wish to use routers to break our address space into a hierarchical arrangement, much like, and probably coinciding with, the zones of our AppleTalk network. The means of doing so is called "subnetting." Since we have sixteen bits of address space to allocate as we wish, we can designate the first eight as subnet identifiers, and the latter eight as device identifiers. Thus, in our address space of 157.22.0.0, the first two numbers will indicate our network, the third will indicate one of 254 subnets of our network, and the fourth will indicate a particular device. Bear in mind that our selection of eight bits for the subnet identifier and eight for devices was utterly arbitrary, and we could as easily have chosen seven bits for the subnet, allowing up to 126, and nine for devices, allowing up to 510. That would not, however, have mapped directly into either the dotted decimal or hexadecimal notations, and would have greatly complicated interpretation of network addresses. For instance, node 10 on subnet 10 (157.22.10.10, or $9B160A0A using the eight-bit scheme) would appear as 157.22.20.10 or $9B16140A under the seven-and-nine-bit scheme, while node 260 on the same subnet would appear as 157.22.21.4 or $9B161504.

The two major benefits of subnetting are, first, ease of navigation for users, since it imposes a logical structure on the addressing of devices, and second, localized broadcasts within a single subnet, which is especially beneficial if your network grows to include slower wide-area-network links to remote locations which could easily become bogged down by excessive broadcast traffic.

Subnets are defined by the difference between the number of bits used by whatever class of address space you have, and the number of masked bits in your *net mask*. The net mask is a 32-bit string composed of two contiguous ranges of ones and zeros which demarcate the part of the address which is host-specific. Thus a class B address would have sixteen bits of network information and sixteen bits of host information. If its net mask had sixteen ones followed by sixteen zeros, individual devices would treat the last sixteen bits as host address. If the net mask had 24 ones followed by eight zeros, devices would treat the last eight bits as host address, leaving the difference, the eight bits in the net mask, but not in the network address, as the subnet address.

The IP address of a Unix machine, its subnet multicast address, and its net mask are stored in a file called /etc/netaddrs. (Macintosh users find it customary to specify pathnames to files with colon delimitation. Under Unix, the

Network Address Range

1,0,0,1,1,0,1,1	0,0,0,1,0,1,1,0	0,0,0,0,0,0,0,0	0,0,0,0,0,0,0,0
157	22	0	0
$9B	$16	$00	$00

Subnet Mask

1,1,1,1,1,1,1,1	1,1,1,1,1,1,1,1	1,1,1,1,1,1,1,1	0,0,0,0,0,0,0,0
	255	255	0
$FF	$FF	$FF	$00

Subnet Multicast Address

1,0,0,1,1,0,1,1	0,0,0,1,0,1,1,0	0,0,0,0,0,0,0,0	1,1,1,1,1,1,1,1
157	22	0	255
$9B	$16	$00	$FF

Network Broadcast Address

1,0,0,1,1,0,1,1	0,0,0,1,0,1,1,1	1,1,1,1,1,1,1,1	1,1,1,1,1,1,1,1
157	22	255	255
$9B	$16	$FF	$FF

Figure 11.3 Subnets and net masks.

slash (/) is used in the same way. Whereas the root level of the Macintosh directory structure is called "Desktop," the root level of a Unix directory is simply named "/". Thus a path name beginning with a slash is an *absolute* path, originating at the root level, while one beginning with another directory name is a *relative* path, originating from the first-named directory. /etc, then, is a directory within the root level, and netaddrs is a file within that directory. The /etc directory, like the Preferences folder on the Macintosh, is used to store many configuration files, among other things.)

Under the scheme we've laid out, our example network can have up to 254 subnets, each containing up to 254 devices. Although there's no standard method of assigning numerical addresses to devices, it's good to establish some system for your site, and documenting it fully is critical. For the purposes of our example, We can reserve the device addresses between 1 and 49 for Unix hosts, between 50 and 99 for routers and other devices, and between 100 and 254 for non-Unix workstations like Macintoshes and PCs. If we want to closely follow our AppleTalk network numbering and zone-naming scheme, it would make the most sense to assign to each network exactly the same subnet number as it currently has AppleTalk network number. Thus, all the subnets below 100 are on Ethernet segments, while all those above are on LocalTalk. This simplifies the decisionmaking process when it comes time to assign an IP address, as well as making those addresses more intuitively decipherable than just a random number.

In addition to an IP node address, each device has ports, much like an AppleTalk device has sockets, subsidiary to its AppleTalk node address. As under AppleTalk, it's the sockets, rather than the node, to which communications are actually being sent, since the sockets (or in this case, ports) are the addresses for specific software processes. In addition, TCP and UDP protocols each get their own identical 16-bit port range, from 0 to 65,535, although the commonly used ports tend to be in the 0–255 range. Thus many software processes maintain both TCP and UDP ports with the same numerical address. As with the node addresses, port addresses are statically assigned. Although it's a very bad idea to change the port that a software process is using, since that's the port at which other processes will try to reach it, the file in which port addresses are assigned to most common networking software is called /etc/services.

11.3   Unix Services

Throughout the rest of this chapter, we'll be discussing the Unix operating system from a very Macintosh-centric point of view: what services Unix machines can provide for Macintosh users, how to set them up, and how to connect to them. For the most part, these fall into the same general areas of service that Macintosh servers provide: electronic mail, file serving, and print spooling. However, Unix machines can also serve as gateways to the global Internet network and allow users much broader access than might otherwise be conveniently achieved.

The remainder of this chapter assumes some familiarity with a Unix text editing application, since nearly all Unix system administration is accomplished by creating and modifying text files on the Unix host. If a terminal connection has already been set up between the Unix machine and a Macintosh or other microcomputer, and you plan to do your administration from there, you may be able to get by with using a local text editor, and copying and pasting between there and the terminal window of your terminal emulation software. To simply display the contents of a Unix file, type:

```
% cat filename
```

You can also use cat (short for "concatenate") to create, and overwrite existing, files. To do so, you direct cat to receive input, and put it into a file:

```
% cat > filename
```

Then paste in your data, begin a new line by typing a <return>, and type <Control>-C, the universal "end this process." command, to end the file.

Although easier in the short run, this approach is cumbersome; if you anticipate actually being responsible for and administrating processes running on a Unix machine, you really should learn at least one Unix command-line text editor, such as vi or Emacs, and become familiar with any window-based text editors available on your Unix system.

11.3.1   /etc/hosts

As under AppleTalk, human-readable names can be assigned to devices, so that end users don't have to remember a numerical address of, for instance, a file server, in order to access it. While under AppleTalk these names are called NBP names, in TCP/IP-lingo they're called "canonical names." In order to facilitate efficient management, under static numerical addressing systems like TCP/IP, name binding services are handled by centralized databases, rather than in the distributed fashion that AppleTalk uses.

There are two kinds of these databases in common use. The first is a simple table which can be queried locally, and has no provision for automatic updating or synchronization with tables on other devices. This table is the file /etc/hosts. It has an extremely simple format: one line, or record, for each device on the network, each line consisting of two or more fields, delimited by spaces or tabs. The first field contains the IP address of the device, the second field contains the name, or Internet address, of the device, and subsequent fields contain aliases which will also be recognized as references to that device. At this point, with only one TCP/IP device on our network, our /etc/hosts file would simply contain the line:

```
157.22.1.1    grommet
```

While /etc/hosts will be entirely superseded on our Unix host by *named,* the next piece of software to be described, it's still important, as machines which use TCP/IP, but aren't running Unix (like users' Macintoshes and PCs), can use local hosts files to improve network performance.

11.3.2   named

Unix devices which perform name-binding services for other devices are called nameservers. They do this by running a program called named (pronounced "name-dee"), which is short for "nameserver daemon." Unix daemons are analogous to Macintosh extensions, in that they can be launched during boot time, and run continuously in the background, unsupervised. Named maintains a database of many different kinds of addresses, not only pairing canonical device names with their numerical addresses, but also pairing aliases with canonical names, and providing e-mail routing information, all in response to queries received locally or from elsewhere on the network via the local host's TCP and UDP ports 53.

In addition to canonical names, which are the simple, one-word names by which our machines will most often be referred to locally, named handles Internet addresses, which are composed of the canonical name and a logical path made up of "domain" names, delimited by periods, or "dots" as they're usually called. Domains are the horizontal groupings within the hierarchic organization of the Internet. Our network will be organized as a domain by registering it with the NIC, just as we did to get an IP address range, and it will be included in a high-level domain, .com, which is short for "commercial." Universities are in the .edu high-level domain, governmental agencies and branches of the military are in .gov and .mil, respectively, Internet connection service providers are in .net, and other types of organizations usually register within .org. Thus, if we register the domain name "grommet," and the name of our Unix machine is also "grommet," its Internet address would be grommet. grommet.com, and the address of a user of that machine would be user@grommet.grommet.com. Since many organizations use one "gateway" machine to handle all incoming and outgoing mail, most nameservers will also recognize addresses which simply specify user@domain.domain (user@grommet.com, in this case), rather than user@machine.domain.domain, if they correspond to a user of that machine.

Named, or BIND, the Berkeley Internet Name Domain server, replaces and supersedes the functionality of the /etc/hosts file on your Unix machine, since /etc/hosts can answer queries only from applications on the local machine, and related to canonical name to IP address resolution.

The most important thing to understand when configuring named is the format of the database it uses. Like most Unix database files, fields can be either space- or tab-delimited, or both, and records are return-delimited. Unlike most, which use the pound sign (#) to indicate the start of a comment, named records use the semicolon (;). The order of the fields in each line is as follows: object name, time-to-live, address-class, record type, record data. Of these, the name field is optional; if left blank it's read as being the same as the immediately preceding record. Time-to-live is also optional, and will be explained in a moment. Thus a typical record might look something like this:

```
grommet  IN A    157.22.1.1
```

This record says that there's a machine on the network called "grommet," that the record is in Internet address format, that the record is of grommet's address, and finally, that the address is 157.22.1.1. All the records in databases for current versions of named will have an address-class of "IN"; that's going to be constant throughout the configuration of named.

The most important of named's configuration files is called hosts. It contains most of the information from which named builds its database. The first record in the hosts file is the *start of authority* (SOA) record. It specifies default information to apply to records which follow it. The name field in an SOA record contains only an "at" character (@), which is interpreted to mean that a new set of records is beginning. SOA records have seven fields in the record data. The first is the origin, the "fully qualified" or full name of the machine on which the database is stored. (In our examples, we're going to assume that American Grommet has only one Unix machine, which will provide all the functions, rather than several working together. If there were more than one Unix machine, others could act as "secondary" nameservers, keeping data from a primary nameserver in memory. The origin is the name of the primary nameserver, the only one to maintain an "authoritative" database, on disk. In our case, the primary nameserver is the only one.) Throughout named's database, addresses which do not end with a dot will have their domain names appended to them to form a fully qualified address. The second field is the *person in charge.* This is the address of the person responsible for maintenance of the nameserver functionality on the Unix host. The third field is the *serial number,* which is left up to the creator of the database to assign and increment upon each revision. The fourth field is the *refresh interval*—the length of time, in seconds, that a secondary nameserver should wait before checking with its primary to see if there are new records.

Although it applies only to secondary servers, the refresh field is mandatory, as are the fifth, sixth, and seventh fields, *retry, expire,* and *minimum.* Retry is the number of seconds after a failure to connect to a primary nameserver that a secondary server should wait before attempting again. Expire is the maximum number of seconds a secondary server should continue to use data which has not been confirmed by a refresh from a primary server. Minimum is the figure, again a number of seconds, which is used as a default when no time-to-live, or *ttl,* is specified in records which follow. The ttl, like expire, is the number of seconds unrefreshed records are kept in a secondary nameserver's database, but ttl's apply to individual records, rather than the whole nameserver. A special property of named databases is that carriage returns which occur between parentheses are not interpreted as the end of a record, but they do indicate the end of a comment. This property is often taken advantage of in organizing SOA records, as follows:

```
@      IN SOA    grommet.grommet.com unruh@grommet.grommet.com. (
    1.0                 ; Serial number
    10800               ; Refresh every eight hours
    300                 ; Retry every five minutes
    3600000             ; Expire after 1000 hours
    3600 )              ; Minimum ttl one hour
```

The SOA record is immediately followed by one NS record for each primary nameserver in the domain. NS records contain no name field entry, and have one data field, which contains the fully qualified domain name, or Internet address, of the nameserver machine. Since we have only one nameserver, and it is, perforce, our primary one, we have one NS record:

```
    IN NS    grommet.grommet.com.
```

The most important of the records which follow are the *A,* or *address* records, like the one used in the first example. In addition to one for the Unix machine, an A record is needed for each machine that's going to be communicating with it. At this point, an address-assignment scheme for your machines should be worked out. For our example network, we'll use the scheme we discussed before; in each subnet, we'll assign addresses in the range 1–49 to Unix machines, 50–99 to routers, and 100–254 to microcomputers. Devices with more than one IP address should be listed once for each; note that in cases with multiple immediately consecutive records for the same machine, only the first need explicitly name the machine. Thus our network administrator decides to name his Ethernet-connected Macintosh "unruh":

```
grommet   IN A    157.22.1.1

fastpath  IN A    157.22.1.50
          IN A    157.22.100.99

gatorbox  IN A    157.22.1.51
          IN A    157.22.101.99

unruh     IN A    157.22.1.100
```

Complementing the A records are HINFO, or host information; CNAME, or canonical name; and WKS, or well-known services records. HINFO and WKS records simply provide information about the host they describe, much like the Responder does on Macintoshes. Both are optional. HINFO records have two fields, one naming the hardware platform, the second naming the operating system. One WKS record should be included for the machine's TCP ports, another for its UDP ports. CNAME records are used to specify aliases, or alternate names, for devices. Thus, if we add the aliases "fp" and "gb" for the Fast-Path and GatorBox, and add HINFO and WKS records, our database is amended as follows:

```
grommet   IN A     157.22.1.1
          IN WKS   TCP TELNET FTP ECHO
          IN WKS   UDP ECHO
          IN HINFO Macintosh          A/UX_3.0

fastpath  IN A     157.22.1.50
          IN A     157.22.100.99
          IN WKS   TCP ECHO
          IN WKS   UDP ECHO
          IN HINFO Router             K-STAR_9.1

fp        IN CNAME fastpath

gatorbox  IN A     157.22.1.51
          IN A     157.22.101.99
          IN WKS   TCP TELNET ECHO
          IN WKS   UDP ECHO TFTP
          IN HINFO Router             GatorShare_2.0
gb        IN CNAME gatorbox
```

```
unruh    IN A    157.22.1.100
         IN WKS   TCP ECHO
         IN WKS   UDP ECHO
         IN HINFO Macintosh         MacO/S_7.1
```

Most of the other record types deal with electronic mail forwarding of different sorts. The *MB,* or *mailbox* record is used in situations like the one mentioned previously, where one mailserver machine handles all incoming and outgoing traffic. MB records specify the machine that mail for a particular user should be forwarded to. The record:

```
unruh    IN MB    unruh.grommet.com.
```

would make sure that all mail sent to unruh@grommet.com or unruh@grommet.grommet.com would be delivered to unruh@unruh.grommet.com, the name of Mark's Macintosh. Notice the trailing dot, which prevents named from appending the domain name, and the machine name from being read as "unruh.grommet.com.grommet.com". This is a common source of problems. *MR,* or *mail rename,* records provide aliasing for user names. Thus the record:

```
mark    IN MR    unruh
```

would guarantee that mail sent to mark@grommet.com would actually be delivered to him, rather than returned to sender with a "no such user" error message. Every site which exchanges mail with any other site is required to have at least one of these, aliasing the name "postmaster" to the electronic mail administrator for the site, so that people at other sites who have difficulty sending mail to your site have at least one constant, one address that they know to be valid.

Records of type MINFO and MG are used for creating mailing lists, that is, lists of people to whom all mail sent to a specific address is forwarded, with the return address pointing back at the mailing list address. This provides a means of facilitating small long-term discussions which wouldn't necessarily be appropriate for public dissemination.

MX, or *mail exchanger,* records are used by sites which are connected to the Internet to indicate to other such sites that they know how to forward mail to some site that isn't connected to the Internet.

In addition to the hosts file, named requires several other, usually much smaller, files to run. These are the boot file, which is read at the time named is launched; the rev file, which provides inverse name-to-address maps; the local file, which defines the loopback address; and the cache file, which contains the addresses of sites higher in the Internet hierarchy. Named, all these files, and the hosts file, are often put in a directory called /usr/local/named or /usr/local/domain. Named reads the boot file when it's started, first to find out in what way it should operate, whether as a primary server or as a secondary server, and then to find out the names and locations of the other necessary files. The record format is simpler than that of the hosts file. The first line of the file specifies the directory named should use for its files:

```
directory    usr/local/named
```

The next records, in any order, specify the domain that's being operated in:

```
domain    grommet.com
```

the fact that this copy of named should operate as the primary nameserver for its domain, and the location of the database that it's to serve:

```
primary  grommet.com              /usr/local/named/hosts
```

the IP address range assigned to the network, and the location of the rev file:

```
primary  22.157.IN-ADDR.ARPA  /usr/local/named/rev
```

the location of its local, or loopback, file:

```
primary  0.0.127.IN-ADDR.ARPA /usr/local/named/local
```

and finally the location of the cache file:

```
cache    .                        /usr/local/named/cache
```

As you recall, the local domain name will be substituted for the dot in the second field of the cache record by named, when it loads the file.

The rev file is used by named to perform name lookups from address information, rather than the reverse, which is named's more usual function. Thus the Internet address and IP address fields are reversed, and the IP address field is reversed internally, as well. The rev file begins with the same Start of Authority record as the hosts file, followed by an NS record. In the first field of each of the following records, only the local part of the IP address is included, and it's reversed:

```
1.1       IN    PTR         grommet.com.
100.1     IN    PTR         unruh.grommet.com.
50.1      IN    PTR         fastpath.grommet.com
99.100    IN    PTR         fastpath.grommet.com
51.1      IN    PTR         gatorbox.grommet.com.
99.101    IN    PTR         gatorbox.grommet.com.
```

Note the record type of "PTR" meaning "pointer," indicating a reverse format record, and the trailing dot after the fully qualified names.

The local file simply contributes the localhost, or loopback IP and Internet addresses to named's database. It also begins with SOA and NS records, just like the rev and hosts files, and has only one other record:

```
1                    IN   PTR          localhost.
```

The cache file, which should be included with your copy of named, contains the addresses of Internet sites which serve as primary nameservers for the high-level domains, like .com and .edu. These addresses are necessary so that name-binding requests originated by your users can be passed upward to the nameserver at the high-level domain in which the addressee's domain resides. In the case of mail, it can be sent to the high-level nameserver, from which it can be routed downward again to its intended destination. It's in the same format as the hosts file, but probably much shorter. The first few lines list the included machines as nameservers for your domain:

```
.                    IN   NS           ns.nasa.gov
.                    IN   NS           terp.umd.edu
```

and the following lines then list the addresses for the nameserver machines:

```
ns.nasa.gov    IN   A            128.102.16.10
terp.umd.edu   IN   NS           10.1.0.17
```

These pairs of lines indicate to named that it can pass mail upward to ns.nasa.gov or terp.umd.edu if it doesn't know how to route the mail itself, and that those machines are good candidates to query for information about other domains. The cache file does not begin with an SOA record.

Once the hosts, boot, rev, local, and cache files have been created and placed in named's home directory, named can be launched, and set to launch at each subsequent booting of the host machine. When launching named, you must pass it the location of the boot file, thus:

```
% /etc/named /usr/local/named/boot
```

so that it can find the other files it needs to construct its database. To make sure that it will be launched at boot time, you can include it in /etc/inittab or /etc/rc, both of which control the launching of daemons at boot time. In this example, we'll use /etc/inittab, which has an interpreted format, rather than simply being run as a shell script like /etc/rc. Each record is colon (:) delimited, with four fields. The first field is a unique process identifier, of between one and four characters. The second field contains a "run level" between zero and six which specifies under which operating conditions the process associated with the record will be allowed to run. The third field specifies what action is to be taken regarding the process; in this case, "wait" specifies that each time the pertinent run level is reached, the process will be launched exactly once.

The fourth field is the command to be passed, in this case to launch named, and pass it the location of the boot file. The inittab entry for our example is as follows:

```
net0:2:wait:/etc/named /usr/local/named/boot    # comment here
```

To make sure that named is running, type:

```
% ps -e
```

to get a listing of all the currently running processes, and look for a line ending with the name "named". After the next subsequent boot of the host machine, this should be repeated to make sure that named was successfully automatically launched. The number at the beginning of the line is named's *process ID,* a unique number which the operating system assigns to each process when it's launched. Named also copies its process ID into a file called pid in its home directory, for other processes to reference. The process ID, or *pid,* is needed to address debugging commands to named.

Named accepts two debugging signals: INT, or interrupt, which causes it to dump a copy of the database as it currently resides in memory into a file called /usr/tmp/named_dump.db; and HUP, or hang-up, which causes named to abandon its current database and create a new one. Both signals are passed as parameters of the kill command. Thus, assuming named's pid to be 169, the commands would appear as follows:

```
% kill -INT 169
% kill -HUP 169
```

The HUP signal is used primarily to cause named's database to reflect changes made to its configuration files without having to kill and restart the whole process. In experimenting with and debugging the configuration files, an iterative process works well: INT and examine the database, edit the configuration files, HUP, and repeat, observing the effect of your changes on the database.

Finally, you may want to create an /etc/resolv.conf file. Resolv.conf contains pointers to the IP addresses of authoritative nameservers, the domain name to append to user-generated host names, and any addresses which should receive higher priority in responses from nameservers. The format of the file is, as usual, one record per line, each record composed of two space or tab delimited fields: a keyword and a value. The three allowable keywords are nameserver, domain, and address. Of those, the ones which we're interested in are nameserver and domain. We want the nameserver record to point back at our nameserver, which happens to be the same machine. This makes more sense than may at first be evident, because by defining the authority explicitly, it helps some software resolve addresses more quickly. There may be up to three nameserver records, and they're tried in the same order as that in which they appear in the file. The domain record should contain the domain name, but no host name. Thus our resolv.conf file should be two lines:

```
nameserver   157.22.1.1
domain       grommet.com
```

11.3.3   Configuring sendmail

Sendmail is the mail-delivering facility most commonly used to perform the delivery of mail that's prepared and submitted by users of the mail and mailx Unix e-mail front ends. Like most Unix services, its code resides in a daemon, sendmail, launched from inittab at boot time. When e-mail front ends submit mail to the mail delivery queue, it waits there until sendmail is next active. Sendmail then parses the header and extracts the address string and return address string, or sender's name. It uses a file called "sendmail.cf" (which contains commands in a complicated text-processing language) to divine from the form of the address what method it should use to deliver the mail, then converts the address and return address in whatever way may be necessary to ensure compatibility with the machine that next has to deal with the piece of mail, and delivers it.

Often as not, the mail is simply addressed to another user on the same Unix host, and the mail is delivered directly, without further complication. If the user is on another host on the same network, sendmail must either determine the name of that host by looking at the address in the header of the mail, or by referring to a mail alias served by named. In either case, the mail will be delivered to the copy of sendmail running on the target machine via a protocol called SMTP, Simple Mail Transfer Protocol, which operates on top of the Ethernet and IP protocols. If sendmail determines that the mail is addressed to someone on a machine that isn't on the local network, things become much more complicated. The sendmail.cf file should always have an outlet pointing "up" the Internet hierarchy, toward a machine which may know what to do with mail that the current machine doesn't know how to deliver. Thus, the sender's machine may know of another machine on the local network which has been designated as a mail gateway, or it may be one itself. If the former is the case, it'll transfer the mail to the gateway machine, using SMTP. If the latter, it must contact a machine on a different network, which is directly connected to the Internet, and can pass the mail on up until it encounters a machine which can route it to its destination. There are two basic methods by which sendmail can transfer the mail to a machine on a different network: either using UUCP, Unix-to-Unix Copy Protocol, a very basic telecommunications transfer protocol, or across an intermittent TCP/IP connection, such as those provided by the SLIP (Serial Line IP) and PPP (Point-to-Point Protocol) protocols. The former method simply requires that sendmail deliver the mail to UUCP in a form it'll recognize as a file to be copied to some other Unix machine it knows about. The latter is more complicated, requiring that an IP connection be brought up across a modem line, prior to sendmail's attempting to deliver the mail using the SMTP protocol.

Sendmail can be launched from /etc/inittab using the line:

```
net8:2:once:/usr/lib/sendmail -bd -qtime
```

where *time* is the interval at which sendmail processes the mail queue. This is expressed in the standard time format, where 2h15m30s would indicate a period of two hours, fifteen minutes, and thirty seconds. Set the delay to a comfortable balance between performance demands on the rest of the machine and delay in the delivery of mail. Five or ten minutes should be reasonable. In this case, the -q option would be set to 5m or 10m.

The -bd flag simply tells sendmail that it should run in the background as a daemon, and listen on socket 25 for incoming SMTP mail.

Mail in the queue can be viewed with the simple command:

```
% mailq
```

Unfortunately, configuration of the sendmail.cf file is beyond the scope of this book. There are other books available which deal exclusively with the subject, and most Unix systems come with a range of preconfigured sendmail.cf files designed to fill different needs. Configuration of the UUCP, SLIP, and PPP wide-area links over which mail to remote sites is transferred are also beyond the scope of the book, and are likewise well documented elsewhere.

11.3.4   Configuring Yellow Pages

YP, Yellow Pages, sometimes called NIS, for Network Information Server, is a utility which manages a database of users, groups, and passwords, originally popularized by Sun Microsystems but now distributed with other vendors' Unix implementations. Originally intended to provide uniformity across networks, by keeping password and similar information synchronized between different machines, we're going to configure it so as to facilitate file sharing with Macintoshes, to be described in the next section.

The YP database contains a wide range of information, culled from /etc/passwd, /etc/group, and similar files on the YP master server. When used on Unix client machines, YP either overrides the local files or concatenates its database onto the end of the local file. It's important that each of the files which are used in the compilation of the YP database be up-to-date on the master server. /etc/passwd should contain entries for all the users on your network, not just the ones you anticipate actually logging into the Unix host with a terminal emulator; /etc/group and /etc/netgroup, a file we'll discuss in a moment, should contain all the access groups you're interested in, just like the groups part of the Users & Groups file on an AppleShare server. Those three are the only files necessary for our minimal use of YP, but if you're planning on adding more Unix machines, you should definitely consult the full YP documentation, and check all the other involved files.

The netgroup file is used to define privilege groups for users who will be remotely mounting directories, rather than using them from the Unix host on which they reside. Each record begins with the name of the netgroup, and is followed by fields containing the names of member entities or subgroups. Fields containing subgroups, other groups defined within the netgroups file, simply contain the name of the subgroup, while fields defining a member entity are described by a triple, consisting of a host name, a user name, and the domain name, comma-delimited and enclosed by parentheses. Empty sub-fields within the triple are construed as wild cards, meaning "any," while characters other than letters, numbers, or the underscore character (_) are interpreted as "none." The character traditionally used to indicate "none" is the hyphen (-).

```
accounting  (-,serventi,grommet)
all         (,,)
employees   mis   r&d   accounting   (grommet,,grommet)
mis         (unruh,unruh,grommet)
r&d         (-,denis,grommet)
```

In the example netgroup file above, five groups are defined. The groups *accounting* and *r&d* each contain one person and no machines. The group *mis* contains one person and one machine. Any person or machine constitutes a valid member of the groups *all*. The group *employees* is a composite group, containing all of the members of accounting, r&d, and mis, as well as anyone with an account on the host grommet.com.

When you've completed checking and updating your passwd, group, and netgroup files, check to make sure that you have an /etc/HOSTNAME file, with two fields, the first being the name of the Unix machine, the second being the name of your domain. (Not, in this case, necessarily your Internet domain name, but a YP domain name, which is associated with exactly one database. If only for simplicity's sake, it's probably best to use the same domain name for both.)

Next, change directories to /etc/yp, and enter the command:

```
% ypinit -m
```

which will begin compiling the YP database. It will prompt you for answers to several questions, and incorporate your passwd, group, hosts, ethers, networks, rpc, services, protocols, and netgroup files, if you have them.

Finally, edit your /etc/inittab file to invoke the two YP daemons, ypserv and ypbind. This should involve changing the contents of the "action" field, or third field, from off to wait, in each of their records. Thus inittab's YP records should appear as follows:

```
nfs1:2:wait:/etc/ypserv
nfs1:2:wait:/etc/ypbind
```

You can then launch the two daemons manually, or restart the Unix host.

11.3.5   Exporting NFS volumes

Network File System, or NFS, allows Unix hosts to share directory structures in much the same way that AFP does for Macintoshes. It works hand-in-hand with YP, in that YP handles user authentication functions, while NFS simply facilitates the remote mounting of directories.

If YP has already been configured with the names, groups, and passwords of the users who will be mounting NFS volumes, setting up NFS simply involves defining the *mount points* or specific directories within the directory structure which will serve as points of entry for remote clients, and setting the NFS-related daemons to be launched from /etc/inittab at boot time.

The file in which mount points are defined is /etc/exports. The format of the exports file requires that each mount point be left-justified, i.e., appear at the origin of a line, without any spaces, tabs, or other characters preceding it. If mounting of an NFS mount point is to be restricted beyond simply requiring a valid login and password, a tab or space-delimited list of authorized netgroups and hosts can follow on the same line. If no groups or hosts are specified, any user with an account can mount the directory from anywhere. As usual, pound signs (#) indicate the beginning of a comment.

```
/       mis                       # Export root to MIS group
/users                            # Export /users to everyone
/usr/tmp accounting mis r&d       # Export /usr/tmp to groups
```

In the above exports file, the root level of the directory structure will be exported, and mountable only by members of the mis group, defined in netgroups as including unruh@unruh.grommet.com. /users is exported as well, and is mountable by anyone with an account on the host. /usr/tmp, a temporary storage area, is mountable by any member of the three named groups, but not by other accounts, as /users is.

The next step is to enable the NFS daemon in inittab, so that it will begin handling incoming NFS requests automatically at startup. The line

```
nfs3:2:wait:/etc/nfsd 4
```

launches the NFS daemon and passes it the parameter "4" meaning that it should start four instances of the daemon. Passing no parameter causes a single instance to be launched. The more instances are running, the more concurrent NFS activity can be handled without remote-user performance degradation.

Next, mountd must be set to launch, either from inittab or from /etc/servers. Mountd processes initial requests from potential clients, and checks them against the privileges specified in /etc/exports. To launch it from /etc/servers, the following line will work:

```
rpc   udp   /usr/etc/rpc.mountd   100005   1
```

After restarting, you should find that the response to a "show all processes" command

```
% ps -ef
```

should include four instances of nfsd and one of mountd. If file systems have actually been exported, exportfs -a will have been called, and it will have placed the names of the exported directories in /etc/xtab, which should contain exactly the same entries as /etc/exports, the file defining what you wanted exported. Any of the commands

```
% showmount -e
% exportfs
% cat /etc/xtab
```

will display the contents of /etc/xtab. Later on, when users are actually mounting NFS-exported directories, the file /etc/rmtab will be created, and will contain entries pairing clients with currently mounted directories.

11.3.6 Configuring GatorBox
NFS-AFP translation

Once your NFS server is up and running, a method of accessing NFS-published directories from microcomputer clients must be found. Generally, the best way to do this is by translating the NFS protocols into AFP protocols, so that the directories can be mounted as normal volumes on the desktops of the clients. There are three points at which this could be done: on the host, on each client, or on another device. Products currently exist in all three categories. Ones in the first category are generally disliked for business use, because they tend to be labor-intensive to install and maintain, and don't accommodate varying user loads gracefully. Translation software running on a client solves the scalability problem nicely, but creates a different kind of administration problem: Suddenly you're responsible for as many instances of the translation software as you have users, all on different machines, in different locations. The third alternative, doing the translation on a third device, frees both the Unix machine and the microcomputers to operate entirely in native protocols, maintains centralized management, and is still relatively scalable. One drawback inherent in the third option, however, is that like a print spooler, it requires that data cross the network twice.

To perform this function, we'll enable an additional function of the Gator-Box router we configured in Chap. 8. First, launch GatorKeeper and select "Servers . . ." from the "Windows" menu, and add an entry for grommet.com.

```
 ▤■▤  BRK_R&D_GB_x5571  ▤
☐ TCP/IP                              ⇧
☐ AppleTalk Routing
☐ DECnet Routing
☐ Download Server
☐ GatorPrint Printers
☐ GatorShare Servers
```

Figure 11.4   GatorShare servers configuration item.

Next, open the configuration window for the GatorBox you want to configure. Open "GatorShare Servers" and select "Add new server . . ." from the "Server Access" menu. Select grommet, and click OK. Grommet should appear in the GatorShare Servers window; if you open it, you'll see a configuration dialog. Enter the name of the AppleShare server you want your NFS server to appear as, in this case grommet, and click on the "User/Group Info . . ." button. Select the "NIS (YP)" radio button, and enter the domain name, in this case grommet again. Click OK, close the configuration window, and restart the GatorBox. In a minute or so, a new AppleShare server named grommet should appear in the zone on the LocalTalk side of the GatorBox.

If mounting an NFS directory doesn't actually work, it's important to take note of what point in the process the error occurs. If passwords are rejected, it's likely that there's a problem with your YP database, and you should check the source files from which it was built. If the password is accepted, but the GatorBox can't get a list of mount points, there's a problem with NFS, and you should check whether the appropriate daemons are running, and whether anything has actually been exported.

Once things are working, you may wish to experiment with the options which can be reached by pressing the "NFS Mount Points . . ." button, at the same level of the interface as the "User/Group Info . . ." button.

AppleSingle and AppleDouble are two ways of dealing with the discrepancy between Unix data files, which tend to be plain text, and Macintosh files,

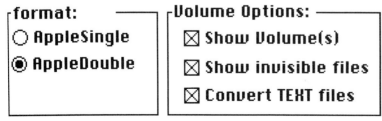

Figure 11.5   Unix to Macintosh file conversion options.

which have two "forks," a data fork and a resource fork. The resource fork of a data file is binary information, while the data fork may be text. AppleDouble stores these as two separate files on the Unix host, while AppleSingle combines them into a single file. AppleDouble creates twice as many files on your Unix disk, but allows the data forks to be edited from the Unix host.

"Show invisible files" allows AFP clients to see Unix files which begin with a dot, and are thus normally invisible on the Unix host. In conjunction with the use of AppleDouble format, this allows users to modify the configuration files for their accounts from a Macintosh. "Convert TEXT files" simply translates Macintosh text files into Unix text files, and vice versa, rather than using AppleSingle or AppleDouble format.

11.3.7 Configuring lpr

The utility used for printing on Unix hosts is *lpr,* short for "line printer," from the days when documents printed from Unix hosts were characterized by huge stacks of green-and-white-striped paper. The utility, however, proved adaptable, and works fine with modern PostScript laser printers. The idea behind lpr is that, on a network of Unix machines, one or more will have serially connected printers. Each machine runs a daemon, *lpd,* which handles print jobs. If there's a locally attached printer, it spools the jobs and prints them to the printer in order. If there's no printer directly attached, it forwards jobs to one of the machines which does have a printer, where they become local jobs and enter the queue. If that machine is unavailable, it queues jobs until it reappears, and then forwards them.

Since our example network has only one Unix machine, it wouldn't be cost-effective to attach a LaserWriter serially, since that would make it much more difficult for the non-Unix machines on the network to use. Instead, we'll enable another feature of our GatorBox, which allows it to act as though it were a Unix machine with a local printer, when in fact it's translating print jobs from the Unix lpr protocol to the AppleTalk PAP protocol, and sending them to one of the LaserWriters or spoolers already on our network.

The spooler daemon, lpd, configures itself by reading a file called /etc/print-cap each time it's called upon to receive a print job. The printcap file uses a file format in which the fields of each record are colon-delimited, and a record can be continued onto the following line by ending a line with a backslash (\). Each record begins with the names by which the printer can be referred to, delimited by pipes (|). The use of the name *lp* defines the default printer, unless the default is overridden by an individual user through the use of the PRINTER environment variable. The following fields, in any order, are labeled with two-letter titles, followed by an equals sign (=), followed by the value of the field. An lp field is used to specify the location of the device driver for a locally connected printer, but is left blank to indicate that a printer is connected to a remote machine. The *rm* field contains the name of the remote machine to which the printer is attached. The *rp* field defines the printer name at the remote machine. The *sp* field defines the location of the local spool directory for the printer, which you'll have to create. The following lines, then, would define two printers, both appearing to be directly connected to the GatorBox router:

```
lp|backbone:\
        :lp=:\
        :rm=gatorbox:\
        :rp=backbone:\
        :sd=/usr/spool/lpd/gatorbox/backbone:

mis:\
        :lp=:\
        :rm=gatorbox:\
        :rp=mis:\
        :sd=/usr/spool/lpd/gatorbox/mis:
```

To create the spool directories, first switch directories to /usr/spool/lpd:

```
% cd /usr/spool/lpd
```

Then make the "gatorbox" directory, and the subdirectories for the backbone and mis LaserWriters

```
% mkdir gatorbox gatorbox/backbone gatorbox/mis
```

Next, change the owner and group to "daemon" so that lpd can access the directory:

```
% chown daemon gatorbox gatorbox/backbone gatorbox/mis
% chgrp daemon gatorbox gatorbox/backbone gatorbox/mis
```

Last, change the permissions, or "mode" of the spool directories, such that anything in the "daemon" group can read, write, and execute files from the directories, and other users and processes can read and execute, but not write.

```
% chmod 775 gatorbox gatorbox/backbone gatorbox/mis
```

The mode of a file or directory is expressed as follows: The hundreds' place represents the owner, the tens' place represents the group, and the ones' place represents other users. In each place, the value is equal to the sum of three values: four for read, two for write, and one for execute. Thus a seven in any place means full access. A five indicates read and execute, but no write privileges, while a four would be read-only, and a zero would mean no access privileges.

You can, if you wish, log lpd errors, by including an *lf* field, with a path to a file that errors can be written to

```
:lf=/usr/adm/lpd.errs:
```

If you do this, be sure to actually create the file you've named, and change its owner and group to daemon and its mode to 664. Creating a new file under

Unix is accomplished by copying an empty file, which is provided with your Unix distribution. Thus the command

```
% cp /dev/null /usr/adm/lpd.errs
```

would create the file needed for logging errors, in accordance with the /etc/printcap field above.

11.3.8   Configuring GatorBox lpr translation

To make the GatorBox begin accepting lpr print requests on behalf of the two laser printers, first open GatorKeeper, open the configuration window for the GatorBox, and select "GatorPrint Printers."

Fill in the name of the printer as it appeared in the rp field of its printcap entry, the exact AppleTalk NBP-registered name of the printer, and the exact zone name in which the printer is to be found. To tell the GatorBox to convert the text files it receives from the Unix host to PostScript files before sending them to the laser printer, check the "Use Text to PostScript Filter" box, and select a point size and font to use. The only reason not to do this would be if you were only going to print pure PostScript documents from your Unix host, which requires a PostScript translator like Adobe's TranScript software running on the Unix host. "Map International Characters" should only be turned

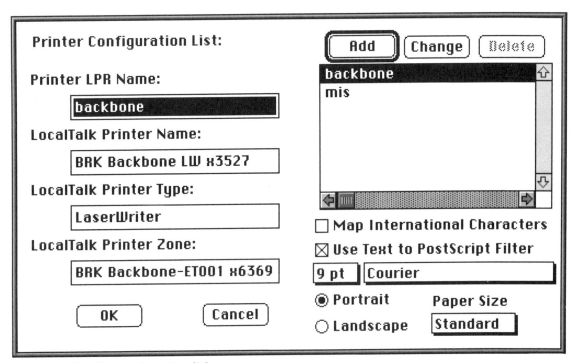

Figure 11.6   GatorPrint configuration dialog.

on if you expect to be printing documents in which characters with accent marks (é, ü, ç, ñ, etc.) are represented by hexadecimal strings.

Make sure all your changes are saved, and restart the GatorBox.

11.4   Macintosh Connectivity

Once networking services have been established on a Unix host, means of accessing them from microcomputers on your network must be devised. The first step in accessing IP-based services from a Macintosh is to get the IP protocol stack running on the Macintosh, so that it can communicate with the server device.

11.4.1   Configuring MacTCP

The Macintosh implementation of the IP protocol stack is called MacTCP. It does several things: First, it turns Macintoshes which are directly connected to Ethernet into native TCP/IP speakers. Second, it allows Macintoshes on LocalTalk to send and receive "encapsulated" IP packets, which are segmented into LocalTalk-sized packets with LocalTalk headers, and exchanged with a MacTCP router. Third, it handles ICMP transactions, like echo requests, just as any AppleTalk node responds to an AEP Request packet.

MacTCP is packaged in the form of a Control Panel. When it's been put into the Control Panels folder and the host Macintosh rebooted, its initial configuration window will contain icons representing the different connection methods available, and a field for the Macintosh's IP address.

In Fig. 11.7, the host machine has EtherTalk selected in the Networks Control Panel, so EtherTalk is available, instead of LocalTalk, as the medium for MacTCP encapsulated packets. If LocalTalk were selected in the Networks Control Panel, and there were no Ethernet cards in the host Macintosh, LocalTalk would be the only option available here, as well. Since the current Macintosh is directly connected to the same Ethernet as our Unix host, we can select one of the two Ethernet cards and use the IP protocols directly, rather than encapsulated. We already figured out the addresses of our Macintosh when we were setting up the named database on our Unix host, so we can fill in the IP address in the appropriate field, and press the "More . . ." button to continue the configuration.

In the dialog shown in Fig. 11.8, we can specify that we want the IP address that we've just assigned this machine to always be used ("Manually"), rather than assigned by a MacTCP router ("Server"). We can specify the address of that router, if we wish, in the Gateway Address field, and we should fill in the domain name and address of our nameserver in the correct fields, as well. Additional domain nameservers can be added on subsequent lines, if you have more than one Unix host running named. These are used, in the order they appear, if the primary one does not respond. By inserting just a period in the "Domain" field of a record, the nameserver at the indicated IP address is designated a valid nameserver for any domain.

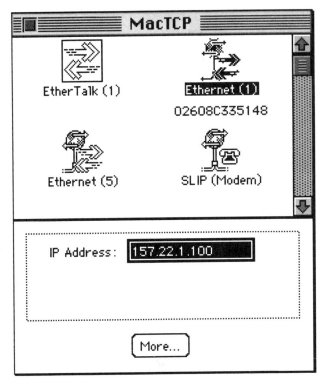

Figure 11.7   MacTCP initial configuration window.

If you recall the discussion of subnet masking at the beginning of this chapter, it's just as critical that we apply it correctly here as it was in setting up the Unix host. First, select the address range class that you were assigned by the NIC from the pop-up menu near the top of the screen. Then drag the small handle on top of the bit-string representation to the correct point, dividing the node address from the subnet address. The number of bits and the subnet and node address below will change as you drag the handle. Close the configuration windows and restart the machine. Any time a change is made to MacTCP's configuration, the Macintosh must be restarted for it to take effect.

It's important to note that unlike AppleTalk, which becomes active during the boot process, MacTCP does not become active until some IP-speaking program opens it for use. There are a variety of programs which can do so, including any telnet-based terminal emulator. Using a system extension which loads at boot time and opens MacTCP can be useful, especially for troubleshooting procedures. There are a variety of such extensions, including publicly distributable and commercial Network Time Protocol clients, and a Trivial File Transfer Protocol server which comes with the Cayman GatorBox, called "GatorBox UDP-TFTP."

You can test whether you correctly configured the address by pinging it from the Unix host. If it's been assigned the correct address, and some program has opened it, each of the commands

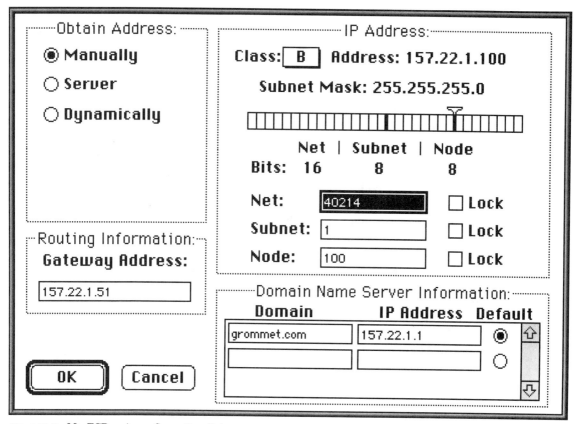

Figure 11.8 MacTCP main configuration dialog.

```
% ping 157.22.1.100
% ping unruh.grommet.com
% ping unruh
```

should result in a stream of lines similar to

```
64 bytes from 157.22.1.100: icmp_seq=0. time=16. ms
64 bytes from 157.22.1.100: icmp_seq=1. time=0. ms
64 bytes from 157.22.1.100: icmp_seq=2. time=0. ms
```

which can be stopped by typing <Control>-C. If only the first works, you know that the address has been correctly configured, but that named on the Unix host, which should resolve names to addresses, is not, and you should begin trying to debug named by dumping and examining its database.

To complete the configuration of MacTCP, you need to put a copy of your /usr/local/named/hosts file into the Macintosh's System Folder, and name it "Hosts". It's important that this file be in the full named-type format, rather than just the simple /etc/hosts style, which will not work. This file serves to "jump start" MacTCP with a list of addresses that it doesn't need to look up from the nameserver. The more complete the hosts file is, the less network traffic MacTCP will generate name resolution requests, but the more work you have to do when you update addresses.

11.4.2 Configuring MacTCP routing

To provide MacTCP service to Macintoshes on LocalTalk, you must configure one or more of your routers to serve as MacTCP-to-TCP/IP gateways. Routers so configured will provide two services: They will accept MacTCP packets, that is, IP packets encapsulated in LocalTalk or even, indirectly, in EtherTalk; and they will dynamically assign IP addresses to Macintoshes which don't have preassigned ones, from a range specified by the network administrator.

In Fig. 11.9, unruh, which is directly attached to Ethernet, can use native IP protocols in transactions with grommet, the Unix host. The two Macintoshes on the LocalTalk networks, however, can't put IP packets onto the networks to which they're attached, since there's no IP packet type defined under LocalTalk, as there is under Ethernet. Thus if the FastPath were configured correctly, and grommet pinged serventi, an ICMP packet would be generated, and grommet would, upon realizing that serventi was in a different subnet, consult its routing table and send the packet to the FastPath's Ethernet address, but with serventi's IP address. The FastPath, recognizing that 157.22.100.0 was the subnet on its other port, would receive the packet, encapsulate it by putting a LocalTalk header on it, treating the entire IP packet as data, and retransmit the new LocalTalk MacTCP (DDP type 22) packet out its LocalTalk port, onto subnet 100, addressed to the MacTCP socket on serventi. The MacTCP process on serventi would then decapsulate the packet and, upon finding the IP packet thus revealed to be an ICMP Echo Request, would generate an ICMP Echo packet addressed to 157.22.1.1. That would be encapsulated in a LocalTalk packet addressed to the router, as specified in the MacTCP main configuration dialog. The FastPath, upon receiving the packet, would decapsulate it, examine the address, and, upon determining that subnet 157.22.1.0 was on its Ethernet port, would send the ICMP

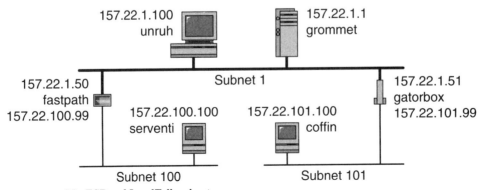

Figure 11.9 MacTCP and LocalTalk subnets.

packet to grommet, using its own Ethernet, but serventi's IP, return addresses.

To make this work, we need three things correctly configured: the MacTCP Control Panel on the LocalTalk Macintosh, the routed ("route-dee," the Unix routing daemon) database on the Unix host, and the MacTCP gateway functionality of the intervening router.

The only difference in configuring the MacTCP Control Panel is that under LocalTalk, a list of zones is presented, and you have to select the zone in which the MacTCP/IP gateway you want to use is located. This is accomplished by choosing the zone name from the pop-up menu beneath the LocalTalk icon which appears in the MacTCP initial configuration window if LocalTalk is selected in the Networks Control Panel. The local zone should appear preselected, by default.

Since we're using subnets on LocalTalk, only the local router's zone should be chosen. Other routers will be configured to handle subnet routing to other subnets, and would be unable to service a node outside their own subnet.

The most difficult part of bringing up LocalTalk MacTCP service is configuration of the routers. Although the conceptual requirements are the same for any router performing this function, configuration software for different vendors' routers often masks this similarity, rather than emphasizing it.

The requirements are these: IP addresses and subnet masks for both LocalTalk and Ethernet ports; one range of dynamically assigned and one range of statically assigned addresses for LocalTalk Macintoshes, together forming a contiguous range immediately following the router's LocalTalk IP port IP address; and RIP (Routing Information Protocol) packets enabled.

First, let's configure the FastPath connecting the MIS LocalTalk network to the Backbone Ethernet network. Shiva's Net Manager software has a single large window for configuring the IP functionality of the FastPath.

First, fill in the Ethernet-side IP address and subnet mask. If you wish, you can leave the IP Broadcast Address field set to its default "0.0.0.0," and the FastPath with calculate its actual value automatically. Next, fill in the address of the Unix host as the Default Router. This is the router to which packets addressed to a locally unknown network will be sent. Specify the Unix machine as the nameserver, as well, in the next field. This field isn't used by the router itself, but it can pass the information to other devices if queried. In the IP Forwarding section, specify a number of static IP clients. This number must be less than or equal to sixty, but really doesn't need to exceed the maximum num-

Figure 11.10 LocalTalk MacTCP zone selector.

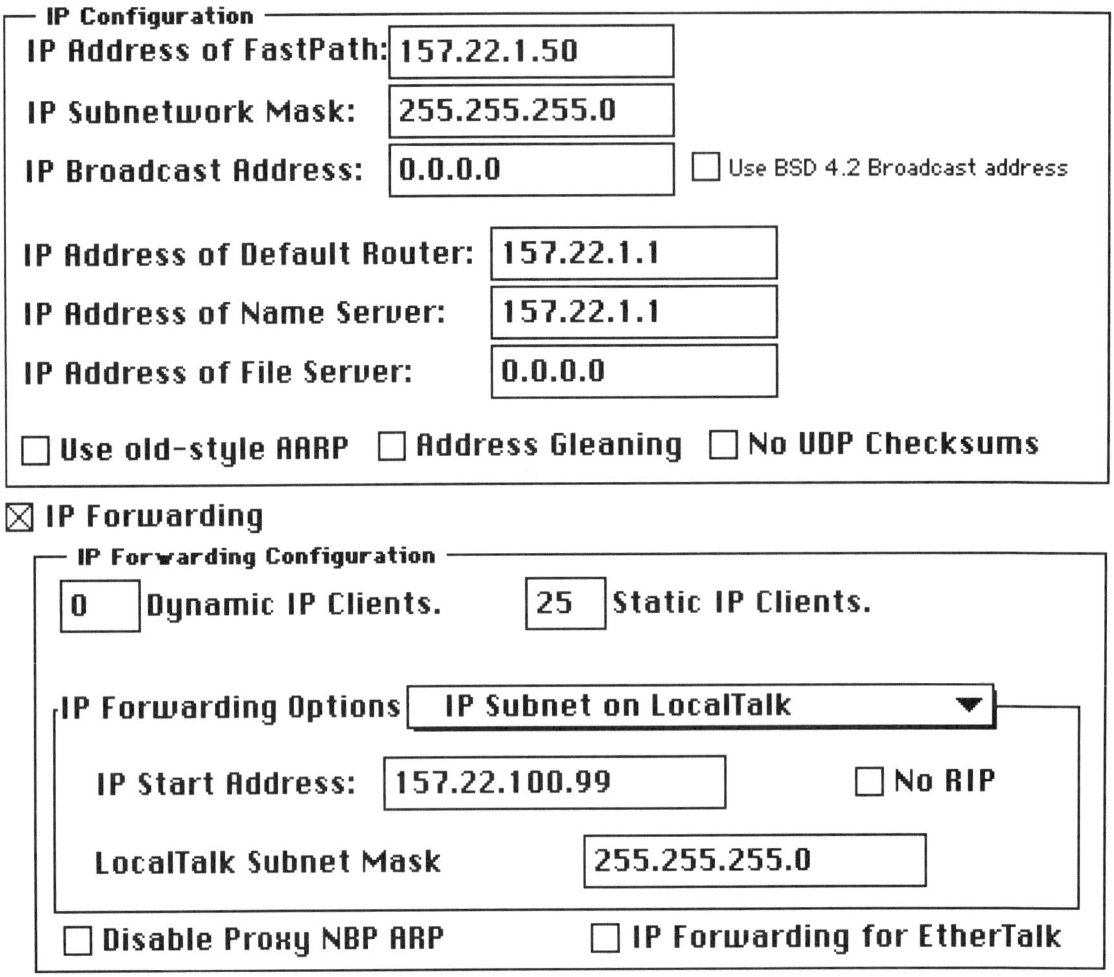

IP Configuration

IP Address of FastPath: | 157.22.1.50

IP Subnetwork Mask: | 255.255.255.0

IP Broadcast Address: | 0.0.0.0   ☐ Use BSD 4.2 Broadcast address

IP Address of Default Router: | 157.22.1.1

IP Address of Name Server: | 157.22.1.1

IP Address of File Server: | 0.0.0.0

☐ Use old-style AARP   ☐ Address Gleaning   ☐ No UDP Checksums

☒ IP Forwarding

IP Forwarding Configuration

0   Dynamic IP Clients.   25   Static IP Clients.

IP Forwarding Options | IP Subnet on LocalTalk   ▼

IP Start Address: | 157.22.100.99   ☐ No RIP

LocalTalk Subnet Mask   255.255.255.0

☐ Disable Proxy NBP ARP   ☐ IP Forwarding for EtherTalk

Figure 11.11   FastPath MacTCP configuration.

ber of machines on the FastPath's LocalTalk port. Next, select "IP Subnet on LocalTalk" from the pop-up menu, and fill in the LocalTalk IP address and subnet mask, keeping in mind that the range of static addresses you've specified will begin with the next consecutive number, in this case 157.22.100.100. Be sure than the "No RIP" box is *not* checked, as this would disallow the FastPath from using Routing Information Protocol packets, the IP equivalent of Routing Table Management Protocol packets. Lastly, select "Save Configuration to File . . ." and "Set Configuration" from the "FastPath" menu, to save the changes you've made and put them into effect.

GatorKeeper, the GatorBox configuration software, uses three nested dialogs to configure the GatorBox IP functionality. They're accessed by selecting "TCP/IP" from the initial configuration window of the GatorBox you're interested in.

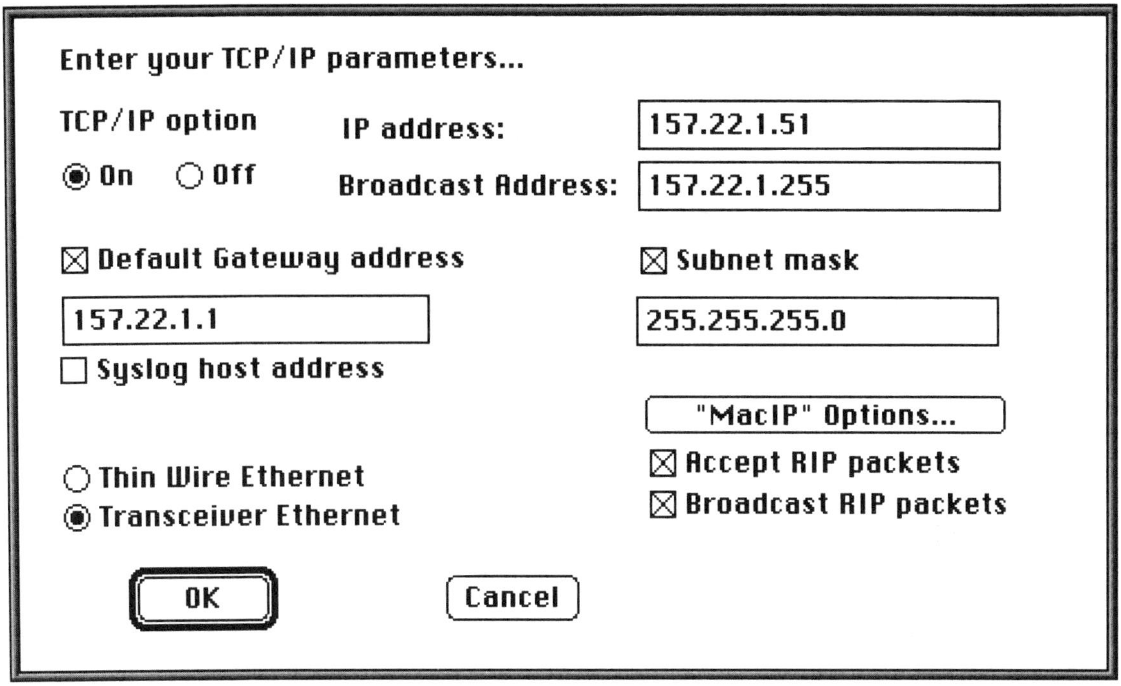

```
┌─────────────────────────────────────────────────────────────────┐
│ ┌───────────────────────────────────────────────────────────┐   │
│ │                                                             │   │
│ │  Enter your TCP/IP parameters...                            │   │
│ │                                                             │   │
│ │  TCP/IP option      IP address:      ┌──────────────────┐   │   │
│ │                                      │ 157.22.1.51      │   │   │
│ │  ⦿ On   ○ Off       Broadcast Address: ┌────────────────┐ │   │
│ │                                      │ 157.22.1.255     │   │   │
│ │                                      └──────────────────┘   │   │
│ │  ☒ Default Gateway address           ☒ Subnet mask         │   │
│ │  ┌──────────────────────────┐        ┌──────────────────┐  │   │
│ │  │ 157.22.1.1               │        │ 255.255.255.0    │  │   │
│ │  └──────────────────────────┘        └──────────────────┘  │   │
│ │  ☐ Syslog host address                                     │   │
│ │                                      ┌──────────────────┐   │   │
│ │                                      │ "MacIP" Options...│   │   │
│ │                                      └──────────────────┘   │   │
│ │  ○ Thin Wire Ethernet                ☒ Accept RIP packets  │   │
│ │  ⦿ Transceiver Ethernet              ☒ Broadcast RIP packets│  │
│ │  ┌──────────┐        ┌──────────┐                          │   │
│ │  │   OK     │        │  Cancel  │                          │   │
│ │  └──────────┘        └──────────┘                          │   │
│ └───────────────────────────────────────────────────────────┘   │
└─────────────────────────────────────────────────────────────────┘
```

Figure 11.12   GatorBox IP configuration.

In the first dialog, turn TCP/IP on, fill in the IP address and subnet mask, and figure out the broadcast address. In this case, we're configuring the broadcast address which applies to the Ethernet subnet to which the GatorBox is attached, number 1. Thus the address is 157.22 (restricting to this network) .1 (restricting to this subnet) .255 (broadcast to all nodes). Then be sure to check both "Accept RIP packets" and "Broadcast RIP packets," so that the GatorBox can maintain its routing table. The Syslog host address field provides an alternate method of error logging. Syslog is an error-logging daemon which runs on Unix hosts. By configuring this option, you can make the GatorBox send its log to your Unix host, rather than keeping it locally, but this adds one more step to any debugging process, and one more link which can fail, so we'll leave it as is. Next, press the " 'MacIP' Options . . ." button.

Here, select the "IP Subnet" radio button, and fill in the LocalTalk IP address and subnet mask. The GatorBox will calculate the LocalTalk subnet broadcast address automatically. Next fill in the IP start address for your LocalTalk Macintoshes, and fill in the number of dynamically assigned addresses, if any. The GatorBox can support up to 64 MacTCP clients, but keep in mind that any dynamic addresses you specify will be taken out of the lower end of that range. Next press the "More . . ." button.

In the final configuration dialog, fill in the Unix host's address in the name-server field, make sure that NBP is selected as the Address Resolution Protocol, and check "Restrict MacIP service to LocalTalk."

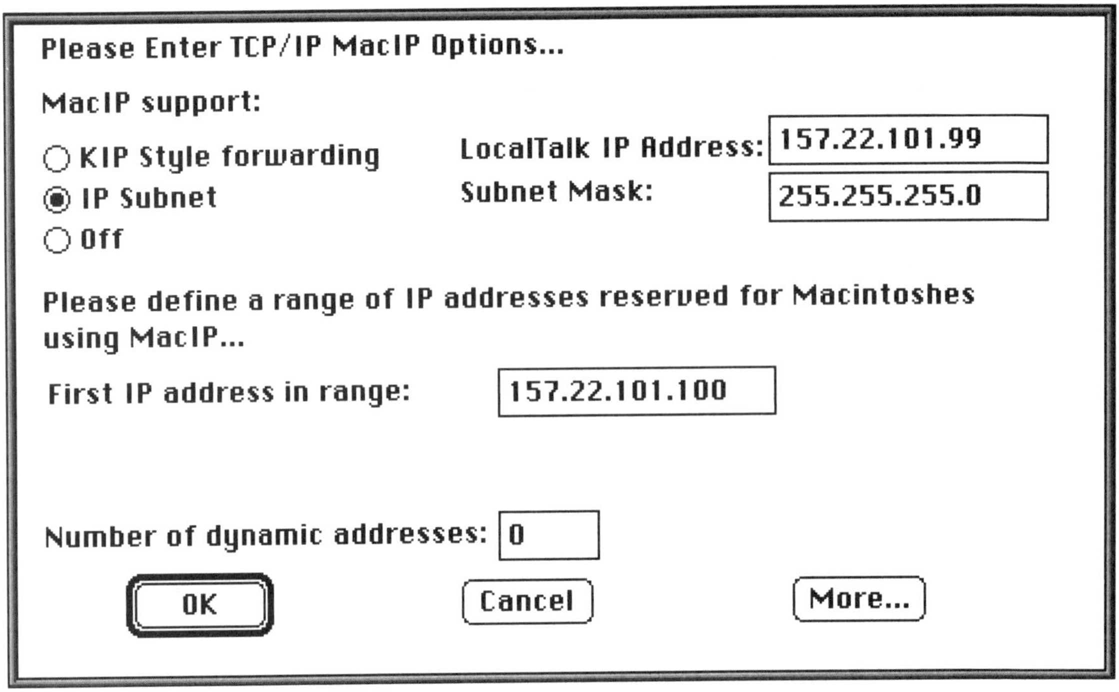

```
┌─────────────────────────────────────────────────────────────────┐
│ Please Enter TCP/IP MacIP Options...                              │
│                                                                   │
│ MacIP support:                                                    │
│  ○ KIP Style forwarding    LocalTalk IP Address: 157.22.101.99    │
│  ● IP Subnet               Subnet Mask:          255.255.255.0    │
│  ○ Off                                                            │
│                                                                   │
│ Please define a range of IP addresses reserved for Macintoshes    │
│ using MacIP...                                                     │
│                                                                   │
│  First IP address in range:      157.22.101.100                   │
│                                                                   │
│                                                                   │
│ Number of dynamic addresses: 0                                    │
│      ┌────────┐       ┌──────────┐        ┌──────────┐            │
│      │   OK   │       │  Cancel  │        │  More... │            │
│      └────────┘       └──────────┘        └──────────┘            │
└─────────────────────────────────────────────────────────────────┘
```

Figure 11.13   GatorBox MacTCP configuration.

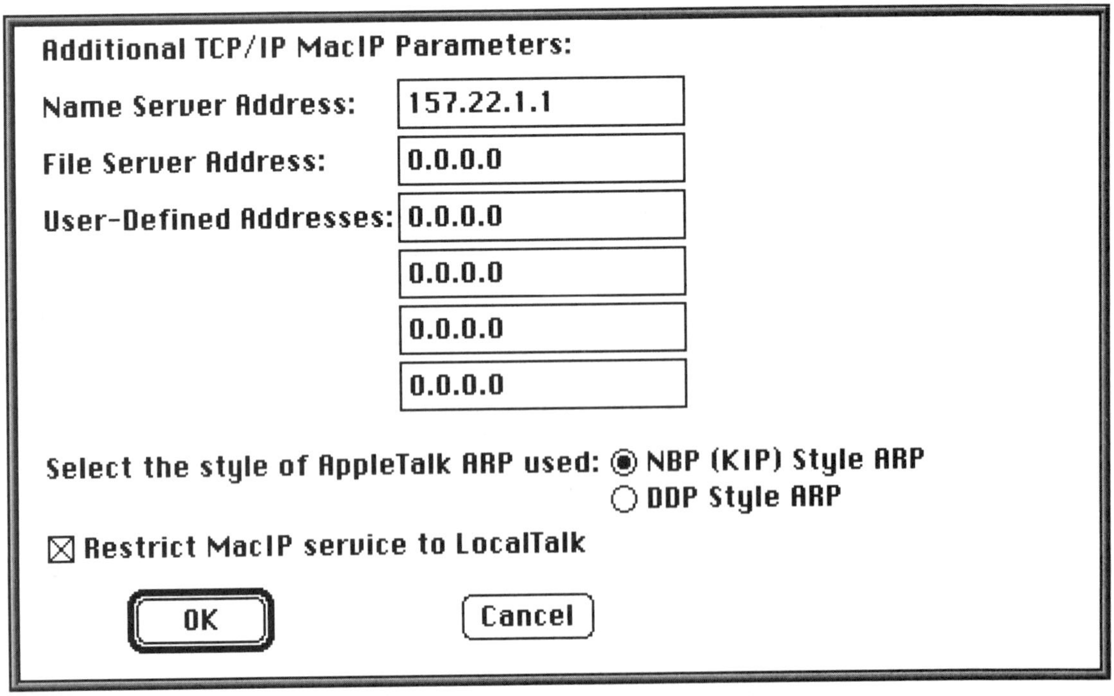

```
┌─────────────────────────────────────────────────────────────────┐
│ Additional TCP/IP MacIP Parameters:                               │
│                                                                   │
│ Name Server Address:    157.22.1.1                                │
│ File Server Address:    0.0.0.0                                    │
│ User-Defined Addresses: 0.0.0.0                                    │
│                         0.0.0.0                                    │
│                         0.0.0.0                                    │
│                         0.0.0.0                                    │
│                         0.0.0.0                                    │
│                                                                   │
│ Select the style of AppleTalk ARP used: ● NBP (KIP) Style ARP     │
│                                         ○ DDP Style ARP           │
│ ☒ Restrict MacIP service to LocalTalk                             │
│      ┌────────┐          ┌──────────┐                             │
│      │   OK   │          │  Cancel  │                             │
│      └────────┘          └──────────┘                             │
└─────────────────────────────────────────────────────────────────┘
```

Figure 11.14   GatorBox MacTCP details configuration.

Lastly, the routing process on the Unix host has to be configured. Since it's not doing any actual routing itself at this point, there's no subnet about which it has exclusive knowledge. Thus it may be able to glean its routing table from the RIP packets being broadcast by the two routers, but we need to be sure that routed is running, and check its routing table to make sure that it has indeed been built.

First, check to make sure that routed is running, by issuing a ps -ef, and look for a line ending in /etc/in.routed, /etc/routerlog, or something similar. To speed up searches for specific processes, you can pipe the output of ps into a searching program called grep, as follows,

```
% ps -ef | grep routed
```

which should return two lines—one for routed and one for the grep process itself—since routed was the parameter you passed it. At any rate, if routed isn't running, it can be enabled in inittab with a line like

```
net4:2:wait:/etc/in.routed /etc/routerlog
```

The commands used in inspecting and modifying the routing table are netstat (network statistics) and ifconfig (network interface configuration). The command

```
% netstat -i
```

will give you a list of the networks which have been contributed to the routing table by the host itself. This should contain two records: one for subnet 1 and one for an internal, or loopback network. Typing

```
% netstat -r
```

will return the whole routing table, which may contain one additional line contributed by each router. The addition of the -n flag specifies IP or "numeric" addresses, rather than Internet addresses.

At this point, the routing table should appear something like this:

```
Destination     Gateway         Flags    Refs     Use     Interface
127.0.0.1       127.0.0.1       UH       3        83      1o0
157.22.1        157.22.1.1      U        12       990     ae0
157.22.100      157.22.1.50     UG       0        0       ae0
157.22.101      157.22.1.51     UG       0        0       ae0
```

If both of the remote subnet records don't appear, there may have been a problem with the RIP enabling on one or both of the routers, or the routing table may simply not have been updated yet. First, check that the network interface is turned on, by using ifconfig:

```
% ifconfig interface
```

where *interface* is the entry from the interface field of one of the records other than the loopback in the routing table, in this case ae0. This should return a line similar to

```
ae0: 157.22.1.1 netmask ffffff00 flags=63<UP,BROADCAST,
    NOTRAILERS,RUNNING> broadcast: 157.22.1.255
```

containing the host's IP address on that interface, the subnet mask in use, the broadcast address for that subnet, and the settings of several parameters, including UP or DOWN. If the line you get reads DOWN, rather than UP, you can enable the interface by typing

```
% ifconfig interface up
```

Next, try restarting the Unix host, and check the routing table again after it's been running for a few minutes. If it's still not getting a full routing table, check the contents of /etc/routerlog, the log file that we passed routed as a parameter in inittab. If everything were working correctly, the last few lines should look something like this:

```
ADD dst 157.22.100.0, router 157.22.1.50, metric 2,
    flags UP|GATEWAY state CHANGED|SUBNET timer 0
ADD dst 157.22.101.0, router 157.22.1.51, metric 2,
    flags UP|GATEWAY state CHANGED|SUBNET timer 0
```

Otherwise, look for error messages in the log.

If you want to manually configure the routing table, you can do it using the route command, passing it the add, remote subnet, router, and hop count metric parameters:

```
% route add 157.22.100.0 157.22.1.50 1
% route add 157.22.101.0 157.22.1.51 1
```

or you can create the file /etc/gateways to do it for you. In a gateways file, each record begins with the word net; the next field contains the subnet address, the next contains the router's address, the next the hop count metric, and the last the word "active," or "passive," depending upon whether routed should expect to be able to exchange RIP packets with the remote router. Thus a gateways file to describe these two routers would contain the following two lines:

```
net   157.22.100.0   157.22.1.50   1   active
net   157.22.101.0   157.22.1.51   1   active
```

The man pages for routed, netstat, and ifconfig explain the IP routing process well, as does the GatorBox Reference manual.

11.4.3   Using telnet tools

At most sites, the main use of IP protocols on Macintoshes is for terminal emulation. A terminal-emulation application on a Macintosh can establish a terminal session with a Unix host, using the telnet protocol, a high-level protocol layered on top of the TCP and IP protocols.

Although a few terminal-emulation applications support telnet through proprietary implementations, most use the Communications ToolBox, Apple's modular and extensible library of communications software components. A number of third-party vendors have written telnet Connection Tools for the Communications ToolBox, or CTB. Although each is different in some small way, they all perform the same basic task, so the fundamental configuration is the same for each of them. They acquire your Macintosh's IP address from MacTCP, but just as a modem tool needs to be told what phone number to dial, telnet tools must be told the address of the host you wish to connect to. Fortunately, most can glean hosts' addresses from your hosts file, if it's present in your System Folder.

In this telnet tool (Fig. 11.15), a hostname is selected from the scrolling list at left, built from the hosts file, and the IP address of the selected host is shown near the top of the dialog. The only other parameter here which should be mod-

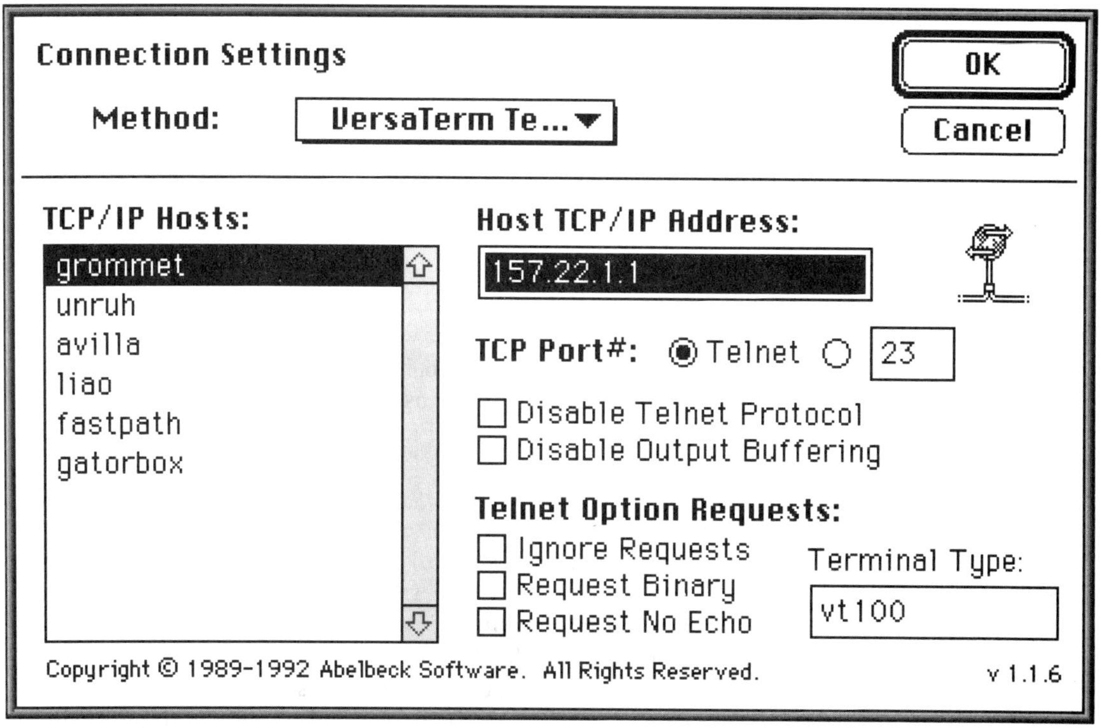

Figure 11.15   Communications ToolBox telnet connection tool.

ified by a user under normal circumstances is the terminal type. Nearly all Unix hosts support vt100, a midrange terminal type which is also supported by an Apple-distributed CTB Terminal Tool. TTY is another choice, if you'd rather have a slightly simpler, teletype-like interface, or vt320, a more powerful terminal type, if your Unix host supports it.

When you've finished configuring the Connection Tool, you should be able to select "Connect" from a menu of your terminal emulator and see a login sequence from your Unix host, something like the one below:

```
Apple Computer A/UX (grommet)

login: unruh
Password:
_____

Welcome to grommet.com

   System Administrator: Mark Unruh
   Mail questions and comments to root@grommet.com
     or call +1 510 427 6369
_____

TERM = (vt100)
Tue Sep 22 14:16:18 PDT 1992
%
```

In this case, the file /etc/motd ("message-of-the-day") has been customized to contain the "Welcome to" message. If the TERM= prompt does not indicate the same terminal type you've specified in your telnet tool, you need to enter the name of the terminal type you're actually using, and then decide which you want to modify—your telnet tool settings or your .login file.

11.4.4   Macintosh FTP clients and servers

File Transfer Protocol, or ftp, is the simplest way of moving files back and forth between most Unix machines, and Macintosh support for ftp has been developed in two forms: Communications ToolBox file transfer tools for ftp client use, and various applications and Control Panels which allow Macintoshes to act as ftp servers.

Communications ToolBox ftp tools are only active while they're in use by the terminal application. That is, using an ftp tool will not allow other people to ftp files to and from your machine; it will only allow you to do so, while you've got a simultaneous terminal session with the same host underway. In Fig. 11.16 you can see the configuration dialog for a typical ftp tool, allowing the selection of a file type for the text files transferred to your Macintosh, and the selection of a default file transfer method, in this case MacBinary. This particular tool also allows the most common ftp commands to be remapped, or aliased.

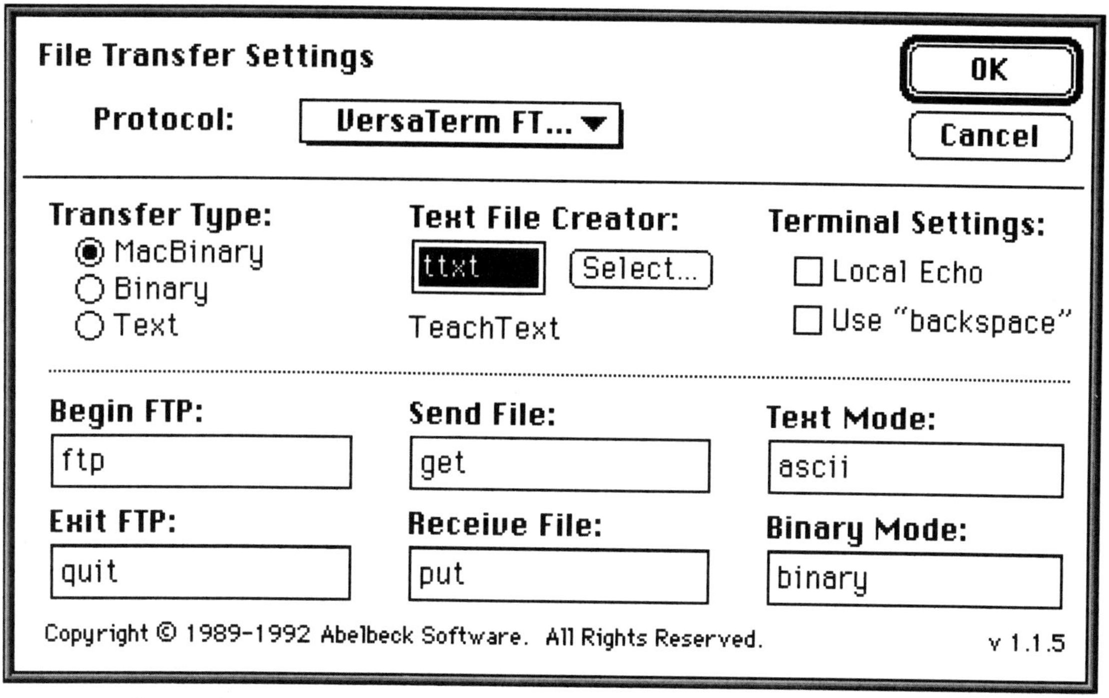

Figure 11.16 Communications ToolBox ftp file transfer tool.

The alternative is a full ftp server process for your Macintosh, which will allow you, or anyone else with the correct password, to log into your machine and transfer files to and from it at any time. The application illustrated in Fig. 11.17 uses a small monitor window to display the names of the users logged in at any time, and to allow you to disconnect them, much like the System 7 File Sharing Monitor.

The configuration window for the server processes illustrated in Fig. 11.18 is very simple, containing settings for the number of simultaneous clients you wish to allow, whether they're to be timed out if idle, whether they may write to the disk, as well as reading from it, and what directory they first appear in when they log in. Also, a password should be entered. This particular server makes provision for only one password, but some other servers allow multiple passwords, each with different access privileges.

If you're logged into a Unix machine, you can initiate an ftp connection to any Macintosh that has an ftp server process running, including a Macintosh from which you're telnetting to the Unix host. To do so, type

```
% ftp unruh
```

If the server is running, and you have a network connection to it, it should respond with a login sequence, prompting you for a user name and password. If your login name is the same on the machine you're ftping from, you should

FTP Monitor
FTP Server Address : 157.22.1.100
This Server is running
Connected Users
Address :
Name :
State :
157.22.1.1 unruh Connected
157.22.1.117 avilla Connected
157.22.102.104 liao Connected
Disconnect
© A.S.C 1991
1.0

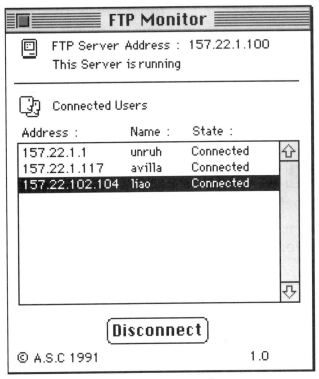

Figure 11.17 Standalone ftp server application monitor window.

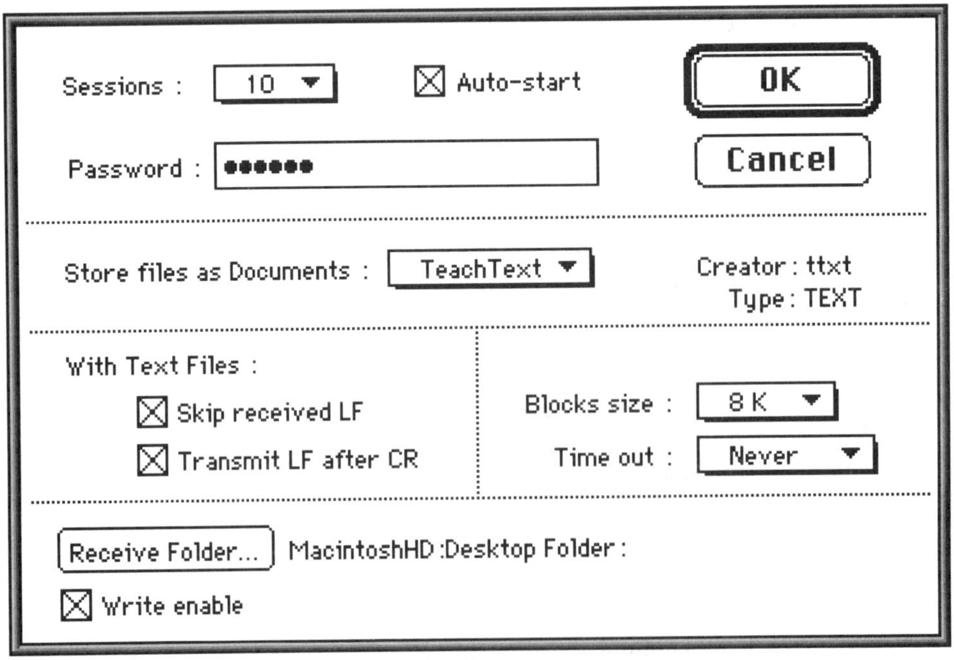

Sessions : 10
Auto-start
OK
Password : ●●●●●●
Cancel
Store files as Documents : TeachText
Creator : ttxt
Type : TEXT
With Text Files :
Skip received LF
Transmit LF after CR
Blocks size : 8 K
Time out : Never
Receive Folder...
MacintoshHD :Desktop Folder :
Write enable

Figure 11.18 Standalone ftp server application configuration window.

be able to just type return at the first prompt, but we've entered the name anyway.

```
Connected to unruh.grommet.com.
220 VersaTerm FTP Server (v 1.1.5), ready.
Name (unruh:root): root
331 Password required.
Password:
230 User logged in.
```

The numbers at the beginnings of response lines are there to make it easier for people to write automated scripts to interface with ftp servers. While the text of a message may change, the numbers serve as a uniform way of indicating the state of the transaction. Next, you'll see ftp's internal prompt. To see a listing of the files and subdirectories within the directory that the ftp server has initially placed you in, type ls:

```
ftp> ls
200 Port Assignment Successful.
150 Opening connection...
Applications & Documents/
Desktop Folder/
NIC Documents/
System Folder/
Temporary Items/
Text Files/
Trash/
Application Folder/
Utilities/
226 Transfer Complete.
146 bytes received in 0.25 seconds (0.57 Kbytes/s)
ftp>
```

The basic commands used in interaction with ftp servers are very similar to those used in the Unix shells. ls lists the contents of a directory; cd changes your current directory to the named one. File transfers are initiated using the commands get and put, depending upon the direction of the transfer, relative to the Unix host. This can become a little confusing if you're logged into a Unix host from a Macintosh and are ftping back to the Macintosh. The backslash (\) character can usually be used to exempt the immediately following character from interpretation as a Unix delimiter or special character. This is particularly useful when dealing with Macintoshes, since spaces and slashes are often found in file names. To change directories into the System Folder, for instance, you would type

```
ftp> cd System\ Folder
```

being sure to correctly capitalize the name of the directory.

If you wish to transfer multiple files from a single command line, the commands mget and mput can be used with standard wildcard characters. For instance, if you were in a directory as follows:

```
ftp> CD MacintoshHD/Text\ Files/RFCs
250 CWD to "/Desktop/MacintoshHD/Text Files/RFCs".
ftp> ls
200 Port Assignment Successful.
150 Opening connection...
rfc768 UDP
rfc791 IP
rfc792 ICMP
rfc793 TCP
rfc821 SMTP
226 Transfer Complete.
220 bytes received in 0.35 seconds (0.61 Kbytes/s)
ftp>
```

the command

```
ftp> mget rfc76*
```

would be a slightly shorter way of getting the first file in the directory than typing

```
ftp> get rfc768\ UDP
```

If you wanted to get the middle three files, you could use the command

```
ftp> get rfc79*
```

which would exclude the first file, which has a six in the fifth place, and the fifth file, which has a two in the fifth place.

11.4.5 Using SMTP mail

The single best reason to install a Unix host at your site is to provide Internet electronic mail services to your users. Once named service has been established, mail can be transferred between any two machines using Simple Mail Transfer Protocol electronic mail software and the IP protocol stack. When sendmail has been configured on the Unix host, mail can be exchanged with local Unix account holders; if it's been configured to use UUCP or you have a SLIP link, mail can be exchanged with any user, at any site, on the entire Internet.

One example of a standalone SMTP mail front-end for the Macintosh is LeeMail. LeeMail provides an extremely simple, if not particularly powerful, user interface.

In Fig. 11.19, the configuration dialog, you specify whether or not to use a nameserver to look up addresses, or to rely upon the local Hosts file; you enter the name, account name, and machine name you want used as your return address; your time zone; and some behavioral preferences. Unfortunately, in order to receive mail, the LeeMail application must be running in the background at all times.

The alternative is an SMTP gateway for your LAN e-mail software. The advantage of such a system is that it provides for simpler management, as it concentrates the new functionality on a single machine and it allows users to continue to receive and dispose of all their mail from a single common interface. StarNine is the predominant vendor of such gateways; they make versions of their Mail*Link software for Microsoft Mail, QuickMail, and InBox.

The gateway configuration interface is the same in each of the three versions, and contains about the same information as LeeMail's. The means of adding users, however, is system dependent.

Under MS Mail, users are added using the "Recipients" submenu of the "Gateways" item of the "Mail" menu, from a client machine logged in as mail administrator.

Under QuickMail, addresses are added to the user list using the "Create . . ." item in the "Users" menu. As you can see, although the differences between the e-mail systems they work within impose some superficial differences, the processes are conceptually identical.

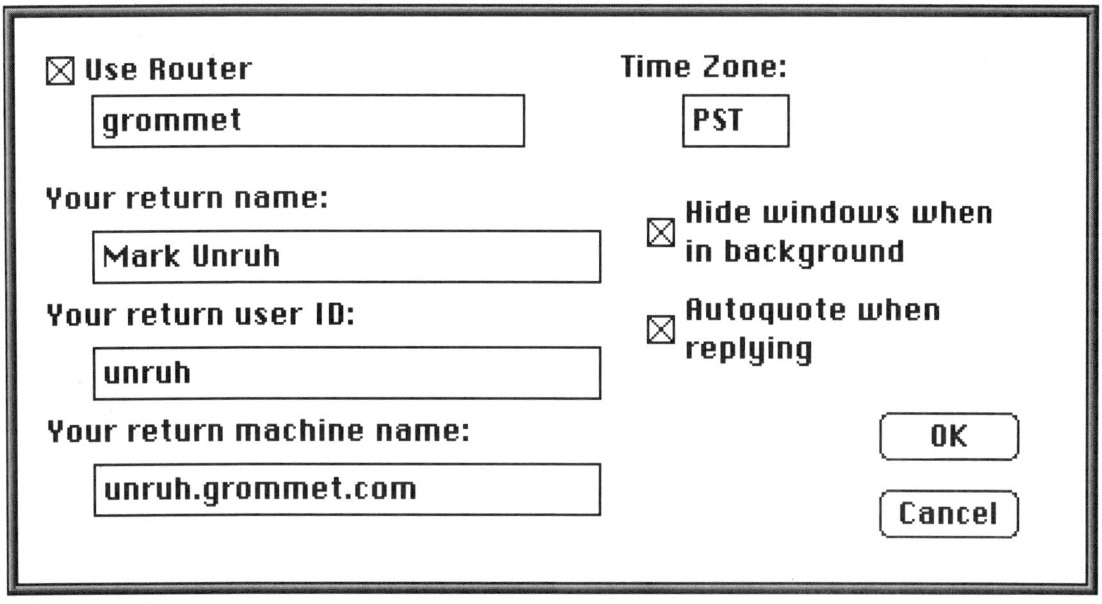

⊠ **Use Router**

    grommet

Your return name:

    Mark Unruh

Your return user ID:

    unruh

Your return machine name:

    unruh.grommet.com

Time Zone:

    PST

⊠ **Hide windows when in background**

⊠ **Autoquote when replying**

    [OK]

    [Cancel]

Figure 11.19 LeeMail configuration dialog.

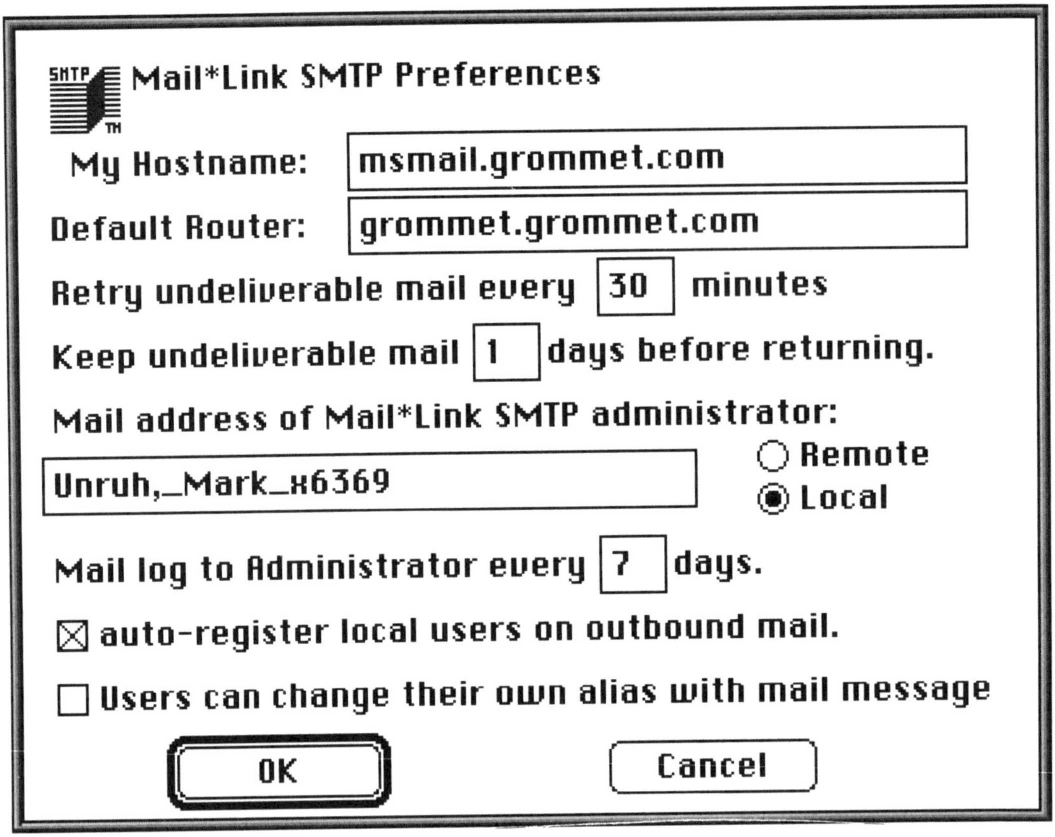

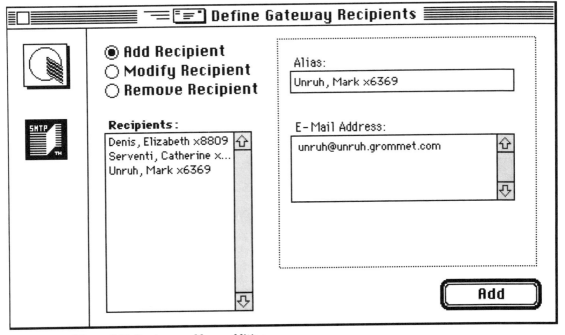

Figure 11.20 Mail*Link SMTP configuration dialog.

Figure 11.21 Microsoft Mail gateway address addition.

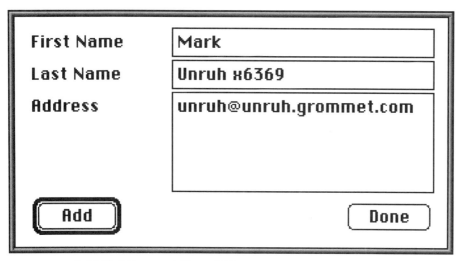

First Name   Mark

Last Name   Unruh x6369

Address   unruh@unruh.grommet.com

Add   Done

Figure 11.22   QuickMail Gateway Address Addition.

11.5   The Solution

Mark decided to go about setting up a Unix host just as he would have gone about setting up any other service: Implement it first on an isolated testbed network, using limited sample data. He set up a Macintosh running A/UX, created several accounts, brought up name service, mail, lpr printing, Yellow Pages, and NFS. He tested each of these as thoroughly as he could from the Unix machine itself, and made his Macintosh a client wherever possible. He experimented with several different methods of accessing Unix services from Macintosh clients, and found that, in general, third-party protocol translators, like electronic mail gateways and GatorBox NFS-AFP translation, worked better than trying to make all the Macintoshes native clients of Unix services. These methods concentrated management in a single point, and allowed users to apply skills they'd already acquired to the new services, rather than requiring them to learn a new set of use patterns.

12

Management and Support

12.1 The Problem

Having finally gotten American Grommet's network installed, routers configured, and services provided, Mark thought his ensuing holiday was well-
earned. As he stepped out of the jetway at Honolulu International Airport,
however, a gate attendant holding a hand-lettered placard bearing his name
caught his eye and drew him aside, handing him a ticket for a return flight
leaving from a gate all the way across the airport in less than fifteen minutes,
as well as a scroll of fax paper many feet long. After sputtering a bit, Mark
examined the fax, and found it to be a list of the problems users had had in the
hours he'd been on the plane. Although he could explain at least half of the
problems ("I keep getting an error message saying 'No printer has been specified. Please select a printer from the Chooser desk accessory and try again.'
What does it mean? What have you done to my computer so it won't print?")
without attributing them to any failure of the network, there were many more
which were described in such fragmentary, baffling terms that he puzzled over
them all the way back to Oakland Airport.

Mark's mistake was that he hadn't thought about his network enough to
realize that simply finishing its construction didn't end his duties. After thinking about the situation a bit more, Mark came to the conclusion that the network could be likened to a delicate piece of machinery being constantly
brutalized and maltreated by its unwitting yet vicious operators, the network
users. He, the mechanic responsible for the welfare of the machinery, must on
the one hand reinforce and safeguard it to make it robust enough to withstand
the continuous assault of daily use, and on the other hand try to educate the
users so that they might see the error of their ways.

Not for laughs alone are users often jokingly referred to by network administrators as the eighth layer of the seven-layer OSI network model. The user
exists atop the protocol stack, fuzzily interpreting the data that percolates up
through the stack, all the way from the physical layer, comprised of the net-

work hardware at the bottom. Unlike the other layers of the stack, the user layer does not utilize rigorously and rigidly defined parsing algorithms to interpret and deal with this data. While this flexibility is what makes people people, it also makes them somewhat unwieldy network components.

Thus ran Mark's train of thought as he gazed out the window of the cab on the ride back to his office.

12.2   Management Policies

One of the best strategies to use in limiting the instances and extent of network failures is to establish stringent policies and procedures anticipating all foreseeable eventualities. For day-to-day operations, this enforces a uniformity of safe and predictable operation which helps limit untoward accidents. When dealing with emergency situations, a response strategy you've plotted out in detail beforehand is likely to be better reasoned than any you could devise under the pressure of adverse circumstances.

From the user side, a network managed in accordance with a comprehensive set of fixed policies is likely to appear more stable, its behavior more easily predictable. If those policies are devised skillfully, with forethought paid the user interface that the network presents, these policies can dramatically improve users' comprehension of the network environment within which they operate, a key step in reducing user-originated questions and complaints.

12.2.1   Naming policies

When users perceive themselves to be operating in a static and comprehensible environment, their actions tend to be more predictable. This is an obviously desirable goal for any network administrator, as it allows one to anticipate user needs and demands with greater accuracy.

These two goals can both be achieved through careful name choice and placement of network services and zones.

User perception of the network tends to be on one of perhaps four levels. Some think of everything as happening within the box on their desk, and don't consider the network connection any differently than they would the power cable. Some think of the network as a "black box" to which their desktop machine is connected, and remember certain strings of actions that will elicit a desired response from the network. Others think of the network in spatial terms, as a physical network, perhaps imagining it something like a system of roads and highways, with data entering and exiting the flow where the computers and devices are attached to the network. Still others, a tiny minority, understand it as a digital communication system, operating on electrical media, carrying packetized binary data.

Of these four models, the first generates a great number of user difficulties, since it provides no framework for users to determine on their own what course to take to achieve a desired end. If the degree to which the user already understands how the network operates forms a starting point for any troubleshooting-oriented conversation between administrator and users, this model provides precious little common ground:

User:	"The memo I was writing yesterday isn't there. I know I saved it."
Administrator:	"Do you remember where you saved it?"
User:	"What do you mean, 'where?' I pressed the 'Save' button."

The second model provides at least a general sense of groups of related actions and responses. If a user associates the Chooser with printing, for instance, the user may be able to navigate through the process of selecting a printer, by trial and error, even though he or she has no conception of how the interface being manipulating relates to the physical world.

User:	"I saved a memo yesterday, on the hard drive that you said was part of the network. Berk Accounting Server, I think it was called. When I go to open it, I can't find that drive on the Desktop."
Administrator:	"Okay, pull down the Apple menu, and select 'Chooser.' Then click on the icon that's labeled 'AppleShare' in the panel at the upper left. Tell me what names show up in the list on the right."
User:	"Okay, I've done it. There's nothing in the list."
Administrator:	"Is there a list in the bottom left-hand corner of the window, called 'Zone List'?"
User:	"No."

Through questions and answers with a user at this level, an administrator can gather basic troubleshooting information, but the process still requires slow, step-by-step, literal instructions, and the user can't operate autonomously to discover the cause of most problems.

The third level, that at which users have a spatial or geographical kind of model of network operation, is by far the most valuable to network administrators. It provides a perfect functional model, within which things can be easily explained, and it provides a source of analogies by which to explain network functions to users. Since users at this level can associate the various means of interfacing with the network at their disposal with real actions, they're much less likely to perform rash or dangerous actions unknowingly. Also, this model allows them to operate autonomously in solving local problems:

User:	"When I turned on my computer this morning my zone's server didn't mount automatically, like it was supposed to. I opened the Chooser, and I couldn't see any of the other zones, so I checked the network connector on the back of the machine and the drop cable to the wall jack, but they looked okay. I guess the problem must be somewhere between there and the other zones."
Administrator:	"Okay. It sounds like there may be a problem with your hub. It should be taken care of in ten or fifteen minutes."

Users beyond that point who actually understand, or think they understand, how the network really works are invariably of the opinion that they can do your job better than you can:

User:	"Hey, you know the router for my zone was down again this morning, so I had to restart it. I changed the zone name to something I liked better, too. You know this is the third time this week I've had to complain to your boss about how you've been handling the network? I'm not going to forget about the time you threw away all my gifs and QuickTime movies from my drop folder!"
Administrator:	"You have a nice day, too."

Users can be encouraged to think of the network in spatial terms by rigorously associating each zone with a specific geographic area. You can use names which tend to reinforce this association both for zones and for devices. For instance, in the network we've been building here, each zone name begins with a three-letter prefix which specifies the city in which the zone is located. That's followed by the name of the department with which it's associated, and that's followed by the network number with which it's associated, since we've stuck to a one-net-per-zone, one-zone-per-net pairing strategy. These net numbers are assigned a three-digit code, wherein the first digit is either zero or one, depending upon whether the net is on Ethernet or LocalTalk, respectively. Lastly, the name ends with the telephone extension number of the person who's responsible for its maintenance. The first two items serve to uniquely correlate the zone with a definite geographical area with which its users are familiar. The fourth item, the phone extension of a responsible person, gives them immediate recourse when something fails. The third item, the net number, is useful to the maintenance staff, eliminating the need to refer back to documentation to figure out which net a zone is associated with, and, with luck, promoting casual memorization of the correspondence.

If you enact a naming policy with similar strengths, and follow it rigorously, your users should be able to easily find any device they're interested in, and should eventually even be able to predict where they could find something, without looking. It's this level of understanding on the part of the users that begins to relieve administrators of questions and problems which are user-related, rather than network-related.

12.2.2 Documentation policies

Another area in which strong policies are useful is with respect to documentation. The idea of documenting changes so as to be able to reverse them in the event of a problem was discussed in connection with wiring in Chap. 5. It's equally important to document changes to router configuration, server user lists, and similar changes. With respect to software changes, this may mean archiving software images of the configuration state of various devices, using a backup program, from which you can later restore network-wide configuration to the state it was in at some particular time.

Log files should also be archived periodically. Obviously, they can't continue to aggregate on servers' disks, and you shouldn't throw them away, since the information in them has value for tracking the effects of changes over time, for determining the direction of usage trends on a large time-scale, and for checking for specific historical incidents (i.e., did employee X send any mail from this site after he was fired, at 5:00pm, March 15, two years ago?). Macro scripts are invaluable for automating this sort of file management, particularly if the clocks of different machines on your network are synchronized so you can make scripts on different machines work together.

HyperCard can also be useful as a text-parsing engine for log files. Hyper-Talk scripts can be written to import data from text files, deal with it on a line-by-line basis, and output it to a different file, in a different format, presumably more appropriate for importation into a spreadsheet or database. Alternatively, analysis can be performed within HyperCard as well, although it's terribly slow compared to real databases and spreadsheets.

In any case, the most pressing reason for both documentation of changes and storage of logs is to provide a base of information from which informed deductions can be drawn when it comes time to troubleshoot a problem. Gathering of information is always the first and most important step in troubleshooting, and precollection of this type gives you a relatively painless leg up on that task.

12.2.3   Troubleshooting

As jokingly noted before, the vast majority of troubleshooting sessions begin with a phone call from a user who says something to the effect of "I keep getting this error message on my machine, '[Network resource X] could not be found on the network.' What's wrong?"

Begin immediately with the first step, information gathering. While the user is still on the phone, find out whether the error message is on their screen. If so, have them read you the exact text of the error message, and copy it down. If they don't have it in front of them, ask them to try to duplicate whatever they did which prompted the error message; if that's successful, copy it down. Contrary to popular belief, error messages are not inscrutable ciphers. They provide an important first step in any troubleshooting process and are usually sufficient to resolve most user problems, if the user stops to read them before calling you, or you're able to explain them to the user. The exact text of error messages which are of identical meaning but displayed by different applications or software processes may vary slightly. This may give you a clue with which process the error message originated, something that may not be obvious to the user, or may be otherwise hard to detect.

Macintosh network problems can usually be fit into one of three categories. First, full or intermittent discontinuity in the physical layer of the network, caused by wiring faults, loose plugs, or faulty or powered-down hardware. Second, software or configuration errors on workstations, consisting of software that's been configured to look for a service in the wrong zone, AppleTalk turned off in the Chooser, the wrong AppleTalk Device selected in the Network Control Panel, et cetera. Third, router configuration errors, usually caused by different routers propagating inconsistent routing table information.

The majority of the "resource not found" problems at most sites can be traced back to the second type, workstation software configuration errors. These simply take a bit of Macintosh expert-user knowledge and a bit of deciphering to work out.

Both the intermittent wiring faults and router configuration errors manifest themselves to users as "ghosting" in the Chooser. That is, zones flickering in and out of the zone list box in the Chooser, and the devices within those zones sometimes being available, sometimes not. Deciding which of these two possible causes is actually responsible is a delicate matter. First, collect information: What zones are being affected? Are the affected zones the same everywhere on the network, or just in one area? Check the routers' logs for error messages. Capture RTMP packets and compare them, looking for any conflicting information which could be causing, rather than just a symptom of, the problem. If you can draw a line across any segment of your network and correctly say "devices and zones on each side of this line are having trouble seeing devices and zones on the other side," then you've probably got an intermittent wiring fault. If, on the other hand, the same few zones are popping in and out most places on the network, then it's more likely that you've got a routing table conflict.

Simple discontinuity is by far the easiest to diagnose. Like intermittent discontinuity, you need to find the line across which you cannot see, from either side. This line intersects your network at the point at which it's down. This may be the result of a device being broken, turned off, or misconfigured, of a loose connector, or of a damaged conductor.

When looking for failures of this type, simple substitution of components is one course to take. Determine exactly what course the network connection that's failed is taking, and attempt to parallel it with another one. If that works, begin substituting segments of the working path into the nonfunctional one. When you get the first one working, back up a step and make sure it fails again, then substitute the component you think is responsible into a working path, and see if it makes that one fail. This method of diagnosis can sometimes be more time-consuming that you'd like, and is often turned to as a last resort, but it's by getting your hands dirty at this level that you really learn what makes your network break, and what it takes to fix it.

The alternative to substitution, which requires a little less legwork, is *pinging* devices. Pinging means trying to bounce echo packets off of a device elsewhere in the network, and checking to see whether they make it back, and if so in what condition, and after what period of delay.

From your management station on the network backbone, try pinging both the machine from which the problem was reported and the device which it couldn't see, using something like CheckNet or Inter•Poll. If you can see both devices, you know they both have network access, but you still have the report that the user couldn't see the resource to explain. If the network resource that can't be found is running on a Macintosh, and it's local or can be reached using Timbuktu, run a copy of CheckNet or Inter•Poll on that machine, and try to ping the user. If the user's machine returns the echo packets reliably over a period of time, especially while the user is reporting that the problem is actually occurring, this confirms that there's no discontinuity between the two machines, and indicates that the problem is a software configuration error on the user's machine.

If one of the machines can't be seen from your management station, try to determine the extent of the cut-off part of the network. Ping other machines on the same net. Ping other machines served out of the same hub. Check to make sure the port of the hub is turned on. If the machine is on LocalTalk, try directly attaching another Macintosh to that port of the hub, use that to ping the machine that's down, and try pinging the newly attached device from the management station. Using techniques like these, you can narrow the range of possible causes of the problem. It may be a problem with a router between the two affected machines. It may be a loose plug or connector on one of the machines. It may be a problem with the hub. It may be a wiring fault, although problems with the cable plant very rarely crop up after the installation period.

12.3   Management Tools

There are a variety of software tools available to help you perform management tasks and gather troubleshooting information. Some of these are a fairly standard part of every network administrator's "toolbox" of software. I'll describe a few representative examples of each genre of tool here.

12.3.1   CheckNet

CheckNet is about as simple as management tools get, and probably the single most frequently used. CheckNet is a small Desk Accessory which lists the NBP-registered device sockets in each net and zone. It can be sorted in any way you wish, and the columns can be reordered and their widths changed to accommodate any information. Filtering is available as well, so that you needn't sift through as much information if you're trying to determine something specific.

In addition to being a quick way to see whether services have gone down, CheckNet, or a CheckNet-like tool, is all you need to determine the location of a break in a daisy-chain or trunk network segment, as demonstrated in Chap. 4.

Perhaps the most attractive feature of CheckNet is that it's one of the least expensive network management tools available, and comes with a multiuser license, so it can be installed on multiple machines, right out of the box.

12.3.2   Inter•Poll

Inter•Poll is among the most venerable AppleTalk administration tools, dating back to 1987. It has a three-level interface. The first level prompts you to

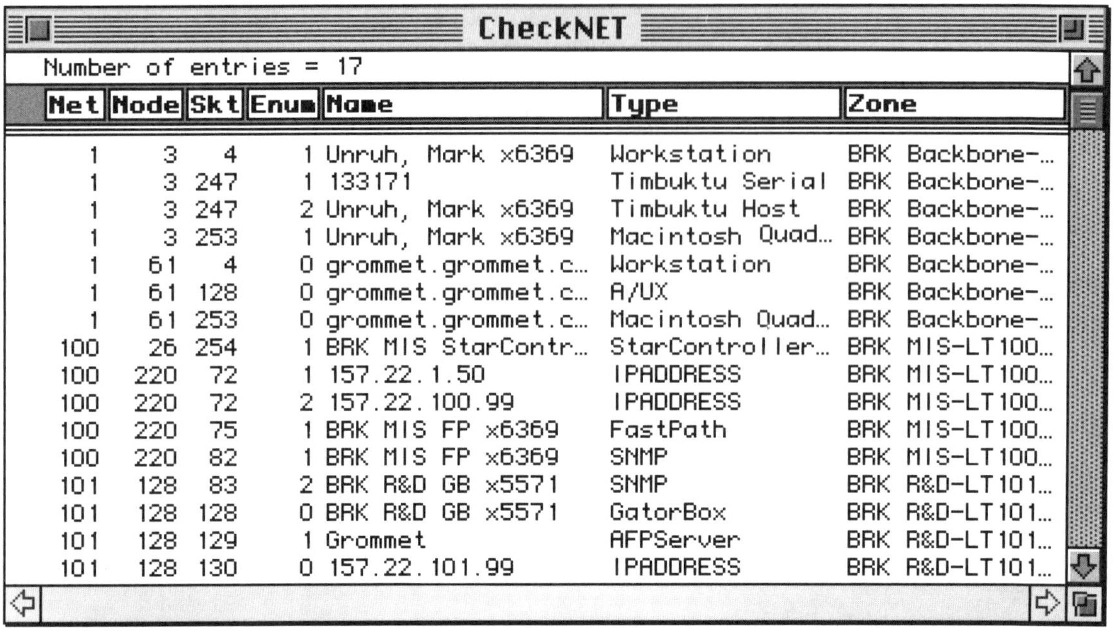

```
╔═════════════════════════════════ CheckNET ═════════════════════════════════╗
║  Number of entries = 17                                                    ⇧ ║
╠═════╦═════╦═════╦═════╦═══════════════════════╦════════════════════╦═════════╣
║ Net ║Node ║Skt  ║Enum ║Name                   ║Type                ║Zone     ║
╠═════╩═════╩═════╩═════╩═══════════════════════╩════════════════════╩═════════╣
║    1     3    4      1 Unruh, Mark x6369       Workstation          BRK Backbone-...
║    1     3  247      1 133171                  Timbuktu Serial      BRK Backbone-...
║    1     3  247      2 Unruh, Mark x6369       Timbuktu Host        BRK Backbone-...
║    1     3  253      1 Unruh, Mark x6369       Macintosh Quad...    BRK Backbone-...
║    1    61    4      0 grommet.grommet.c...    Workstation          BRK Backbone-...
║    1    61  128      0 grommet.grommet.c...    A/UX                 BRK Backbone-...
║    1    61  253      0 grommet.grommet.c...    Macintosh Quad...    BRK Backbone-...
║  100    26  254      1 BRK MIS StarContr...    StarController...    BRK MIS-LT100...
║  100   220   72      1 157.22.1.50             IPADDRESS            BRK MIS-LT100...
║  100   220   72      2 157.22.100.99           IPADDRESS            BRK MIS-LT100...
║  100   220   75      1 BRK MIS FP x6369        FastPath             BRK MIS-LT100...
║  100   220   82      1 BRK MIS FP x6369        SNMP                 BRK MIS-LT100...
║  101   128   83      2 BRK R&D GB x5571        SNMP                 BRK R&D-LT101...
║  101   128  128      0 BRK R&D GB x5571        GatorBox             BRK R&D-LT101...
║  101   128  129      1 Grommet                 AFPServer            BRK R&D-LT101...
║  101   128  130      0 157.22.101.99           IPADDRESS            BRK R&D-LT101...⇩
╚═════════════════════════════════════════════════════════════════════════════╝
```

Figure 12.1   CheckNet window.

select the zones you wish to examine. The second level lists the NBP-registered AppleTalk devices in those zones. The third level, reached by double-clicking on one of the devices displayed in the second level, is probably the most interesting.

In this window (Fig. 12.2), you can choose a type of packet to bounce off of the device you've selected. Any AppleTalk device should be able to respond to a short (6 data bytes) AppleTalk Echo Protocol packet, and most should be able to respond to a long (511 data bytes) AEP packet. Printer status packets are PAP packets, and are thus only answered if the device in question is a printer. System info packets are queries to the "Responder" socket on a Macintosh. The Responder is a piece of system software which simply opens a socket and waits to be interrogated. When this happens, it responds with the information which you see displayed in the "Status" box at the bottom of the illustrated dialog. The sending parameters are configurable, including the number of packets to be sent (1–32,767), the minimum interval between sent packets (0–99,999 seconds), and the amount of time to wait for a response before declaring a packet lost (0.2–99,999 seconds). Running averages and totals are displayed in the "Packets Sent" box in the middle of the screen. Hops away is, of course, the number of routers each sent packet has to pass through to reach its destination, while delay is the amount of time it takes for an answer to come back.

Don't take Inter•Poll's manual too seriously. It calls routers bridges, and assumes all AppleTalk networks are LocalTalk daisy chains; it's an artifact of an era before Apple conceived of "enterprise networking."

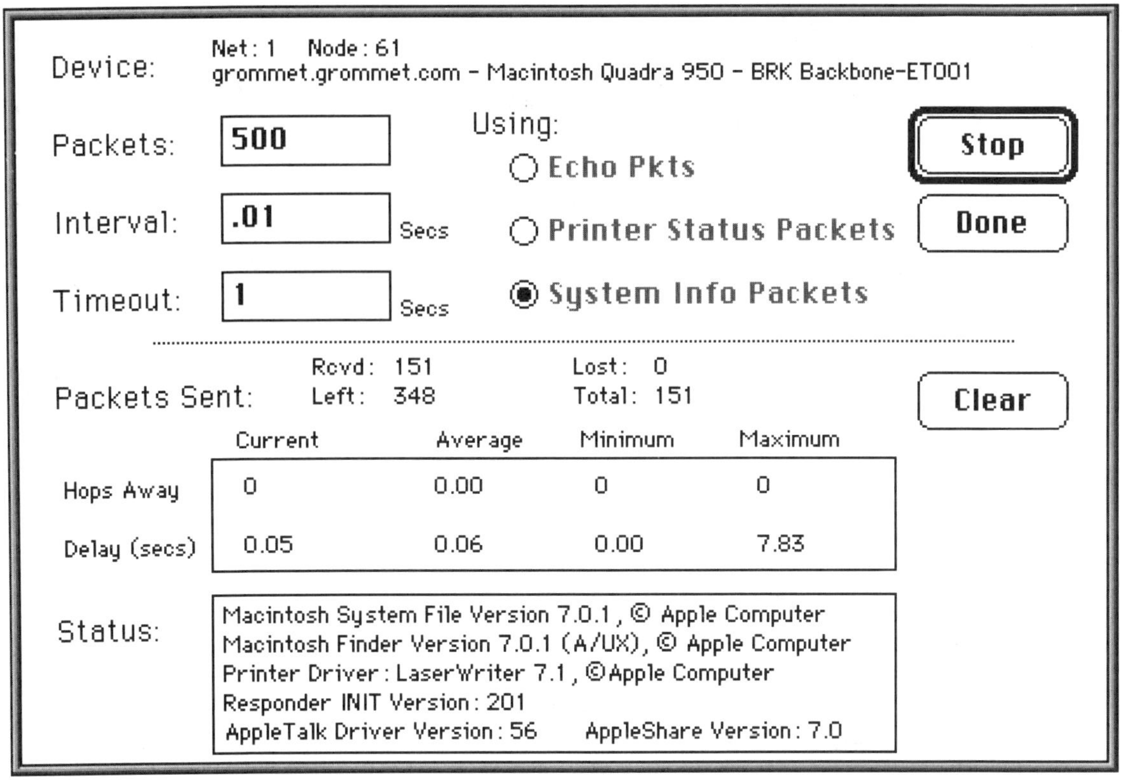

Figure 12.2   Inter·Poll device interrogation dialog.

12.3.3 RouterCheck

RouterCheck is an invaluable tool for monitoring the status of routers on your network. It collects configuration information from many different kinds of routers, for you to view side-by-side, all in the same format. It makes spotting zone name and network number conflicts easy, and it does a pretty good job of identifying the node numbers associated with the non-NBP-registered ports on routers.

RouterCheck's main window lists router ports, and tries to associate them with each other or, failing that, labels them with their net range and start, as you can see in the case of node 175 in Fig. 12.3. There's a save function, which captures a record of the state of your routers at any given time, so you can view the results of the current lookup, or historical data, for comparison. The data in this window can be sorted upon any of its fields.

The row of buttons along the bottom of the window provide access to specific features of RouterCheck. The first, "Query . . . ," brings up a general-purpose data-display window (Fig. 12.4), in which you can view port, network, zone, route, or software version and serial number information gathered from the currently selected router.

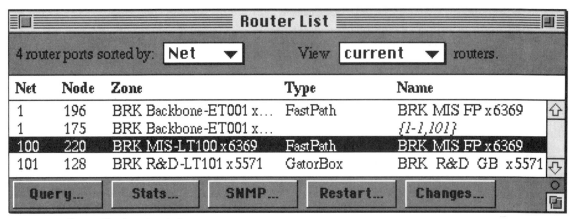

Figure 12.3   RouterCheck main window.

Figure 12.4   RouterCheck Query Window

The second button, "Stats . . . ," displays a long list of packet and error statistics for each network interface, which is updated continuously. Double-clicking on any line of this listing brings up another window, in which the data is graphed in real time, as it comes in.

In Fig. 12.5, the line showing the number of Ethernet packets sent since the last reset was selected, and this window shows the number of packets sent, quantified at five-minute intervals, as a percentage of total bandwidth. Much longer or shorter intervals may be selected, depending upon your needs.

The third button, "SNMP . . . ," queries any SNMP MIB, or Simple Network Management Protocol Management Information Base, that may exist in the selected router. SNMP is a standard management protocol which is, at the time of this writing, and for the last several years, only partially implemented by any vendor of AppleTalk routers. SNMP management consoles, which display information on a management station, use a common set of protocols to talk to SNMP MIBs, which are the information databases that reside within devices. MIBs come with a small interface which can be compiled into any console, so generic interplatform management should be possible. Unfortunately, security shortcomings within the SNMP protocol have dissuaded vendors to delay full implementation at least until the revised specification for SMP, or Secure Management Protocol, is finalized.

The fourth button, "Restart . . . ," simply asks you whether you really wish to reboot the selected router and, if you tell it to proceed, does so. This is useful when you wish to force the propagation of a zone name or network number change.

The fifth button, "Changes . . . ," initiates periodic monitoring of routers for changes in their zone name and net number lists.

Like CheckNet and Inter•Poll, RouterCheck is a basic tool that's hard to do without, when managing any network with very many routers.

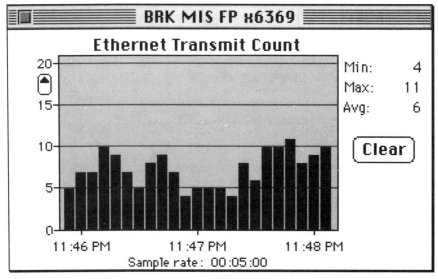

Figure 12.5 RouterCheck packet statistics graph.

12.3.4 EtherPeek and LocalPeek

These two packet analyzers, like similar products made by a similar company, perform the same function in Macintosh software as PC-based hardware protocol analyzers that cost well over $10,000. They allow you to watch each packet that goes by on the network, open up ones you're interested in, and examine the headers and data inside in a decoded form. They cover not only the AppleTalk protocols, but IP, Digital's DECNet and LAT, Novell's IPX, and Banyan Vines, as well.

Within the scrolling list of packets that have gone by there are several columns (Fig. 12.6). The first is a sequential number assigned to the packet while it's in the list. The second and third columns denote the sender and the intended recipient of the packet, while the fourth column may contain a "flag" indicating some condition or other; here, the dot simply indicates that these are all 802.3 Ethernet packets. The fifth column describes the packet type in moderate detail, the sixth indicates its size in bytes, and the seventh column contains a time stamp which can be viewed in absolute time, as here, relative to the beginning of the session, or as the interval since each previous packet.

In this list of captured packets, we can see three basic transactions between the three devices represented here. In packet 26 (Fig. 12.7), grommet.com, our Unix host, is broadcasting a Zone Information Protocol GetNetinfo Request. In packets 31 and 32, the GatorBox and FastPath respond with ZIP GNI Responses. In 27 and 29, the GatorBox and FastPath are querying grommet.com with AppleTalk Address Resolution Protocol Request packets, to which it responds with AARP Responses in 29 and 30.

To examine packet 26 in greater detail, we can double-click on its line to open it. The decode appears as in Fig. 12.7. We can pretty safely ignore the Ethernet

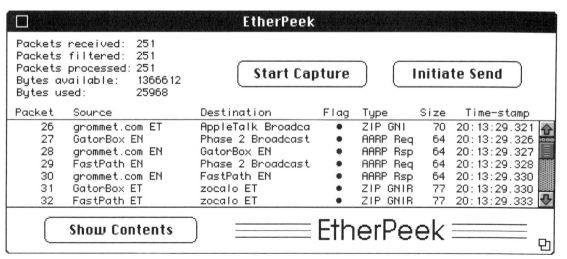

Figure 12.6   EtherPeek main window.

and 802.2 headers, and proceed to the AppleTalk headers, further in. The DDP header shows that this was indeed a broadcast packet, sent to 255, the broadcast address, by 1.61, the current address of grommet.com. It's being sent to and from ZIP sockets, as it should be, since its DDP type, 6, is that of a ZIP packet. Within the ZIP header and data, we can see that this is a GNI Request, ZIP function 5, and that the zone about which information is being requested is "BRK Backbone-ET001 x6369."

By pressing the right one of the two little arrows in the bottom right hand corner, we can proceed through the packet decodes to packet 31, the first of the two responses.

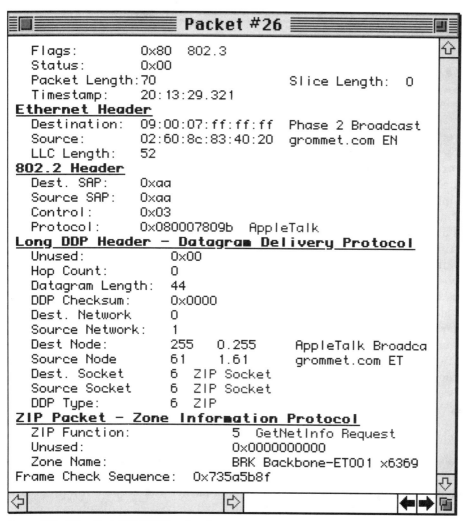

Figure 12.7   EtherPeek ZIP GNI Req decode.

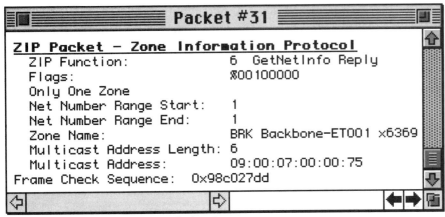

Figure 12.8   EtherPeek ZIP GNI reply decode.

We can see that this is a valid response, from what we know of the network we've built. Indeed, there is only the one zone associated with this Ethernet segment, and the net start and range are both 1, as well. The zone name is correct; if we were to calculate the multicast address out, it's a fair bet that it'd be correct as well.

It's when something is obviously not working, however, that protocol analyzers are most valuable. No other tools allow this kind of in-depth investigation of the working mechanism of network processes, so no other tools can give you the information you need to fix things that are broken at this deep a level.

That doesn't mean, however, that you should wait until things go wrong to pull out a protocol analyzer. Quite the contrary. Like any collector of data, it's worthless if it's used only in a state of abnormality. When your network is working well, or at least you think it is, you should capture packet streams from different parts of it as different network transactions take place, and store them for use as controls against which you can measure later packet samples taken during network malfunctions. Taking some time to come to understand the normal operation of your network at the packet level is good, as well. Like learning a language, it happens fastest under great duress (when you're in a foreign country, for instance, or in this case, when your network is already broken), but anything you've learned before that point, while it probably won't have made as deep an impression, can only serve to make your later task easier to understand and less productive of anxiety.

12.3.5 TrafficWatch

Like a packet analyzer, TrafficWatch puts the network interface into promiscuous mode, accepting packets to all addresses. Instead of capturing the whole packet, however, it simply notes the type of packet and keeps a running total of various statistics related to the traffic. Obviously, it can only observe packets in the zone the host machine is in, since it can't see through routers.

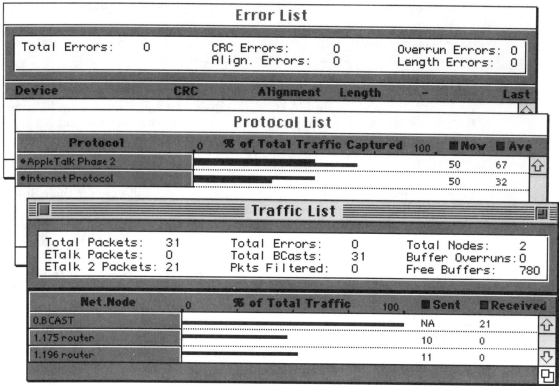

Figure 12.9 TrafficWatch.

TrafficWatch provides real-time graphing of the levels of traffic each device in a zone is responsible for, graphs the relative amounts of traffic of each protocol type, and graphs the different kinds of errors which occur.

Perhaps the most important feature of TrafficWatch is its ability to automatically save tab-text files containing matrices of the number of packets between each pair of machines in the zone over time, measured to a granularity of as little as five minutes.

When used as data for statistical analysis, this is an extremely powerful tool. It can very precisely model traffic flow over the course of days, allow you to find the peak load times for different resources and parts of the network, and find devices which access resources in other zones frequently, so you can consider moving them to a more appropriate zone.

12.3.6 Net Watchman and NetWorks

These two products exist in a nearly identical niche. Both poll with AppleTalk Echo Protocol packets to confirm the presence of devices at a regular interval. NetWorks can also use Internet Protocol ICMP Echo packets to poll TCP/IP devices. Both allow a variety of alerts when devices turn up missing, including dialog boxes, sounds, and alphanumeric paging, and NetWorks adds electronic mail and synthesized voice notification. Net Watchman offers slightly more flexible polling, which helps take hop-induced delays into account on large networks, while NetWorks has an easier-to-use interface.

The function they serve is to make sure that the network administrator is the first person to know, rather than the last to know, when a network service goes down. If you're the first to know, this gives you a fighting chance to bring the service back up before anybody (or at least everyone) notices that it's broken. Thus the pager support.

12.3.7   StarCommand

StarCommand is Farallon's proprietary management software for their StarController line of LocalTalk and Ethernet network hubs.

Farallon's combination of hardware and software confer an advantage over some other vendors', since they provide both in-band and out-of-band management. That is, the StarCommand software can find and control hubs either by signaling them through the network, using AppleTalk packets, or it can do so using a separate, proprietary two-wire connection. The advantages of out-of-band signaling are that it frees the network of traffic, it's potentially much faster, and it'll work even when the network isn't.

StarCommand's main window (Fig. 12.10) lists the StarControllers which it can find, in the order it finds them. It defaults to displaying which ports are turned on, and which off, but I've set it here to display running totals of the number of packets, and the percentage of bandwidth utilization, using the pop-up menu at the center of the window. Error-tabulation and hub interconnection views are available, as well. The green bars in the Traffic column move dynamically to show the relative amount of traffic graphically, and the little circles in the Errors column light up red, like little LEDs, whenever errors occur.

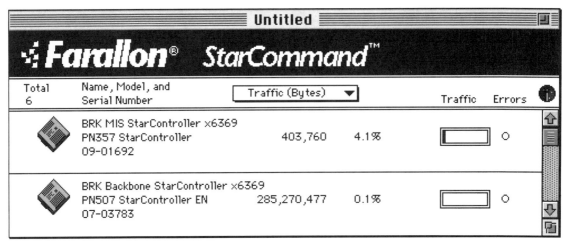

Figure 12.10   StarCommand main window.

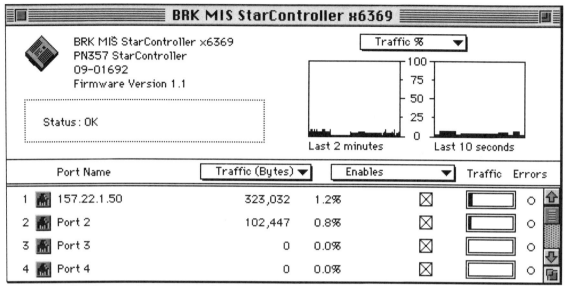

Figure 12.11   StarCommand secondary configuration window.

To inspect any particular StarController in greater detail, double-click on its line in the main window. A secondary configuration dialog (Fig. 12.11) is brought up, showing traffic and errors for each port. Some models are able to determine the NBP name of the device on each port, as well. Again, running error totals can be viewed instead of traffic totals. By double-clicking on any of the port icons, or on the icon for the StarController at the top of the window, you can view specific packet statistics, broken out by type of error.

StarCommand is an invaluable tool for debugging network problems, but unfortunately it's only useful if your network hubs are Farallon-made.

One word of caution: When StarCommand is opened, it defaults to searching both on AppleTalk, looking for in-band connections, and on your modem port, looking for out-of-band ones. If your StarControllers are all linked by an out-of-band system, turn off the AppleTalk searching in the Preferences window, opened from the File menu. If the machine on which you're running StarCommand isn't connected to the out-of-band system, then tell it to search all zones, and turn off the modem port searching. You can save a settings document, much like one for a telecommunications program, to which these preferences will apply. You can thus set up one document to open when you have access to the out-of-band system, and one for in-band use.

12.3.8   Nok Nok A/S

Nok Nok A/S is an AppleShare server management utility. It provides two basic services: logging and notification of user logins, and the enforcement of administrator-set limits on the duration of user sessions and idle time.

The logging and notification are configured separately. The logs are in the form of tab-delimited text files, which can be opened, sorted, and manipulated by spreadsheet applications.

The logging function is activated by the check-box at the top of the window (Fig. 12.12). As the log file can become quite large, logs can be limited in size, or new ones can be started automatically at the beginning of each day, on the same day of every week, or at the beginning of every month. As an optional security feature, Nok Nok can shut down the server if it finds itself unable to continue logging user sessions.

Nok Nok logs the date and time of each login, whether the user logged in as a registered or guest user, the account name they used, the name, zone, net, and node number of the machine they logged in from, the total length of time they were logged on, and the reason they were disconnected.

Notification of new logins can be accomplished in one of three ways: Nok Nok can display a dialog box with the user's name and machine name in it, it can play a sound, or it can bring the AppleShare application, and its monitor window, to the foreground.

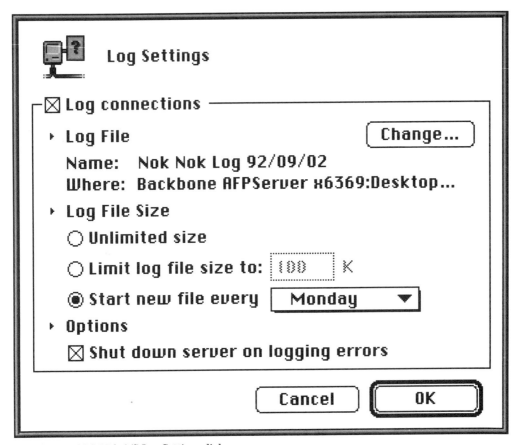

Figure 12.12   Nok Nok A/S Log Settings dialog.

Date	Time	UserType G-Guest R-Registered	UserName	MachineName	ZoneName	Net	Node	TimeOn	Disconnect 0-Connected 1-Normal 2-Idle 3-MaxTime 4-ShutDown 5-BadPassword 6-UnknownUser
9/2/92	8:55:11	R	Boyd, Grace x7716	Boyd, Grace x7716	BRK R&D-LT101	101	112	000:09:12	1
9/2/92	9:02:42	R	Denis, Elizabeth x8809	Denis, Elizabeth x8809	BRK R&D-LT101	101	87	002:48:19	2
9/2/92	9:27:38	G	Guest	Passarella, Ray x7241	OAK Prod-LT104	104	82	000:30:00	3

Figure 12.13 Nok Nok A/S User Log

For any user, Nok Nok-initiated disconnection is predicated upon the meeting of certain criteria, which are set in the dialog box in Fig. 12.14. Time limits can be set separately for registered users and people using the guest account, and different messages and alert times can be displayed for time-limit and idle-time disconnections. The "Ignore" options are useful to allow yourself an unlimited login duration, and to avoid cutting off users with files open in memory from the server-based originals.

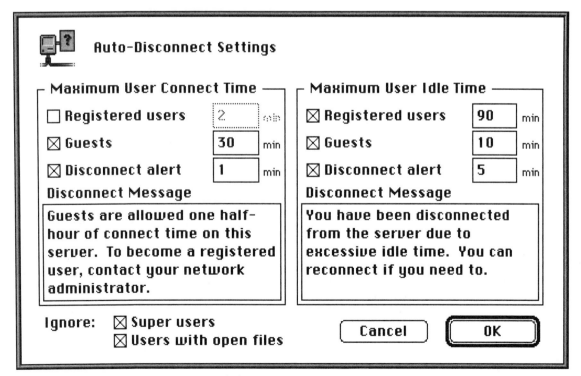

Figure 12.14 Nok Nok A/S Auto Disconnect dialog.

12.3.9 Spreadsheets and databases

It sounds odd, but two of your most valuable management tools will be your spreadsheet and database applications. The need for a database for cable-plant management was discussed at the end of Chap. 5. The same techniques can be used in tracking equipment that's been assigned to users, and the exported data from programs like StatusMac. Spreadsheets are often even more valuable, as they allow you to coalesce large masses of raw data that you've collected into some simple, concrete piece of knowledge. For instance, login data from copies of Nok Nok A/S could be used in calculations to evaluate the relative merit of different departments' requests for hardware upgrades for their AppleShare servers, or in association with AppleShare Server disk usage logs to calculate interdepartmental recharges for the use of server time and disk space. Alternatively, you could use data collected with TrafficWatch to help you determine when different nets should be upgraded from LocalTalk to Ethernet. Combining data from both these sources would give you a fairly good picture of when people performed the most work on AppleShare servers, and how that related temporally to their login times.

12.4 Support Tools

Another genre of software tools are aimed more at dealing with users than with the network itself, but since users are the eighth layer of the protocol stack, and usually fall within the network administrator's area of responsibility in many ways, some of these tools are equally important.

12.4.1 Timbuktu

As a management tool, Timbuktu is in something of a category all to itself. Unlike other such tools, it doesn't collect data per se. It's kind of a "remote control" for Macintoshes elsewhere on the network. It allows any user possessed of the correct password to view the screen of one or more other Macintoshes, behave as though his or her own mouse and keyboard were directly attached to each of the remote machines, and transfer files and the contents of the clipboard to and from them.

Timbuktu's control window (Fig. 12.15) is used primarily for selecting the Macintosh you want to access, and the type of control you wish to exercise over it.

Once you've initiated a session, the screen of the remote machine appears in a window on your desktop. The window is rather odd in appearance (Fig. 12.16), but that helps distinguish it from others on your desktop and keeps you from "getting lost." When you move your cursor into the window, the remote cursor leaps to match its position, and follows it until it leaves the window. The window can be set to auto-scroll, so that moving the cursor near the edge of the window prompts the window to scroll to keep the cursor inside.

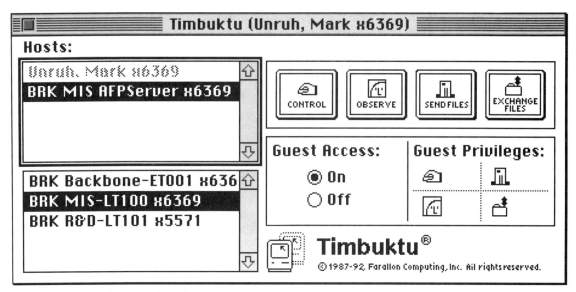

Figure 12.15   Timbuktu control window.

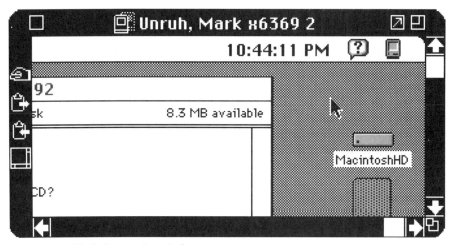

Figure 12.16   Timbuktu session window.

Timbuktu works by sending QuickDraw commands across the network, using ADSP, Apple's data stream protocol. QuickDraw is the language used inside the Mac to draw things on the screen. It's used almost universally, but some programs that use bitmapped images, notably HyperCard, can be very slow to redraw the screen, since the whole bitmap must be sent across the network, rather than just a few lines of update commands.

Timbuktu quickly achieved popularity with network administrators, since it allows one to remotely control Macintoshes which don't even have monitors, mice, or keyboards attached. This is advantageous for server machines for two reasons: First, it lessens the cost of the server, and second, it discourages physical tampering with the server machines. Servers administered and secured in this fashion are usually referred to as "headless servers."

Timbuktu can be used with machines which have no video card, either, but this takes additional RAM from the machine, since the machine can no longer use the video RAM on the card, and must block out some memory to use as a "soft screen" that Timbuktu can read. Thus if you configure a server of some kind with a video card in, and a screen attached, and it works fine, but when you remove the card it crashes during the startup process, or the server process never successfully launches, it's probably run out of memory. This is obviously not a problem on machines with built-in video circuitry.

The main use of Timbuktu, however, is in user support and remote diagnosis of problems that aren't locally visible. If a user reports a problem, you can log into the user's machine and view it for yourself, or perhaps explain to the user why what they're seeing doesn't constitute a problem. You can step them through processes they may not be able to get the hang of with verbal instructions alone, like configuring MacTCP or changing the network connection method.

12.4.2   Likewise

Apple's Likewise utility is designed primarily for "lab" applications, as in schools, where a group of machines, often all within one zone, need to be identically configured.

As you can see in Fig. 12.17, Likewise's capabilities are limited, but it's extremely easy to use. In the Client Settings area, you can set the name of the boot volume of each client to the same name, and you can do the same for User and Machine names. Leaving any of these fields blank tells Likewise to leave whatever value is currently being used on client machines untouched. The Monitors pop-up menu allows you to set the client machine monitors to the maximum number of colors supported by the video drivers on each machine, the maximum number of shades of gray, or to black and white. In the Actions area, you can tell Likewise to delete all the files on the client machine's disk before copying new ones over, delete only unlocked files, or to delete only those files which are replaced by the software that's being distributed. Checking Update Settings applies the changes specified in the Client Settings area. Update System Folder copies the System Folder form the current machine to all the client machines. This will include settings like mouse tracking speed, background pattern, map location and time zone, and views, as well as copying whatever Control Panels, System Extensions, and the like you may have on the administrator machine. Synchronize Clocks does just that, resetting the clocks to match the time on the master machine.

When working on a wide area network, Synchronizing Clocks is a bad idea if you've got clients in different time zones. Since Likewise updates the map

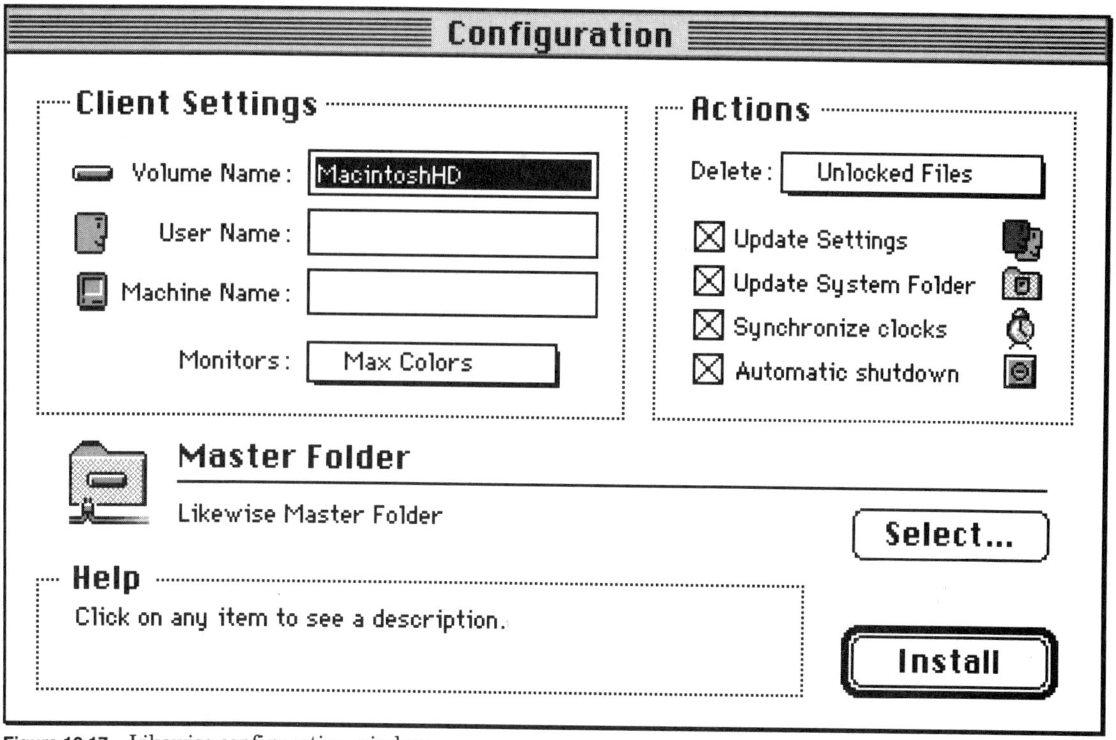

Figure 12.17   Likewise configuration window.

location and time zone settings to match those of the master machine, it has no way of synchronizing clocks while keeping them in different time zones. Automatic Shutdown shuts each client machine down when the updating process is through. Remember, though, that some machines must be physically turned off, as well as shut down, and it cannot do that. Pressing the "Select . . ." button allows you to specify one folder other than the System Folder to copy to the client machines. This folder may contain as many subfolders as you like. It should contain all the applications you want client machines to have, unless you want them to be run at startup, in which case they should be in the Master Machine's Startup Folder, and Update System Folder must be checked.

The client side of the operation requires that each machine be booted from a special boot disk. There are both double-density (800K) and high-density (FDHD) client boot disk images distributed with the package. The disk launches a client application at startup, which waits for the update to occur.

Back at the master machine, press the Install button. You'll be prompted to select zones to update. Likewise uses broadcast packets to send the updates, so you don't need to select individual machines to update; any machines running the client software in a selected zone will be updated. The update process occurs at about the same rate that a network backup would: about one megabyte per minute on LocalTalk, faster on Ethernet. An estimated time to completion will be displayed on the master machine during the update process.

If the System Folder and settings do not need to be updated, the Likewise client application can be run from the client machines' normal hard disks. If you are going to update the systems on multiple machines from a single one, it's crucial that you install complete System software on the master machine, rather than just support for whatever model of machine the master itself is. To do this, run the System installer on the master machine, and select "Custom" instead of "Easy Install." Choose "System Software for any Macintosh" from the list of available options, in addition to anything else you may wish to install. If you don't do this, resources that other kinds of machines need to boot up will not be present; after you copy the System to other machines, they won't be able to restart.

12.4.3   StatusMac

StatusMac is one of several similarly featured management applications which started life as facilities-management tools, more than as network administration ones, but have evolved since. Basically, they allow *profiling* of the hardware and software configuration on machines on the network, with the goal of allowing administrators to track the need for client hardware and software upgrades, track the spread of computer viruses, and assess the capabilities of existing machines. Many of these functions are of use to network administrators, as well as to facilities managers; those two duties are, as often as not, invested in the same person or department in many companies in any case.

The program's main window (Fig. 12.18) simply displays a list of the machines it knows about, including the model, machine name, zone name, and the date on which the most recent information about the machine was collected. Collecting information is a simple affair for the administrator, requiring only the compilation of a list of the machines to be polled. The poll requests are sent off to the user machines, where they're received by a client Control Panel which alerts and allows the user to commence the profiling immediately, after a delay or upon shutdown. The profiling process takes three to five minutes on most machines. When the profile has been completed, it's returned to the Control Panel on the administrator's machine, which then passes it back to the administrator application if it's open and the "Auto Import" box is checked. If the administrator's machine is not available on the network at the time the profile is completed, it's stored on the user's machine for later delivery. This store-and-forward approach sets StatusMac apart from its competitors, which don't currently support this delivery method.

Once a profile has been completed, returned, and imported into StatusMac's database, which should all happen automatically, it can be viewed by simply double-clicking on the associated line of the main window. The data is displayed (Fig. 12.19) using a window reminiscent of the pre-System 7 Control Panel, using a scrolling list of categories on the right hand side to limit and organize

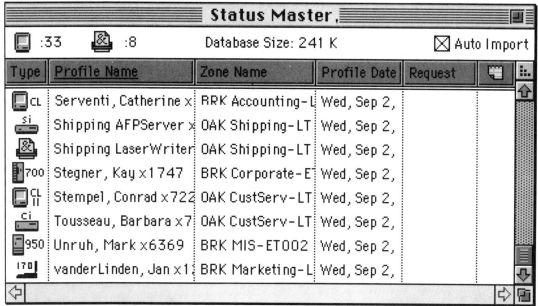

Figure 12.18   StatusMac main window.

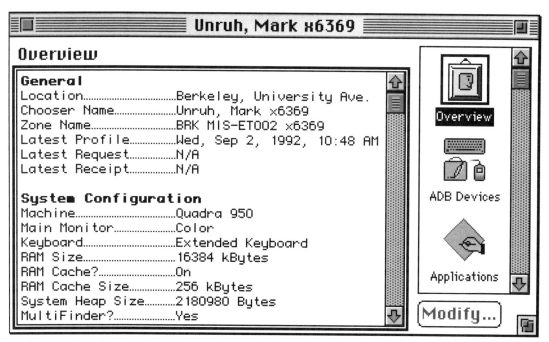

Figure 12.19   StatusMac profile window.

the data being displayed in the data field. The range of information collected by these programs is astounding, ranging from the creation and modification dates of applications and extensions on the disks of users' machines, to the characteristics of the disks themselves, to the size of the bit-depth of each monitor. Of particular interest to network administrators, however, are the Ethernet hardware address, IP address, current AppleTalk LAP, AppleTalk version, networking-related driver code loaded, and similar information.

StatusMac also allows administrators to create their own reports, which serve as both filters and templates for the display of data. In this example (Fig. 12.20), included with the application, we've simply narrowed the data down to the currently installed System software version for each user. A set of logical operators is available as well, including *and, or, not,* and qualifiers like *greater* and *less than,* where appropriate. As an example, we can construct a simple filter to find people who might need RAM upgrades and can't use virtual memory, by specifying:

```
RAM < 8 megabytes
    and
System Heap > 2 megabytes
    and not
32-Bit Clean = Yes
```

Alternatively, a more complicated filter might check the size on disk, modification date, version, and other characteristics of several applications to check for corruption or infection.

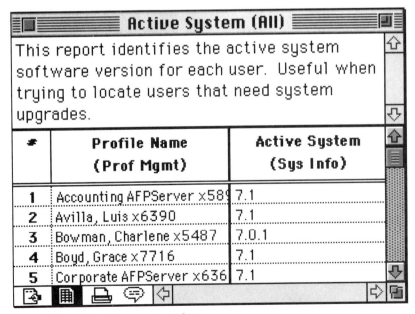

Figure 12.20   StatusMac report window.

12.4.4 NetDistributor

NetDistributor is a utility which facilitates the remote installation of software on users' machines. It allows you to create a "package" of software to be installed, incorporating many of the same kinds of logical operators that StatusMac does. These packages are then transferred to the user machines and executed. Each one checks the parameters of the user's machine on which it finds itself, performs the logical operations needed to decide whether and what to install, and performs the installation.

NetDistributor combines many of the best features of Likewise and StatusMac, in a useful conglomeration.

Figure 12.21 is an installation script associated with a package containing a MacTCP upgrade. Although it may look complicated at first glance, it's really quite simple, although not all the details are visible at this level. In the first line, we look for a preexisting copy of MacTCP, of version 1.1 (the version in

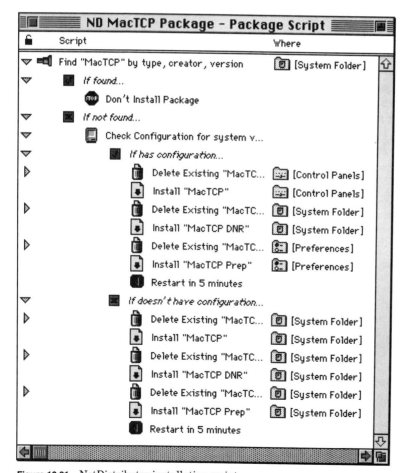

Figure 12.21 NetDistributor installation script.

this package) or newer. If one is found matching this description, the script terminates without installing anything. If none are found to match this criterion, the script proceeds to check whether the System version is 7.0 or newer. If so, it deletes any existing copies of MacTCP and its associated files from the Control Panels, System, and Preferences folders, immediately installing replacements from the distribution package. If the System is of a version previous to 7.0, it won't have a Control Panels or Preferences folder within the System folder, so the installation works entirely within the System folder. Once one of these two possible installations has taken place, the user is given five minutes to save any open files and quit what they're doing, and the machine restarts to load the new software.

Although this example is rather trivial, and could easily be accomplished without reference to the manual, much more powerful operations are available, allowing the installation of fonts, desk accessories, and even sounds, under both System 7 and previous System versions.

12.5 The Solution

Mark's conclusion? That by gaining a better understanding, himself, of the processes at work in his network, by instituting a set of stricter and more completely thought-out policies, by delineating a chain of command for dealing with network problems, and most importantly by buying airline tickets under a false name, he may be able to enjoy his vacations undisturbed in the future.

13

Ethics and Security

13.1 The Problem

Mark, our network administrator, cognizant of the evil that people do, is aware of two problems as yet undealt with.

The first, an ethical issue, is that he's reasonably sure that although American Grommet owns many copies of quite a range of different commercial software packages, the company doesn't own as many copies of some specific programs as there are people using the software. He's seen the small print in every box of software, and has begun having nightmares involving tiny software police jumping out of those boxes.

Problem number two is the result not of his own, but of the company president's paranoia. She's deathly afraid that the wily and devious agents of the competition, National Eyelet Corporation, will engage in industrial espionage, and steal the trade secrets which have lead to American Grommet's domination of the particularly crucial bushing market. Since security is his boss's concern, it must, perforce, be Mark's as well, and he resolves to investigate both matters.

13.2 Software Licensing

Although you might not think it, the license agreements included in commercial software packages can be fascinating reading. The agreements by which, in theory at least, you become bound as soon as you open the envelopes which contain the disks, usually explain that you haven't actually purchased a copy of the software, but instead have licensed the right to install and use it on one computer at your site.

Most license agreements lay out terms and conditions which generally follow these lines:

- You may make one copy of the software for backup purposes, or you may install the software onto a hard disk and retain the original copy as your backup. You may not make any further copies, whether they be on floppy disks, through the network, or part of a tape backup.

- The manufacturer owns the software and sometimes even the disks on which it's shipped. What you've purchased is a nonexclusive license to use it on a single machine, which the manufacturer can revoke at any time.

- The working copy may be used at a single machine, and usually may not be accessed over the network.

- You may not modify your copy of the software, by changing the icon or any of the dialog boxes for instance, and you're especially forbidden to remove any copyright or trademark information.

- You may not rent use of the software to someone else.

- You may not try to figure out how the software works, for the purpose of creating a competing software package.

- You may transfer the license (resell your package of the software), provided the buyer agrees to the terms of the license agreement, you destroy any copies which aren't transferred to the buyer, and the manufacturer is notified in writing.

- The manufacturer disclaims liability for damages caused by the software to the greatest extent that it may do so under local law.

The effect on network administrators is many-fold. First and most obvious, most license agreements effectively preclude the sharing of software on file servers. If you install the software onto the server, it constitutes your working copy, which can only be legally used on that computer, rather than from another computer, over the network. And if someone copies the file onto their own machine and runs it, there then exist three copies, which again violates the agreement. Fortunately, many software companies take this into account, and have special "site licenses" which allow several users to run the software simultaneously, and sometimes even allow more than that number of copies of the file to exist on different computers, provided that no more than the licensed number are in use at any particular time.

In practice, what usually satisfies both the manufacturer and the users is the purchase by a company of as many copies of the software as are going to be simultaneously in use by employees during periods of peak usage. Thus, if a company had forty employees, and twelve of them used FileMaker, but only eight of them would ever use it simultaneously, the company would purchase eight copies, and install one of them on a file server. This solution is not officially recognized by some companies, however, and brings up two more problems: First, if software is launched across the network, it runs at a considerable performance disadvantage and increases the level of traffic on the network; second, if users are allowed to copy the software onto their own disks, the network administrator loses the ability to limit the number of copies in simultaneous use.

As discussed in Chap. 6, AppleShare has the capability to both copy-protect files which reside on the server, and to limit the number of concurrent users. In Fig. 13.1, we've applied all available security measures to a copy of Claris File-

Maker Pro. The number of concurrent users has been limited to five, so as not to exceed the number of copies owned; the file has been copy-protected, so that users cannot transfer copies of it to their own machines and run them there, where AppleShare has no control; and the file has been locked, so that users cannot modify it.

If you can afford the performance degradation imposed by launching software from an AppleShare server, the applications can be copy-protected and launch limiting can be enabled, to keep users from making illicit copies and to enforce license compliance. If software is to reside on enduser workstations, the administrator no longer has that ability. By entering serial numbers into copies of software yourself, and keeping a log of the location of each copy, you can however begin to achieve the same effect, especially if you perform occasional internal audits to confirm the location of each copy, and there are no extraneous copies as well. Software such as Sassafrass Software's KeyServer alters each copy of an application in such a way that it cannot be launched without checking out a "key" from a centralized server, much like the launch-limiting functionality in AppleShare. This way, modified copies can be freely distributed among user workstations, and will be useless if they are removed

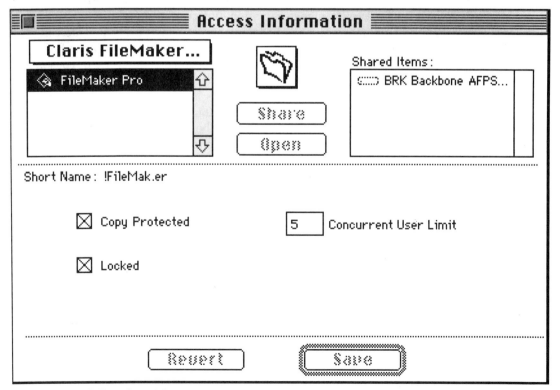

Figure 13.1 AppleShare launch limiting.

from the network, or if the number of copies in use is as great as the number of copies which have been licensed. KeyServer also keeps detailed usage logs, which you may be able to use to justify the licensing of more copies of applications of which all copies are frequently in use. Although this certainly represents the spirit of most software licenses, it does violate not one, but two of the clauses common to many agreements, since it involves modifying the application's code, as well as distributing more than the licensed number of copies to your users. Management software like Status•Mac and GraceLAN, which were discussed in Chap. 12, greatly aid the process of internal auditing. Renaming copies of serialized applications to include an identifiable part of the serial number can help as well, although users can easily rename the applications.

Another, and more minor, consideration which license agreements serve to highlight is that one shouldn't include application software in backups, whether they be of users' computers or of server volumes. First, under the terms of the license, this would constitute a third copy of the software; second, any corruption which the software may have been subjected to in use will be carried through in the backup. It's both more politic and more prudent to replace software on restored disks with copies from the original distribution disks. Most backup software is intelligent enough to allow filtering-out of application software, while still including things like preferences files and user dictionaries, which contain customization and user-supplied information.

Although the manufacturers of Macintosh software rarely pursue contract violators themselves, there is a well-funded organization, called the Software Publishers Association, which was formed specifically for that purpose. The SPA operates on anonymous tips, and coordinates raids with local law-enforcement agencies on corporations which are suspected of license violations. The investigators create a list of all the software found on each computer or server, contact the manufacturers, compare the number of copies found with the number of copies registered, and sue for the dollar value of the difference, on behalf of all the manufacturers. This can often be a staggering sum.

Although the licenses (those printed on stickers are called, amusingly, "licenses of adhesion") were once strictly grounds for civil suit, as of October 1992 medium- and large-scale software piracy can now be prosecuted as a felony as well. 1992 Senate Bill SB893 makes the possession of ten items of pirated software, or any number of items with a total value greater than $2500, punishable by up to a year imprisonment and a $250,000 fine.

Whatever one's opinion on the enforceability or propriety of such licenses and laws, the SPA and SB893 should stand as a caution to all network administrators to take responsibility for deterring misdeeds on the part of their endusers, lest that responsibility be placed upon them after the fact.

13.3   Representation of the Company

The virtual space people are in when they communicate with each other via electronic means has been called "cyberspace." This space is no longer populated solely by hackers and pioneers, but has been colonized by business. Universities, banks, research organizations, the military, and corporations of all sorts have staked out claims in this space, and are actively using it to conduct business and business communication.

Just as the physical premises of your company, its offices, and grounds may convey some distinct impression to visitors and casual passersby, so too will its appearance on the Internet or any smaller networks on which the company or its employees have a presence.

Thus, it's important that whatever values your company holds, regarding proper conduct and comportment of employees and the appearance of the organization, be extended to apply to the virtual space of the computer network as well. The electronic "public image" of a company is apparent in two ways: statements made by recognized employees in postings or electronic mail directed outside the company, and the organizational structure of any computing resources which are accessible from outside the company.

13.3.1 Electronic mail

As we saw in Chaps. 7 and 11, whenever electronic mail is sent through the Internet or virtually any other electronic mail medium, a return address is prepended to the message in an address header. This return address identifies the writer with the site from which the message was sent or posted, possibly your company. In addition, it's common practice to use *signature files* or *.sigs* which are automatically appended to outgoing messages of all kinds, to provide the same kind of information in more human-readable form. A typical .sig might read as follows:

```
Elizabeth A. Denis                        denis@grommet.com
Senior Scientist—Materials Research    ...sun!grommet!denis
American Grommet, Inc.                  voice +1 408 555 8809
4200 Caribbean Drive                      fax +1 408 555 1537
Sunnyvale, CA 94089-1999               home +1 510 555 1212
```

Figure 13.2   A typical signature file.

Many .sig files also include witticisms or quotes, but the majority are perfectly formal, just like this one. The problem is that this in effect attaches company imprimatur to every outgoing document, without regard to the content, much as though it were printed on company stationery.

Both studies and observation show that people using electronic media feel less socially constrained and, while possibly being more productive, also engage in more outright and contentious disagreement. Between individuals who are used to electronic communication, this is called "flaming" and is generally taken in good humor. When an individual appears to be representing or speaking on behalf of a company, however, it can lead to embarrassing misunderstandings and potentially even to litigation.

In response to this problem, some companies modify their Unix mail software to automatically append a disclaimer to all mail, or require that employees include it in their signature file. Most disclaimers are quite simple and straightforward, although they're frequently satirized by employees. Thus:

```
Elizabeth A. Denis                      edenis@grommet.com
Senior Scientist—Materials Research     ...sun!grommet!edenis
American Grommet, Inc.                   voice +1 408 555 8809
4200 Caribbean Drive                      fax +1 408 555 1537
Sunnyvale, CA 94089-1999                 home +1 510 555 1212

Disclaimer: The views expressed above are those of the author, and do not
necessarily represent the opinions or policies of American Grommet, Inc.
```

Figure 13.3 Signature file with disclaimer.

In most companies the right to express and define corporate policy is limited to individuals in a few positions, and there is a system of accountability already in place. For instance, official correspondence with customers is usually handled by customer service departments and correspondence with the media by public relations. There must be some official channel for expressing the opinions which are those of the company in electronic form as well, and it follows that the same policy which applies to paper and telephone correspondence should be extended to electronic representation of the company. Thus it's necessary to set up some accounts without disclaimers; such accounts should be accessible only to those authorized to make official statements. Accounts of this kind are often used to moderate mailing lists, answer questions in newsgroups and on online forums, and receive correspondence from customers. In this last case, the address must be either intuitive or easily remembered. Account names commonly used for such communication are "info" and "support" or, in this case, "info@grommet.com" and "support@grommet.com".

13.3.2 Accessible resources

The appearance of the network to outside observers will differ greatly depending upon where the viewer is located, what means they're using to observe the network, and who they are. First and most obvious, if your company maintains an anonymous ftp site on the Internet, care must be taken to keep the directory structure orderly and easy to understand.

To this end, and to limit liability and retain control, the vast majority of ftp sites maintain read-only access privileges for anonymous users. The only two legitimate uses for anonymously writeable directories on ftp servers are for individuals at other sites to deposit files for users at the host site, or to submit new files for review for inclusion in the ftp library. In either case, the primary addressee should be an employee of the host company, and since ftp-able machines are certain to support mail as well, there's little reason to make user-writeable directories available for anonymous use.

Many sites have documents in each directory which detail the purpose of the directory and describe each of the files in it. Such documents are usually named "00readme.txt" or something similar, such that they appear at the top of any alphabetical listing, their purpose is evident, and it's obvious that they're in simple ascii form.

In Fig. 13.4, directories which are accessible via anonymous ftp are in bold-face while those to which access is restricted are not. As you can see, the most potentially dangerous directories, etc/, bin/, and dev/, are not accessible, while the pub/ or "public" directory is. Publicly accessible directories on Unix systems are universally named pub/ so that, although the temptation to change the name of the directory to something one feels to be more intuitive may be strong, submitting to it would in fact achieve the opposite effect. Subdirectories within pub/ contain different kinds of public information and documents, for instance, customer service contact information, lists of local dealerships in different regions, press releases and announcements, and answers to frequently asked questions or "FAQs."

Subscriber-controlled subdirectories, or "forums" on online services such as CompuServe, GEnie, AppleLink, and America Online, serve much the same purpose as ftp sites, but pose little security threat, since the directories are maintained on remote hosts which are not connected to your network. They generally provide a means of communication with customers who are less technically astute than those who would have Internet access, but more than those who have no telecommunications resources at all. Online services are expected to be more user-friendly than the Internet, and a good organizational scheme is therefore critical in the forums they contain. Since there's no reason to keep any private information in such a forum, the whole forum is somewhat akin to the pub/ directory at an ftp site, and the subdirectory structure outlined for that application would be equally appropriate in a forum.

13.4 Security

At most computerized companies, there are many potential targets for those with technical acumen and illicit motivation. The press often terms such peo-

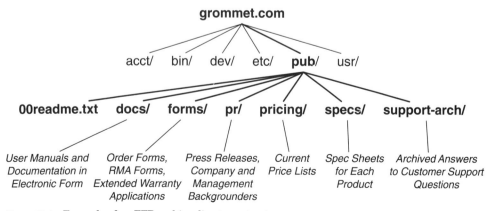

Figure 13.4 Example of an FTP archive directory structure.

ple *hackers*, which is neither accurate nor politically correct in many circles. In more proper usage, a hacker is someone who can create "hacks," that is, programs or pieces of computer code which are quick and dirty, but effective. People with the ability to do so are highly respected within the programming community. People who break into other people's computer systems, on the other hand, are *crackers*, the subset of those people who destroy things they find on those systems are *trashers*, and those who duplicate software without paying for it are *pirates*. Again despite popular characterization, such behavior is tolerated even less within the computer industry than outside of it. After all, the victim of an act of software piracy is not the person from whom the software is copied, but the author/programmer of the work; and who has more to lose at the hands of hackers and trashers than a computer company?

In the following discussion of cracking and the means and technologies of its prevention, it should be borne in mind that fewer than one quarter of all computerized firms take any steps toward securing their systems against attack, and the majority of those have not been ill affected as a result. Thus these are *potential* measures, rather than strongly suggested ones. For the most part, they do place some burden upon users, and each company has to decide for itself where to draw the line of compromise between convenience and security.

13.4.1   Modeling the problem

Measures can be taken by any company to reduce the risk of both intrusion and piracy. The first step in doing so is to model the situation. If one is to erect barriers against such misdeeds, one must decide what the barrier is to delineate; that is, what is to be on each side of the barrier, and who can cross the line that it creates.

One simple model creates two areas: one inside the company, one outside the company. With two areas, there are four possibilities (shown in Fig. 13.5) for any instance of wrong-doing: entirely within the company, from outside the company directed within, entirely outside of the company, and from within the company directed to the outside.

Securing a site is a matter of tradeoffs. As a general rule, any form of security imposes some task or burden upon both legitimate and illegitimate users. Ideally, a balance can be reached which sufficiently frustrates crackers that none are able to enter, while not annoying your own users so much that they don't try to use the secured services. The trick is in finding security procedures which prove to be a greater barrier to illegitimate users than your own users. This could be a criterion by which to pass qualitative judgment on any security procedure: Efficient security measures raise the barriers to entry proportionately higher for illegitimate users than for legitimate ones.

13.4.2   Inside-In

Examples of problems which occur within companies are not hard to come by; misuse of computing resources for personal ends, making copies of software

Figure 13.5 Matrix of mechanized malfeasance.

out-of-license, and illicitly accessing payroll or personnel records are but a few of them.

Misuse of resources is a problem not easily subjected to technological limitation; we've already discussed a few methods of enforcing license compliance, and the rest of these problems center around the use of shared files which reside on file servers. Control is achieved primarily through the rigorous use of both individual and group access privileges. Try to get your users to think in the same terms as well, so that upon beginning new projects of a sensitive nature, they'll discuss the creation of an appropriate privilege group and folder on a server volume with you. Encourage your users to think in terms of limiting liability: If they can show that they never had access to information which has been leaked, they won't be under suspicion. Similarly, if they operate from a default position of granting limited access, rather than unlimited access to information, they're less likely to be accused of impropriety if it falls into the wrong hands. Remember that even the best individual and group access schemes are rendered useless if users tell each other their passwords instead of using appropriate shared spaces to transfer files. Another way AppleShare security is commonly breached is almost ridiculously simple: Users log into servers and leave them mounted on their machines while they're away from their desks. Not only does this allow anyone who happens to pass by to reassign folder privileges (something that is unlikely to be noticed, if done carefully, since the icon won't change, and most people don't routinely check the access privileges of their folders), but a skilled cracker can read the user's AppleShare password for each mounted volume out of the client machine's memory. A simple way to discourage users from casually making unauthorized use of each others' machines is to employ any one of a number of screen savers which, when "woken up," request a password before relinquishing control of the Macintosh. Although easily bypassed by rebooting the computer, this does present a first line of defense, since most people would hesitate to reboot another user's workstation, especially when they have no way of discerning whether it contains unsaved work.

Although packet-capturing utilities like LocalPeek, which we used in Chap. 2, are a great boon to troubleshooting, they are a security risk as well. In Fig. 2.9 we watched the contents of a printed document being sent from a Macintosh to a LaserWriter. Anyone else using a similar tool could capture and read both this and many other kinds of network traffic, since very little software supports encryption of data transmitted over the network. Thus, it's crucial to limit the availability of packet-capturing utilities to members of your network support staff who have a legitimate need for them. Again, the lists of applications on users' machines which can be generated by Status·Mac and GraceLAN are invaluable in finding copies of such utilities. Any time you're hunting for specific files on a network, be aware that users may be storing them on servers instead of their local disks, or even on floppy disks, which aren't visible to you at all. Although users can easily change the names of applications in order to disguise them, the means of changing their creation date, creator signature, and size are slightly more obscure. The database capabilities of management software packages make searching through such clues fairly easy.

Fortunately, versions 1.1 and higher of LocalPeek and EtherPeek register sockets of type "monitor" which can be seen on the network, and utilities like NetWatchman, which can watch for the appearance of specific socket types or names, can be used to log the use of these two packet-capturing utilities. Socket registration can, however, be defeated if the user turns off AppleTalk on their machine before running the utility. Other utilities like Apple Peek, Cayman's Watch, and Neon Software's NetMinder Ethernet and NetMinder LocalTalk, have no such provision. Since they must turn AppleTalk off in order to switch to promiscuous mode and capture packets addressed to other people, the Macintosh on which they're running becomes invisible on the network while they're running; this provides a small clue as to their use.

13.4.3 Outside-In

The most widely popularized form of cracking, examples of outside-in security breaches are mostly the result of casual experimentation by kids with modems and too much spare time, although there is, of course, espionage which occurs in some industries. This poses a greater potential threat.

The goals of casual crackers are often hard to anticipate, but, from looking at documented cases, the most common ones are simply to gain complete access to a system without necessarily doing anything with it, or to create user accounts which appear legitimate and can be used in the future for browsing through a system or storing data on disk. The vast majority of documented break-ins have occurred on Unix machines connected to the Internet. These provide tempting targets for several reasons: They're available on a 24-hour basis and are most likely unsupervised during crackers' primarily nocturnal hours; since they maintain full-time connections, they're more likely to be useful for a storage place or as a point of departure for a further crack (to be discussed further in Sec. 13.4.4, Outside-Out); they use a common language and set of protocols so the cracker needn't be familiar with the particular machine that's being targeted; and due to the complexity and continual state of development of the Unix operating system, new security loopholes are being found, publicized, and documented constantly. Moreover, Unix is the system of choice at nearly all universities, so many people are exposed to it, usually in an environment where security breaches are either overlooked or not punished rigorously. Local Area Networks, on the other hand, are often not directly connected to the Internet, and use simple but proprietary protocols. Thus the number of crackers who could successfully break into a Unix machine probably outnumber those who could do anything at all illicit on an AppleTalk network by a hundred to one. The motivation is much less in any case.

The obvious first step in securing any Unix machines on your net is to decide whether or not to make a full-time connection to the Internet. As was discussed in Chap. 11, the benefits of such a connection are mostly in being able to access other Internet sites and being directly accessible to others on the Internet, and faster delivery of mail and other services. Through a periodical dialup connection to a UUCP mail feed, rather than a full-time connection, there's very little that a cracker can hope to achieve, since he's limited to sending mail, rather than personally appearing "in your machine" via rlogin, telnet, or ftp. A second step, which may seem counterproductive, is to avoid leaving large amounts of disk space on Internet-accessible machines unutilized. Although having a lot of freespace on your disks prevents fragmentation and other problems, it's also a temptation to anyone who needs someplace to cache or buffer data. If you consider freespace a form of conspicuous consumption, it's easy to see why avoiding it may make you less of a target.

If your network has a full-time connection to the Internet, there are still measures you can take to keep your data inaccessible to those who aren't legitimate users. First of all, keep important documents on Macintosh-based Apple-Share servers, since they don't run Unix and won't be as vulnerable. If you're using NCSA Telnet to transfer files between your workstations and Unix machines, you should be aware that by default it publishes your Macintosh or PC's hard drives as an ftp server, does not require a password, and gives full read and write privileges to all files. This feature can be turned off each time the application is launched, using the appropriate menu command, or the line "ftp=no" can be added to the config.tel file. Alternatively, to use NCSA Telnet's ftp functions with password protection, you can use the included Telpass utility to create a table of users and passwords for ftp clients.

There is an organization which collects and distributes information on patching security holes in different vendors' implementations of Unix, called the Computer Emergency Response Team/Coordination Center, or CERT, for short. CERT maintains a mailing list for its bulletins, to which you can subscribe by mailing to cert@cert.org. CERT is housed at Carnegie Mellon University, in Pittsburgh, Pennsylvania, and maintains a 24-hour hotline at +1 412 268 7090.

Probably the most common form of security, and the most widely touted, is dial-in security. This encompasses any security procedures which are imposed upon people who wish to make a connection to your network, or some particular machine on your network, from a remote location. To connect to a network like we've built in this book, they might want to dial into some form of AppleTalk Remote Access server, create a half-routed connection with a Shiva device on your net, or establish a terminal session with a Unix machine. Although all three of these devices include their own password security, many people feel that a single password is insufficient protection. Thus another device or process must be added to impose a second security measure.

The most common alternative is the dial-back modem. Dial-back modems keep registers of names, passwords, and phone numbers. When users connect to a dial-back modem, they are prompted for a name and a password. The modem then compares the entered name and password to its table; if they're valid, it hangs up and calls the user back at the associated phone number. The liabilities of this system are obvious: First and foremost, there is no inherent provision for valid users who must dial in from more than one location, or do not know in advance the phone number of the location they're calling from. Furthermore, consider the number of situations in which a dedicated data line is not available to the caller, to answer the return call: In hotels and motels the telephones are answered by the front desk, which then forwards the call, a situation the modem cannot provide for. Similarly, salespeople at customer sites are unlikely to be able to commandeer a direct phone line that does not pass through a receptionist or automated attendant. Dial-back security is often unworkable in situations which require automated connections, since many calling devices aren't programmed to do the hanging up and answering of the call-back necessary to complete a connection with dial-back modem. Worst of all, whenever a phone number has to be added or changed, the administrator must reprogram each modem individually, an unenviable task at best. The advantages of the dial-back system are not to be scoffed at, however, and can weigh heavily in its favor in situations which do not require the flexibility which it's unable to provide. For instance, if a small number of engineers who work for your company have computers at home, and need to be able to access network services at night and on weekends, it may be a good solution. Their phone numbers are unlikely to change frequently; if they already have computers and modems at home, they may already have dedicated data lines installed as well, and if anyone tries to enter the network using their name and password, they get a call at home, alerting them to the problem.

One means of providing for remote users who aren't at a fixed location, which admittedly negates much of the value of dial-back security, is to assign a 700 number to traveling users. 700 numbers offer variable call-forwarding, with only a single termination point. Thus when a user is at a location with a phone line that can receive calls, he or she can call the 700 number, enter the PIN, or password, and tell it to forward calls to that location. Next, they initiate a call to the dial-back modem, which returns a call to the 700 number, which terminates on the user's location until redirected. 700 numbers are currently available only through AT&T, but work internationally.

It's interesting to consider that since the security of the dial-back system depends not upon the name and password, but upon the security of the telephone to which the call is returned, the name and password need not be different, nor particularly secure or unguessable in and of themselves. The lack of control a network administrator may usually exercise over a phone line installed at a user's house can be a serious drawback, however. Since local telcos rarely, if ever, confirm the addition of new service orders with subscribers, a cracker could easily add busy call-forwarding to the home phone service of a user, thus making it possible to extend calls which should terminate at the legitimate user's location out to his own. Such a deceit would not be noticed until the end of the next billing period, by which time, presumably, the cracker would have made his move, since the user's normal dial-in operations would not be effected. When the cracker wanted to intercept a call, he would use a second line at his own location to dial the user's data line, just after the dial-back modem has hung up, thus busying it out, and momentarily activating call-forwarding at the crucial instant that the dial-back modem returns the call. While in practice the cracker would not forward the call directly to his own number, but rather through some diversion, the scheme remains the same.

A more recent and direct innovation requires the use of a "box" which the cracker places between his modem and telephone line. He uses his own modem to call the target site, enters any user's name, and the box simulates the sound of the line being disconnected. It waits a few seconds for the target site's modem to go off-hook again, simulates the sound of a dial tone, accepts any outgoing touch-tones, and simulates a ring tone on both sides of the box, completing the connection as soon as the cracker's modem goes off-hook to answer the call. The box is, in effect, masquerading as a legitimate telephone switch, while never actually relinquishing control of the line back to the telephone company's equipment. Simpler still, a cracker could just use a laptop computer and modem with a pair of alligator clips to connect directly to the legitimate user's phone line, at the point at which it enters the user's house. In short, the problem with dial-back security is that it relies upon nonexistent physical security at remote locations, outside the administrator's authority, but unfortunately still within his or her responsibility.

The dial-in authentication devices currently viewed as most secure and reliable are those which use effectively random passcodes. There are two basic methodologies that have been devised. Both require that users carry security tokens, which are tiny electronic devices frequently made in the form-factor of credit cards, since they're easily carried and presumably hard to lose. The first method, time-based authentication, uses a token with a clock chip in it. Each card is serialized; using the serial number and current time as seeds, it generates a new passcode every second or so, from a secret algorithm. Each user carries a different token, and memorizes a PIN number, just like those used with auto-tellers. When a call is placed, a device or software process at the secure end requires a password, composed of the PIN number of the user, and that user's current passcode. It then looks up the PIN number in a table, finds the serial number of the token associated with that user, runs the algorithm using that serial number and the time of the call, and permits or denies the connection to proceed accordingly.

The second method requires a slightly deeper level of integration between the security system and the thing to be secured, as well as more work on the part of the user. In this system, the user still has a PIN number, but is now issued a series of numerical challenges. Each series of numbers is entered into a keypad on the user's token, which then displays the appropriate numerical responses. If the PIN number is valid, and each challenge is correctly answered, the connection is made. Both systems rely upon the PIN number to secure the card, since the card will still work if it's been taken from the valid user. Authentication features like retinal scanning can be added to the token as well, but this defeats many of the design objectives of the token: to be conveniently portable, inexpensive, and easily replaced. If a token is lost or stolen, the person to whom it was issued should ideally be able to cancel its validity from the host's lookup table from a remote location, obviously without having the use of a token to do so. Neither system is proof against users under duress, unless an alternate PIN number can be assigned for use in such situations.

Regardless of the hardware and software you place between callers and the network, there are a few inexpensive common-sense measures that can be taken to reduce the risk of dial-in security breaches. Most are so simple that they're often overlooked, both by network administrators and by crackers.

First of all, be sure that your data lines are unlisted and haven't been assigned numbers in the same numerical sequence as your voice lines. Make sure that they're not in sequence with each other, not in sequence with anyone else's data lines, and preferably from blocks assigned primarily to residential use, rather than to other businesses. Remember that an obscure number is rendered valueless if you publish it anywhere, or if it becomes well known. Thus if your Regional Bell Operating Company (RBOC) offers Caller•ID, you should find out whether they also offer per-line call-blocking, so that the phone number of your data line is never passed on to any sites that your users may call. If per-line call-blocking is not available, odds are that per-call call-blocking is. Per-call blocking requires that you dial a short prefix string before any outgoing call for which you want your number to be masked. Bellcore specifies the string *67, but you should check with your local telco to make sure that they haven't implemented the feature with some other string. Caller·ID is the phrase used to identify calling-party number identification in local telephone service. Its long-distance equivalent is Automatic Number Identification (ANI). ANI is passed to operators of 800 and 900 numbers, the former because they have a right to know who's calling them, since they're paying for the call, the latter for billing purposes. Although there's no telco service means of blocking number delivery on long-distance calls, a device called a toll restrictor can be placed between each modem and each outgoing telephone line.

Toll restrictors listen to the touch-tone or pulse digits being dialed on outgoing calls, and cut off the phone line if they hear any strings which you've put on their "forbidden" list. This is an appropriate method of blocking calls to both 800 and 900 numbers and can be used with the local equivalents of 900 numbers, which have different prefixes in different areas. In Pacific Telesis country, California and Nevada for instance, the local equivalent uses a 976 prefix. Another trick is to get your data lines "foreign prefixed." This means paying a small monthly charge for a telephone number with a prefix (assigned on the basis of what telco central office, or CO, your local service originates from) from a different CO, preferably one which is as geographically far from your actual location as is possible within your area code, or as numerically far from the prefixes served by your local CO. This way, if someone "demon dials" all the telephone numbers in your area, looking for your data lines, they won't find them. In large area codes, there are hundreds of thousands of assigned telephone numbers, so the demon-dialing method, which may take as long as 30 seconds per attempt, is usually only used if a cracker can narrow his target down to the one or two COs serving a single city. Another simple, if slightly annoying, measure is to increase the value of your answering modem's S-register zero setting. The number in S0 is the number of times the modem will allow the line to which it's connected to ring before answering. Since each ring lasts five seconds, and the principle of demon-dialing requires speed, few crackers are likely to have their software wait more than four or five rings before writing off a phone number as an unanswered voice line. Thus, setting S0 to 9 would mean that legitimate callers would have to wait 45 seconds before their call was answered, but it would also be likely to escape demon-dialing attempts. Just like passwords, data lines are more secure if their numbers are changed periodically. Again, unless you have a large number of data lines, this is not a prohibitively expensive undertaking.

Since the security of the telephone service providers themselves has frequently been demonstrated to be less than impervious, and billing departments are particularly subject to constant attack, it could be argued that having the data line service billed to a name and address other than that of either the company or any of its employees is not without merit. Unfortunately, many telephone companies will not send bills to USPS post office boxes, but there are many private mailbox providers who assign customers suite numbers, rather than box numbers.

On data lines which are used exclusively for outgoing calls, you can set the modems to ignore incoming calls, so the phone just rings and is never answered. This is also done using the S0 register, set to zero, or "autoanswer off." Although if you aren't using a line for any dial-in functions, it may not be crackable anyhow, you may want to use it for more sensitive applications in the future; this is one way of preserving its obscurity until that point, since if it isn't answered at all, it won't show up in the results of any demon-dialing done in your area.

A less obvious and more difficult, but effective, way of obscuring dial-in phone lines is by hiding them as extensions on your own office's phone switch, or PBX. For the same reasons that it's difficult to make dial-back work with automated connections, this is problematic as well, but is workable if your PBX has an automated attendant. That is, if there is some facility in your PBX for an incoming phone call to be answered with a recorded greeting or message, like "Welcome to American Grommet. If you know the extension of the party you're trying to reach, dial it now, otherwise dial zero, or stay on the line to speak to an operator." Your dial-ins can be attached to the PBX as extensions, each with a separate numerical code, usually two or three digits long. You can reassign extension numbers at no cost whenever you feel the need to, and you can assign hunt groups easily as well. Since the call is answered by a voice, rather than a modem, again the number won't show up in demon-dialer results. The means of automating the connection is simple: In the dialing string of the calling modem, instead of simply having a seven-digit number, you include enough commas (commas in a dialing string are usually defined as a two-second pause in AT-command-set compatible modems) to get you past the ringing and into the voice message, and then add the extension number. Thus to get to extension 487 on a trunk with the number +1 408 555 1212, you would have a dialing string which read 14085551212,,,,,,,487. One problem with this method is that it makes it very hard to trace an incoming call since, unlike full-size CO switches, PBXs don't usually support call-tracing, making it impossible to ascertain on which trunk line an illegitimate call to an extension is coming in. A few recent models of PBX are specifically designed for use with dial-in lines, and can track and alert an administrator to large volumes of short-term calls, consistent with a brute-force crack.

If you can designate a specific group of phone numbers which will only call each other, and your local RBOC offers Centrex or equivalent business-class service, you may be able to have those phone numbers turned into a nonenterable network. Callers who aren't calling from one of the other designated phone numbers get a recorded message to the effect that "The number you are trying to reach cannot be dialed from your calling area." In many cases, this is a less intrusive alternative to dial-back security, and is useful not only between dedicated data lines in employees' homes and a main office, but between electronic mail servers in different offices, as well, since it's fully transparent, as dial-back is not, and will not impede automatically supervised connections. Better yet, if the numbers are served out of the same CO, intercom service can be ordered as well, and you will effectively have local calls billed at an inexpensive flat rate, a service not offered to business customers in most areas.

One way to maintain an audit trail is to terminate an 800 or 900 number on your dial-in POTS (Plain Old Telephone Service. Yes, that's really what it stands for—I'm not trying to make an obscure techie joke.) line. Many local telcos, as well as nearly all the long-distance service companies, now sell 800 and 900 service, and many companies now offer numbers which are dialable from Canada and Europe, as well as the United States. The advantage of this scheme is that you no longer have to give your POTS number to anyone. It's still dialable, but it's only likely to be found by accident, since the only parties who know what it is are you, your local telco, and your 800 or 900 service provider, who may be one and the same. At the end of every month, or immediately in emergencies, you get a list of all the phone numbers from which calls you received originated. You can compare this to any databases of callers you might have generated in other ways, for instance as logs of QuickMail dial-in users, to check for discrepancies. If, for instance, one user logged out at the office at 5:15 p.m., and logged in via the telephone at 7:20 p.m., you might not find anything odd. But if you knew that they'd called from a telephone on the other side of the country, you would have good reason to suspect a problem. As mentioned above, unlike Caller·ID, the ANI service provided to 800 and 900 subscribers cannot be blocked, so your audit trail will be complete unless your POTS number is discovered. 800 and 900 numbers may be desirable for two other reasons, as well. If your employees are traveling, an 800 number may provide a less expensive way for them to call in than the rates many hotels and COCOTs (customer-owned coin-operated telephone, or "pay phone") charge; if you're providing customers with services via a dial-in line, a 900 number is one (admittedly somewhat sleazy) way of charging them for downloads or information. The POTS lines on which 800 and 900 numbers are terminated generally do not support the dialing of outgoing calls, reducing the risk that an outgoing call to a Caller·ID or ANI number will betray the POTS number.

One security measure, which is so basic as to be frequently overlooked, is to simply physically disconnect modems from telephone lines whenever you know for certain that they won't be needed.

13.4.4 Outside-Out

As mentioned earlier, one of the reasons crackers defeat security at many sites is so that they may use the site as a stepping stone to other, or primary, targets. This technique may be used for any number of reasons, foremost as a means of diverting anyone who may try to trace telephone and Internet connections back to them. The more sites they go through, the greater the number of people who must coordinate any tracing effort, the more leeway they have between the time they're detected and they must disconnect from a system, and the greater the likelihood that they will get away unidentified. Stepping-stone sites also provide crackers with a means of limiting their own telephone toll expenditures, and can provide places to cache any data stolen from more hardened target sites for later recovery.

A site is useful as a stepping stone only if there are ways both into and out of it. Thus a site with dial-in or dial-out capabilities and a full-time Internet feed is a candidate, as are ones which have full-time Internet feeds and a Unix machine on which the cracker can set up an account for himself, or use an existing account, and sites which have simultaneous dial-in and dial-out capabilities. For small sites, outside-out cracking is a minor problem, since most sites wouldn't have Internet feeds, and many would have only a single telephone line connected to their network, so *simultaneous* dial-in and dial-out are literally impossible.

A means of combining this simple principle with some of the methods in the outside-in section might result in a system which had an 800 number terminating on a POTS line which supports outgoing calls, connected to a modem on an AppleTalk Remote Access and dial-out modem server. A second 800 data line is connected to a modem on an e-mail server, but enduser dial-in services are not enabled on this line, only connections to other mail systems and gateways. A third data line, connected to a second e-mail server, is part of a nondialable Centrex network, by which the e-mail server is assured secure communication with subsidiary sites, and with important users who have dedicated home lines. Also in the Centrex network are two more modem servers, with toll restrictors on their modems, so that they will not accept dialing strings other than those of other numbers within the Centrex network. This system has several important features, mostly as a result of combinations of different techniques. First of all, there are only two numbers which can be dialed from anywhere: the main data line and one of the lines to the e-mail server. Both of these have audit trails courtesy of the 800 service provider. Since the e-mail server provides a bulletin-board-like front end, crackers could not get through it to the network. At worst, a clever one might find a way of sending mail onto your network. Conversely, if a cracker entered via the dial-in line, there is no way the e-mail line could be used to do anything other than send outgoing mail. The same is true of the second line attached to the e-mail server, and it cannot be reached from outside the Centrex network at all. The other modem servers are available to anyone else calling from a number within the Centrex network and, because of the toll restrictors, can only be used to connect to other numbers within the network. These would be used by employees to call into work from home, or call home from work. If this is to prove secure, none of the other sites on the Centrex network may have networked modems which can place calls to numbers outside the network.

13.4.5   Inside-Out

As discussed in the Outside-In section above, a dialup Internet connection limits the abilities of crackers tremendously. This bottleneck works in both direc-

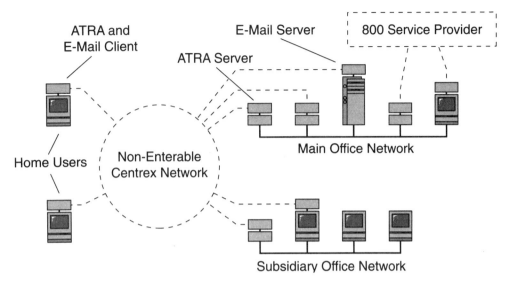

Figure 13.6 A network hardened against break-in.

tions, limiting employees' potential means of egress as well. While this is probably the converse of what you're trying to achieve, it is worth passing consideration; if your company is large enough to have a legal department, they may have an opinion on the matter. The issues here are largely the same as those discussed earlier regarding representation of the company: the possibility of an employee having the power to force the company to assume some liability. The traditional use of toll-restriction devices is precisely for that purpose, to block outgoing calls to 900 or other specially billed numbers, or to block all long-distance or toll calls. This limits the employee's ability to place the company in debt to the telco unexpectedly. It's much harder to prevent employees from using company facilities to facilitate cracking or piracy, while still giving them flexible communications with the outside world.

Obviously, if their means of outside communication is limited to electronic mail, there will be no practical way to crack anyone else's security from your site, and any piratical acts could only occur with outside assistance. E-mail forgery is still a consideration, but tends to be difficult in practice. If modems are served to network users, and there are only a limited number of valid destinations for outgoing calls, again, a toll restrictor may be your best solution. Keep in mind, however, that if the destination isn't under your control, it may be call-forwarded to any destination. If employees must be able to dial any number, however, you have no means of determining the legitimacy of the calls they make, discounting the unlikely possibility that your organization can establish some method of accounting which will make auditing of telephone bills practical. That could only occur at the end of each billing cycle, or once per month. If your employees are given full-time access to the Internet, there is no practical way of limiting their actions, save monitoring them continuously, and even that makes the uncomfortable assumption that the employees lack the ingenuity requisite to successful disguise of their actions.

13.4.6 Password security

One of the crucial lynchpins of nearly any security scheme is password security. While it might seem a simple matter to keep passwords secure, there are a nearly infinite number of ways a password can lose its integrity. The two most common are users either voluntarily or through carelessness disclosing their password to others, and users choosing passwords which are easily guessable.

In the first case, it's often hard to prevent users from disclosing their passwords, since it's often difficult to impress upon them the import or value of a secure password. What an administrator can do, however, at the risk of appearing a martinet, is lay down simple rules and guidelines for the handling of passwords. First of all, writing passwords down is always a mistake. Make sure that users know that if they forget their password, they can come to you and get a new one, and that you'd prefer to go to that trouble than have them put it on a Post-It note on the front of their Macintosh. Make sure they understand how to move files between their own folders on shared volumes, and those of others, so that they won't think that it's simpler to confide their password in someone else. Above all, stress to them that *no one* has *any* legitimate reason to ask them for their password and that any such request is cause for immediate suspicion, and should be reported to you, the network administrator. The most common and successful technique crackers employ is something they call "social engineering." It simply means amassing enough trivial little bits of information about a business that they can appear (usually over the telephone) to any employee to be another legitimate employee, and usually to be a network administrator in the company. A typical socially engineered phone call might run as follows: "Hello, Myrna? This is Bob, up in MIS. Yeah, sure we've met . . . Don't you remember once last year, at the Christmas party? Anyway, what I was calling about, we've been having trouble with your file server. I wonder if you could try logging in from there, and then have me log in to your account from here? Yeah, we'll need your password." Surprisingly, this works most of the time, since most users simply don't think of security as a constant process.

The next technique, discovering passwords by guessing them, is accomplished in one of two ways: through brute force or by trying words which are particularly likely.

The more possibilities there are for a given password, the less useful a brute force approach is. Thus, longer passwords are inherently harder to break than ones known to be short, and programs like AppleShare, which are case-sensitive (distinguishing uppercase and lowercase letters as separate values) are more difficult to crack than non-case-sensitive ones. Also important is the number of tries a cracker can execute in a given period of time. Many dial-in and network security processes, AppleShare being one such example, allow a certain number of tries, with a short delay in between, and then disconnect, forcing the cracker to establish a new login session.

You can use AppleShare's administrative features to require users to select passwords of more than zero characters, or indeed set any minimum up to eight characters, which is unfortunately the maximum allowed length, but keep in mind that placing any restrictions whatsoever reduces the total potential number of possible passwords, although some restrictions do make dictionary cracking more difficult. As we saw in Chap. 6, an AppleShare administrator can require that users update their passwords at regular intervals, and can require the entry of a new password the first time the user logs in, as well.

The most common means of cracking Unix password security is to gain access to the machine first, then take the /etc/passwd file, which contains encrypted versions of all the users' passwords, encrypt a dictionary of English words and names, and compare the two, looking for matches. When one is found, backtracking reveals which word matched, and that's the password. If hardware security on an AppleShare server is maintained, this specific approach doesn't work, but dictionaries can also be applied to automated login attempts. Dictionary approaches work with high frequency when users are allowed to choose their own passwords. Several studies have showed that the password most commonly employed by American computer users is "sex," while that most common in Britain is "Fred." These two rather amusing examples, as well as many more, are well known to most anyone who makes a hobby of guessing passwords. Other common, and bad, choices include names or birthdates of either one's self or family, driver's license or automotive license plate numbers, or the make or model name of one's car or computer.

In a Unix system dictionary crack I observed recently, the majority of the approximately three hundred users' passwords were discovered, over the course of a few hours. Most of these were the users' own names, and nearly half of them were also in use as the passwords for accounts held by the same users on other machines on the same network.

The most common method of frustrating dictionary cracks is to require that users include special characters, like punctuation or symbols, in their passwords or on case-sensitive systems, to require odd patterns of capitalization. Unfortunately, such requirements are nearly impossible to enforce.

One tradeoff many sites make in order to assure themselves of sensible passwords is to generate and distribute passwords centrally, rather than make users individually responsible for their own passwords. Although this alleviates one problem, it creates several new ones. First, the means of distributing the passwords must be secure. In practical terms, this means verbally instructing users behind closed doors, since transferring them over the network by e-mail is dangerous, and if they were distributed on paper, in all likelihood users would either retain the paper or dispose of it in an unsecure fashion. Since users are unlikely to be able to remember completely generic passwords

("4MiR8%hU" or "hR&NbpFe," for instance), schemes for developing easily remembered passwords have been devised, similar to those used to generate project codenames at many sites. The results of such programs ("tanplant" or "quickhog," for instance) are something of a compromise, since they merely combine words according to simple rules, and can thus be broken using a method which takes longer and is more tedious, but no more difficult, than a dictionary crack. As long as users do not forget their passwords constantly, it makes more sense, and is more secure, to generate new ones when old ones are forgotten, than to keep lists.

Administrators at some sites run password-cracking software periodically themselves, and notify users whose passwords are successfully guessed that they have to come up with better ones. This form of internal auditing is a useful precautionary measure, but can become time-consuming if performed very rigorously.

Encourage users to take a common-sense approach to looking out for their own security: Just as they might change their door locks and notify the police if their homes were burglarized, users should change their passwords and inform their network administrator immediately if they suspect that someone else has gained access to any of their password-protected services. Similarly, as they wouldn't use the same key for their car, their house, and their safe-deposit box, it's advisable to use different passwords on different services, so that the compromise of one doesn't endanger the rest.

Lastly, remember that keeping valid passwords out of the hands of unauthorized users means that you have to invalidate existing passwords of users who are no longer authorized to access data. The most common example of such a case is when an employee leaves the company. Failing to immediately change that employee's passwords on all services is a breach of security.

13.4.7 Hardware security

Perhaps the most straightforward aspect of securing any computer installation is creating and maintaining a secure physical premises within which to work. For many sites, this simply means locking servers in a wiring closet to which only a few people have keys, and this is probably enough for most applications. Since there are few software security measures which can't be broken if physical access to some point on the network is achieved, however, it is at least as important and deserves equal thought.

Awareness of the precise routing of the cables which make up your network is a good starting point. Although retrofitted telephone cabling is sometimes affixed to the outside of buildings to avoid the expense of routing it through preexisting walls, it may pay to run network cables inside, despite the expense, since a passive tap on your network would probably be less readily noticed than one on your telephone lines, not to mention easier to accomplish and more potentially damaging. If outside runs cannot be avoided, affixing the cable high enough that it's out of arm's reach from the ground and enclosing it in tubular galvanized steel conduit are deterrents, although conduit can conceal tampering as much as prevent it. If the option is available, telephone service from a subterranean feed, which opens into your building's basement, is preferable to an aerial feed, since aerial drops are hard to secure and could potentially be tampered with anywhere along the local loop which connects your building to the telephone company's central office.

The routing of your network's cable inside your building isn't quite so critical as that of any parts of it which extend outside, since tampering would presumably be more readily noticeable, and harder to accomplish. Nevertheless, routing cable inside walls is preferable again, since then only the locations of the walljacks can easily be determined, and this limits the number of spots which may be attacked. Inside conduit is usually of little security value, since most is designed to be easily reenterable, to facilitate wiring modifications. I've heard, however, of airtight pressurized conduit, which can be monitored with a pressure gauge, so that any form of tampering lowers the internal pressure and trips an alarm. This is probably excessive. Cable bundles stapled to baseboards are typical of the style of installation often employed in retrofitted office wiring, and this doesn't afford much of any deterrent to tampering.

Securing wiring closets and computer rooms is especially important, as they offer centralized points of access to the wiring and data of which your network is composed. Lock and key is a must, but an alarm system with a credit-card reader is a good idea as well, since it provides an audit trail and discourages anyone who is inclined to rely upon anonymity. I've always found it rather amusing that many contracts which bind people to securing spaces specify that "the walls must reach both the ceiling and the floor," but this makes obvious good sense. Partitioned offices are the least secure space in any building, and nearly any closet or locking space is preferable, even if inconvenient. Separating access by need or function, as you would do using groups on an AppleShare server, is a good tactic in the real world as well. High visibility is also a virtue. Thus, separating your demarcation blocks from your service and distribution punchdown blocks by putting them onto backboards in separate areas may make sense. Putting the demarc blocks in a glass-faced locking cabinet in clear view of the lobby, where they afford easy access to telco employees, and tampering would be highly visible, and removing all the service and distribution blocks to the computer room/main wiring closet where only authorized employees need have access, would be a rational means of applying this approach. Although punchdown blocks are of necessity cluttered, if they've been laid out with a clear plan in mind, cross-connected neatly, and covered with transparent hinged covers, tampering should be revealed under close scrutiny by anyone who's sufficiently familiar with the wiring to understand the model, and where wires should be routed.

In Chap. 4 we discussed the security advantages of packet-switched hubs, and later we introduced routers. Each of these forms of filtering can be thought of as a security measure of sorts, since it segregates network traffic and minimizes the amount of data that could potentially be intercepted from any one point. Routers do this in a top-down manner, separating whole zones from your Internet, while switched hubs work from the bottom up, isolating individual devices from each other.

Although it isn't directly related to networks, it's worth noting that a great deal of the information which crackers gather in the process of social engineering is supplied to them in bulk by the very companies they're trying to penetrate, in the form of garbage. "Dumpster diving" is one means of putting together a profile of the traits and activities which characterize a company and its employees, as well as gathering specific, if relatively randomly occurring, tidbits of concrete information. The only real means of heading off security lapses in this area are the bulk shredding of paper trash and an awareness on the part of employees that anything they put into the trash may be used against them later.

13.5 The Solution

After a thorough investigation of both the license and security problems, Mark reached several conclusions. Regarding software licensing, he saw that he was right to worry about the legality of American Grommet's software use habits, and moved quickly to collect statistics on employees' software use habits, so as to be able to justify the purchase of more copies of software, simultaneously strictly regulating the number of copies of each program which could be simultaneously launched to the number of boxes he actually had in hand. At the same time, he decided to investigate the possibility of reduced-rate site licenses for the packages most frequently used, and began dreaming of a future in which electronic banking would make it possible for him to configure his server to require the eleventh user of a ten-pack to electronically sign a purchase order for the additional copy.

As for the question of security, he'd quickly realized that there existed no pat answer, and that what was required was a skillfull compromise which would provide security against attacks both from within and without, while not impeding users' work habits overly much, appeasing his boss's worries. He decided that he should concentrate most of his security-enhancement efforts on placing elementary barriers against casual snooping by kids, rather than investing in the high-tech systems needed to deter industrial spies.

While pondering these problems, Mark had stumbled across the issue of the company's electronic façade. Although American Grommet didn't really have any online representation, this still provided exactly the excuse he needed to stamp out one of his pet peeves, so he laid a strict injunction upon the sales and marketing departments to stop using the company fax machines (which emblazon the company name and phone number across the top of every outgoing fax!) to send their friends at other companies cartoons, top-10 lists, and lewd jokes.

Chapter 14

Postscript

The Future of AppleTalk

AppleTalk is a continuously evolving protocol suite, and the demands of the AppleTalk network environment change as well. As the past few years have seen the development of Phase 2 addressing, AppleTalk Data Stream Protocol, and the introduction of ARAP, the years ahead will see further development and the introduction of other new services.

At the time of this writing, the two-most eagerly anticipated are AppleTalk Update-based Routing Protocol, or AURP, and the AppleTalk Simple Network Management Protocol MIB.

AURP is a second-generation routing protocol, designed to interconnect already-large AppleTalk networks across limited-speed or foreign-protocol wide-area-network connections. Where the increase in the percentage of RTMP traffic on a network grows linearly with the number of routers and zones, AURP is designed to minimize routing traffic by informing other routers only of the changes to the existing state of the network, rather than exchanging complete routing tables every ten seconds. At the same time, it must be capable of mediating the conflicts that arise when AppleTalk internets, with different and perhaps otherwise incompatible net numbering schemes, are connected by remapping the remote network numbers. AURP is designed to be portable, so that it can carry AppleTalk traffic in encapsulated form over many different kinds of network connections and protocols. The initial version will most likely support encapsulation within IP packets.

SNMP, as mentioned earlier in this book, is a platform-independent management standard. By utilizing modular components with standard interfaces and a single universal protocol which runs atop the IP stack, the same management tools can be used whether the management station happens to be a Macintosh, a Unix workstation, or a PC. Similarly, a wide variety of network devices support the basic SNMP protocol, each with its own set of statistics and manageable features. These different individual sets of statistics and features are called the Management Information Base, or MIB, for that particular device. A MIB template should be included with any SNMP-supporting device, which can be compiled under any SNMP management console, on any kind of management station. Nearly all AppleTalk routers and network hubs have an SNMP "agent" which can respond to SNMP queries with information from their MIBs, and Macintoshes should be no exception. Apple has designed a Responder replacement which uses an SNMP MIB and can communicate either via IP, if the protocol stack is available, or via AppleTalk if not. It currently seems likely that SNMP queries will be gatewayed between the IP protocol stack and the AppleTalk stack as a new DDP type 8, associated with a new reserved socket number, also 8.

Apple's protocol-development groups have turned increasingly to networking product developers and the networking community for input and guidance on new protocols; the Internet Engineering Task Force, the standards-setting body of the Internet, has at various times actively collaborated with them in the specification of new protocols. It's expected that this trend will continue, ensuring ever greater interoperability between AppleTalk and other networking environments.

Glossary

10Base-5 See **Thick Ethernet**.

10Base-T A physical medium for Ethernet networks in common use. Sometimes confused with **Twisted Pair Ethernet**, an earlier implementation of Ethernet running over twisted-pair wires, upon which the 10Base-T specification was loosely based. The cable consists of two 24-gauge unshielded twisted pairs, which is the same as nearly all telephone wiring. The outside jacketing is usually beige or gray, although **plenum cable** jacketing is usually semitransparent white. The insulation of the wires themselves is striped in color-coded pairs. The diameter of the cable is dependent upon the number of pairs. Two-pair cable is about an eighth of an inch in diameter; four-pair cable is two-tenths of an inch in diameter; and twenty-five pair cable is four-tenths of an inch in diameter. 10Base-T uses pins 1, 2, 3, and 6 of **RJ-45** connectors for Rx+, Rx–, Tx+, and Tx– signals, respectively. 10Base-T absolutely requires one home run per device, with a multiport repeater at the other end. Hubs in a hierarchical arrangement do not attach to their parent hubs via client ports, but through a separate **cascade** port. Individual home runs may be up to 330 feet in length, and are not terminated with a resistor. Most 10Base-T hubs have twelve client ports. Devices are usually connected to the wall jack at the end of the home run with a drop cable, which must also be of 24-gauge twisted-pair cable, plugged into an RJ-45 jack on the back of their Ethernet card. Devices which only have an AUI jack may be connected as well, by using 10Base-T transceivers, which usually have an AUI plug on a pigtail on one side, and an RJ-45 jack on the other.

66-Block See **Punchdown Block**.

110-Block See **Punchdown Block**.

802.3 The IEEE standard which defines the use of **CSMA/CD** access methods in Ethernet networks. When Ethernet is discussed in the generic sense, rather than a specific type of Ethernet cabling scheme, it's sometimes referred to as 802.3 Ethernet.

AAUI See **Apple Attachment Unit Interface**.

Access Control Method An algorithm by which each device on a network can determine when it will successfully be able to transmit data without fear of collision. All access control methods attempt to prevent any two nodes from transmitting simultaneous, or overlapping, signals. See **CSMA/CD** and **Asynchronous Transfer Mode**.

Active Star A **star topology** network which has a multiport repeater at its center, repeating packets from each machine back out to all the others.

Address An identifier which serves to uniquely identify or locate an area of a network, a device, a software process running on a device, or even in some cases a discrete function of a single process. A full AppleTalk address is of the form

"Network:Node:Socket:Enumerator." While unique addresses are required so that computers can deal with each other, they're hard for people to remember and use, so Apple Talk provides a means of associating names with addresses, using **Name Binding Protocol**. While these Apple Talk NBP names are not assigned in a meaningful way, it is possible under other protocols to assign informative names, which use a hierarchical structure to allow routing to take place.

Address Resolution Protocol   ARP is used on **Internet Protocol** networks to perform name binding between a device name and its address. Reverse-ARP, or RARP, performs the opposite type of correlation. The name-binding process is sometimes generically referred to as arping. ARP is described in **RFC** 826.

ADSP   See **AppleTalk Data Stream Protocol**.

AEP   See **AppleTalk Echo Protocol**.

AFP   See **AppleTalk Filing Protocol**.

American Wire Gauge   AWG, or simply gauge, is the measure of the diameter of a conductor. Like shot, a smaller number indicates a larger diameter. Telephone wiring is generally of 24-gauge solid-conductor wire, and occasionally of 22- or 26-gauge. By contrast, 110-volt power wiring is often between 10- and 16-gauge.

Amphenol Connector   The common name for a 50-pin connector used in many telephone and network installations. See **RJ-21**.

Analog   Anything which is continuously variable. Analog signals tend to be represented as waveforms. Analog data is often described as "directly measurable," which means that an analog information source, such as a rotating shaft or a wave emitter, can be measured with greater precision, ad infinitum, without ever being fully described. The data can only be measured approximately, or translated into another analog form. Analog is generally taken as the opposite of **digital**. Thus a normal touch-tone or rotary-dial telephone sends and receives an analog electrical wave representing the analog force of the sound waves directed against the microphone. An **ISDN**, or digital, telephone measures the intensity of the sound wave, assigns it one of a finite and fixed range of values, and sends the value, numerically encoded, to the receiver, which interprets it and reproduces the sound. It's important to remember that all electrical signals are analog regardless of the intention of the transmitter; they're simply interpreted in a binary fashion by the receiver, which matches the incoming signal to a threshold to make its decision.

ANI   See **Automatic Number Identification**.

Apple Attachment Unit Interface   AAUI is Apple's proprietary adaptation of the standard **AUI** interface normally used between Ethernet cards and Thick Ethernet transceivers.

AppleShare File Server   A piece of Apple software which makes a Macintosh share volumes with client users across the network. Early versions required that the Macintosh be "dedicated" to this task, and run only one or two other pieces of software, at most, but since version 3.0, the file-serving process runs in the background of the Finder like any other application. AppleShare File Servers use the AppleTalk Filing Protocol to control the exchange of data between themselves and their clients. There are other AFP server implementations sold by other companies, but the word AppleShare is the specific name of Apple's software product.

AppleShare Print Server   A central print spooler that's included with Apple's AppleShare File Server. It can NBP-register itself as several networked printers, accepting jobs on their behalf very quickly, and then assume the responsibility for sending them on to printers. AppleShare Print Server can spool jobs for any networkable printer, whether PostScript or dot-matrix.

AppleTalk Data Stream Protocol   ADSP is AppleTalk's connection-oriented reliable delivery protocol. It rides atop **DDP**, providing a "virtual circuit" connecting any pair of AppleTalk nodes. This circuit's primary attraction is that it ensures that data is delivered at the recipient's socket in the same order that it's sent, and that it doesn't require that each packet be individually addressed by the application layer software; neither feature is provided by **ATP**, which is more suitable for shorter transactions. Although ADSP is in the Session layer of the ISO-OSI model, it rides directly atop DDP, supplanting the Transport layer entirely. ADSP was not included in the initial AppleTalk specification, but was added in 1989.

AppleTalk Echo Protocol   AEP packets are used to test for the presence of other machines, test round-trip packet delivery times, or test the error rate (percentage of packets lost) between any two points on a network. These actions are often referred to as "exercising the network." A machine wishing to initiate an AEP exchange sends an AEP Request packet with some data in it to another AppleTalk device. The addressee doesn't even examine the contents of the packet, but simply creates a new packet, an AEP Response, puts the data back in it, and sends it back to the originator of the transaction, who can then examine the packet for errors or check how long it took to receive a reply. AEP is in the Transport layer of the ISO-OSI model. See also **ICMP**.

AppleTalk Filing Protocol   AFP is the protocol used between AppleShare file servers and their clients. Apple has two AFP server products, AppleShare File Server and System 7 File Sharing. Many other vendors also make servers which use the AFP protocols. Novell's Macintosh NLM (Netware Loadable Module) and Cayman's GatorShare are notable examples which run on hardware platforms other than the Macintosh. AFP servers are also available to run under Unix and VMS, as well as a host of other platforms. AFP operates primarily within the Presentation layer of the ISO-OSI model, atop the AppleTalk Session Protocol (which isn't used for anything else) and ATP.

AppleTalk Remote Access   Apple's software which implements the endpoints of an ARAP connection. AppleTalk Remote Access, or **ATRA**, comes in two parts: a client and a server. The client software can connect a single remote Macintosh to a Macintosh, on a network, running the server software via a pair of modems. The ATRA user license allows the use of three copies of the client software.

AppleTalk Remote Access Protocol   ARAP is a protocol designed specifically to minimize the disadvantages of slower-than-usual (often wide-area) AppleTalk network connections. ARAP is a very low-level protocol which combines some aspects of a routing protocol and some aspects of a link access protocol. In its routing function, it tries to minimize the amount of repetitive data transferred across the connection by caching tables of network number and zone information at the remote end, and trapping for (watching for and diverting) RTMP packets and ZIP requests. In its link function, it passes higher-level protocols transparently to the other side of the connection. ARAP specifies the use of Microcom Network Protocol (**MNP**) on the dialup connection between devices. Future implementations may use **Point-to-Point Protocol** instead of Apple's proprietary data-link level. Apple has implemented ARAP in a software server and client for dialup connections, while third parties have built hardware servers.

AppleTalk Transaction Protocol   ATP is AppleTalk's transaction-oriented reliable delivery protocol. Its function is to add reliability to the lower-level **Datagram Delivery**

Protocol. ATP is in the Transport layer of the ISO-OSI model. See also **AppleTalk Data Stream Protocol**.

Apple Update-Based Routing Protocol   AURP is a second-generation routing protocol, under development by Apple at the time of this writing, designed to supplant RTMP in wide-area networks. Its two main goals differentiate it from RTMP: first, it's designed to minimize routing overhead traffic, and is thus "update-based," propagating only those parts of a routing table which have changed, rather than gratuitously exchanging complete tables on a regular basis. Second, it includes network number remapping, which allows two large AppleTalk networks to connect to each other, even if they include network segments with numbers which duplicate some on the other net. Such segments are assigned proxy net numbers on the remote network, and the AURP routers simply perform substitution on traffic to and from them.

ARAP   See **AppleTalk Remote Access Protocol**.

ARP   See **Address Resolution Protocol**.

Asynchronous Transfer Mode   ATM is a time-division **access control method** which works by assigning each node a periodically occurring time-slice of variable size, in which to send data. As such, it allows very high utilization of bandwidth without any adverse saturation effects. It's particularly valuable for transferring video and sound in real time, as it guarantees the sender regular and predictable access to the network, as CSMA/CD does not.

Asynchronous Transmission   The means of passing data used by most modems on normal phone lines, whereby the beginning and end of each byte is indicated by a start bit and a stop bit. See also **synchronous transmission**.

ATM   See **Asynchronous Transfer Mode**.

ATRA   See **AppleTalk Remote Access**.

Attachment Unit Interface   AUI is the standard for cables and plugs connecting Ethernet cards to Ethernet transceivers, when the card does not inherently support a direct network connection. AUI cables are theoretically limited to 165 feet, but are actually usually not more than two to three feet long, and they use DB-15 connectors. See also **Apple Attachment Unit Interface**.

Attenuation   The reduction in voltage of a signal sent over a distance of any transmission medium, often measured in decibels per unit of length.

AUI   See **Attachment Unit Interface**.

AURP   See **Apple Update-Based Routing Protocol**.

Automatic Number Identification   ANI is a service provided to 800 and 900 service subscribers by long-distance carriers, which gives them the phone number of the calling party. With automated reverse-directories, most ANI receivers translate this information into names and mailing addresses. ANI is the long-distance equivalent of **Caller·ID**.

Backboard   Soft plywood, usually ¾" thick, covering the walls of a wiring closet, for the purpose of mounting **punchdown blocks**, **mushrooms**, and other networking and telecommunications equipment. Backboards should be mounted solidly and permanently to structural members, rather than just nailed to the wall or attached with sheetrock anchors.

Backbone   In its simplest sense, a backbone is the cable which forms the bus in a trunk network, but does not include the drop cables by which individual machines are connected to the bus. In more macroscopic usage, a corporate backbone is the main trunk of a regional, national, or global corporate network to which departmental or local networks are attached. In a wiring plant sense, the backbone is the system of **risers** which vertically connect wiring closets on different floors to the main wiring closet, or equipment room, in the basement.

Backplane   The interconnections between devices in a **rackmount**. In a rackmount of Ethernet hubs, for instance, traffic between individual hubs might go through either an Ethernet backplane, an FDDI backplane, or a router backplane, depending upon the design of the rackmount or concentrator.

Balun   From BALanced/UNbalanced. A device like a LocalTalk connector, which transforms a balanced signal (like that on a twisted-pair network) to an unbalanced one (like that the Macintosh expects on its serial ports).

Bandwidth   Used in two senses, both applied to transmission media. In an electrical sense, the difference between the highest and lowest frequencies which are useful or practical for transmitting data, expressed as a value in Hertz. In LANs, however, bandwidth is often used as a synonym for throughput, that is, how many bits per second can be passed through a given medium. Although the two figures are related, throughput depends also upon the robustness of the transmitted signals, the sensitivity of the receiving device, and a host of other factors.

Baseband   A network on which each transmitted signal is transmitted across the entire usable bandwidth of frequencies. Thus only one signal may be transmitted at a time, and an access control method like CSMA/CD is required to keep multiple devices from transmitting simultaneously. Contrast with **broadband** networks.

Baseboard Raceway   A conduit system which emulates architectural baseboards lying against the intersection of the walls and the floor of an interior space.

Baud   A measure of end-to-end throughput. A connection between two modems using V.32bis as their data protocol is limited to 14.4kbps, or 14,400 bits per second. If the modems are employing compression protocols, or even if the data which is being sent has been compressed using an application on the host computer, the number of bits going into one end and coming out of the other can be much higher. This higher figure is expressed in baud. Since compression is not specified as a part of either the AppleTalk or TCP/IP protocol stacks, speed of networks in this book is always measured in bits per second; since modems used in examples in the book usually use compression protocols, modem speeds are usually referred to in baud.

BDF   Building Distribution Frame. See **Distribution Frame** and **Main Closet**.

BIX Block   A proprietary punchdown block used in some Northern Telecom installations. Termination is similar to that on 110 blocks, and the form factor is somewhat similar. The blocks themselves come in a great many varieties, designed for different kinds of distribution, bridging, and adapting. Each block supports 25 pairs. **BIX** blocks are of sufficient quality to support ISDN telephone service and 10Base-T Ethernet.

BNC   The standard connector for **Thin Ethernet** components and cables. The female "barrel" connectors are about a quarter of an inch in diameter, with two prominent bayonets. The male connectors are about four-tenths of an inch in diameter, with an internally notched rotating cuff which engages the bayonets on the female connector, and holds in place with an internal spring, once engaged. Cables are terminated with male connectors, and the T-connectors used to attach machines have two female connectors along one axis, with a single perpendicularly oriented male connector. Cards and devices have female connectors.

Bonding   A term for the interconnection of electrical grounds on equipment throughout a building, to ensure that there won't be a difference in electrical potential between any two devices which could overload circuitry. Bonding between buildings of a campus is generally considered impractical, and fiber-optic, radio, infrared, or other information-transmitting systems which don't convey electrical potential are used instead.

Bridge   A device which connects two networks, either of similar or dissimilar speed and protocol, indiscriminately. That is, it passes all the packets it sees on each side through to the other side, regardless of where they're addressed. Unlike **Routers**, bridges do not delimit new zones.

Broadband   A type of network which carries multiple simultaneous signals at different frequencies. A cable television distribution system is a common type of broadband network. Contrast with **Baseband** networks, which are more commonly used by computers.

Broadcast   To address a packet to "all." There is an address in most network protocols, AppleTalk and TCP/IP included, to which packets can be addressed so that all devices on the network will receive them. In AppleTalk, that address is node 255. In TCP/IP, it is 255.255.255.255. At an even lower level, there is a raw Ethernet broadcast address, as well, which would be received by both AppleTalk and TCP/IP devices on an Ethernet network: ff:ff:ff:ff:ff:ff. See also **Multicast**.

Brouter   A device which **routes** some protocols, and **bridges** those it doesn't know enough about to be able to route.

Bus   A single cable connecting multiple devices. Thick and thin Ethernet networks use topologies which are busses, and LocalTalk trunks are busses. Busses are also characteristically flat address spaces, where every connected device sees every signal, but only pays attention to those with appropriate addresses. See also **Trunk Topology**.

Cable Grip   A flexible mesh-basket-like assembly which is placed over the end, or around the middle of, a length of cable, and contracts around the cable in the manner of a Chinese finger trap, when pulled in the correct direction. Faster and cleaner than using tape to ensure a firm grip on cable as it's being pulled.

Cable Plant   The sum total of all the communications cable installed in a building. See **Premises Wiring**.

Cable Tray   See **Raceway**.

Caller•ID   One feature of the **CLASS** local value-added telephone service, Caller•ID provides the called party with the phone number of the calling party, after the first ring, if the called party's telephone or modem supports the service. Either per-line or per-call blocking are available in most areas, so that the calling party can withhold the number from which they are calling, but block-blocking is available in some areas as well, so the called party can automatically refuse messages from callers who withhold their numbers. See also **ANI**.

Carrier Sense Multiple Access/Collision Avoidance   CSMA/CA is a modification of the CSMA/CD access control method for use with the LocalTalk **Link Access Protocol**. Since LocalTalk hardware has no way of determining whether a collision has occurred, more precautions must be taken in sending data, so a "handshake" is performed prior to any network transaction. First, the sender waits for a period of at least 400 microseconds (called minimum interdialog gap, or IDG), plus an additional, randomly selected period of time. Then the sender transmits a Request To Send, or RTS, packet to the intended recipient. The receiver of the RTS must then respond with a Clear To Send, or CTS, packet within 200 milliseconds (called interframe gap, or IFG). Upon receipt of the CTS, the sender proceeds to send its data packet, within the next 200 milliseconds. The reason for the 400-millisecond wait is to listen for other transactions which may be beginning on the same wire. By definition, any other transactions would generate traffic within any 400-millisecond period, since they're only allowed interframe gaps of 200 milliseconds of silence. If RTS packets collide, the senders receive no CTS responses, and "back down" for a period of time based upon a random seed and a multiplier which is dependent upon the number of recent collisions. The more collisions occur, the longer the "back-down" period is, and the longer it'll take to get any data sent.

Carrier Sense Multiple Access/Collision Detection   CSMA/CD is the logical basis for the collision-avoidance protocols incorporated into most network and bus protocols, including Ethernet. Multiple access means that more than one device can be connected to a cable; carrier sense means that devices wait until no other device is transmitting before they themselves transmit; and collision detection means that it can be determined whether sent packets have reached their destination, so they can be resent if a collision has destroyed them.

Cascade   To connect devices in a hierarchical arrangement. Usually applied to arrangements of hubs in star-configured networks, wherein several hubs are connected to each other via the client ports of a hub higher in the hierarchy.

CDDI   Copper Distributed Data Interface. The original name for twisted-pair-based analog to **FDDI**, now trademarked by a vendor. See **TPDDI**, the generic term.

Centralized   A term for any service which is concentrated in a single device, rather than provided in a **distributed** fashion, by a number of devices acting in conjunction. A centralized database would be accessed by querying a machine which possessed the whole database, while in a distributed database, each participating device would possess a portion of the database. See also **Server**.

CERT   Computer Emergency Response Team. A center at Carnegie Mellon University which coordinates the dissemination of information regarding Unix and TCP/IP-related security holes and new viruses to network administrators. CERT can be reached at cert@cert.org, and they maintain a twenty-four-hour hotline at +1 412 268 7090.

Circuit Switched   A circuit-switched connection uses a single address to establish a contiguous, end-to-end connection. A POTS, or analog, telephone connection is probably the most common example. The advantages of a circuit-switched connection are that the addressing overhead is limited to a single transaction at the beginning of the exchange, and the full bandwidth of the channel in use is available for the exchange of data between the two devices in communication. The limitation is that a device cannot generally engage in simultaneous transactions with multiple other devices. See also **Packet Switched**.

CLASS   Custom Local Area Signaling Services. Originally developed by AT&T as LASS, to run on A1 ESS switches, this is the software which provides users with an interface to the services provided by **SS7**. CLASS features include **Caller·ID**, Call Blocking, Distinctive Ringing, and other less-used functions. CLASS is being gradually implemented by local **telcos**, now that SS7 is in common usage.

Clear Text   Textual data sent across the network unencrypted. It's generally considered undesirable to send passwords or other sensitive data in clear text, because they can be intercepted with packet analysis tools, and thus constitute a security risk.

Client   A subscriber to a service. The AppleShare Chooser device, for instance, is the client which complements the AppleShare, or AFP, server. Network services tend to require both a client and a server process, which communicate across the network. Both client processes themselves and the machines on which they're running are commonly referred to as clients.

Coax   Cable like that used in thick and thin Ethernet networks, which has two conductors, the "tip," which is solid or stranded and in the center of the cable, and the "ring," a cylindrical braided conductor which shares the same longitudinal axis as the central conductor. Thus the name coaxial cable. The ring conductor serves to shield the tip conductor from interference and induced voltage, allowing very high data rates. Unfortunately, it also makes coax cable thick, inflexible, and expensive.

Collision   What happens when two devices connected to the same cable send packets simultaneously. The sent packets collide and pass through each other, each leaving the other somewhat garbled and often unintelligible. Collision-avoidance protocols are incorporated into network communication protocol stacks to avoid this problem. See also **CSMA/CD**.

Concentrator   A longer name for a network hub, or multiport repeater. The word "concentrator" tends to imply a larger scale, however; for instance, a rackmount capable of holding multiple multiport repeaters, such as those made by Cabletron, Synoptics, Farallon, and others.

Conductor   Anything capable of conveying an electrical potential. Usually used to refer to a single strand of copper, electrically isolated from each other one, in a wire or cable.

Conduit   A system of pipe-like tubing running inside walls, through which wire can be drawn without reopening the walls. Also applied to reenterable enclosures affixed to the outside of interior walls, and to metal tubing on the outside of buildings, as well. Wire guides and troughs running above suspended-tile ceilings are usually called raceways or cable trays.

Cross-Connect   To connect terminals of one punchdown block to terminals of another, using **cross-connect wire**. Wire is generally routed up the side of the punchdown block from the point it was punched down, past any blocks above that one, draped over the mushroom at the top of the column and horizontally over others until it reaches the mushroom above the destination punchdown block, and then back down, in a similar manner, leaving at least several inches of slack to aid in tracing and to provide for repunching down in the future.

Cross-Connect Field   A large contiguous array of punchdown blocks in a wiring closet. Sometimes called a **distribution frame**.

Cross-Connect Wire   A single twisted pair of 24-gauge wire used to effect connections between terminals on different punchdown blocks. Cross-connect wire is white-blue/blue-white, although occasionally yellow-blue/blue-yellow wire is used. See also **Cross-Connect**.

Crosstalk   The interference generated on wires as a result of undesired electromagnetic coupling with other nearby wires. It's a byproduct of the fact that the electrical current flowing in each conductor generates a magnetic field. The fields of nearby wires interact, producing perturbations which manifest themselves as changes in the current of the wire. The term originated in the telephone industry, where crosstalk most frequently makes itself evident as faintly audible traces of other conversations, ring tones, and busy signals during telephone calls. Analog telephone lines are not subject to significant crosstalk from data networks, and vice versa, due to the difference in frequencies at which they operate, but crosstalk between two or more different network connections can become a problem if non-twisted-pair cabling or many connectors are used, and ring tones from telephone lines can occasionally cause problems, since they're at a much higher voltage (often 40V) than ordinary signals.

CSMA/CA   See **Carrier Sense Multiple Access/Collision Avoidance**.

CSMA/CD   See **Carrier Sense Multiple Access/Collision Detection**.

Cut Down   See **Punchdown Block, Punchdown Tool**.

Daisy Chain   Used as a noun, a daisy chain is a **topology** in which all devices are connected in serial, in a long chain. Like the old example of a string of Christmas tree lights, machines connected in serial are more vulnerable to network service outages than those connected in parallel, in a trunk or star topology.

Datagram Delivery Protocol   DDP is the AppleTalk protocol responsible for the delivery of datagrams (packets) between any two sockets on a network. It's in the Network layer of the ISO-OSI model, and rides atop any of the Link Access Protocols.

DDP   See **Datagram Delivery Protocol**.

DECnet   A network protocol stack used primarily by Digital Equipment Corporation VAX computers running the VMS operating system. DECnet runs primarily over Ethernet cabling. DECnet drivers for the Macintosh are available from Digital and various third parties. These drivers allow Macintoshes to act as clients to services like e-mail, videotext, and databases, provided by the VMS operating system.

Demarcation Punchdown Block   The punchdown block, or set of blocks, on which telephone-line service arrives in a building. The USOC code for such blocks is RJ-21X, but they're usually called demarc blocks, or just demarcs. Telephone company documents sometimes refer to them as Network Interfaces, since they're the point at which the premises wiring meets the public telephone network. Under Public Utility Commission tariffs, local telephone companies are only required to assume responsibility for wiring up to the outside of the centerline of each demarc block, while the customer is responsible for wiring up to the premises side of the centerline. Demarc blocks can usually be quickly identified by their bright orange hinged covers, which should have the incoming phone numbers listed on the inside, next to the rows of pins upon which they terminate. Under most circumstances, it's a violation of the terms of your telephone service to tamper with the wiring on the telco side of the demarc block.

Dialback   A method of securing a telephone connection. A remote user initiates the connection by calling the destination and identifying him- or herself. The destination then hangs up, compares the user's identification to an internal table of phone numbers, and calls the user back at the preassigned phone number.

Digital   Based upon numbers. Today's computers are all digital, and work with discretely quantifiable values, rather than analog, or infinitely variable values. Digital does not imply electronic; there were electromechanical digital calculators before there were electronic computers, and even an abacus is digital. Nor does it imply binary; there are computers which use counting systems with bases greater than two.

Direct Inside Wire   See **Inside Wire**.

Distributed   A term for any service which is supplied by a number of different devices, operating in conjunction, rather than by a single one. The opposite of **Centralized**. See also **Peer-to-Peer**.

Distribution Frame   A large contiguous array of punchdown blocks in a wiring closet. Also called a cross-connect field.

Distribution Punchdown Block   The punchdown blocks upon which **home runs** terminate. Distribution blocks are cross-connected to blocks where services terminate, Star-Controller punchdowns and demarc blocks, for instance, to extend those services out to the walljacks in user work areas.

DIW   See **Inside Wire**.

Driver   Code implemented in hardware, firmware, or software, which allows a specific piece of hardware to perform its function. Sometimes called a "device driver." The EtherTalk and LocalTalk drivers are examples of such things on the Macintosh.

Drop Cable   See **Line Cord.**

Drop Folder   A folder on an **AFP**-served volume which has access privileges such that users other than the owner can make changes, but only the owner can open the folder. The net effect is that of an "in box" by which documents can be delivered to the folder's owner.

DSS1   Digital Subscriber Signaling System 1. The signaling protocol used on the subscriber side of endpoint central offices in an ISDN connection. DSS1 is the protocol which conveys dialing and **mux**ing information over the ISDN D channel. Above the D channel physical layer, there is a data link layer and a network layer which carries all the signaling and switching information, and contains a 16-bit address field. DSS1 packets always have priority over those of other protocols on the D channel. See also **SS7**, which is used to convey signaling information between central offices.

Duplex   In both directions. Connections which allow data to be transmitted in both directions simultaneously are described as full-duplex, while connections which allow transmission in one direction at a time are described as half-duplex or "ping-pong."

Dynamic Address Assignment   The method of assigning each node a unique numerical address used by the AppleTalk protocol stack. Each node is assigned a number which is checked for uniqueness at the time it's booted. Some other network protocols stacks use static address assignment, which requires that an administrator preconfigure each device with a numerical address before it's attached to the network. Dynamic address assignment is the single largest contributor to the "plug-and-play" ease of AppleTalk network configuration.

E-Mail   Electronic mail. Messages exchanged between the users of one or more computers, usually transferred over a network or modem connection. E-mail can, and often does, include data, like files which one user may want to send to another, or even pictures, voice recordings (voice mail), and video clips. Although there are many different logical models upon which e-mail systems are built, most operate within one of three general categories: central, wherein all mail is kept on a single machine and read remotely; client-server, which uses a networked server to forward mail from the computer of a sending client to that of a receiving one; and distributed, in which there is no server, and clients must deliver mail directly to each other. See also **Interprocess Communication**.

EIA/TIA 568   The Electronics Industry Association/Telecommunication Industry Association building wiring specification. This document is the primary definition of correct wiring practice for commercial and industrial cable installation. Unlike AT&T's **PDS** and IBM's Cabling System specification documents, EIA/TIA 568 is entirely nonproprietary.

ELAP   EtherTalk Link Access Protocol. The **Link Access Protocol** which allows AppleTalk packets to be sent across Ethernet networks.

Encryption   The process of encoding data to prevent its being deciphered without the use of a secret key code. Many modern encryption schemes use a mathematical algorithm which uses a password as a "seed" number with which to process the data. For instance, if our data were the number 7, and the password I chose were the number 3, a simple multiplication would result in the encrypted data 21. If I gave this to someone who knew that the password was 3, they could run another algorithm, division in this instance, and retrieve the original data. More advanced "public key" encryption schemes use two different passwords, one which is "public" and can be distributed freely, with which data may be encrypted only, and the other, the "private" key, retained in secret by the user, which can be used to decrypt data encrypted with the public key.

Entrance Facility   The point in a building at which utility services enter. Usually located in the basement, in the mail wiring closet, or in the equipment room. This is the point at which utility/premises demarcation takes place: where the incoming wires stop being the property and responsibility of the electrical and telephone companies, and become yours.

Enumerator   When a software process wants to use a socket that it's opened for more than one purpose, usually to send and receive packets, it can assign a finer level of addressing granularity, called an enumerator. Thus an address might be 4027.126.152.2, where the first number is the net number, the second the node, the third the socket, and the fourth the socket's enumerator.

Ethernet   The physical layer of many high-speed networks. Described in IEEE 802.3, Ethernet specifications have been met on several different media. On local area networks, Ethernet operates at a data rate of 10 megabits per second. See also **Thick Ethernet, Thin Ethernet**, and **10Base-T**.

EtherTalk   Apple's implementation of AppleTalk on Ethernet. An Ethernet card or adapter is required for a Macintosh to use EtherTalk. Like any Ethernet protocol, it runs at 10 megabits per second, but since the Macintosh hardware isn't explicitly optimized for the use of an Ethernet interface, as it is for LocalTalk, and due to bottlenecks in hard-drive access and other areas, the maximum data throughput is only about ten times greater than that of LocalTalk, rather than forty times greater, as one might expect. EtherTalk packets can be recognized on multiprotocol networks by their IP protocol type code, which is $809B.

Extended Network   See **Phase 2**.

FAQ   Frequently Asked Question. There are documents called "FAQ Lists" available on the Internet, usually via both an FTP site, and periodically published and revised in a topical newsgroup, which answer frequently asked questions on a seemingly endless variety of topics. These include not only technical issues like sendmail or router configuration, but real-life pursuits like Chinese cooking and kite repair, as well.

FDDI   See **Fiber Distributed Data Interface**.

Fiber Distributed Data Interface   FDDI is the LAN standard for fast communication over optical fibers, rather than copper wires. FDDI allows 100-megabit-per-second data rates over distances of several miles, and uses a dual counter-rotating ring topology, much like IBM's **Token Ring** LANs, although one class of network device can operate while connected to only one of the two rings. The actual layout of an FDDI network still uses home runs; the signal just goes out on one conductor and comes back on the other, for each ring, rather than being an actual star.

Fiber-Optic Cable   Fiber-optic cable is made of flexible glass or plastic fibers formed into an extremely thin cylinder, and covered by a cladding material with a high index of reflection and a low index of refraction, the opposite of the fiber itself. Pore silica is usually used for the cladding compound. There are two general types of fiber cable: incoherent and aligned. Incoherent cable is much easier to make, and will transmit light, but not an image. Aligned fiber cable uses equal-length fibers, which are all aligned parallel to each other and the axis of the cable, and are thus capable of transmitting an image. Aside from the much higher data rates which can be achieved using optical transmission in place of electrical methods, the dielectric quality of the cable means that it's ideal for connecting sites which don't share a common ground, as it can't convey imbalances in electrical potential or, worse, the extreme spikes caused by electrical storms.

File Server   A machine which stores documents and applications, and makes them available to **client** machines across the network.

Firewall   A firewall machine or router separates a company network from the Internet, or divides a corporate network internally, for security reasons. Some firewall machines allow only the passage of electronic mail; others allow but limit or log and audit through network access in one or both directions.

Fire Walls   Walls which run all the way from the structural floor to the true ceiling, above any suspended tiles, and serve to control the spread of fire, in case of a conflagration. Fire walls are required by building codes, and it's important to maintain the integrity of function of such walls, and of the floors and ceilings, as well, when passing cable through them. This is accomplished by sealing with a nonflammable material the unoccupied space in conduit or holes which penetrate the fire barriers. Various cements and caulks are available for permanent installations, while prefabricated pillows are used to create reenterable seals.

Fragile   Used to describe a practice or implementation which may be technically compliant with specifications but is not to be desired for reliability reasons. Contrast with **robust**. Fragile situations are often recognized and endured as part of a trade-off of some kind, in exchange for some benefit realized elsewhere. For instance, a passive star network might be tolerated in one part of an office, if it was only being subjected to casual use, and the monetary savings effected could be used to make a heavily used area of the network more robust.

Frame   Used in two senses. Most often, frame is used in the same sense as the word packet; it means the same thing, an address and protocol header followed by data. In its physical sense, a frame is a wiring distribution area, like a **backboard** of **cross-connects** or a rackmount of **patch panels**.

Frame Relay   A kind of packet-switched public data network offered by many telephone companies that is inefficient for use with network protocols like AppleTalk and TCP/IP, which frequently employ broadcasts and multicasts.

FTP   File Transfer Protocol. A lowest-common-denominator means of point-to-point file transfer between Unix machines interconnected by an IP network.

Furniture Walls   The moveable upholstered partitions, generally four to six feet tall, from which office cubicles are formed. Many contain provision for the running of cable to convenient places in associated modular furniture, and all provide sufficient vertical clearance that cable can be run between the bottom edge of the wall and a carpeted floor.

Gateway A device or software process which translates transmissions between the higher levels of two different protocol stacks, but doesn't deal with the lower levels. Something which converts AFP calls to NFS calls, for instance, is a gateway, as is something which converts electronic mail in QuickMail format to SMTP.

Gauge See **American Wire Gauge**.

GFCI Ground Fault Circuit Interrupter. An electrical circuit-breaker which detects even small differences in potential between its positive and negative sites, and trips itself immediately if it detects a grounded circuit. GFCIs are used primarily in damp or below-grade electrical installations, to prevent electrocution of people or equipment. They are, however, subject to occasional accidental tripping, especially as loads are applied or taken off the circuit.

Ghosting The repetitive appearance and disappearance of a zone or network entity in the Chooser or other NBP interface. Ghosting is a symptom of severe network problems, which may stem from a wide range of sources.

Ground Any conductor which eventually makes firm electrical contact with the earth, allowing electricity to discharge, completing a circuit. In a computer, the ground is a system of conductors which serve as a standard against which the presence or absence of voltage in signal-carrying conductors is measured.

Group Usually used to indicate a collection of authorized users of a computer system, file server, or e-mail system, who can be addressed collectively by a single name, or upon whom access privileges can be granted or disallowed collectively.

Guest An anonymous user of an AFP file server, who need not enter a password or specific user name. Most AFP server implementations allow guest access to be turned off, and none allow guests to own folders or directories.

Half-Bridge A LAN-to-LAN bridge formed by two symmetrical components, each comprised of a network-to-modem bridging device and a **modem** or **mux**. The two modems are then connected over telephone lines or a large-scale data network, and the two bridges appear to form a unit equivalent to a single bridge connecting two networks in the same location.

Half-Router Similar to a **half-bridge**, except that it uses the limited bandwidth between the two LANs more efficiently, because it emulates a router and, as such, filters traffic before sending it across the connection between its two halves. On a pay-per-packet public network, this reduces the cost of a connection, while on a limited-bandwidth telephone connection, it increases effective throughput and speed.

Hardware Address A network address fixed in hardware by the manufacturer of the hardware. The LocalTalk protocols don't employ hardware addresses, but all Ethernet devices have hardware addresses. Ethernet hardware addresses consist of six bytes, normally represented in hexadecimal format, of which the first three are a manufacturer ID and the latter three are an individual serial number. Apple's ID is 08:00:07, while 3Com (the manufacturer of Apple's original Ethernet cards) uses 02:60:8C. Cayman GatorBoxes are identifiable by their vendor ID of 00:00:89, while Shiva FastPaths use 08:00:89.

Header The addressing and routing information which precedes the data in a packet. Although headers normally only appear at the beginning of a packet, the term "encapsulation" is often used to describe the wrapping of a header around a data packet, or an already formed packet with preexisting headers already attached. In this way, headers are often thought of as forming an "onion skin" of layers surrounding the data at the core. The receiving node must remove each layer before it knows how to go about interpreting and removing the next layer. The order of the layers corresponds with the OSI reference model order of the protocols represented: The outermost header is the lowest level, a Link Access Protocol header, while the innermost, directly adjacent to the data, is the highest-level protocol.

Home Run   A single run of cable directly connecting one wall jack in a user work area with an area on a punchdown block in a wiring closet. It's often interpreted as meaning a single physical piece of wire unbroken by punchdowns or terminals.

Hop Count   The number of routers an AppleTalk packet has passed through. A packet traveling to an adjacent net should have a hop count of one, since it's traveled through one router to reach its destination. The current maximum hop count is fifteen, after which the packet is discarded, on the assumption that it's entered a closed loop between routers. The hop count occupies the first six bits of the DDP header, and is incremented by routers during retransmission.

Horizontal Wiring   All the wire on one floor of a building, emanating from a single riser/backbone closet. Also referred to as a horizontal subsystem.

Host   A computer on which software is run, under the control, often remote, of a user at a **terminal**, which may not have any computing power of its own. Interaction between Macintoshes and mainframes or Unix machines is often of the host-terminal variety, as contrasted with **client-server** and **peer-to-peer** transactions, which are more common between computers of the same type, and connote computing power or "intelligence" on the part of both devices. Host-terminal interaction is most efficient in situations in which a user runs a "batch" type program, which requires very little input, a lot of processor time, and produces very little output. Client-server and peer-to-peer transactions, on the other hand, work best in situations where a lot of input can be translated into a very simple transaction, which may then result in a lot of output—graphing the output of a complicated but precise database query, for example.

Hub   A multiport repeater which forms the center of an active star topology network. Hubs are usually standalone boxes which are connected to either a service punchdown block or a patch panel by one or more Amphenol cables.

IBM Cabling System   IBM's building wiring specification document. Of the three major specs, IBM's is the oldest (not a good quality), but in some ways one of the most flexible. This is also not necessarily desirable.

IC   See **Intermediate Closet**.

ICMP   See **Internet Control Message Protocol**.

IDC   Insulation Displacement Contact. Any one of a number of different types of contact or terminal which forms an electrical connection with a conductor while displacing the insulation around it. IDCs are found on punchdown blocks and in some more modern jacks.

IDF   Intermediate Distribution Frame. See **Intermediate Closet**.

Impedance   The opposition to the flow of current presented by a circuit, measured in ohms. If two possible paths are available, the first with impedance X and the second with impedance Y, the current will travel across both paths, but in reverse proportion to their impedance. Thus the first path would carry Y/X+Y of the current, while the second path would carry X/X+Y, or the remainder of it.

Inside Wire   Also called IW, Direct Inside Wire, DIW, Network Communications Cable, or NCC. Standard 24-gauge twisted-pair cable, with PVC insulation and jacketing. Commonly available in 2-, 4-, 12-, and 25-pair cables. This is as opposed to Quad cable, which isn't twisted-pair, and is four-conductor only, or Plenum cable, which is fire-insulated with Teflon jacketing, so as to meet the NEC specifications for wire to be run through ventilation ducts, or plenums. See also **Premises Wiring**.

Interim CDDI   A de-facto standard for the propagation of 100-megabit **FDDI** over shielded twisted-pair wires established by a consortium of five FDDI vendors in May 1991. It allows run lengths of up to 330 feet.

Intermediate Closet   A wiring closet in which vertical and horizontal cables are cross-connected. There are one or more ICs on each floor of most modern buildings, located no farther than 300 feet from any user work areas.

Internet   Used in two senses. The Internet (capital "I," proper noun) is the global network composed of many participating users' private, corporate, public, and academic networks. It uses TCP/IP protocols, and has additional standards for the interchange of news, electronic mail, and a wide variety of other services. Your internet (lowercase "i"), on the other hand, is the sum of all the logical networks at your site.

Internet Control Message Protocol   The ICMP protocol family is notable primarily for its inclusion of ICMP Echo Protocol, IP's analogue with AppleTalk's AEP Echo Protocol. Other ICMP are used primarily to inform hosts of a packet transmission failure, in the case, for instance, of an unreachable network, host, or port, or to inform a host of a more efficient route. The ICMP protocol is defined in RFC 792.

Internet Engineering Task Force   The IETF is a standards-setting body composed of technically astute Internet users, who are typically engineers in networking and telecommunications companies. The IETF issues **RFCs**, or "Requests for Comment," defining protocols and standards of usage and behavior on the Internet. The IETF is, for instance, the body which has defined the **Internet Protocols**.

Internet Protocol   The Internet Protocol is the "native protocol" of Unix computers, and the protocol upon which the global Internet is built. Macintoshes can use IP protocols if they've been configured with **MacTCP** drivers. Unlike AppleTalk, IP is based upon a fixed, rather than dynamic, addressing scheme, so name resolution tends to rely upon lookups from name/address tables which must be propagated across the network from name server to name server, rather than upon lookups directed to an individual host, using the "distributed database" approach that AppleTalk does. Aside from that, many of the specific IP protocols have fairly direct analogs in the AppleTalk stack, and most other basic principals are very similar. The Internet Protocol is defined in RFC 791.

InterNIC   Network Information Center. The organization responsible for assigning ranges of TCP/IP addresses to, and registering unique Internet domain names for, networks and individuals. The InterNIC also provides network "maps" which can be used in configuring electronic mail routing paths across the Internet, and it maintains a database of Internet-connected sites, accessible using the *whois* command on many Unix machines. The InterNIC is a service contracted for by the U.S. government, administered by the National Science Foundation and, at the time of this writing, jointly held by AT&T, CERFnet, and Network Solutions. It provides services to users anywhere on the Internet, regardless of physical location or nationality. The InterNIC can be reached by telephone at +1 800 444 4345 or +1 703 742 4777, or via electronic mail at info@internic.net or hostmaster@rs.internic.net. "RS" stands for Registration Services; RS is maintained by Network Solutions. The InterNIC's other two machines are DS (Directory Services, maintained by AT&T) and IS (Information Services, maintained by CERFnet). DS provides queriable databases of network and user information, and IS serves a variety of mailing lists and discussion groups, disseminating information about services available on the Internet.

IP   See **Internet Protocol**.

IPTalk   See **Kinetics Internet Protocol**.

IPX   IPX, or Internetwork Packet Exchange, is the Ethernet-based protocol that Novell Netware servers and clients use. A Macintosh native implementation called MacIPX is underway as of the time of this writing, which should function in much the same way that MacTCP does.

ISDN   Integrated Services Digital Network. The digital telephony standard that is gradually replacing analog **POTS** lines in business and residential use. ISDN telephones and equipment have **RJ-45** connectors, and use pins 4, 5, 7, and 8, or pairs one and four for the data, while the other four pairs are used to supply backup power to connected devices. One of the benefits of ISDN, however, is that between the subscriber's premises and the central office it runs on a single pair. This requires simple equipment (called an NT1, or "Network Terminator 1") at the demarcation point to convert the signal from two pairs to one. An additional benefit of the service is that multiple channels of information can be "multiplexed" into the stream of bits carried on that single pair. There are two kinds of digital channel which comprise ISDN service. B, or bearer, channels carry **circuit-switched** digital voice or data at 64kbps, while D channels are used to send **packet-switched** addressing and control information back and forth between the subscriber's telephone or data terminal and the telephone company's central office at 16kbps, using the **DSS1** protocol. The remaining bandwidth of the D channel can be used for packet-switched connections to other subscribers or services. The most common form of service, which is sold to most residential and small business customers, is called BRI, or Basic Rate Interface, and has "2B+D" or two bearer channels and one D channel. PRI, or Primary Rate Interface, is aimed at larger businesses, and has 23 B channels and a 64kbps D channel.

ISO   International Standards Organization. The body responsible for establishing many networking and telecommunications standards, the Open Systems Interconnect reference model, or **OSI model**, among them.

IW   See **Inside Wire**.

Kinetics Internet Protocol   KIP is an encapsulation scheme devised by Kinetics, the original developers of the FastPath router. KIP encapsulates LocalTalk packets within IP packets, so that they could be passed through IP routers which didn't understand AppleTalk.

KIP   See **Kinetics Internet Protocol**.

Krone   A little-used type of punchdown block which fits into the same space (and uses the same type of **standoff brackets**) as a 66-block, but has a lower maximum bandwidth useful only for voice and low-speed networks, and uses a different and incompatible punchdown tool. Krone terminals use a silver plating, which has proven subject to corrosion and tarnishing which impede the formation of clean electrical contacts.

LAN   See **Local Area Network**.

LAP   See **Link Access Protocol**.

LAT   See **Local Area Transport**.

LEC   Local Exchange Carrier. See **Telco**.

Line Cord   The cable which connects a client device to a walljack. For a LocalTalk or telephone connection, for instance, the drop cable is a length of modular flatwire terminated with RJ-11 plugs. With a 10Base-T connection, it's a twisted-pair cable terminated with RJ-45 plugs.

Link Access Protocol   Once all the higher-level protocols have put their headers onto a packet, the Link Access Protocol adds any headers that are media-dependent, providing node-level addresses and packet types. Apple has created three LAPs: LLAP for LocalTalk, ELAP for EtherTalk, and TLAP for TokenTalk, while third-party vendors have introduced a couple of others for proprietary media. Link Access Protocols are in the Data Link layer of the OSI model, immediately above the Physical layer.

LLAP   LocalTalk Link Access Protocol. The **Link Access Protocol** which allows AppleTalk packets to be sent across LocalTalk networks.

Local Area Network   A Local Area Network, or LAN, is a group of networked devices in one geographically contiguous area. LANs typically use high-speed transmission protocols which assume low error rates, like LocalTalk, Ethernet, and FDDI. LANs combine to form **Wide Area Networks**, or WANs.

Local Area Transport   LAT is a bidirectional data stream protocol used by the VMS operating system for communication between hosts and terminals. Some LocalTalk-to-Ethernet routers support LAT bridging for LAT terminal emulation on LocalTalk-connected Macintoshes.

Local Router   The term which describes each of the one or more routers directly connected to the physical network segment upon which a device under discussion is connected. It is from one of its local routers that a device would receive zone information, for example.

LocalTalk   The proprietary communications protocol built into every Macintosh. LocalTalk operates at 230.4 kbaud, or approximately a quarter-megabit. Apple's LocalTalk connectors and PhoneNet-type connectors convert the Rx+, Rx–, Tx+ and Tx– signals coming out of the Macintosh's serial port to a balanced, polarity-insensitive signal suitable for transmission over a single twisted pair. Since it's polarity-insensitive, like standard telephones, the two wires can be switched, and the system will continue to work, unaffected, as it shields itself from electromagnetic interference and **crosstalk** when running on twisted-pair wire.

Loopback   A test in which one device sends a complex signal to another device, which returns it for comparison by the sender. Often used in stages to determine the source of a problem in a faulty connection. The Apple utility Inter•Poll uses AppleTalk Echo Protocol packets to conduct loopback tests on AppleTalk devices, and many high-performance modems have loopback functions built into them. Most IP devices support a "loopback address" of 127.0.0.1, which simply returns sent packets to the network interface's receiver. In the most simple loopback tests, a physical cable is used to connect the input and output of a single device, so that it can talk to itself.

MacTCP   Apple's implementation of the Internet Protocol stack for the Macintosh. When equipped with the MacTCP Control Panel, Macintoshes can use both AppleTalk and IP.

Main Closet   The Main Closet, or MC, is the wiring closet from which vertical cables distribute network and telephone services to Intermediate Closets. It's usually located in the basement of your building, directly below the Intermediate closets, and also serves as a **demarcation point**, or point-of-entry, for services coming in from outside providers like the telephone company.

MAU Used in two senses. A Medium Attachment Unit is a an external adapter which connects a network adapter to a kind of physical wiring it's not able to connect to directly. For example, a LocalTalk connector is a MAU, as is a box which connects an **AUI** port to a 10Base-T network. In the second sense, a Multistation Access Unit is a simple wiring hub which allows several devices to connect to a network at one point. They're commonly used to reduce costs on types of networks which are inherently expensive to create new connections to; i.e., **10Base-5** Thick Ethernet, and most kinds of **ring topology** networks.

MC See **Main Closet**.

MDF Main Distribution Frame. See **Main Closet**.

Medium The physical channel through which a signal passes. Examples of different media are copper wire, optical fiber, and floppy disks transported by hand.

MIB Management Information Base. The database of information that's maintained by any **SNMP**-managed device, containing information on its current state, its configuration, error logs, and the like. The MIB can be retrieved through a query mechanism from an SNMP management console, or parts of it may be voluntarily sent out if the device discovers that it's malfunctioning.

Microcom Network Protocol MNP is a series of data link protocols used in telecommunications. Some provide data compression, while others provide error checking. While most modems suitable for use in wide-area networking applications include implementations of MNP levels one through five or higher, AppleTalk Remote Access and other ARAP servers must implement MNP before handing off data to the modem, so it's not required in modems which will be used solely for ARAP connections. Microcom, the developer of MNP, is a commercial telecommunications company which licenses MNP to other vendors to promote its protocols as a standard. MNP level 10, and other recently developed levels, have been aimed at improving performance over wireless links such as those provided by analog cellular telephones.

Mini-DIN 8 The type of jack used for the Macintosh's serial ports. It's a circular connector with eight pins, about five-sixteenths of an inch in diameter. The larger "regular DIN" plugs are sometimes used for power to modems and in stereophonic equipment. Apple's LocalTalk connectors and the ADB bus both use Mini-DIN 4 connectors, which are similar, but have four pins, and are also used by Super-VHS video equipment.

MNP See **Microcom Network Protocols**.

Modem From MODulator/DEModulator. A device which converts binary digital signal to and from analog waveforms. Used in pairs to create connections between digital devices using analog telephone lines.

Modular Flatwire The flat four-conductor cable usually used as drop cables from telephones or PhoneNet-type connectors to wall jacks. The jacketing is usually silver in color and contains red, green, black, and yellow-clad conductors. It should never be used in Ethernet networks, as the wires are side-by-side, rather than twisted-pair, and thus provide no shielding from crosstalk. Modular wire comes in 2-, 4-, 6-, and 8-conductor varieties. On the eight-conductor wire, conductor 1 is blue, 2 is orange, 3 is black, 4 is red, 5 is green, 6 is yellow, 7 is brown, and 8 is white. The smaller cables are color-coded as subsets of that, removing pairs from the outside. Two-conductor modular wire is not used for LocalTalk networks, and is recognizable by its very small diameter and its occasionally blue-tinted jacks. In modular flatwire, the individual conductors are 28-gauge stranded, composed of seven very fine strands. This raises impedance, but makes the cable more flexible and resistant to breakage.

Mount   The process of connecting to a file server and making its served volumes locally accessible.

Multicast   A transmission which is sent to multiple addressees simultaneously, but is not addressed to all users. That is, it's not a broadcast, but it's similar in that it's a broadcast upon which constraints have been placed. Under AppleTalk Phase 2, devices in different zones on the same Ethernet wire use zone multicasts where Phase 1 devices would use broadcasts. In TCP/IP, a multicast address is assigned to each subnet and called the "subnet broadcast address."

Multiplex   See **Mux**.

Mushroom   A mushroom-shaped peg, of beige or white plastic, one and a half inches in diameter at the top, and three inches tall. Mushrooms are used in the routing of cross-connect wire on telephone and network backboards. They form the radius of each 90° bend at the top of the path of a cross-connect wire, and support horizontal runs of cross-connect wire across the backboard. Mushrooms are mounted two inches above, and vertically centered upon, the screw which secures the top left-hand side of the top punchdown block in each column.

Mux   Mux, or multiplex, can be used in two senses: As a verb, it means the action of combining digital signals from several sources into a single analog or digital signal. Demuxing is performed on the opposite end, separating the signals out again. As a noun, a mux is a device which performs muxing and demuxing.

N-Type   Also called "N-Series," these connectors are the standard termination for thick Ethernet cabling. Otherwise similar to BNC connectors, N-Type connectors are threaded, rather than bayoneted, and the male connectors are slightly larger than half an inch in diameter.

Name Binding Protocol   An AppleTalk protocol used in name resolution. When a device wants to find the AppleTalk address of another device it knows by name, the name of a device at a certain address, or find all instances of a certain kind of device, it can issue an NBP Request, which would be answered with NBP Responses. NBP is the query language for the "distributed database" of names and addresses on an AppleTalk network. NBP is in the Transaction layer of the ISO-OSI model.

National Electric Code   A national building code issued by the NFPA, or National Fire Protection Association, and ratified by ANSI, which specifies standards for electrical wire installation. It does not relate primarily to telephone wiring, but does require that all wire passing through ventilation ducts must be flame-retardant, necessitating the use of plenum cable.

National Research and Education Network   See **NREN**.

NBP   See **Name Binding Protocol**.

NCC   Network Communications Cable. See **Inside Wire**.

NEC   See **National Electric Code**.

Network   A collection of devices which are able to communicate using a common set of protocols. The communication may take place over copper wires, optical fibers, radio or light waves, or anything else capable of conveying information.

Network Communications Cable   See **Inside Wire**.

Network File System   NFS is the IP equivalent to AppleTalk File Protocol. The NFS protocol contains fewer commands, and is somewhat simpler, but most user interfaces to it are more complicated than the AFP client software.

Network Information Center   See **InterNIC**.

Network Number   The 16-bit numerical address of an AppleTalk logical network. This forms part of the full hierarchical address which distinguishes each node. AppleTalk networks are often simply referred to as "nets," and should be clearly distinguished from **zones**. See also **Phase 2**.

Network Range   Under Phase 2 AppleTalk, networks on Ethernet and Token Ring may have more than one **network number**, or logical network, associated with each physical network segment. The network numbers must be sequential, however. A network range is the range of network numbers associated with a physical network segment, and is expressed in the form "first-last" or "1-3" where the network numbers on the physical net would be 1, 2, and 3.

Network-Visible Entity   Any AppleTalk device which has registered a name using NBP, or Name Binding Protocol. The few things which do not register names tend to be physical-layer devices, such as repeaters and bridges. Most routers only register a name on one of their ports, and are not network-visible from the other side, if traffic is not passing through. Entity names are composed of three parts: an object name, a type, and a zone name. Entity names are not guaranteed to be unique. For example, two objects both named "LaserWriter Ilg," both of type LaserWriter, could coexist on the same network.

NFS   See **Network File System**.

NIC   Network Information Center. The organization which assigned TCP/IP address ranges and registered Internet domain names until March 31, 1993. In association with the formation of the **NREN**, the NIC was dissolved and replaced by an organization called the **InterNIC**, performing the same service. For most of its duration, the NIC contract was held by the Stanford Research Institute, and later by Network Solutions Inc.

Node   A single device attached to a network. Under AppleTalk, each node is identified by an eight-bit Node Number or Node ID which, in combination with the node's **Network Number**, serves to uniquely identify the node.

Non-Extended Network   See **Phase 1**.

NREN   National Research and Education Network. The portion of the Internet funded in part by the United States government, and administered by the National Science Foundation. In time, the NREN is intended to supersede NSFNet. It is intended to provide service first to universities and research labs, and may perhaps later be extended to lower education, business, and individuals. NSFNet connects NSF grant recipients, primarily universities, and does not carry commercial traffic. The NREN is a sign of a more liberal attitude on the part of the U.S. government, intended to open the "data highways" to commercial use.

NVE   Network-Visible Entity. Any AppleTalk device or process which has NBP-registered itself on the network.

Ohm   The measure of **impedance**. LocalTalk network **termination** is accomplished using resistors which present 120 ohms of resistance to current.

Open Systems Interconnection See **OSI Model**.

Optical Fiber A very thin glass fiber through which signals may be transmitted in the form of pulses of light. The light is generated by a laser diode at one end, and received by a photocell at the other end. Fiber networks typically have much wider bandwidth and higher maximum frequency than electrical ones, and are unaffected by electromagnetic disturbance. The most common standard for fiber-optic networking is **FDDI**.

OSI Model Open Systems Interconnect reference model. The standard seven-layer conceptual model against which network protocols and devices are often measured. The seven layers, from top to bottom, are: Application, Presentation, Session, Transport, Network, Data Link, and Physical. The Application layer is simply the application software processes which are running on each machine. The physical layer is composed of all the physical, tangible components of which the network is constructed. The layers in between are protocols which form an "onion skin" of layers of addressing information successively wrapped around data at one end of a connection, and unwrapped at the other. The OSI model was established by the ISO, or International Standards Organization, and is also recognized by the CCITT.

Packet-Switched A method of routing data whereby the data is packetized, and each packet may have an individually addressed header. Each packet is then individually routed to its destination. This is the way nearly all computer networks operate. Contrast this with **circuit switching**, which is the stream-oriented connection method used for telephone switching.

PAP See **Printer Access Protocol**.

Patch Panel A rack-mountable panel, with modular jacks of some kind on the front, and either Amphenol connectors or punchdown terminals on the back. Patch panels are used where punchdown blocks would be inappropriate because connections must be changed frequently. Cross-connections between pairs of patch panels are formed using plug-terminated modular cables called patch cords, rather than cross-connect wire, and can thus be interminably rearranged without damaging either the panel or the cable. One disadvantage of patch panels is that they provide an electrical connection of far inferior quality to that provided by a punchdown block. Another is that, since they appear to be familiar technology, users are more likely to run amok and try to rearrange them.

PCS/PCN Personal Computer Services/Personal Computer Networks. An acronym used primarily to describe microwave radio-based public data networks.

PDS See **Premises Distribution System**.

Peer-to-Peer A general class of transaction in which the communicating devices are performing comparable tasks. In a distributed processing task, for instance, separate copies of an application may be running on different hosts and cooperating to solve a problem. This approach is often used to harness the power of multiple workstations on a network in solving complicated mathematical or imaging problems, which can be easily divided into component tasks. This is as opposed to client-server transactions, in which a client applies to a server for some service, or **host-terminal** interaction, in which the host does all the processing, including even that associated with input and output on the terminal.

Phase 1 An AppleTalk network in which each physical network is associated with exactly one logical network and one zone. Zones may, however, include multiple logical networks. LocalTalk networks are always Phase 1. The use of Phase 1 EtherTalk has been in decline since Phase 2 was introduced, and, since the beginning of 1991, Apple has been releasing new products which don't support Phase 1 EtherTalk.

Phase 2   In an AppleTalk Phase 2 network, physical networks may contain multiple logical networks and may be associated with multiple zones. Two routers delimiting an extended network might know about seven networks and three zones existing on the length of cable between them. Again, zone names may span several physical networks. This introduces a new form of addressing: the **multicast**, which allows a packet to be addressed to all the devices within one logical network, while devices on the same physical network, but other logical ones, ignore it. The practical consequence of this is that more than 254 Phase 2 AppleTalk devices can be connected to the huge, unrouted, physical networks, typical of the Ethernet backbones found in large corporations. It's possible for Phase 1 and Phase 2 devices to exist side-by-side on a single physical network, and to communicate with each other if there is a transition router connected to that physical network, although this is not a robust practice. All versions of AppleTalk since v.53, which was released in August 1989, have implemented Phase 2 protocols where appropriate.

Pigtail   A cable and plug depending directly from a device, as opposed to a jack on the device, into which a cable which is connectorized on both ends fits. The mini-DIN 8 plugs on LocalTalk connectors are on the ends of pigtails.

Plenum Cable   Cable which is designed to comply with the National Electric Code, which requires highly fire-resistant jacketing material on cable which is run through ventilation ducts and risers. Plenum cable is generally Teflon clad, and costs two to four times as much as nonplenum cable. Plenum cable is more ubiquitous in buildings built after more stringent codes were enacted in 1988. The standard code for plenum cable specified in NEC article 800 is CMP, as opposed to the general use CM cable and residential CMX cable.

Point-to-Point Protocol   A protocol which is designed to underlie multiple higher-level protocols simultaneously, and transport them over synchronous or asynchronous wide-area network connections. As of this writing, PPP is not yet widely used, although it's expected to supplant **SLIP** in the future.

POP   Used in two senses. A Point of Presence is a local dial-in port for a network which may span a large area. For instance, the CompuServe network is a commercial service which spans a large part of the globe, and has banks of modems in someone's rented basement in nearly every major city. By dialing into any modem at any of these sites which may be local to you, you're connected to the network on an equal basis, without paying additional long-distance charges. In the second sense, Post Office Protocol is an electronic mail protocol occasionally used between Unix mail servers and microcomputer clients.

POTS   Plain Old Telephone Service. Used to distinguish ordinary telephone service from Centrex, ISDN, CLASS, special data lines, or any other specialized variety of service provided by the telco.

PPP   See **Point-to-Point Protocol**.

Premises Distribution System   AT&T's Systimax Premises Distribution System, or simply PDS, is a telephone wiring specification which is at least loosely followed during the construction of most new office buildings. At the simplest level, most buildings wired in this manner have 24-gauge unshielded twisted-pair home runs from each wall jack to central wiring closets (called riser/backbone closets) on each floor, and risers from these closets descend to a main closet in the basement. Star topologies evolved as a part of this arrangement. PDS is described in AT&T document number 100-142-456.

Premises Wiring All the wire for which the telephone customer is responsible, from the "premises-side" of the demarcation block's centerline all the way out to the wall-jacks in the user work areas.

Print Spooler A process which accepts print jobs and queues them by acting as a proxy for the intended printer, later standing in as a proxy for the original sender in delivering the print job to the computer. Print spoolers are employed for two purposes: increased accountability and quicker return of the user's machine to user control after sending a print job.

Printer Access Protocol PAP is the protocol used between AppleTalk printers and their clients. Like ADSP, it's connection-oriented, and provides same-order packet delivery. PAP operates in the Session layer of the ISO-OSI model, riding atop NBP and ATP.

Protocol A common "language" used by multiple devices, so that they can intercommunicate. Most devices speak many different protocols, grouped into one or more different families, or **protocol stacks**.

Protocol Stack A family of protocols, wherein certain "low-level" protocols are shared universally between devices, and serve as a basis for initial communication, and specialized task-specific "high-level" protocols are layered on top of them, to provide communications channels tailored for more specific needs. The conceptual model against which nearly all protocols stacks are measured is the **OSI**, or Open Systems Interconnect model, which contains seven protocol layers, numbered from seven (low) to one (high).

Punchdown Block Any one of a number of types of dielectric blocks which hold matrixes of reusable terminals upon which wires can terminate and be interconnected. Punchdown blocks are available in several standard styles, each with its own set of incompatible tools and techniques. The most common are 66 and 110. Most 66 blocks have fifty rows of four terminals each. These are coded from 1A in the top left-hand corner to 50D in the lower right-hand corner, but they're also assigned to pairs, from 1 at the top to 25 at the bottom, each pair consisting of a "tip" on top and a "ring" below it. In addition, blocks are available either "common" or "split," depending upon how the pins in each row are connected to each other. On common blocks (66M1–25), all four terminals in each row are connected to each other within the punchdown block, while on split blocks each row consists of two pairs of terminals, one on each side, not connected across the centerline of the block. On split blocks (66M1–50), the pairs are numbered on either side of the centerline, as follows: pairs Left-1 through Left-25 from top to bottom on the left side, and pairs Right-1 through Right-25 on the right side. Distribution blocks are usually common, while demarcation blocks are always split. Other wiring configurations are available, but less common. 110 blocks feature four horizontal rows, each containing fifty positions, but are further complicated by the fact that punchdowns occur on two planes. In the rear plane, cable runs are terminated against the block. A connector block is placed over the terminated wires, contacting them, and providing additional IDC contacts on its face, being the front plane. The front plane then solely facilitates interconnection between terminated (and no longer accessible) cable runs.

Punchdown Tool A tool used to terminate a wire on a terminal of a punchdown block. Interchangeable bits are often available for different types of punchdown blocks. Punchdown tools generally perform two actions every time they're used: They create an electrical connection between the conductor and the terminal, and they trim off excess wire on one side of the terminal. 66-block tools are unkeyed, which means that you have to hold them correct-side-up to avoid cutting off the wire before the terminal rather than after it, while 110 tools are keyed, which means that they won't work if they're upside down.

Quad Cable An inexpensive four-conductor cable used in some telco installations, the insulation of the wires in quad cable is color coded red-green-black-yellow, like modular flatwire. The jacketing is usually beige or gray. Station wire is not twisted-pair, but all four wires are twisted around each other, using a less expensive process. It is thus inappropriate for any networks which depend upon twisted pairs to shield balanced signals, like 10Base-T, and it decreases the potential range of LocalTalk networks. Quad cable also fails to meet the minimum requirements for ISDN telephone service.

Raceway An open rack of welded metal straps which, like **conduit**, serves to hold a large number of cables. Unlike conduit, it's only used where directly accessible. Its purpose is to facilitate easy rearrangement of the cable it supports. It's normally used only in wiring closets and above suspended-tile ceilings. Also called cable trays or cable racks.

Raised Floor The floors of computer and equipment rooms are often raised by eighteen to twenty-four inches, using a system of support girders and hard plastic tiles, usually four feet square. Much like an inverted suspended-tile ceiling, the tiles lift off the framework for access to the space below, through which cable is run between devices.

RBOC Regional Bell Operating Company. Any of the so-called "Baby Bells."

Repeater A device which performs electrical, rather than logical, operations on signals to clean them up before sending them out another port. Most LocalTalk **hubs** are multiport repeaters, although the earliest repeaters had only two ports and were used to extend the length of trunk networks. See also **Bridge** and **Router**.

RFC Request for Comment. RFCs are the documents issued by **Internet Engineering Task Force** Working Groups, defining technical issues associated with the Internet and the Internet Protocol stack.

RG-8 See **Thick Ethernet**.

RG-58U See **Thin Ethernet**.

RIP See **Routing Information Protocol**.

Riser A large wiring conduit vertically connecting wiring closets on different floors of a building to the main wiring closet, or equipment room, in the basement.

RJ-11 The type of plugs used to terminate telephone line cords. RJ-11 plugs are defined as having only two active contacts, the center pair, pins 3 and 4. These are not useful with either LocalTalk, which tends to be carried on the outside pair, not present on these plugs, or with Ethernet, which requires two pairs.

RJ-11C The "C" suffix indicates a jack, rather than a plug. The same is true of the other RJ-series connectors.

RJ-11W The "W" suffix indicates a wall jack that's equipped with a special faceplate to facilitate the direct mounting of a wall-mount telephone set.

RJ-12 The type of plugs used to terminate telephone handset cords. These plugs and jacks have only four positions, but are fully populated, with four contacts. RJ-12 connectors are not currently used for any networking purposes, and are only found in a computing context on Macintosh 125, 512, and Plus keyboards and keyboard cables.

RJ-14   The most common of the three types of common "telephone" plug, RJ-14 jacks use the center four of six possible pins. The pins are numbered 2, 3, 4, and 5 from right to left, viewing the plug head-on, with the tab down; or left to right, viewing the jack from the front, tab down. 2 and 5, and 3 and 4, are always wired as pairs when connected to twisted-pair cable, and correspond to the first two, or white-blue/blue-white and white-orange/orange-white pairs in the color-coding scheme. When connected to station wire or used with modular flatwire, pin 2 is black, 3 is red, 4 is green, and 5 is yellow.

RJ-21   The standard 25-pair, or 50-pin connector used for many networking and telecommunications applications. It consists of a row of 25 pins on each side of a central ridge, enclosed in a trapezoidal shield. Also occasionally referred to as "Amphenol connectors," that being the name of a company which produces a large portion of the RJ-21 connectors in use.

RJ-21X   The telco designation for a 66-style **demarcation block**, usually including an RJ-21 connector on one or both sides, wired to the pins on that side of the block.

RJ-25   An elaboration on the **RJ-11–RJ-14** theme, RJ-25s have all six pins populated, adding 1 and 6, which are white and blue, respectively, and connect to the white-green/green-white pair in a twisted-pair cable.

RJ-45   Similar to **RJ-25** telephone connectors, but about half again as wide, with all eight possible pins present. Different proprietary variations on the standard RJ-45 connector are "keyed" with tabs extending from the side of the plug, such that it cannot be plugged into a jack which is not also keyed. The RJ-45 connector is the standard for cable termination under the **10Base-T** spec, while keyed versions are often used for the connection of "dumb" data terminals. The RJ-45 uses a slightly different pin-numbering scheme from that used in the RJ-11. Pins 4 (red) and 5 (green) are still the first pair, and connect to the white-blue/blue-white pair, but pins 1 (blue) and 2 (orange) now form the second pair, and connect to the white-orange/orange-white pair; pins 3 (black) and 6 (yellow) form the third pair, and connect to the white-green/green-white pair; and pins 7 (brown) and 8 (white) form the fourth pair, and connect to the white-brown/brown-white pair.

RJ-61X   See **RJ-45**.

Robust   A relative term used to describe a practice or implementation which is fault-tolerant and not fragile, or likely to fail. In software, code which is able to cope with a wide range of expected situations, and is able to exit gracefully and in an informative manner from unexpected situations, would be described as robust.

Router   A device which resides on two different networks, filters traffic, and passes packets through to the opposite side if they're addressed to nodes on or beyond the network on the other side. Routers can be used to delimit new AppleTalk zones.

Routing Information Protocol   RIP is the TCP/IP equivalent to AppleTalk's RTMP. IP routers use RIP packets to exchange routing table information. RIP packets are multicast across directly connected subnets every thirty seconds.

Routing Table Management Protocol   RTMP is the protocol used by AppleTalk routers to exchange routing table data. Every AppleTalk router broadcasts its routing table in an RTMP packet out each port every ten seconds. When the router is using a **Split Horizon** routing table update method, it sends only the information related to networks connected to other ports, so as to minimize the size of the RTMP packets. RTMP operates in the Transport layer of the ISO-OSI model.

RS-422 A standard which describes data communication over a certain class of connectors, much like RS-232. LocalTalk ports use RS-423, a dual-use port type, which can comply with either RS-422 or RS-232, depending upon whether it's being used for LocalTalk or serial communications.

RTMP See **Routing Table Management Protocol**.

Server A machine or process on a network which provides centralized services to clients. Common examples are **AFP** and **NFS** file servers, and print spoolers.

Service Entrance See **Entrance Facility**.

Shielded Twisted Pair Twisted-pair cable with some form of static shielding surrounding the pairs of conductors. There are three common forms of shielding: Single-shield cable has a single layer of aluminized mylar foil wrapped just inside the jacketing. Double-shield cable has a woven conductor of tinned copper between the jacketing and the mylar. Individually shielded pair cable has a separate foil wrapping around each pair of conductors. Although shielding does reduce interference, it also keeps signal reflections from dissipating, reducing possible run lengths. STP is not recommended for use in LocalTalk networks, and does not comply with the 10Base-T Ethernet spec. STP is, however, required by the **Interim CDDI** spec. See also **Unshielded Twisted Pair**.

Silver-Satin Cable See **Modular Flatwire**.

Simple Mail Transfer Protocol SMTP is the standard electronic-mail protocol used in the IP protocol stack. SMTP is not the only means used to transfer mail between IP hosts, however; UUCP, or Unix-to-Unix-Copy-Protocol, is often used where an IP connection between two hosts does not exist. SMTP is defined in RFC 821.

Simple Network Management Protocol SNMP is a standard means of collecting management information from, and sending configuration information to, dissimilar network devices. It's modular, such that each device has a compliant management interface, which can be used in any SNMP management "console." This interface then queries the "SNMP agent," which maintains a socket on the SNMP-managed network device. The agent responds with data from its MIB, or Management Information Base, which the console then displays through the interface's display template. In addition, agents can send out warning or SOS messages unprompted, in the event of malfunctions. These are received by "SNMP trap listeners," which may be socket listeners associated with management consoles, or may be independent store-and-forward processes.

SLIP Serial-Line Internet Protocol. A version of the Internet Protocol designed to be run over synchronous or asynchronous wide-area network connections. See also **PPP**.

SMDS Switched Multimegabit Data Services. An extremely high-bandwidth packet-switched wide-area network protocol which, as of the time of this writing, is being tested in several regions for possible future use. Although it's packet-switched, rather than circuit-switched, and thus transaction-oriented, rather than connection-oriented, there's some feeling that it's in competition with Primary Rate ISDN; whichever of the two first becomes widely available to business users may well stifle use of the other.

SMTP See **Simple Mail Transfer Protocol**.

SNA See **Systems Network Architecture**.

SNMP See **Simple Network Management Protocol**.

Socket Sockets are unique numerical addresses assigned to different software processes operating on the same **node**. Any packet must be addressed to a specific socket, even if it's being broadcast to many different nodes. In this sense, the socket is the most essential part of any network address. Sockets may be further subdivided, by the software process that owns them, into **enumerators**.

Solid Conductor Cable Cable in which each conductor is a single piece of solid copper, annealed to make it resistant to breakage and snapping, rather than one made up of many smaller strands. Solid conductor cable is a must for long runs and high-speed networks, and should be used by default in all situations except drop cables in user work areas. See also **Stranded Conductor Cable**.

Split Horizon An innovation in AppleTalk Phase 2, whereby AppleTalk routers try to send only the network and zone information that's needed in each RTMP packet that they broadcast. Thus if a network contained two nets, 1 and 2, and one router between them, it would only send information about net 1 to net 2, and vice versa, rather than telling each network about all the networks that it knows about. The motive for this is to reduce the size of the RTMP packets broadcast on large networks.

Spudger A nonconductive tool that looks something like a dental pick, used for untangling, separating, and tracing wires in a cross-connect field. Also useful for removing trimmed wire ends caught in the terminals of a punchdown block.

SS7/CCS Signaling System 7/Common Channel Signaling. A common set of protocols in use by both local telcos and long-distance service providers, which enables the passing of call-description data to all the switches routing a telephone call by digitizing the voice message and interleaving data with it. Before SS7 voice and data could not share the same channel. It's SS7 which makes Caller•ID and ANI possible, by sending the telephone number of the originating phone, along with the call itself. See also **DSS1**.

Star Topology A topology in which each device is connected in parallel to a central point by means of a **home run** of wire which leads directly from a single point in the user work area to a single point on a distribution punchdown block. There are two types of stars, active and passive. Active stars use **hubs** to repeat signals down each run of wire, and are nearly universally preferable. Passive stars use simple cross-connections formed on a punchdown block, which greatly limits the distance and number of devices they can connect.

STP See **Shielded Twisted Pair**.

Stranded Conductor Cable Cable which uses many fine strands of copper wire, twisted about each other, to form each conductor. Like a piece of string, it's very flexible, and doesn't break or snap easily, but it has fewer beneficial electrical characteristics than **solid conductor cable**. Stranded cable should only be used in situations where the cable will be handled frequently, like drop cables in user work areas.

Subnet A division of a TCP/IP network with some properties similar to those of an AppleTalk net, and some similar to those of an AppleTalk zone. Subnets are areas of an IP network which have been demarcated by routers, and assigned different subnet addresses, which come between the network address and the node address. They allow the use of subnet broadcasts, a form of **multicasting** which decreases traffic propagation across routers.

Suspended Tile A type of ceiling in common use in commercial buildings. Large rectangular molded-fiber tiles, usually two feet by four feet, rest at their edges upon a thin metal lattice, which is suspended by steel cables from the true ceiling, usually at least two feet higher up. In this two feet, conduit, ventilation ducts, cable trays, and electrical wiring all coexist.

Switched Multimegabit Data Service   See **SMDS**.

Synchronous Transmission   The means of passing data used by most networks and some leased-line modems, whereby the steam of bits is expected to be constant in speed, and the beginning and end of each bit is mapped to the timeframe in which it is expected to arrive. See also **Asynchronous Transmission**.

Systemax   See **Premises Distribution System**.

Systems Network Architecture   An IBM network protocol stack which, although supported by a few Apple products, is almost unheard-of in Macintosh environments.

T1   A one-and-a-half-megabit-per-second digital leased-line service standard that's available from telephone service providers throughout much of the world. T1 often requires a coaxial cable from the telco's central office to the subscriber's premises.

TCP   See **Transmission Control Protocol**.

TCP/IP   See **Internet Protocol**.

Telco   The Telephone Company. Used to refer either to the provider of your local telephone service (your LEC, or Local Exchange Carrier) or to equipment which is in standard telco usage. Thus RJ-11 and Amphenol connectors are sometimes referred to as telco connectors, while BNC and DIN connectors are not.

Telnet   An IP terminal session protocol. Telnet is used by terminals or terminal-emulation software to establish a terminal data session with a host or terminal server, across an IP network. Telnet is one of the most common ways of "logging in" to a Unix host, whether from a microcomputer or from another Unix machine.

Terminal   Used in two senses. In the electrical sense, a terminal is any kind of point at which two conductors may coterminate. That is, a device, usually very small and simple, which holds two wires together securely but not permanently, such that a good electrical connection is formed between them, yet they can be released and the terminal reused at a later point in time. Both the pins of a punchdown block and the screws and washers in a wall jack are terminals. In the computing sense, a terminal is traditionally a hardware device with a screen, keyboard, and sometimes other input/output devices, but no computing ability of its own, which is connected to a computer that may be remote. In more modern times, most terminals are actually software processes running on workstations and personal computers, which offer a "terminal window" in which communication with the remote computer can happen. Software terminals are usually preferable to hardware, since they allow the user to manipulate data from the remote computer (or "host" computer) in an intelligent fashion, locally, thus making more efficient use of the network or telecommunications resources used to connect the terminal to the host.

Terminate   Also used in two senses. The most common use is to denote the method of ending a piece of cable: **Modular flatwire** is usually terminated with an **RJ-11** plug, for instance; or to denote the action of cutting a cable (you terminate **cross-connect** wire with a **punchdown tool**). In the second sense, many network media require the presence of a resistor across their conductors at some points in the topology to absorb reflected signals and nonsignal garbage. These are called terminators, and the act of putting one of these across your network is referred to as terminating it. The sense of the word can usually be gleaned from the context. Terminating a network almost always refers to putting a resistor across it, while terminating a wire usually refers to ending it.

Thick Ethernet   A physical medium for Ethernet networks that is no longer often used in new installations because of the high cost and difficulty of routing the thick and inflexible cable. Usually called ThickNet, sometimes 10Base-5 or, more derisively, "EtherHose." The cable is coaxial, 11.5-gauge, 0.41 inches in outside diameter, and usually color-coded bright yellow. The cable spec is RG-8; DEC specification number BNE2B is compliant. The connectors are called **N-Type** and are similar to, but larger than, **BNC** connectors. Individual thick Ethernet cable segments may extend to 1640 feet, while a single network may not exceed 2.5 miles. Each end of a cable run is terminated with a 50-ohm resistor, and no more than 100 machines may depend from a single segment, with an absolute minimum of 8.2 feet between them. Machines are attached using **ThickNet transceivers**.

Thick Ethernet Transceivers   Much like scaled-up versions of PhoneNet connectors, these perform an equivalent service in the connection of a device to a **thick Ethernet** network. Typically they are about three inches high and wide, and an inch thick, with an extruded aluminum clamp on top which pierces the jacketing of the ThickNet cable to provide a "nonintrusive" connection, the installation of which doesn't cause an interruption in network service to other users. Occasionally one runs across N-Type transceivers, which have a threaded N-Type connector at the top, on each end. The transceiver or "tap" is connected to the host machine by an **AUI** cable, which plugs into the Ethernet card or adapter on that machine.

Thin Ethernet   A physical medium for Ethernet networks in common use. Usually called ThinNet, sometimes 10Base-2, and occasionally "CheaperNet," to distinguish it from the more expensive thick Ethernet cable. The cable is coaxial, 21-gauge, two-tenths of an inch in outside diameter, and often color-coded black or a medium blue. The cable spec is RG-58U, not to be confused with RG-59U, a similar cable used in Wang networks with a 75-ohm impedance, or RG-62U, an IBM cable standard, with 93-ohm impedance. ThinNet cable uses BNC connectors, and is terminated with a 50-ohm resistor at the end of each cable segment. The maximum length of a single physical network is 606 feet. No more than 30 machines may be connected to a single physical network. Although the specifications say that each machine may be up 165 feet from the BNC T-connector which connects it to the trunk, in practice the male side of the T-connector is connected directly to the Ethernet card or adapter on the client machine.

TLAP   TokenTalk Link Access Protocol. The **Link Access Protocol** which allows AppleTalk packets to be sent across **Token Ring** networks.

Token Ring   The name of a proprietary IBM network architecture, it also describes a class of networks which share a similar ring-shaped topology, rather than the ones more common to LocalTalk and Ethernet networks. In token ring networks, the cable literally forms a ring connecting the client devices, and each machine relays messages to the next, until the message is delivered to its addressee or returns to its sender. **FDDI** uses a ring topology.

TokenTalk   The implementation of AppleTalk which runs over IBM Token Ring-type networks.

Topology   The physical layout of a network. There are several workable LocalTalk topologies, including daisy chains, trunks, and stars, while under Ethernet, options are constrained by the specific medium. 10Base-T, for instance, can only be used in a star topology, although the stars themselves may be cascaded to other 10Base-T stars, or attached to a thick or thin Ethernet trunk. Thick and thin Ethernet are usually used in trunk topologies, although it's perfectly possible, if not cost-effective, to use them in active-star topologies.

TPDDI ANSI X3T9.5 Twisted-Pair Digital Data Interface. An adaptation of the **FDDI** high-speed network system to use copper conductors, rather than optical fibers. As of the time of this writing, it's hoped that the proposed standard can be ratified in late 1993. Most development work is aimed at achieving reliable operation and multivendor interoperability at the standard 100-meter home-run distance, over grade-five unshielded cable.

Transition Router A router which has been configured with two logical ports connected to the same physical network, one using Phase 1 addressing, the other using Phase 2 addressing. Transition routers allow Phase 1 and Phase 2 devices to coexist on the same physical network, theoretically during transition periods during which the Phase 1 devices are upgraded or eliminated. Transition routers are widely considered inherently evil devices, and the transition state, in which the two addressing methods coexist, is not one to be desired.

Transmission Control Protocol TCP is the Internet Protocol's connection-oriented reliable-delivery protocol, equivalent to, but much more common than, AppleTalk's **ADSP**. TCP is defined in RFC 793.

Trunk Topology A topology in which all devices are connected in parallel to a single bus of wire. LocalTalk networks may operate on trunk topology cabling, and both thick and thin Ethernet are trunks by definition, but 10Base-T Ethernet will not operate in a trunk.

Tunnel A tunnel is a point-to-point network connection between two encapsulating devices. For example, two LocalTalk-to-Ethernet routers performing **KIP** encapsulation of LocalTalk packets in IP packets would form a tunnel between each other, through the IP network. Each encapsulating device may support multiple tunnels to different other encapsulating devices elsewhere on the intervening network.

Tuple A synonym for record. Each record of an RTMP packet is referred to as a tuple, and the same terminology is used in some databases.

Twisted-Pair Ethernet Often confused with 10Base-T, twisted-pair Ethernet was a precursor to 10Base-T, promoted primarily by Synoptics. Like 10Base-T, it ran on 24-gauge unshielded twisted-pair cable in a star topology. Although many twisted-pair Ethernet devices will work with 10Base-T devices, run lengths often need to be shortened to 180–200 feet before they will successfully communicate, due to differences in the propagation characteristics of the signals. Twisted-Pair Ethernet has not been in common use since 1989.

UDP See **User Datagram Protocol**.

Uninterruptible Power Supply A device composed of lead-acid or other rechargeable batteries, charging and discharging circuitry, and power-quality and level-monitoring circuits. UPSes isolate devices from the outside power lines, and supply clean power through brownouts, spikes and surges, and power outages. They're often used in computer rooms and wiring closets to provide guaranteed power to critical devices like network hubs, routers, and servers, and to telephone equipment. The number of devices a UPS can support, and the length of time which it can support them, are dependent upon the size of the battery pack. While small UPSes capable of supporting several hubs and routers, or a single microcomputer for 30 to 45 minutes, are typically several hundred dollars and less than fifty pounds, large ones, designed to support multiple servers or a mainframe, can reach into the low thousands of dollars and usually weigh more than a hundred pounds.

Unshielded Twisted Pair   By far the most common form of cable in use in office buildings today, UTP is the best choice for **LocalTalk** networks, and is required by the **10Base-T** Ethernet spec. Inside UTP cables, individual wires are arranged into pairs and color-coded, so as to be easily distinguishable. Each pair of conductors is then twisted about itself. The twisting of pairs around each other serves as a substitute to shielding, in that the signal is being sent as the difference between the voltages on the two wires, or the difference mode voltage. Since the conductors are twisted around each other, on average, neither will be closer to any source of interference than the other, so they will be equally effected, resulting in an equal amount of induced noise on each, at the end. Since the voltage of the noise is the same on each, it's referred to as the common mode voltage. The ability of the receiving device to distinguish the signal from the noise is dependent upon how successful it is at removing the noise that's common to both conductors, leaving the signal, which is the difference. This is called common mode rejection. The color-coding scheme used in twisted-pair wiring is a base-five counting system, in which white (wht), red (red), black (blk), yellow (yel), and violet (vio) correspond to 0, 1, 2, 3, and 4 in the fives place, and blue (blu), orange (orn), green (grn), brown (brn), and slate (slt) correspond to 0, 1, 2, 3, and 4 in the ones place. In each pair, the conductor whose jacket is predominantly the fives-place color, with bands of the ones-place color, is punched down above its complement. Using two digits then, we can count from 0 to 24, which gives us enough combinations to distinguish each conductor in a 25-pair cable. Obviously this requires counting from zero, rather than one, but since it's almost never necessary to make conversions to base-ten, and the base-five system quickly becomes second nature, this is almost irrelevant. To give an example of this system, positions one and two (the first pair) on a punchdown block correspond to the white-blue and blue-white conductors; forty-nine and fifty (the twenty-fifth pair) correspond to violet-slate and slate-violet; and twenty-one and twenty-two (the eleventh pair) correspond to red-blue and blue-red.

UPS   See **Uninterruptible Power Supply**.

User Datagram Protocol   UDP is the Internet Protocol stack's connectionless reliable-delivery protocol, analogous to AppleTalk's ATP. UDP is described in RFC 768.

UTP   See **Unshielded Twisted Pair**.

WAN   See **Wide Area Network**.

Wide Area Network   A group of **Local Area Networks** in different places. Common means of connection are **half-bridges** and **half-routers**, using either proprietary protocols, modem protocols like **V.32**, digital telephone protocols like **ISDN**, leased-line protocols like **T1**, or public data network protocols like **X.25**.

Wiring Closet   A room containing a distribution frame or backboard full of punchdown blocks, where incoming services are cross-connected to cables which lead, finally, to walljacks in user work areas. There are three types of wiring closet: the main closet, computer room, or equipment room, located in the basement, where telephone, outside network, and electrical services enter the building; the backbone/riser closets, which are located in a vertical column above the main closet, one per floor, and connected by large-diameter riser conduit; and satellite closets, which may exist as tertiary distribution points at other places on each floor, receiving service cables from the backbone/riser closet on the same floor.

ZIP   See **Zone Information Protocol**.

Zone   A named area of a network, delimited by routers. On **nonextended** networks, each physical network is associated with exactly one zone, while extended networks allow flexibility in the number of logical networks and zones which are associated with each physical net.

Zone Information Protocol   ZIP is AppleTalk's mechanism for exchanging zone name and network number correspondence information. It's primarily used between routers, but is also employed by user nodes to determine their own zones and get zone lists for use by the Chooser and other application-layer software. ZIP is in the Session layer of the ISO-OSI model, but some queries ride atop ATP, while other queries and all responses ride directly atop DDP, bypassing the Transport layer entirely.

Zone Multicast   See **Multicast**.

Index

ABOUT THE AUTHOR

Bill Woodcock is president of Zocalo Engineering, an
AppleTalk and TCP/IP network design and installation con-
tracting firm based in Berkeley, California. He is a prominent
speaker, consultant, and columnist, and is the moderator of
MacNetAdmin, a nationwide electronic forum dedicated to
the discussion of AppleTalk networking and administration
issues. He is on the board of directors of the Apple Network
Managers Association, writes a column for its monthly
newsletter *ANMA Notes,* and is a coauthor of *Network Solutions Guide: Distributed Computing for the 1990s.*